WRITING AND THE MODERN STAGE

It is time to change the way we talk about writing in theater. This book offers a new argument that reimagines modern theater's critical power and places innovative writing at the heart of the experimental stage. While performance studies, German *Theaterwissenschaft*, and even text-based drama studies have commonly envisioned theatrical performance as something that must operate beyond the limits of the textual imagination, this book shows how a series of writers have actively shaped new conceptions of theater's radical potential.

Engaging with a range of theorists, including Theodor Adorno, Jarcho reveals a modern tradition of "negative theatrics," whose artists undermine the here and now of performance in order to challenge the value and the power of the existing world. This vision emerges through surprising new readings of modernist classics – by Henry James, Gertrude Stein, and Samuel Beckett – as well as contemporary American works by Suzan-Lori Parks, Elevator Repair Service, and Mac Wellman.

JULIA JARCHO is an OBIE Award-winning playwright and director with the company Minor Theater. She is an Assistant Professor of English at New York University where she teaches courses in modern drama, modernism, theater studies, critical theory, and playwriting. New York productions include *The Terrifying* (2017), *Every Angel is Brutal* (2016), *Nomads* (2014), *Grimly Handsome* (OBIE Award for Best New American Play, 2013), *Dreamless Land* (2011), and *American Treasure* (2009). Her scholarly work has been published in *Modern Drama* and *Critical Inquiry*. *Minor Theater*, a collection of her plays, is published by 53rd State Press.

WRITING AND THE MODERN STAGE

Theater beyond Drama

JULIA JARCHO
New York University

CAMBRIDGE
UNIVERSITY PRESS

University Printing House, Cambridge CB2 8BS, United Kingdom

One Liberty Plaza, 20th Floor, New York, NY 10006, USA

477 Williamstown Road, Port Melbourne, VIC 3207, Australia

4843/24, 2nd Floor, Ansari Road, Daryaganj, Delhi – 110002, India

79 Anson Road, #06-04/06, Singapore 079906

Cambridge University Press is part of the University of Cambridge.

It furthers the University's mission by disseminating knowledge in the pursuit of education, learning, and research at the highest international levels of excellence.

www.cambridge.org
Information on this title: www.cambridge.org/9781107132351
10.1017/9781316450888

© Julia Jarcho 2017

This publication is in copyright. Subject to statutory exception and to the provisions of relevant collective licensing agreements, no reproduction of any part may take place without the written permission of Cambridge University Press.

First published 2017

Printed in the United States of America by Sheridan Books, Inc. in 2017

A catalogue record for this publication is available from the British Library.

ISBN 978-1-107-13235-1 Hardback

Cambridge University Press has no responsibility for the persistence or accuracy of URLs for external or third-party Internet Web sites referred to in this publication and does not guarantee that any content on such Web sites is, or will remain, accurate or appropriate.

for Cody

Contents

Preface	*page* ix
Acknowledgments	xvi
PART I MODERNISM'S NEGATIVE THEATRICS	1
1 Introduction: Negative Theatrics	3
2 "Something stranger yet": Theatrical Distractions in Henry James and Gertrude Stein	23
3 "Gesture towards the universe": Theater as Utopia in *Waiting for Godot*	68
PART II BEYOND THE PRESENT: PLAYWRIGHTS AT THE TURN OF THE MILLENNIUM	107
4 Introduction: Staging Writing Today	109
5 The Promise of "Playwrighting": Suzan-Lori Parks	131
6 "Small, fierce creatures": Mac Wellman's Auratic Theater	172
Notes	215
Works Cited	248
Index	264

Preface

In his 1999 book *Certain Fragments*, director Tim Etchells describes "the spectacle of 'new playwrights' at a 1997 conference in London's Royal Court Theatre": the writers' "biggest (almost only) topic of conversation seemed to be long pontifications on the understanding of a comma ... Hard for me to understand," he continues drily, "having never much cared for punctuation ... Never cared much for playwrights" (104–105).

Etchells is the founder and artistic director of Forced Entertainment, the United Kingdom's highest-profile experimental theater company. He is also a writer, and the essay that contains these remarks, "On Performance Writing," expands on the kind of text that might ultimately make those pedantic "playwrights" obsolete: this is theater's newfound "gabbling voice composed of scraps and layers, fragments, quotations" (99). In this vein, the essay makes a case for the theatrical power of writing, something Etchells's subsequent work has never stopped exploring.[1] And yet he seems to dismiss the playwrights for taking the *writing* of writing, its literary mechanics, too much to heart: "How directors and actors can't understand a comma these days. The terrible shame of it" (104). The implication, of course, is that directors and actors have more important and exciting things to worry about. If a writer wants to hang with theater's advanced guard, she'd better put down her MLA guide and jump into the fray.

As a fan of Etchells, but a playwright myself, I come back to this passage now and then with mixed feelings. Its relatively good-humored dig caps off a century of related gestures, often more adamant: for Antonin Artaud, playwrights were "human snakes" (*Theater* 45), and a number of other artists and theorists have offered their own variations on the theme of dethroning, demoting, or outwitting the playwright, thereby setting theater free.[2] By the turn of the millennium, this trajectory had coalesced into common sense, from the Berlin artistic director rolling her eyes at "text theater" to the US grant-maker explaining that putting on plays isn't normally considered an experimental practice. Not that playwrights themselves are an endangered species; in America, they keep on streaming through MFA programs, and their work finds appreciative audiences in regional theaters throughout the country and Off-Broadway. But – rightly or wrongly – theirs is not a theater that often gets called experimental; and it's not a theater that tours internationally, on the circuit where Forced Entertainment and other European artists cross paths with downtown New York companies like the Wooster Group, Elevator Repair Service, and Nature Theater of Oklahoma.

While I don't want to contribute to the reification of a de facto divide, and at the risk of eliding some real innovations, I think it is still accurate to say that the theater of big-budget American plays is largely (though not entirely) governed by a realist dramaturgy that evokes the storytelling norms of movies and TV. This means that young artists who feel alienated from mainstream cultural production and deeply attracted to the self-conscious experimentation of the last century's avant-gardes are likely to find themselves drawn to the "other" field of theater – even when they're writers. Anyway that's what happened to me. For a while, in my twenties – in New York and, more briefly, in Berlin – I tried characterizing the things I was writing and directing as "performance pieces," vaguely hoping this would affiliate me with the avant-garde companies I admired, but no one was fooled. They're plays. I still stand by the claim to affiliation, but I've stopped pretending not to be a playwright – and someone who does care a lot about commas. And I've learned that Gertrude Stein cared a lot about them too.

This book is an attempt to understand what it can mean to be an experimental playwright now, by investigating what it meant for certain writers at the beginning, middle, and end of the twentieth century. More broadly, however, this book is about the relationship between theater and literature. It's my contention that the study of theater today would do well to turn *toward* the literary – not least because the suggestion sounds so perverse. How could this be anything but a critical regression? The recognition that writing is just one of theater's many materials has been getting brought home to us with such force, and for so long, that it's hard to imagine seriously thinking otherwise. But theater discourse still seems to suffer from its own version of the "medial panic" Rebecca Schneider has observed among performance artists in the world of visual art, who "go out of their way to say that their work is *not* theatre and *not* dance" (129). Ironically, we in theater keep doing something similar, continuing to reiterate that real theater is not literature.[3]

This habit has been reinforced in recent years by the discourse on "postdramatic" theater, a term coined decades earlier by Richard Schechner (in English) and Andrzej Wirth (in German), but launched into widespread scholarly use by Hans-Thies Lehmann, particularly in his influential *Postdramatisches Theater* (1999).[4] Lehmann applies the term to modes of theatrical experimentation that have arisen in response to the "omnipresence of the *media* in everyday life," a development he dates to the 1970s (22). He argues that the theoretical and critical paradigm of theater as *drama* is no longer applicable to this work, which consciously moves beyond the dramatic norms that have long organized Western theater. Whereas drama uses theater as a means of guiding spectators through a fictional narrative, postdramatic theater rejects the "fictive cosmos" as such (22, 31). "If texts and staged processes are perceived according to the model of suspenseful dramatic *action* [*Handlung*, also "plot"]," Lehmann explains, "the *theatrical* conditions of perception, namely the aesthetic qualities of theatre *as* theatre, fade into the background … These elements (the form), however, are precisely the point in many contemporary theatre works" (35/51). The substance of these works is inseparable from their form, inhering in their temporally and spatially specific performance. Postdramatic theater thus irreducibly concerns "the eventful present, the particular semiotics of bodies, the gestures and movements of the performers, the compositional and formal structure of language as a soundscape, the qualities of the visual beyond representation, the musical and rhythmic process with its own time, etc." (35).

The works I discuss in this book similarly tend to subordinate the engrossments of fiction to explorations of these medial concerns, with special emphasis on the first entry in Lehmann's list, "the eventful present." (Indeed, theater's space, time, embodiment, and sociality are all tightly bound up in the problematic that this term generates.) But the majority of these works, unlike the ones Lehmann discusses, are not theater productions – they're pieces of writing. It might therefore seem absurd to expect postdramatic discourse to have anything to say about them: "postdramatic theatre," Lehmann writes, "presents itself as a meeting point of the arts and thus develops – and demands – an ability to perceive which breaks away … from literature as such" (31). Lehmann never suggests that text has *no* place in the postdramatic, and in recent years he has strenuously objected to the idea "that the postdramatic is non-textual," which he calls a "downright misunderstanding" of his argument ("Decade" 31).[5] His translator Karen Jürs-Munby, a leading scholar on the author Elfriede Jelinek, has been especially active in contesting this notion and exploring applications of Lehmann's theory to written works. Nevertheless, *Postdramatic Theater* presents its paradigm as emerging through a "drifting apart of text and theatre" (46) or, put more agonistically, through a coup in which "the dominance of the text" that had characterized drama (54) gets overthrown. Writing may still have a role to play, but we're repeatedly reminded that the text is *no longer in charge*.

Throughout the past two decades' critical discourse on experimental theater, this gesture recurs with impressive regularity – especially where texts themselves are the objects of analysis. In reading after reading of experimental plays, in German and in English, we're reminded that "the literary text is no longer the uncontested center and goal of theatrical performance, but is noticeably regarded as the linguistic material of an autonomous stage art and used as such" (Poschmann 20); that on "closer reading," postdramatic texts are "seen to be merely one, albeit significant, element of the performance text" (Tomlin 60). Postdramatic text can "offer itself as an active agent in performance," but the "textual basis of postdramatic theatre is only a small part of the phenomenon. The words themselves, one of the dominant elements of the dramatic theatre, become just another element in a theatrical mode that militates against hierarchies in performance" (Barnett, "When" 23, 16). It "is not a question of a renewed dominance [*Vorherrschaft*] of the text over other elements a performance has to offer; rather it is a question of texts in which the refusal of dominance is anchored" (Jaeger 9).[6]

Such accounts of contemporary innovation have met with criticism from scholars who challenge the assumption that dramatic theater – or any theater – could really have been "dominated" by text in the first place. In *Drama: Between Poetry and Performance* (2010), W. B. Worthen points out that "this vision of postdramatic theatre begs the question: is a 'text' always – or ever – 'staged' in this way, translated in some direct manner into speech and depiction, 'declamation and illustration'?" (*Drama* 86). Worthen argues throughout *Drama* that the answer is no: a playtext can only ever be an "agency" or tool of performance, and performance will always exceed and subvert the written words it draws into its event. Dramatic theater, that is, was never a fundamentally "literary" form, so it makes no sense to conceive a *post*dramatic break from literature. Worthen reads a series of canonical plays, showing how they allegorize the fact that text is something performance *uses*; in this vision, performance subverts, exceeds, and outpaces text at every turn, as "a specific kind of doing that lives outside the text" (55) and "cannot be kept captive to its writ" (109).

Similarly, Benjamin Bennett's provocative *All Theater Is Revolutionary Theater* (2005) describes "*all* theater" as the subversion of text: theater is "a kind of training in revolutionary resistance to the otherwise unchallengeable conservatism of writing" (68). For Bennett, the "exposure of writing to performance" (64, 67) is the radical subjection of writing to "chance, disorder, contingency, negativity," which only performance makes possible (120).

It's hard to overstate the importance of these interventions. Amidst a critical discourse that often seems to privilege automatically whatever work "does not begin with a writer or take a dramatic text as its basis" (Crawley 11), one feels that arguments like Worthen's still haven't quite been heard as they should. In this book I'll take a different tack, however, prompted by an equally striking convergence that joins scholars like Worthen and Bennett to the "postdramatic" critics: they all emphasize what text *doesn't* do. Whether the referent is postdramatic theater, drama, or "All Theater," our field now seems to require the gesture of diminishing the script, as if the best reply to complaints like Etchell's – or Artaud's – were something like: "don't worry, the playwrights know they aren't really running the show." In order to refute the notion that "text theater" is inherently outdated or conservative, its scholars assure us that, in theater, the text does not come out on top. They may disagree about the dramatic/postdramatic distinction, but they share a vision of theater as something that inherently eludes or exceeds writing. It's a vision I want to challenge.

This book is about writing as a disruptive theatrical force in its own right. In the following chapters, I examine twentieth-century texts that do theatrical work on the page. I don't just mean that they are specially crafted for performance, though many of them are; or that they engage with the subject of theater, though all of them do. Rather, I am saying that these works posit, simulate, and situate themselves in moments of theatrical performance in order to discover the rifts and insufficiencies of those moments. They enact a *heightened negativity*: a specifically utopian response to the *heightened actuality*, or presentness, that has often seemed to distinguish performance from other kinds of art. In doing this, they turn the theater into a place where the determining force of *how things are, here and now* can be confronted and shaken. They do so not by presenting an alternative world, but by variously attacking, exploding, hyperbolizing, and contesting the present as such. This possibility depends on the reference to performance: it's only in relation to the prospect of theatrical enactment in a concrete space and time that the texts can work this way.

But in performance, their writtenness is never superseded. It's *as writing* that they make theater lodge a complaint against the here-and-now.

Does insisting on the theatrical importance of text automatically return theater to a dramatic model? Only if we take "dramatic" to mean "based on text" – but an entire theoretical and aesthetic tradition urges us not to. As this book's subtitle suggests, I believe postdramatic discourse is right to see the push "beyond drama" as a central impetus of modern experimental theater. But as long as we identify drama with the presence – or the "dominance" – of a script, we will miss the more fundamental critical impulse at work in the drive to move beyond drama: the desire to push *against the experience of the present*. For this negative project, writing isn't just something theater "uses"; it's something theater needs.

This book consists of two parts, each of which begins with a theoretical introduction. In Part I, "Modernism's Negative Theatrics," I read works by Henry James, Gertrude Stein, and Samuel Beckett; I explore the theatrical accomplishments of their writing, which often inhere in the very features that mark that writing as writerly, or palpably literary. In Part II, "Beyond the Present: Playwrights at the Turn of the Millennium," I turn to contemporary artists. Chapter 4 introduces this section of the book by very briefly surveying the current landscape of text as a component of experimental theater, and engaging with a recent production which, while not itself a play, can help us think more expansively than usual about what a text might ask of performance: Elevator Repair Service's *Gatz* (2006). The subsequent chapters discuss late-twentieth-century plays by the American playwrights Suzan-Lori Parks and Mac Wellman. Throughout Part II, I take a particular interest in what it means for certain works to *be* plays, bearing recognizable textual conventions appropriated from drama (such as character-distributed speech). Such pieces are not just "theater texts" offered as material for a directorial or devised assemblage; rather they are scripts that – far from any "refusal of dominance" – promise to structure a corresponding theatrical event. Building on Part I's analysis of *Waiting for Godot*, my readings of Parks and Wellman attend to this outlandish promise of the play as a form, arguing that it marks a crucial strand of contemporary experimental theater.

The gap of time that falls between Parts I and II – say thirty-seven years between the premiere of *Godot* in 1953 and the premiere of Parks's *The Death of the Last Black Man in the Whole Entire World* in 1990 – is not meant to be polemical. I don't claim that the theatrical negativity I am tracing disappeared for decades, only to resurface at the end of the century. The highly textualized stage of writer-director Richard Foreman, from the late 1960s on, would be one obvious place to look for continuity.[7] I suspect a trajectory could also be drawn through the work of, for example, Sam Shepard or Adrienne Kennedy; all three writers are treated at length in Marc Robinson's 1994 study *The Other American Drama*, which extends from Stein through a group of contemporary playwrights including Parks and Wellman. But neither would I want to suggest that today's negative theatrics are exclusively American, even though my two privileged examples are; in this respect, I hope the reader will forgive what may be a certain provincialism. I'll return briefly to the question of "Americanness" in Chapter 4, but I should confess at the outset that the idea for this project sprang from the weird, wild work I have loved since my New York adolescence, particularly Wellman's plays; that's the major reason why this book ends up where it does. Scholars like Robinson, Elinor Fuchs, Una Chaudhuri, Bonnie Marranca, Andrzej Wirth, and Lehmann himself have already explored patterns of theatrical affiliation that range across the twentieth-century decades and across national borders, and while none of these genealogies focuses on the specific tendency that concerns this book, I think they do obviate the urgency of showing *that* continuity exists – indeed, they would make this very difficult to deny. My aim is not to provide an exhaustive history of influence, but to consider manifestations of a negative engagement with presentness that rises to prominence in modernism – its literature and, especially with Theodor Adorno, its aesthetic theory – and continues to shape new forms of playwriting after the century's end.

What these texts share is a perception that writing can collude in the theatrical project of contesting the present as such, wielding a negativity that attacks (itself as) what is. "Space thinks, Something something something," Wellman writes of theater; "Time thinks, This will kill that" (*Speculations* 24). As we'll see in James and Stein, theatrical space can attack the "something something something" of time, too. Such assaults takes place in the name of something *else*:

RAYMOND: And what will this new sky look like?
SUSANNAH: I told you I don't know.
 Like a sprig of blossoming mustard. (Wellman, *Murder* 32)

Through their negative theatrics, these texts strain against the world as we have lived it, as we are living it. This study tries to trace their furious blossomings.

Acknowledgments

This book began as a dissertation in UC Berkeley's Rhetoric department, which I hope will always be a home for miscellaneous weirdos who like theory. My advisor there, Shannon Jackson, was a tireless, rigorous, generous reader and teacher; she taught me how to be part of the world of scholarship, and how to write this book. Dan Blanton was also incredibly generous right from the start of the project, asking incisive questions and helping me find my way. I might not have made it to that point, though, without Felipe Gutterriez, who took the time to supervise me in a year-long independent study on philosophy and theater and helped me figure out what I actually cared about. Two seminars with Robert Kaufman introduced me to Adorno – and more specifically to the Adorno who inspired this project. Studying with Barbara Spackman showed me how beautiful a theory laying hold of a text could be. I was also lucky to have the help and support of Anthony Cascardi, Daniel Boyarin, David Bates, and Marcus Norman.

Soon after beginning work on this project, I attended the Mellon School of Theater and Performance Research at Harvard University, where I benefitted from a dissertation workshop led by Katherine Biers and a seminar taught by Martin Harries. Since then, Martin has been an ingenious and wonderfully kind interlocutor, who has been willing to read this work and think about it with me on numerous occasions. I want to thank everyone from that summer who has been willing to keep the conversation going, including Nicole Jerr, Matt Cornish, Jacob Gallagher-Ross, and especially Shonni Enelow, whose feedback and comradeship have been invaluable. Thanks also to my theater-studies pals from Berkeley, Brandon Woolf and Shane Boyle, who are so good to talk to.

Since I joined the Department of English at NYU, Una Chaudhuri and Richard Halpern have been unfailingly generous with their feedback on this project, and their advice and moral support have meant a lot to me. I also want to thank Elaine Freedgood, Juliet Fleming, Maureen McLane,

Greg Vargo, Bill Blake, Nick Boggs, Pat Crain, and Chris Cannon. I don't know what I would do without Sonya Posmentier and Wendy Lee, who are sources of continual wisdom and comfort.

I'd like to thank Zach Samalin, who has been in this academic thing with me since the beginning, and everyone who has discussed pieces of the project with me along the way, including Michael Bachmann, Geoffrey Baker, Lauren Berlant, John Brenkman, Elin Diamond, Jonathan Flatley, Elinor Fuchs, Chris Grobe, Dennis Johanßen, Joshua Kotin, Douglas Mao, Simon Porzak, Nicholas Ridout, Rebecca Schneider, and Damon Young. I'm grateful to Vicki Cooper for bringing this book to Cambridge University Press, and to Kate Brett, Marianna Prizio, and Rebecca Jackaman for seeing it through.

Then there are the people who've shaped my life as a playwright and director, and given me the stake I have in thinking about theater. Mac Wellman has been the number one daemon, through his essays, conversations we've had, and especially his plays. I suspect it will be clear to anyone who reads all of this book that Mac is at the center of it, though he only really comes to the fore in Chapter 6. He's warped my mind, and it's probably permanent; he's also left his mark on pretty much everything there is to love about "the American theater" today. A portion of the chapter on Mac was first published as "Mouthing Off: The Negativity of Monologue in Mac Wellman's *A Murder of Crows*" in *Modern Drama* 57.3 (Fall 2014): 293–314, and I'm grateful to *Modern Drama* for the permission to use it here. I'd also like to thank Elevator Repair Service and Big Dance Theater for giving me access to performance video, and of course for the work they do, which keeps the rest of us on our toes.

I don't think I could stand writing about theater if I weren't also making some, so I want to thank everyone who's done that with me over the past several years: the actors, designers, production teams, institutions, and friends who have made it happen. They know who they are; I've thanked them before, and I hope I'll have lots more occasions for thanking them again. So for now I'll just say thanks to Richard Maxwell, Jenny Seastone, Ben Williams, and especially Ásta Bennie Hostetter, who has spent so many hours with me over the past twenty-odd years, hashing out what the hell it is we think we're doing up there anyway.

I want to thank two more people: my mother, Fredrica Jarcho, for bringing me to the theater in the first place; and Cody Carvel, who makes it all possible and who is always on my mind, whatever's happening.

PART I

Modernism's Negative Theatrics

... what is wants the other:
   the artwork is the language of this wanting. (Theodor Adorno)[1]

CHAPTER I

Introduction

Negative Theatrics

ESTRAGON: *[gesture towards the universe]* This one is enough for you?
(Samuel Beckett, *Waiting for Godot*)¹

The Presence of the Stage, Again

Of all the voices ever raised against textual "dominance" in theater, Antonin Artaud's is surely the most piercing. "We must get rid of our superstitious valuation of texts and *written* poetry," he proclaims in 1938's *The Theater and its Double* (78). Artaud calls for a Theater of Cruelty more "immediate and direct" than anything written down: "a poetry in space," not in words (74, 38). He was not the first to decry written plays as a perversion of theater, but the searing power of his polemic keeps drawing us back with the pull of a primal scene. It sometimes feels as if contemporary theater discourse has never really left Artaud's presence, as if we still bore the "ineffaceable scar" he hoped to inflict on his audiences (77).

Lingering with Artaud, however, doesn't always mean reasserting his program. Almost as significantly as Artaud's own work, Jacques Derrida's essays on Artaud in *Writing and Difference* (1967) reset the terms within which theorists of theater could conceive their object. Derrida characterizes Artaud's vision as a theater of "pure presence" (*Writing* 247), where the live event of performance would restore its participants to an original state of immediacy. Conventional theater, with its script and its storytelling, always represents something else, someplace else, another time. It divides us from the present and from ourselves. By contrast, Artaud's Theater of Cruelty would make us find ourselves, here, now, at the actual scene of the performance. For Artaud, Derrida suggests, this possibility is what constitutes and distinguishes theater as a live medium. That vital promise is obscured by the tradition that converts the stage into a medium of representation. At issue here is not only the representation of fiction through theatrical mimesis, but, as Derrida emphasizes, the re-presentation of a written work (the script) which exists outside and apart from the performance present, and hence divides the present event from itself (*Writing* 237). Artaud's ideal of a theater "without works" springs from a sense of writing as "that which dispossesses me and makes me remote from myself, interrupting my proximity to myself" – whereas performance, as an "art of life," should be able to put me right where I am (ibid. 183). In a much-quoted passage, Derrida argues that this ideal of presentness must ultimately defeat itself, because its very accessibility *as* an ideal occurs through its opposite, representation. "The present offers itself as such, appears, presents itself, opens up the stage of time or the time of the stage only by harboring its own intestine difference, and only in the interior fold of its original repetition, in representation ... Presence, in order to be presence and self-presence, has always already begun to represent itself, has always already been penetrated" (248–249). "Presence" means that which is not re-presentation, a state of being that is just *here, now*. But to conceive presence, or to experience presence *as* presence, is "always already" to cast it within a system of past and future identifications, corrupting the very actuality that was supposed to define it.

The last half-century of theater and performance scholarship has exhibited a kind of selective amnesia when it comes to Derrida's critique, now acknowledging and now forgetting that "presence" is a problematic term. A theater discourse that positions itself against the "dominance of the text" still frequently also asserts, à la Artaud, the priority of "presence over representation" (Lehmann 109). This way of characterizing postdramatic theater or "live art" seizes on the waning of drama's internally coherent make-believe worlds, and interprets this as a shift away from representation itself, toward an immediate production of meaning here and now. "Meaning is no longer *represented* by theatrical signifiers, but *produced* in the aesthetic playing space between stage and house" (Poschmann 319) – just as, for Artaud, the Balinese theater seemed to offer a "language without meaning except in the circumstances of the stage" (*Theater* 61).[2] And it's hard not to hear an echo of Artaud in Hans-Thies Lehmann's claim that postdramatic theater "offers not a representation but an intentionally unmediated experience of the real" (134).[3]

This familiar vision of theater, as a medium in which what is *really present* can supplant representation, is exactly what Derrida deconstructs. But the fact is, we seem to need some account of presence (or "the present") in order to distinguish performance from other kinds of art. Some theorists have sought to reconcile this imperative with deconstruction by flipping the script: since performance cannot be the site of presence, it becomes the site where we feel presence's "impossibility" (Derrida, *Writing* 249) most keenly. Thus in Peggy Phelan's important work on performance as disappearance, theater becomes a medium of absence, dispossession, and loss.[4] Accounts like Phelan's strive to preserve the medial specificity of performance, not through appeals to the full presence of performer and audience, but by reference to a sense that, as the time of performance passes, we are never quite present enough. The impossibility of Artaud's theater thus becomes the very lesson of performance, which emerges as *the* deconstructive art form par excellence.

Despite repeated references to theatrical "presence," Lehmann evinces a similar understanding when he turns to this topic with more sustained attention. The "presence" of postdramatic theater, he explains, is really better understood as a "present," in the sense of an "experience of lack [that] takes place at the seam of time ... *The present* [Präsens] *is necessarily the erosion and slippage of presence* [Präsenz]. It denotes an event that empties the now and in this emptiness itself lets memory and anticipation flash up" (143–144/258–260). Even before Phelan made this argument a staple of performance theory, Elinor Fuchs had offered a similar reading of contemporary experimental theater in her important 1985 article "Presence and the Revenge of Writing: Re-Thinking Theatre after Derrida." Fuchs describes a series of recent pieces, including a 1975 Mabou Mines production done with mirrors: "The actors performed the entire short piece from a balcony above and behind the spectators; we saw only their ghostly reflections. Such a staging undermined habitual expectations of bodily presence and actor-audience contact" ("Presence" 164).[5] This emphatic deprivation of immediacy, Fuchs argues, typifies a new kind of theater, marked by the Derridean awareness that presence is always contaminated by the doublings of representation.

Other scholars, however, have felt that this critical emphasis on absence, mediation, and textuality in theater threatens to occlude the embodiedness that is also fundamental to the medium. Stanton Garner's 1994 *Bodied Spaces* criticizes what he sees, in poststructuralist theory, as a pervasive "uneasiness with the body ... as a site of corporeal and subjective elements that always resist reduction to the merely textual" (26).[6] Garner suggests that the post-Derridean presence embargo has encouraged a critical tendency to ignore, or evade, the corporeality that constitutes theater as the "most bodied of all mediums" (39). He therefore proposes a renewed phenomenology of theater, one which would incorporate poststructuralist insights and resist falling back into a naïve confidence in presence "as a stable essence, given in itself within the perceptual act" (43). Theater's "phenomenological complexity," Garner writes, "comprehends, indeed is fueled by, difference and absence" (ibid.). But these factors need not be seen as eliminating presence altogether; on the contrary, it is the way presence sustains their assault that constitutes theatrical experience. In particular, this complexity defines the condition of language in theater. "Although theatrical language may aspire, in the hands of certain artists and theorists, to the condition of pure textuality, it maintains its inherence in a field of embodied utterance, even when it subjects this field to transformation, substitution, or dispersal" (123). Garner thus hopes to rescue the specificity of theater (and of writing in theater) by conceiving its presence as both metaphysically unstable *and* experientially real.

Now, it seems to me that this argument does not fully address the depth of Derrida's critique, since it still rests on a binary conceptual distinction between embodied presence and signification, even while it presents the two as mutually inextricable. Early in *Bodied Spaces*, Garner asserts that "not only are such rigid oppositions as sign/phenomenon unnecessary, they are also theoretically untenable" (16). But throughout his breathtaking readings, phenomenal presence still tends to appear as something other than, or beyond, linguistic meaning, something that "infiltrate[s]" and disturbs representation (123).[7] When Garner proposes to "complemen[t] the 'always already' of signification with the 'always also' of the subject's corporeal fields" (39), his "also" signals an immanence not recuperable within representation, a claim that cannot be fully reconciled with the deconstructive argument. The Derridean retort would be that there is no phenomenality that cannot itself be (or has not itself been) captured as a sign.

Nevertheless, part of what makes theater phenomenology like Garner's so compelling, and doubtless also lies behind less cautious espousals of "presence" in other theater scholarship, is the same thing that lends Artaud's manifestos their own irresistible conviction: the fact that it *does* seem to make a difference to us when our fellow beings are performing here and now. It may well be that this experiential fact (or "effect") is bound up with what Derrida calls the "closure" of our "historico-metaphysical epoch" (*Grammatology* 4) – that any experience of performance as such is only possible within that closure.[8] If we accept this limitation at least provisionally, we can shift our focus from the question of how much presence there "really is" in theater, to the question of how various artists have registered the *experience* of a distinctly present medium, and have devised their innovations in response to that experience. We need not ask whether these innovations bear out a particular thesis about the ontological status of presence/presentness in theater: in this book, I ask instead how the perception of theater's heightened phenomenal presence, or here-and-nowness, pushes writers to discover countervailing powers of negativity within the theatrical.

In the chapters that follow, therefore, my own analyses take as a premise the conviction so carefully articulated by Garner, and reaffirmed more recently by Cormac Power: that the spatial, temporal, corporeal, and intersubjective dimensions of theater always produce at least the potential to call our attention to the present *as* present, even or especially when it also exposes that present as "a *function* of signification" (Power, *Presence* 198), or in poststructuralist terms, as a presence effect.[9] I think it is indisputable that theatrical signs operate, as Bert States writes, "not simply by signifying the world but by being *of* it" (*Great* 20). Taken one way, of course, this description applies to all signs; it also has special application to photographic media.[10] But because of the simultaneity and spatial contiguity of production, presentation, and reception that distinguish live performance from other art forms, "the world" that theater's human and nonhuman materials are "of" is, emphatically, *ours*; it is *this* world, sharing our moment in history. If there were an earthquake or a bombing or the paradigmatic fire, we would all go down together. And when, on the contrary, the show goes on, this fact bespeaks the greater going-on of the world in which we watch it. The successive moments of a production, its ongoingness before our eyes, prove that the systems that support our present reality are more or less functioning; and as an audience, we are on the scene of – we take part in – that functional success.

This emphatic going-on of the world as we know it can feel like a triumph; it can also feel awful. For the artists whose works I will be reading, the present is above all something to break out of. We ought to recognize, with Derrida, that any present already harbors its own (and our) disappearance; but to totalize this aspect of performance's presentness is to ignore the historical weight we invoke when we speak of "the present," its *reference* to *what is*; what testifies to having been perpetrated; what we are tolerating and perpetuating. Theater can make this burden of actuality palpable. And in so doing, it can prompt the search for actuality's opposite: that which is *not* here or now, that which would be radically different.

Resisting the present thus doesn't simply mean embracing representation, or turning metaphysics on its head. It is true that, insofar as representation in the Derridean sense *undoes the actual* by marking its dependence upon what *is not here*, there is at least a gestural parallel between representation and the negative theatricality that interests me. But as Derrida also argues, the concept of representation is still bound up in a hierarchy that asserts an erstwhile present as the origin and source of value. The works I read exhibit no such nostalgia. Their logic is much closer to the operation that Derrida suggests "representation" is meant to cover over: *writing*, which is never truly just the copy or mark of a presence, but enacts an unrecoverable dissemination of difference. Writing "displaces the *proper place* of the [spoken] sentence, the unique time of the sentence pronounced *hic et nunc* ... " (*Grammatology* 281). A theater that seeks to displace us from the site where we are, but *not toward a second, imitative present*, is neither a theater of presence nor a theater of representation. It might, however, be a theater of writing.

This possibility returns us to Elinor Fuchs's argument that "Writing, which has traditionally retired behind the apparent presence of performance, is openly declaring itself" in late twentieth-century theater ("Presence" 163). Whereas Fuchs saw the aim of this tendency as specifically deconstructive, the artists I examine are less concerned to discredit the concept of presence than to escape the experience of it. Still, their work, like the work she describes, teaches us to value writing as disruptive of the present. In fact, Lehmann also notes that postdramatic theater continues a modernist valuation of "the written text as an interruption of the self-sufficient imagery of the stage" (146).[11] Even more suggestively, he offers writing as an analogy for the entire theatrical event, arguing that the most highly "visual" postdramatic theater operates "like a text, a scenic poem" (94; cf. 61, 74, 85). These observations point us toward a theater whose relationship to writing is especially intimate, *because of the way writing complicates the actual*.

Drama and the Present: Peter Szondi and Bertolt Brecht

In the readings that make up this book, I show that a utopian desire to negate the present lures writers to the theater, and opens theater up to writing. The next section of this chapter will start to ground this claim in a reading of Theodor Adorno's aesthetic theory, the philosophical source to which the book will return most often. First, however, I want to explain why – given that my argument seems to be at odds with some basic tendencies in postdramatic theater studies – I have retained what I take to be that discourse's central insight: the notion of a theater that pushes beyond drama. In order to do this, I'd like to turn to the classic study that theorized drama itself as the very form of presence and presentness: Peter Szondi's *Theory of the Modern Drama*.

Writing in the mid-1950s, Szondi interprets the history of modern dramaturgy from Henrik Ibsen through Arthur Miller as a series of responses to an aesthetic "crisis": drama proper could no longer accommodate "the problems of contemporary life" (5), and so, as per Hegelian aesthetics, changed content was "precipitated" as changed form (4). Szondi declines to articulate programmatically the contemporary situation that has produced these changes, insisting that analysis should stick with the "technical contradictions ... internal to the concrete work itself" (5). But the implied historical shift clearly entails a loss of confidence in the social sphere as the site of truth. Ideal drama had emerged in the Renaissance, when

> a newly self-conscious being ... sought to create an artistic reality within which he could fix and mirror himself on the basis of interpersonal relationships alone. Man entered the drama only as a fellow human being, so to speak. The sphere of the "between" seemed to be the essential part of his being; freedom and obligation, will and decision the most important of his attributes. The "place" at which he achieved dramatic realization was in an act of decision and self-disclosure. (7)

The growing inability of "freedom and obligation, will and decision" to account for daily experience, however, meant that by the late nineteenth century, the drama could no longer serve as a form of expression. "Modern drama" therefore exists in tension with itself: it consists of a series of incursions into the dramatic form, efforts that unmake what is proper to drama even as they try to adapt the genre to contemporary reality. Harking back to a generic binary instituted by Aristotle, revived by Weimar classicism, and reanimated again by Bertolt Brecht, Szondi takes the opposite of "drama" to be "epic"; the decline of drama in modernity thus implies the encroachment of epic elements on theatrical texts. The most fundamental of these elements, for Szondi, is the "epic *I*." In ideal drama, consciousness is realized *as* the actions of characters in an interpersonal space; in epic, consciousness remains apart from such events, and the subject "stands facing the others," evaluating the social world rather than finding herself realized in it (37). This construal echoes Brecht's famous claim that the subject or "I" of epic theater – as opposed to drama – "must not simply put myself in [people's] place, but must place myself opposite to them" (Brecht 243).[12] For Szondi, this estranged confrontation displaces not only Brechtian theater, but modern theater more broadly, into the realm of epic.

Introduction: Negative Theatrics

In *Postdramatic Theater*, Lehmann criticizes Szondi's "conception of the epic as *the* successor to the dramatic," an assumption Lehmann claims has been buoyed by Brecht's "overpowering authority" (29). Postdramatic theater as Lehmann conceives it is importantly "post-Brechtian" (33); part of the impetus for Lehmann's project is precisely the sense that the model of "epic theater" cannot account for more radical innovation. Epic, as an Aristotelian category, still implies the dominance of a fictional plot; but in postdramatic work, Lehmann argues, "the idea of theatre as a representation of a *fictive* cosmos in general has been ruptured and even relinquished altogether" (30–31). The works he examines frankly defy Brecht's maxim that the "'plot' is the theatre's great undertaking" (Brecht 250); properly speaking, postdramatic works are thus not "epic" at all.

In that sense, neither are the works I will be reading here. What epic theater shares with drama – the prominence of plot – renders it an unsuitable category for these works. But Szondi's and Brecht's analyses can still illuminate them, because a central aspect of epic's *difference* from drama (and, for that matter, from some obviously "postdramatic" performances) remains highly relevant to what the works I am studying want to do. I believe that some of the same anti-dramatic tendencies Szondi identifies as "epic" also appear in an alternative tradition of theatrical experimentation that runs through the twentieth century. This tradition remains active today, resisting a norm that Szondi and Brecht both see at the heart of drama, and that continues to dominate a wide range of theater practice: the *affirmation of the present as such*.

"In the Drama," Szondi writes, "time unfolds as an absolute, linear sequence in the present" (9); "Its presence is pure actuality" (38). Today's readers might well be surprised to find the following description attached to drama, rather than to postdramatic theater or to performance art: "It is not a (secondary) representation of something else (primary); it presents itself, is itself. Its action, like each of its lines, is 'original'; it is accomplished as it occurs" (Szondi 9). Or again: "An action which represents is not dramatic: the events in the Drama, absolute in themselves, can stand for nothing beyond themselves" (36). Szondi's scare quotes around the word "original" reflect two facts: 1. drama is a written text before it is a performance, and 2. it is a fictional story. But the former fact is rigorously suppressed by the play itself, which occludes its own author through the very consistency of the second fact. "The dramatist is absent from the Drama," Szondi observes. "He does not speak; he institutes discussion. The Drama is not written, it is set. All the lines ... are spoken in context and remain there" (8). For Szondi, dramatic fiction does not take us away from the present, in either spatial or temporal terms. Rather, drama absolutizes the here-and-now, ideally producing what Derrida, glossing J. L. Austin, would call the "total context": that scene where "no *remainder* escapes the present totalization" ("Signature" 322). Speeches and actions that interrupt the consistency of the fiction, reminding us of the elsewhere of its poetic composition, also perforate the actuality of performance. They thereby break with drama, which consistently affirms and even institutionalizes the performance present.

There is undoubtedly a risk, here, of eliding key differences beneath polyvalent terms. As Power points out, "Presence in theater means different things at different times to different people" (*Presence* 12). Is the kind of "presence" or "presentness" typically attributed to experimental theater and performance really the same as the "absolute" present Szondi accords to drama? One objection might be that drama's actuality excludes the audience, whereas the here-and-now of other performance forms constructs itself openly as a "co-presence" with the audience.[13] But this is where Brecht's analysis becomes especially relevant, suggesting that the distinction cannot be so clear-cut. Drama may not overtly make a place for the audience within its closed circuit of fictional relationships, but the internal magnetics of this circuit draw us in through empathetic identification: ideally, we are absorbed into the present so fully that no elsewhere, no other time remains to us.

The ideally dramatic work never incorporates its audience explicitly, like Peter Handke's *Offending the Audience* ("You become aware that you are sitting in a theater. You become aware of the size of your limbs ... You become aware of your tongue. You become aware of your throat" [20]). As Brecht observes, however, drama operates no less directly on the audience's bodies, calibrating those bodies to the actuality inhabited by the actors *and*, with all its social and political implications, by us. Drama's spectators, "strenuously ... tensing all their muscles, except where these are flabby and exhausted," are drawn into the closed world of the same fiction that disavows them, and closure becomes the principle of their own world too. Brecht summarizes this effect in resonant phrasing: in drama, he writes, "everyone can say at once: yes, that's how it is [*so ist es*]" (237/ VII: 25).

In dramatic theater, then, we are *more firmly present* than ever: fascinated by the tautological affirmation of "how it is," we grasp at our actuality and cling to it as such. What distinguishes dramatic actuality from that of other performance forms is thus not so much drama's putative exclusion of the audience as its occlusion of any other scene from which the shared present might have diverged – or derived. The perception that drama fixes us within the present of its own occurrence motivated Brecht's call for the "literarization of the theatre" (71), a phrase that is terrifically suggestive for experimental work today.[14] Just as Szondi aligns drama's absolute present with its disavowal of writing ("The Drama is not written, it is . . . spoken in context"), Brecht thinks the *inclusion* of writing can dislodge us from this kind of fixation. Thus he defends his use of title cards in productions:

> Someone with an academic approach to drama might object to the titles on the basis that the playwright should be able to say everything that needs to be said through the action of the play – that the literary work should be able to express everything within its own confines. The corresponding attitude for the spectator is that of not thinking about a subject but within the confines of that subject. But this practice of subordinating everything to a single idea, this urge to propel the audience along a single track where *it can look neither right nor left, up nor down*, is something that the new dramatic writing must reject. The use of footnotes and the comparing of points *on different pages* need to be introduced into dramatic writing too. (72, my emphases)

In fact, it's not at all obvious that reading inherently offers more critical freedom than theater (cf. Puchner, *Stage* 148). We'll consider in the next chapter how the page can maintain a dramatic immediacy of its own. But Brecht's notion of the literary, here, arises through the question of what writing might do *in performance*, and more specifically what it might do to a theater dominated by dramatic habits. Brecht's sense that writing undermines the "single track" of dramatic affirmation by producing *alternate sites* will emerge as a fundamental tenet for the artists considered in this study. For them, Brecht's idea of "literarization" has its most profound resonance not in the epic self-possession of a reader mastering a text, but in the ways writing can beckon us outside the moment of performance, undermining the self-sufficiency of the performance's here-and-now.

"[C]onscious of nothing outside itself" (Szondi 8), drama's significance is ideally exhausted within the time and space of the play, so that no *other knowledge* is necessary. By contrast, the epicized forms of "modern drama" that Szondi analyzes expose and emphasize the performance present as continuous with factors that are not precisely onstage or "in the room." So, of course, do multiple avant-garde performance traditions. For example, fin-de-siècle cabaret, as Lehmann observes, "is based on the possibility of allusions to everyday reality shared by players and audiences and hence contains a performance moment that is inseparably connected to urban life" (62). Many decades later, when asked if a "happening" should be lifelike, John Cage responded: "Not that it should be lifelike but that we should be able to consume it in relation to our lives. So that it would introduce us to the other things in our lives which we consume" (qtd. in Kostelanetz 54). There is indeed a significant difference between the perceived actuality of such forms and that of dramatic theater, one which we might express as follows: where dramatic actuality is bounded, these forms' actuality would be limitless; an intensive, impervious present contrasts with an extensive, inexhaustible present. But the latter ideal, just as much as the former, threatens to affirm *what is* at the expense of any radical alterity.

In *Looking Away* (2009), the theorist Rei Terada excavates a modern philosophical and aesthetic tradition of "discomfort with the coercion of the given" (5), a resistance to the prevalent conflation of how things are with how they ought to be (known to philosophers as the fact/value conflation). Terada focuses on a response she calls "phenomenophilia," a powerful desire to linger with private experiences of ephemeral perception, like "looking away at the colored shadow on the wall" (4). These perceptions, precisely because they make no claim on our acceptance as fact *or* value, offer "fleeting relief from the pressure to endorse what Kant calls the world 'as is'" (ibid.). Brecht, dedicated to a theater firmly focused on material, historical concerns, would be an unlikely phenomenophile; but what his scornful formulation of the dramatic "*so ist es*" indicts is precisely the "pressure to endorse" the given world that Terada describes. Indeed, where Terada shows how resistance to the given as such flares up with particular urgency in the wake of Kant's epistemology, Brecht points to the ways in which theater – as a space of embodied, collective, here-and-now reception – can intensify this urgency, by threatening to become a chamber for that "pressure."

The negative theatrics I'll be tracing are not exactly phenomenophilic; the ephemerality of performance isn't their dominant value. But the artists discussed in this book all approach theater as a site for "looking away" from the present, and theatrical writing as a technology for doing so. In the context of this field, Terada's work might offer a check on the critical tendency to identify theater's value entirely with shared actuality – the assumption that *real* theater, unlike literature, is all about what's happening in the room. Against this norm, which contemporary theater discourse often carries over from drama, the artists I'll consider court utopia: that which is not yet. Utopia would be, precisely, that which is still *not happening* – "the longing for the new, not the new itself" (Adorno,

Aesthetic 32). This negativity characterizes the theater that will emerge, in different forms, throughout the following chapters.

The "Wrong Life" of Performance: Adorno and the "primacy of the text"

Adorno has not commonly been regarded as a major resource for theater and performance studies, although this is now beginning to change. The antipathy to his theory is understandable: where many performance scholars have devoted themselves to discovering meaningful social resistance within popular forms, Adorno's work maintains an unpalatable bitterness toward mass culture; where theater scholars have continually returned to Brecht in theorizing the political and phenomenological aspects of the medium, Adorno appears as an infamous Brecht detractor.[15] But by the current norms of these discourses, the most objectionable feature of Adorno's work (though not the most widely known) is probably his assertion of "the primacy of the text over its performance" (*Aesthetic* 100) – an assertion he applies to theater as well as to music, with which he is much more closely engaged. For the study of performance forms today, "the primacy of the text" appears less as a serious challenge to prevalent assumptions than as an outmoded piece of antitheatrical modernism.[16]

Those of us invested in the theory and practice of theater, however, should take this notion seriously – and not only because it might unsettle certain disciplinary complacencies about performance's punk-rock status. Adorno's argument signals a way to value text within the performance context as something performance does *not* simply instrumentalize, exceed, or undermine; to value the script as a form apart. In suggesting that we heed this claim, I don't mean simply to reverse the poles of the prevailing hierarchy, making *text* the radical and *performance* the conservative term. Such an exercise might be invigorating but would certainly be irresponsible, both to my own sense of what theater is, and to the richly complex and dialectical theory that lies behind Adorno's "primacy of the text." What I do want to do is suspend the assumption that this "primacy" is a fallacy that we of the performance disciplines have long moved past. Instead, I hypothesize that Adorno's privileging of the textual artifact over the performance event corresponds to a crucial *problem* with performance, a problem whose negotiation marks the emergence of certain major formal innovations.[17]

That problem is, as I suggested above, the "eventful present": the phenomenological fact that performance happens, as we are so often reminded, here and now. Drama celebrates this fact, but celebration becomes difficult if, to put things baldly, "here and now" names a horror – a "wrong life" that, as Adorno famously said, "cannot be lived rightly" (*Minima* 39). We need not commit to a total abomination of life as we know it, or pretend there is nothing we love here and now, in order to grant the legitimacy and the ethical necessity of acknowledging that our present, sustained by institutionalized global suffering, is unacceptable; and that all that exists is in some way complicit with this suffering. The relentlessness with which Adorno's writing asks us to keep this in mind has made his work unbearable for many readers, and surely there are other readers whose instinctive sympathy with this "dark" outlook has made them uncritical enthusiasts of the critical stance. The critical attitude that drives Adornian negative dialectics is exactly not a whole-scale dismissal of "everything," but a commitment to engage at the minute level of the most particular, to interrogate phenomena in their utmost specificity. Nevertheless, Adorno's works are full of references to a *bad totality*, in which the fundamental operation of both art and theory is defined as the refusal of positivity: the operation of differing with what is.

The more effectively our present presents itself as the only possible one – "*so ist es*" – the harder this imaginative labor becomes. "The here and now is a prison house," writes José Esteban Muñoz at the beginning of *Cruising Utopia* (2009). "We must strive, in the face of the here and now's totalizing rendering of reality, to think and feel a *then and there*" (1).[18] Adorno's work is dedicated to theorizing the ways in which art and thought, while utterly implicated in and conditioned by historical reality, imaginatively exceed that reality by negating it. The prospect of thus exceeding what is real motivates philosophy's "contradictory effort to say, through mediation and contextualization, what cannot be said *hic et nunc*" (Adorno, *Lectures* 74), as well as art's "determinate negation of the existing world order" (*Aesthetic* 344). Adorno's insistence that art must be understood in this way, as a determinate negation that gestures *beyond* the real through a recognition of itself as *within* the real, will be the central theoretical premise of this book.

This configuration defines art's *autonomy* – a term that has sometimes served as a straw man in contemporary academic discourse. For Adorno, the autonomy of an artwork is not a matter of its standing outside history, independent of the forces and relations of production, immune to the marketplaces of labor and taste, or impervious to ideology. To begin with, he explains, art's claim to autonomy is itself a historical phenomenon, as "a function of the bourgeois consciousness of freedom that was itself bound up with the social structure"; the individual work, too, is obviously socially conditioned, both in its "mode of production" and in its "thematic material" (*Aesthetic* 225). But while Adorno continually warns against any inclination to dehistoricize art, his major theoretical target is less this bourgeois mythology than strains of Marxism that value art for its social efficacy. Such reckoning places art squarely in the current of existing reality, subjecting it to instrumental reason. It is against this sort of demand for an "engaged" art that Adorno develops the notion of aesthetic autonomy as negativity – which is itself, he argues, art's most profound social engagement. "[A]rt becomes social by its opposition to society, and it occupies this position only as autonomous art. By crystallizing in itself as something unique to itself, rather than complying with existing social norms [including revolutionary norms] and qualifying as 'socially useful,' it criticizes society by merely existing" (225–226).[19] Autonomy is the "historical gesture [that] repels empirical reality, of which artworks are nevertheless part" (227). The artwork is autonomous in its insistence on differing from what is, what it itself is: the here-and-now, the compromised reality of existing social, economical, political relations.

Autonomy, then, is art's protest against the actuality to which it belongs. For Adorno, this protest is inherently processual: the artwork needs to be understood as an ongoing process because it never achieves the total self-determination or alterity it seeks, but is continually confronted with its own dependence upon the material realities it also continually transcends. "[A]rt's dynamic," he writes, is "an irresolvable antithesis that is never brought to rest in the state of being. Artworks are such only *in actu* because their tension does not terminate in pure identity with either extreme" (*Aesthetic* 176). The paradox of art, its inability to achieve itself completely, marks it off from the world of instrumental reason; art's constitutive unfinishedness is, one might say, both its difference from itself and, thus, its difference from a world governed by the "reality principle," the ideology of self-preservation. If the work were able to overtake its disparate elements and unite them into a seamless whole, it would have definitively sacrificed their otherness for the sake of its own self-constitution. It would therefore no longer *be* a work of art, since what art seeks is "the identity of the identical and the nonidentical" (ibid.) – a goal that the finished achievement of pure self-identity would betray. Because art's nonidentical identity can only exist as an ongoing project, never as a static outcome, its essence is process.

This might seem like an aesthetic theory that would privilege the utterly processual, time-based medium of performance. For Adorno, however, the work's internal conflict is maintained as such *within* the delimiting sphere of a fixed artifactual form. The work's violent life is forged, that is, through its "objectivation": its coalescence into a formed thing. Adorno writes:

> it is only as finished, molded objects that they [artworks] become force fields of their antagonisms; otherwise the encapsuled forces would simply run parallel to each other or dissipate ... The movement of artworks must be at a standstill and thereby become visible ... What crackles in artworks is the sound of the friction of antagonistic elements that the artwork seeks to unify; it is script [*Schrift*] not least because, as in linguistic signs, its processual element is enciphered in its objectivation. (*Aesthetic* 176–177/263–264)

The work's objectivation, its taking the form of a static object (a piece of written text, a musical score, a painting or sculpture), is what captures and intensifies its processuality. We might say that objectivation is a kind of constitutive crisis for the work, whose conflicting forces are thereby locked up together in an echo chamber that magnifies and sustains their "antagonisms." The clash between processuality and fixed form also redoubles the conflictual dynamic that produced the processuality in the first place: the dialectic between the work's identity and its nonidentical elements reappears as the dialectic between *that* dialectic and the static form that confines its processuality, so that here too the work "negates itself" (176). Art's difference from the world's tyranny of identity, art's fundamental negativity and allergy to affirmation are thus at work most robustly in the self-negating aesthetic *object* – for which writing (*Schrift*) offers a privileged model.

Adorno's remarks on performance suggest that its capacity for protest is compromised not only by its ephemerality – which is, in fact, a feature of all art (3, 80) – but more specifically by its spatial and temporal inseparability from its own production. "The fixation through print or scores is not external to the work; only through them does the work *become autonomous from its genesis*: That explains the primacy of the text over its performance" (100, my emphasis). I understand this statement as follows: performance is bound to its own genesis in a way text is not, by the very fact that performance *is* its own genesis: its existence is coextensive with its arising, which it can never outlast. And since its genesis is what anchors it in worldly economies, that is to say, in history, performance itself is more emphatically worldly than objectivated forms.[20] Whereas the object-work abides both within and in excess of the actuality that has determined it, becoming "foreig[n] to the world" (183) within the walls of its "force field," performance erects no such extraterritoriality: it is constantly being *born here*, its citizenship reconfirmed at each instant. As we saw, phenomenologists of theater have theorized this insistent presentness as fundamental to performance, where "actuality continually infuses the alterity that seeks to displace it" (Garner 41).[21] In a different register, Brecht bemoaned theater's institutional tendency to engulf each new play "so that the play no longer represents a foreign body within the apparatus" (71). For an Adornian sensibility, this reassertion of the actual realm as against the alterity of the "foreign" constitutes a problem at once aesthetic, political, and ethical.[22]

Adorno is of course not advocating the abolition of performance, but he does insist that performance – theatrical and musical – be referred to its text, that its aesthetic value be located *apart from its actual occurrence*. This stance becomes especially clear in Adorno's condemnation of the "happening," a performance ideal very much on the rise at the time of his writing. I want to dwell on Adorno's vision of the happening for a moment, without testing it against the real events (engineered by Allan Kaprow, Cage, and many others) which would certainly have complicated Adorno's account, had he let them.[23] It seems to me that his remarks on the happening are most illuminating, not as criticism of concrete works, but as the articulation of a threat that seems to inhere in all performance, the degree-zero of its dependence on *happening* in the everyday sense of the term (he uses the English word).

Specifically, Adorno sees "the happening" as a culmination of art's tendency to "becom[e] its own enemy, the direct and false continuation of purposeful rationality" (*Aesthetic* 103). The happening's extension of purposeful rationality is "false" both because it can never fully escape the aesthetic "semblance character," the unreality, it wants to leave behind, and because it inevitably fails by purposeful-rational standards (103–104; cf. Sarkoparnig 62–66). I am not going to enter into the debate about Adorno's contention that artworks are "cut off from real political effect" (*Aesthetic* 104), which is the question of whether and how art might enact a meaningful protest *within* the purposeful-rational procedures that sustain reality.[24] Instead, I want to focus on the idea that the happening's continuity with purposeful rationality is (in a remarkable but typical moment of dialectical condensation) not only "false," but also "direct," that is, that there *is* a continuity. This would work out as follows: eschewing the dream of autonomy, the happening tries to throw itself wholeheartedly into the real, where purposeful rationality reigns supreme. Embracing an ethos of the immediate, the happening tries to shut down the utopian dimension that the work, in its struggle to differ from life, holds open. And if the work's utopian protest *is* its only meaningful "engagement," then the happening is doomed to complicity.

Now, the happening is just one specific mode of performance, apparently as different as can be from other modes – for instance, from the theatrical performance of a scripted play. And yet *as performance* of a text, as the move to a medium where exposure to contingency constantly compromises autonomy, the theater piece seems to manifest a kind of will-to-happening. The project of performing a text could even be considered a more emphatic rejection of aesthetic autonomy than the unscripted performance event, since the former actively compromises a level of objectivation that has already been achieved. To repeat: performance is the form for which "autonomy from its genesis" is least available: by definition, performance *is* its own genesis, which means that it never stops asserting its implication in the material reality that (not only has produced it, but) is producing it. If all art is the determinate negation of what exists, producing reality's other by way of immersion in reality, performance specifically threatens to block this transcendence at every moment by being *too insistently* immersed, and thus disabling the dialectical reversal. The choice of live performance, as medium, just *is* the choice of ongoing susceptibility to the real. And in a society becoming more and more "total" and "contract[ing] to a unanimous system" (*Aesthetic* 31), this means susceptibility to laws that constantly threaten to corral the work's difference, drawing it into society's mechanics. The problem with the happening, in other words, was already a problem with theater.

One possible response to this understanding of performance would be to point out its consistency with millennia of antitheatricalism; another would be to set about deconstructing the performance/text binary in Adorno, although it seems to me that his dialectical understanding of both terms goes a long way toward anticipating any such critique.[25] At present, however, I am less concerned with whether Adorno is "right" about performance than with the question of what his apprehensions might do *to* performance, *were they shared, consciously or not, by some of its practitioners*. How might they reinvigorate theater's aesthetic negativity, driving it to new levels of utopian vehemence? For the artists I consider in the following chapters, the heightened actuality of performance no longer, as in drama *and* some avant-garde forms, defines the theatrical ideal. But neither does this revaluation imply a rejection of theater itself. Instead, the prospect of being caught up in an ongoing present leads these writers to discover resources for contesting that present *within* the dimensions of theatrical performance, illuminating the ways in which this medium resists being reduced to its own "happening."

Writing is key among these resources, invoking the resistant force of its own objectivation even while providing for performance. It will come as no surprise that of all the artists considered here, Samuel Beckett – poster child of Adorno's modernism – forges the most rigorously dialectical relation between text and scene. For Beckett, writing gestures toward utopia amidst a totalizing present that engulfs the stage; it does so, however, only by indicting its own complicity with this present. In contrast, someone like Gertrude Stein may seem a less likely fit for the negative poetics of a "bad reality," or the deployment of writing *against* the actuality of performance.[26] But this is because for Stein, as for Henry James, theater always harbors something other than the presentness drama exploits – an alterity manifest not only in text, but in the very space and time of the theatrical situation itself. Their poetics are based in a sense of theater's dimensions as *disrupting* or *dispersing* its own present; writing does not so much intervene in this dynamic as describe, anticipate, and expand it. For Beckett at mid-century, this has changed: the experience of radical multiplicity has all but vanished in a world of what Adorno calls "unanimous system." Theater's promise therefore comes to reside in its dialectical construction of what *isn't here*: theater becomes a site for utopia, and writing takes on the agonized function of both refusing and promising a constitutively unrealized alterity.

As we'll see in Part II, this orientation reappears in the texts of late twentieth-century playwrights, who continue to work and rework the relation between writing and a problematic theatrical present. They do this in part by cultivating the disruptive force of monologue that Beckett unleashes in *Godot*; as we'll see, monologue becomes a crucial device for shaping performance as the performance *of text*, in a specifically nondramatic sense. But they also find many other ways to point us toward an unplaceable site of writing, straining against the "direct continuation" of what goes on here and now. And at the same time, they also reach back past the certainty of a bad totality, grasping for the alterity that still quivers just out of sight in the theaters of James and Stein.

The Readings

Before launching into this argument, I want to address what might seem like a methodological peculiarity: only half of the works I read in Part I are plays. My reading of James focuses on his late fiction, and while most of my Beckett chapter concerns *Godot*, it ends with an analysis of Beckett's novel *The Unnamable*. In a book that will ultimately want to make a claim about playwriting, why devote so much time to texts that were never meant to be staged? The answer is that I do not believe we can understand how text is disposed *in* theatrical performance without investigating text's resources *of* theatrical performance. Approaching a theater text from the perspective of what can be done with it (or to it) onstage may be extremely fruitful, but the results will also depend on what the text itself does. This is a literary question, and it is answered (though never settled) by searching out the text's ways of writing – verbal qualities that it will turn out to share with other verbal texts, only some of which will have been written for the theater. There is no reason to assume that texts can only engage with theater by being destined for performance. Ultimately, the question of what writing can bring to theater, and more specifically of *what theater* writing can bring to theater, demands that we explore all the texts whose relevance to theatrical problems impresses us, whatever their genre. To restrict this field to theater texts would eliminate from consideration certain texts whose engagement with theater is profound and fascinating – including works like James's which, since they will not "get their theater" in production, exert themselves all the more spectacularly to fabricate a theater of the page.

For these reasons, I have not limited my study of textual theater to a study of theater texts. But as the very names of James, Stein, and Beckett suggest – names that will hardly catch anyone in theater or performance studies off-guard – I have let myself be guided by the fact that each of these authors does engage explicitly and extensively with theater *qua* theater: that there is reason to hypothesize from the outset that theater takes up space in each author's imagination, and hence in that of the work. This approach amounts to recognizing these texts not merely as examples of, but also as authorities on the theatrical. When I shift my focus to contemporary writers, I present Parks and Wellman as picking up their modernist forebears' negative textual theatrics, and delivering this tendency over to the production theater of a "postdramatic era." In order to understand what today's playwrights are doing for and to theater, it will behoove us to have seen what the earlier writers were doing *with* it.

It would be disingenuous, however, to pretend that this book's engagement with James, Stein, and Beckett is motivated entirely by an interest in possible theatrical "results," or what can happen when this kind of writing is brought to the stage. To resort to this justification would be, once again, to instrumentalize writing as "material," or to value it as a potential that waits to be fulfilled through the event of production.[27] But the texts themselves contest the hierarchy that makes actual enactment the locus of ultimate value. This is not to say that they reject the theater, but rather that they *envision theater as the site where this contestation of what actually "happens" can most powerfully occur*. People who care about theater should take an interest in these texts, not only because they can broaden our understanding of what writing offers to theatrical practice, but also because they confront us with their own radical theory of what theater can be.

CHAPTER 2

"Something stranger yet"
Theatrical Distractions in Henry James and Gertrude Stein

> The scene, that evening, at which ... I did not assist, is one of the most ineffaceable in my tolerably rich experience of the theatre.
> (Henry James, 1903)

> I think my first play really was *Pinafore* in London but the theatre there was so huge that I do not remember at all seeing a stage I only remember that it felt like a theatre that is the theatre did. I doubt if I did see the stage.
> (Gertrude Stein, 1934)

> He said, Can you tell me, Miss Stein, what authority you have for so frequently using the split infinitive? Henry James, said Gertrude.
> (Alice B. Toklas, 1963)[1]

In *The Autobiography of Alice B. Toklas*, Gertrude Stein identifies Henry James "quite definitely as her forerunner," James having been "the first person in literature to find the way to the literary method of the twentieth century" (78). Depending on what version of Henry James comes most readily to your mind, this claim of affiliation might or might not be startling. Perhaps the clearest link between the two writers is the impetus both offer for thinking about how a "literary method" might also be a visual one: James, with his perpetual recurrence to the vocabulary of "picture," his legendary development of "point of view," and the exquisite phenomenology of seeing he presents in works like *The Turn of the Screw*; Stein, whose historical and aesthetic involvement with cubism not only appears throughout, but very often serves as a heuristic for her formally radical writings.[2] It's no surprise, then, that both James and Stein have also often been read for their texts' relationship to theater – the *theatron* being, etymologically, a "place for viewing." And indeed, like many others of their respective generations who were "in literature," they devoted serious time to writing for and about the stage.

Beyond registering this fact, what might it mean to call them both "theatrical" writers? Especially in James's case, it has meant various things: critics have presented highly diverse characteristics of his writing – from representational economy to affect to ethics – under the sign of theatricality. Meanwhile, Stein's pioneering contributions to experimental theater continue to place her prominently within the genealogy of the contemporary stage. As Sarah Bay-Cheng puts it, "the history of experimental theater and drama in America is virtually inconceivable without her influence" (1–2; see 115–142); Stein's influence on such seminal artists as Robert Wilson, Richard Foreman, and Elizabeth LeCompte (all of whom have staged her plays) is well known.[3] At the same time, however, both writers have also been understood as *anti*theatrical: James, in light of his incessant complaints, in fiction and nonfiction, about the fate of the dramatic text in the coarse hands of theatrical production (a fate he famously bore in person at the disastrous premiere of his *Guy Domville*); Stein, because her invention of the "landscape play" allegedly arises from a similar, modernist distaste for inherent properties of the theater medium. In this account, Stein's alliance with visual modernism does not feed into an alliance with theater but, on the contrary, crystallizes her orientation against it.[4]

In this chapter, I suggest that a rigorous conceptual distinction between drama and theater can help clarify the theatrical/antitheatrical problematic that arises in the critical discourse around each author. It's no anachronistic imposition to speak of a theater "beyond drama" in James's and Stein's texts; rather, it's what the texts themselves imply. By treating drama and theater as separate concepts, we can begin to see a theatricality in James that is directly in conflict with his own attachment to dramatic norms; in his later fiction, a theatrical desire to see drama foiled perpetually disrupts a supposedly dramatic narrative. In Stein, a quite different picture emerges: her theater is not the ongoing downfall of drama but is, rather, what emerges when drama is simply set aside (one is tempted to say, ignored). Critical accounts of Stein's theater as antitheatrical have as their premise a fundamentally *dramatic* understanding of theater as defined by "spatial and temporal continuity" (Puchner, *Stage* 110). But I'll argue that the idea of theater that Stein elaborates, both in her 1935 lecture "Plays" and in her plays themselves, already exceeds such a framework.

Much closer to both Stein's and James's sense of theater is the theatricality theorized by poststructuralist scholar Samuel Weber in his 2004 *Theatricality as Medium*. Weber's analysis rarely engages with concrete instances of theatrical performance, and at times his notion of theatricality "as medium" – as in-betweenness, separation, and the disruption of self-identity – becomes so powerfully conceptual that its relationship to theatrical experience slips from view. While neither James nor Stein appears in Weber's analysis, I find that their writing lends a more concretely theatrical determination to his theory, and I will refer to him repeatedly throughout the following pages. In fact, Weber's relative lack of interest in the prevailing norms of existing theater, even while he explores its mediality, gives his approach an especially Steinian accent: while James's theatricality finds itself in direct conflict with the dramatic standard of his day, Stein's tends to bypass that standard entirely. Certainly, and indeed unlike James, Stein wrote plays that fly in the face of dominant theater norms; but her own writing encourages us to read these plays, not as a gesture of opposition to drama (much less to theater), but as arising out of alternative experiential possibilities that theater itself harbors.

In both authors, then, what has sometimes been seen as a rejection of theater is in fact an enthusiastic and canny appreciation of the theater medium, an embrace of theater's possibilities beyond the dramatic. In making this distinction, I don't mean to misrepresent the dialectical nature of antitheatricalism, particularly as theorized by Martin Puchner: his readings in *Stage Fright* trace the ways in which antitheatrical, diegeticizing impulses have *generated* crucial new forms of theater, including Stein's plays.[5] Since this book also theorizes a theater that takes issue with its own "happening," it might seem odd that I don't ally myself more fully with this critical tradition. My resistance to doing so comes from my belief that theater always bears the potential for such contestation – and that the awareness of this potential lies at the heart of the texts I read. Theater's present-tense occurrence may come under attack, as in James; it may undergo a radical dispersion, as in Stein; or it may sustain a dialectical negation, as in Beckett. But for all these writers, the "anti-" lies *within* the scope of theatricality itself, and determines theater's profound appeal. Theorizations of "antitheatrical theater," by contrast, must at some point conceive of the theatrical as a more or less stable positive quantity, upon which negativity (or, say, modernism) supervenes as if from without. If one has defined theatricality in this way, one can quite properly show that a range of experimental texts repudiate it; but I find that such a conception of theatricality is false both to my own experience of theater and, more importantly, to the sense of theater that emerges in the texts examined here. To put it another way: the sense of distress that overtakes some of these writers when they go to the theater does not mean that they'd rather stay home.⁶

In Chapter 1, I began to describe an aesthetic wherein theater would actively undermine the actuality of its own performance, reflexively attacking the shared here-and-now. Such theater produces distance, discrepancy, and discontinuity, qualities that, as I'll argue, determine the theatricality of writing for James and Stein. But if this is true, then Stein's theatricality in particular may need to be "rescued," not only from readings of her texts as antitheatrical, but also from readings that assert her pro-theatricality through a simple identification of theater with concreteness and total presence. Such readings identify an uncomplicated theatrical presence with Stein's well-known poetics of "entity" (orientation toward the thing-in-itself) and of the "continuous present." Thus, for example, in her stunningly comprehensive study of Stein's 77 plays and their performance legacies, Betsy Alayne Ryan writes:

> The theatre's *concreteness*, its relational movement within the limitations of the performance, and its *purely present existence* could not help but strengthen her concepts of entity and time ... she could *incarnate* them for the theatre in a way that literature never would. What better way of 'giving what I was realizing at any and every moment of them and of me until I was empty of them' – and of having it *directly and immediately perceived* by an audience as it occurred – than to do it through the theatre? What better way to insist upon the entity of a work than to isolate it from the world in a finite space and *present its solid reality* to an audience? (37, my emphases)

Compelling as Ryan's work is, her conception of what theater offered Stein threatens to miss, or misconstrue, the most radical qualities of Stein's playwriting. I'd suggest that neither the "Plays" lecture nor the landscape plays themselves espouse theater as "solid reality" or as purely immediate, concrete presence.⁷ Rather, as we'll see, Stein activates the spatial dimensions of theater to divide the concrete present from itself. Perhaps surprisingly, James can help us identify this maneuver, since the spatial logic that links his theatricality to Stein's is even more clearly opposed to any "solid reality" that could be "directly and immediately perceived." As the first two epigraphs to this chapter suggest, then, I will be offering a reading of James and Stein that emphasizes the extent to which each writer's sense of theater depends upon what is not "solidly" present: a sense of the stage as a place that, so to speak, keeps itself *apart*.

This is precisely how Samuel Weber theorizes theatricality. Framing theatricality as the operation of *"parting with"* (17–22, 158), Weber writes:

> Place as separable is the stage. However defined its borders may be, they must still remain in contact with what they exclude and yet presuppose. Such contact may be temporarily forgotten, excluded from consciousness, but its effects do not disappear. Separation, in short, does not dissolve the relation to the other or to the outside, nor does it reduce the other to a goal or purpose that would complete a story and make it intelligible. Rather, separation communicates with that from which it distances itself... (294)

Both James and Stein explore the intuition that theater functions as the separation and interrelation of place(s) and time(s), fracturing the dramatic present. For James as for Stein, theater rends the here-and-now into irreducibly distant *parts*.

Throughout what follows, I hope to show how this theatricality aligns James's writing with Stein's most striking literary innovations – perhaps to a greater extent than Stein herself allowed. Indeed, readings that present Stein's work in terms of either cubism or twentieth-century technology, as Stein herself frequently did, tend to imply that a figure like James, culminating master of "nineteenth-century" literature, could have had only a transitional ("proto-modernist") relationship to her modernist achievements. If Stein's work is "Cubism," then James's is still "Realism" (Caramello 164). If Stein's work manifests twentieth-century physics, responding to a "universe where multidimensionality, not directionality, seemed the defining characteristic" (Ryan 10), we might well assume that James, too old to catch on to this zeitgeist, must have been outpaced by its literary manifestation. Glossing Stein's account of airplane travel in "Picasso," Ryan writes: "Driving in a car within the landscape on a road naturally resulted in a vision of progress or development – travel through time – where points of the journey are perceived in order, according to the movement of the car. The airplane, on the other hand, freed the traveller to order the journey as he wished while hovering over the whole landscape . . . an experience of time had become an experience of space" (9). And yet the dispersion of progressive time through a differential space is likewise, as I'll suggest, a major project of James's late fiction. With Stein, we can picture this kind of project forming from an airplane window; but James helps us imagine it forming, just as urgently, from a rather uncomfortable seat at the theater.

1 Henry James

The intensity of Henry James's relationship to theater is not only a biographical fact; it has also become a critical commonplace. A theatrical vocabulary dominates his essays and his fiction, where narrators and characters alike seem to process almost every experience in terms borrowed from the stage. But this register has been marshaled for widely diverse interpretive purposes; throughout literary studies, the elucidation of Jamesian theatricality has referred to everything from a "rigid economy" of representation to a perceptual politics of "surveillance," from a moral concern with promiscuity to an investigation of group psychology to an erotics of display.[8] I want to trace a rather different sense of theater that I find emerging in James's later fiction. On the one hand, this theater not only exceeds but challenges "dramatic" storytelling tendencies, and on the other, its qualities are not reducible to perceptual experiences of "seeing" or "showing." As such, James's texts begin to delineate a negative theatrics that will go on developing in the work of subsequent writers who engage the stage.

David Kurnick hints at James's movement beyond drama when he argues that *The Awkward Age* "strains against the novel toward a kind of performance, [while] it also resists the actually existing theater," a "naturalist drama" which in James's day was rapidly "adopting a notion of psychological truth in turn borrowed from realistic fiction" ("Horrible" 111). The alterity of the "kind of performance" toward which James's late fiction strives is what I want to elucidate here. I will also be making the related claim that theatricality in James belongs to what is not straightforwardly seen or shown, an approach suggested by John Carlos Rowe's argument that "there is no perception, no impression in the ocular or present sense possible in James's epistemology" (202).[9] Through close readings of passages from "The Beast in the Jungle" and *The Ambassadors*, and drawing upon the critical work of Leo Bersani and other theorists, I consider how James's refusal of the present – which is also the refusal *to* present – drives his discourse into deeply strange configurations. Narratologists' accounts of reading as a process of "linear detailing through time" (Chatman 107) will help establish the challenge James faced in importing his disintegrative sense of theatricality into a page-bound medium. This challenge was functionally analogous to the dramatic norm that confronted him in theater, but it was in his prose fiction that James attacked it most decisively. For James, theater's multidimensionality tends to explode the sense of ongoing immediacy that characterizes both drama and reading; at the same time, it undermines the planar integrity of the image, as we'll see in the second section below. In turn, writing becomes theatrical by simulating the disruptive multiplicity of a deeply distracting space.

The Beast in the Sentence: Writing Theatrical Space

Born a century before Robert Wilson, Henry James might seem an unlikely candidate for "postdramatic" status. But James's own approach to temporality would seem to smile on critical anachronism: *having been going to have been* postdramatic is exactly the kind of description his writing invites us to apply. The following sentence, from the fourth chapter of James's 1903 tale "The Beast in the Jungle," exemplifies such tortuous syntax beautifully: "It deepened the strangeness to see her, as such a figure in such a picture, talk of 'horrors,' but she was to do, in a few minutes, something stranger yet – though even of this he was to take the full measure but afterward – and the note of it was already in the air" (523). These typically Jamesian acrobatics have a specific temporal function: what begins as the conveyance of a temporally immanent response – "it deepened the strangeness to see her" – soon abandons that immanence, splitting one moment into three. The "scene" is not allowed to unfold in anything like a continuous sequence; instead, the present becomes the site of a doubly proleptic distraction, a graph-like surface on which multiple times are rendered.

Of course, a narrator's reference to what's going to happen, the dear-reader-if-she-only-knew technique, may just be a device for creating suspense – a ploy typical of literature's "hermeneutic code" (Barthes, *S/Z* 61–63). But such usage normally affirms that one moment will lead to the next, making us relish the vector that points inexorably toward a payoff at the end of the read. In James's sentence, by contrast, we get a promise of a promise of a retrospection: to move forward will not be to arrive at a climactic present but to continually negotiate a paradoxically simultaneous future and past. In fact, as the last few words of the sentence suggest, there is no such thing as a discrete moment: the space of the scene, its very "air," is "already" inhabited by a time that exceeds it. This is what Leo Bersani describes as the "Jamesian tendency to extract all events, as well as all perspectives on them, from any specified time, and to transfer them to a before or after in which they are de-realized in the form of anticipations or retrospections" (Bersani and Phillips 23). As Bersani also observes, "The Beast in the Jungle" is remarkable in that it not only exhibits but "thematizes" this default of event (ibid.). John Marcher is, James tells us, "*the* man, to whom nothing on earth was to have happened" ("Beast" 540).

Still, why characterize James's attack on the present as theatrical? After all, theater – and performance as such – is often described as the medium *of* the present, the form whose only time is now. While many theorists have sought to deconstruct the notion that theater offers full presence or immediacy, the very insistence of this "debate" shows how forcefully theater's actuality continues to summon our attention. As we saw in Chapter 1, Szondi and Brecht suggest that dramatic theater directly affirms this actuality, asserting the here-and-now of performance and excluding the prospect of any alternative site. For Adorno, performance's heightened actuality becomes a problem in that performance, constantly emerging into the real, fails to achieve the artwork's constitutive "foreignness to the world." And yet Adorno's objection to the presence of performance is an objection that theater itself is also uniquely posed to make. Precisely because theater demands simultaneous, spatially adjacent appreciation, it can become a site for the contestation of the present. We'll see in the following chapter that Beckett's early theater seizes on drama's "absolute present," exacerbating it to the point of dialectical reversal. For James and Stein, however, theater's power and pleasure arise from properties that *always* threaten to undermine presence. In James's theater, what we will (borrowing from Bersani) call the medium's "other parts" keep rising up against the centralizing force of the dramatic present. Accordingly, to read James is to see how theater might appeal to a sensibility critical of the present as such.

From such a perspective we can acknowledge that drama's affirmation of actuality exploits a fundamental aspect of performance, while also seeing that dramatic logic works *in reaction against* other elements of the theater medium. This chapter's first epigraph is drawn from a 1903 work in which James remembers being excluded from a family trip to the theater when he was little: the play "at which ... I did not assist," he writes, became an "ineffaceable" theater experience (*William* 259, qtd. in Caramello 84–85) – not in spite of but *through* having missed the show. The passage exemplifies the Jamesian approach to experience that Kevin Ohi has described as a queer "erotics of belatedness," in which "the regret for the life one missed *is*, paradoxically, the life one missed" (150, 156). But it also ties that erotics specifically to theater experience, as constituted in this primal "scene" of James's relationship to the stage: theater's *happening* becomes seductive precisely by being something we can miss.[10] Attending the theater doesn't dispel this promise, either: on the contrary, every show confronts us with the looming possibility that a performance will offer too much for us to synthesize "now." James describes this sensory surfeit in *The Ambassadors*, when the protagonist Strether attends a play at a London theater:

> He felt as if the play itself penetrated him with the naked elbow of his neighbor, a great stripped handsome red-haired lady who conversed with a gentleman on her other side in stray dissyllables which had for his ear, in the oddest way in the world, so much sound that he wondered they hadn't more sense ... He had distracted drops in which he couldn't have said if it were actors or auditors who were most true, and the upshot of which, each time, was the consciousness of new contacts. (92)

At once unsettling and thrilling, theater is a field where "new contacts" loom on every side, where "distracted drops" ongoingly divide our attention. Amidst all these solicitations, there is little chance of our focusing on the plot.

In an attempt to prevail against this field of distractions, drama pursues an ideal of maximal *clarity*. This ideal still organizes contemporary dramaturgy to a remarkable extent;[11] in James's day, it was even more pervasive. H. G. Wells could write, in his review of James's play *Guy Domville*, that "[a] play written for the stage may very well be compared to a pen-and-ink drawing that is to undergo reproduction by some cheap photographic process. Delicate turns, soft shades, refinements of grey *must* be avoided; bold strokes, black and firm – that is all that is possible" (qtd. in Edel 212–213). In reading James's play, though, one is struck by its relative shortage of "delicate turns" – verbal or psychological – compared with his fiction. It is difficult to imagine words like the following in the novels or stories James would write after his "dramatic years":

MRS. PEVEREL. You speak for him as if – *(Breaking down with excess of feeling. Re-enter FRANK HUMBER and LORD DEVENISH.)*
GUY. As if I didn't love you to passion – heaven hear me! And as if – heaven hear me! – I hadn't come down here to *tell* you so! (Edel 199)

James himself tended to account for such straightforwardness as a concession to the theater audience's mental limitations. "In that art," he bitterly writes his publisher in 1894, "one must specify one's subject as unmistakably as one orders one's dinner – I mean leave the audience no trouble to disengage or disentangle it. Forget not that you write for the stupid – that is, that your maximum of refinement must meet the minimum of intelligence of the audience, in other words, of the biggest ass it may conceivably contain" (qtd. in Margolis 85). This is the classically "antitheatrical" James, raging against "that art" with a mixture of throbbing resentment and wry self-incrimination. Evidently, he hoped to write well even under these daunting conditions; as Anne T. Margolis observes, he was "quite capable of regarding these conditions as a challenge rather than as a barrier" (72). Margolis offers a convincing portrait of James as a writer deeply worried about his audience, even "obsessed with his dream of ... winning the approval of the multitudes" during his playwriting years (84) – a dream for which he would willingly "sacrifice[e] every note of subtlety" in his work (56). Certainly, James's solicitude for "the biggest ass" in the theater can account for the "bold strokes" of his plays; but his hyperbolic efforts to make things clear also bespeak his *own* sense of how persistently theater mediates against clarity.

The directness (by James standards) with which his stage characters express themselves suggests his awareness of performance as threatening a phenomenal overload. Like Wells, James was attuned to the ways in which theater's "turns" could undermine drama's "bold strokes." The "incorruptibility of line" that the protagonist of another James tale ascribes enthusiastically to "the dramatic form" ("Nona" 5) is drama's defensive response to a theatrical potential for distraction: the danger that a viewer or performer will lose the thread of her own experience. Ideally, each instant of the drama would offer itself to immediate comprehension and thus ease us along to the next, producing the "pure actuality" (Szondi 38) that sustains the continuity of the dramatic timeline.

When we recall the baffling contortions of our sentence from "The Beast in the Jungle," James's writing looks like a terrifically unpromising candidate for any such communicative immediacy. And yet the lines from *Guy Domville* suggest that when it came time to contribute to the theater of his day, James tried to abide by dramatic standards. Indeed, he often expressed frustration with the ways actual theater confounded dramatic law.[12] When characters in his story "Nona Vincent" describe the transition from page to stage as "a sudden descent" into "vulgarity" (6), they may well be speaking James's own conviction. But James's keen *frustration* with the ways theatrical production departs from the "pure art" ("Nona" 6) of drama is only the obverse of his equally keen awareness of theater *as* precisely this departure, or difference. I do not believe we can make sense of his continued return to the theater without supposing that he got a tremendous charge from the "distracted drops" of theater's continual, constitutive "descent." This theatrical charge is the thrill of taking pleasure in perversion. "I want to intensely," says the playwright when asked if he wants "to be acted," "but I'm sorry I want to" (ibid.).

Ultimately, as Kurnick suggests, the dramatic conventions of James's day – conventions he himself tried to abide by – prevented him from realizing his own polymorphous theatricality in works for the stage. Those conventions were (and are) geared toward repressing precisely the experience that James knew so well: the expansive, disintegrative moment of *falling apart*, the rending of the dramatic moment from itself. Turn-of-the-twentieth-century British theater would not willingly house such an art of disintegration; James therefore transplanted his sense of theater to the field of prose fiction.

But what does it mean to make theater on the pages of a story or novel? For James, this becomes a question about *reading* versus *attending*: what would prose fiction have to do to fabricate a theatrical experience for its reader? What basic differences between these activities would such a hybridizing project need to surmount? We have already encountered one answer in Brecht's converse idea of "literarization." For Brecht, reading's appeal resides in the way the page lies open to investigation, *meeting* my gaze; theater, by contrast, threatens at once to compel and to dodge my attention.[13] This account of reading finds corroboration in the work of narratologists such as Gérard Genette and Seymour Chatman. According to Chatman, written narrative describes by way of a "linear detailing through time" (107): it presents its objects by doling out their information in a sequence of units, producing them in a forward temporal movement that corresponds to the progress of our eyes over successive characters on the page. We get our information as we go; the written text "has no other temporality than what it borrows, metonymically, from its own reading" (Genette 34). Funneling all information through the channel of my uptake, the text has no room for an *other* time. The now of my reading is all there is, temporally, to this activity. Anything more can only come in its turn; that is, when I turn to it.

Of course, the notion that I could ever be fully coincident with what I read, that a piece of language could really be delivering its whole meaning to me at any moment, has long been recognized as theoretically untenable. As we will see, Stein in particular complicates the understanding of written narrative as a continuous stream of immediate communication, through her explicit insistence that most texts harbor "two times" as well as through her writing itself. Nevertheless, I think the narratologists' account does speak to a normative experience, or expectation, of reading: a page of text will tend to *present itself as* a direct stream of information, where the reader can regulate the stream's flow in order to access each moment's content. She accesses the text in her own time; there is nothing given there that she can't, in principle, receive.

In theater, by contrast, there is always a potential for overload. Events occur with or without our uptake, distributed across a differential space of "naked elbows," "stray dissylables," and other things, bodies, and places that can compete for our attention. James's writing boils with the specific awareness that even the most unassuming drawing-room scenery threatens to rear up, in its recesses and furnishings, and distract us from whatever is going on at center stage. Theater's constitutive simultaneity, the fact that its "here" can always be divided into "there, there, and there," means that in any given moment there is always, phenomenally, more than what we attend to in that moment; this excess is part of the medium itself. Here, any stream of consciousness flows over rough terrain, which always threatens to interrupt and divert it: "linear detailing" cannot describe the course. Instead, the spatial dimensions of the medium house a time other than mine. If drama aims to reduce this plurality to a single, emphatic *now*, it does so in the face of an ongoing danger: I might fall out of step with that present, something else in the room might suddenly call me away.

A novelist with a longing for theater, then, might seek strategies for undoing the effect of immediacy that reading seems to offer. And if she had to remain within the parameters of the textual medium, she might try to simulate theatrical interference *on the level of narrative*. A writer with an inveterate desire for theater, that is, might look for ways to set forks in the stream of her story, to pull open a disruptive additional dimension, to achieve a pseudospatiality in writing. Such a "theatricalization of literature" would in one sense constitute a kind of anticipatory countermove to Brecht's "literarization of theater": a repudiation of epic clarity and control, a subjection to the rhythms of a realm not cognitively my own. It might seem that James's Strether, in his throes of elated frustration, could not be farther from Brecht's ideal of the "literarized" theatergoer: relaxed, self-possessed, "watching-while-smoking" (72). And yet as we saw in Chapter 1, Brecht's "literarization" also fundamentally works to diversify spectatorial attention, pulling us away from the "single track" of drama (ibid.). In *this* sense, Jamesian theatricality is already highly "literarized"; Brecht and James converge in seeking analogies between the two media's possibilities for disrupting dramatic focalization.[14]

Throughout James's later work, this project amounts to what I have called his attack on the present – exactly what we see in our passage from "The Beast in the Jungle," which I will quote again here: "she *was to do*, in a few minutes, something stranger *yet* – though even of *this* he was to take the full measure *but afterward* – and the note of *it* was *already* in the air" (523, my emphases). Tenses and disparate temporal markers proliferate: "was to do," "but afterward," and "already" pull the intensifier "yet" toward its temporal meaning. Pronouns accumulate, their referents perpetually deferred: "something," "this," "it." The elaborate refusal to give us any temporally intact moment or simply *show us anything now* stretches our attention toward multiple points at once, so the *time* of the narrative takes on a back-and-forth movement that simulates the distracting multidimensionality of theatrical *space*. James scatters the "now" of reading into a field of other moments, inaccessible alterities.

Bersani might well be thinking of passages like this when he observes, in "The Jamesian Lie," that "James's habit of giving us the consequences and the implications of a thought or a fact before giving us the thought or the fact itself shifts the organizing principle of the text from the temporal logic of a character engaged in the story's movement to the spatial perspective of a narrator who ignores his character's time for the sake of his own designs" (*Future* 143). We could take this remark as an invitation to see James simply privileging space over time, but I don't believe this is the most productive reading of either James or Bersani. After all, as the next section of this chapter will emphasize, movement along the temporal axis plays a key role in James's disruptive theatrics. In this passage from "The Beast," what we witness is less a subordination than a reorganization of time, such that temporality itself takes on the discontinuous multiplicity of theater space. Narrative sequence is thus driven, as it were, to distraction: not one thing after another, but each thing always behind, before, beneath, beyond something else – "something stranger yet."

Bersani does not discuss James's work in terms of theater, but his writing on performance offers terms for understanding the way Jamesian narrative explodes any unified or "immediate" present. In another essay published in the same book with "The Jamesian Lie," Bersani discusses contemporary experimental theater, exemplified for him by the work of Robert Wilson. Such work, he writes, is "engaged in decentralizing the audience's attention" (*Future* 284). Whereas "[n]umerous aspects of traditional theater work to centralize our attention" and "the movement toward climaxes or *dénouements* could be thought of as a way of closing in, during the time of the drama, on its central significance," the phenomenal multiplicity of Wilson's productions works the opposite way (ibid.). "The action [is] always somewhere else," Bersani writes, noting: "If we look intently at one part of a Wilson tableau, our attention is peripherally solicited by *other parts* of the tableau" (284–285, my emphasis). Interestingly, James makes a similar point, though with a different slant, in his glowing 1891 review of *Hedda Gabler*: "such a production asks the average moral man to see too many things at once" (*Scenic* 252–253). Through the heightened experience of what Bersani calls "other parts" – what James calls "too many things at once" or, in *The Ambassadors*, "the consciousness of new contacts" – theater resists the dramatic ideal of continuous presentation. James's prose becomes theatrical in fabricating the same resistance.

It may therefore be time to revisit an old *topos* of James criticism, sprung from James's own accounts of his work: the famous "scenic method." This term refers to various ways in which, as is commonly held, James's fiction models itself upon theatrical presentation. Leon Edel's classic account of James's vexed relationship to theater, for example, suggests that fiction is scenic wherever conversations "unfold without the intervention of the narrator" (115). Seeking a more rigorous definition, Joseph Wiesenfarth explicates the theatrical provenance of James's fiction in terms of "intensity," "economy," and "objectivity" (3). Such readings once again construct theater, and by extension James's "scenic" writing, in terms of a heightened immediacy – an association that should by now appear thoroughly problematic. On the contrary, James works from a feel for theater, and hence for scene, that emphasizes theater's potential *interference with* immediacy, the heterogeneity and distraction that can counteract the temporal unity of spectatorial attention and narrative "stream."

James himself discusses his work's "scenic consistency" in the Preface to *The Ambassadors*, a novel I will return to in the following section of this chapter. James designates one particular passage of *The Ambassadors* as "an excellent *standard* scene" (47–48); before coming back to "The Beast in the Jungle," therefore, it seems worthwhile to inquire how this apparently exemplary Jamesian scene plays out. In fact, it is the same episode that includes the passage about theater I quoted earlier. In this scene, the American protagonist Lewis Lambert Strether goes to a play in London with his new friend Maria Gostrey; between the acts, he explains to her how and why he has become the "ambassador" for a wealthy New England family, on his way to Paris with orders to bring home their wayward son, Chad Newsome. This definitively "scenic" scene does begin with several lines of dialogue between Strether and Gostrey; but if we expect this shining specimen to be devoid of narrative "intervention," we are mistaken. About halfway through the scene, Strether and Gostrey are discussing the identity of "the article produced" at Woollett,

Massachusetts, the source of the Newsomes' (and potentially Strether's) fortune. She tries to guess; "he persuaded her to patience. But it may even now frankly be mentioned that he in the sequel never *was* to tell her. He actually never did so ... She could treat the little nameless object as indeed unnameable – she could make their abstention enormously definite. There might indeed have been for Strether a portent of this in what she next said" (97–98). Even in its most "standard" edition, then, the Jamesian scene refuses to let the time of the story unfold with the continuity proper to drama. Instead, it labors to create the sense of a theatrical "more": a content in excess of the present action. James proleptically adapts the "always somewhere else" of theater for written prose, by creating a narrative that is always some*when* else.[15]

If we are quick to identify theater with the immediate here-and-now that defines drama's ideal, we won't be able to grasp the way such maneuvers in themselves constitute a "scenic" poetics. A reading attuned to theatrical possibilities beyond drama, however, can recognize theater in the way these scenes *deny* the possibility of a self-contained moment. James's own characterization of the ideal scene enacts this very denial: "copious, comprehensive, and accordingly never short, but with its office as definite as that of the hammer on the gong of the clock, the office of expressing *all that is in* the hour" (*Ambassadors* 48). Itself a spatialized image of time, the simile divides our attention; the sentence's syntax encourages us to accept the clock's office *as* the scene's – which might bring us close to a traditional understanding of scenic temporality – but the emphasis at the end suggests that clock and scene really have opposite functions: where one expresses the hour, the other expresses *all that is in* it. The scene, that is, turns the hour inside-out, subjecting temporal flow to the distractions of heterogeneous copia. As the passage from *The Ambassadors* shows, what is "in" the hour for James includes what is, by the standards of the clock, definitely outside it.

In the midst of all this material, what dissolves is the dramatic event itself: the striking of the hammer, which would register temporal progress, never even *happens* in James's parable; instead, the hammer hangs suspended in the strange phrase of its "office on" the gong.[16] These scenes hardly lack content, but the very abundance of their content makes them resistant to actualization, stretching them insistently beyond the "now." In forsaking drama's presentism, they also fight against the flow of readerly consciousness, simulating the distractions of theatrical space.

If we return to "The Beast in the Jungle," we can identify the moment that would, in a truly "dramatic" writer, be the story's climax; instead, it becomes the climax of a decidedly different, Jamesian theatricality. Recall that our original passage referred to "something stranger yet" that May Bartram "was to do"; I want to turn now to James's account of this strange action. We have also been told that John Marcher "was to take the full measure [of it] but afterward"; as this foreshadowing suggests, Marcher's retrospective rearticulation of this scene will constitute the story's final crisis. The passage in question, which begins when the dying May tells Marcher "it's never too late" (526) but ends by her affirming that "what *was* to" happen has happened (527), is exactly a compositional space kept open for subsequent interpretive recrossings: May's, Marcher's, and our own. It is *not* the narrative transmission of anything we (or Marcher) can immediately recognize, in the "now" of our reading (of his beholding), as an event. In marking out this empty space, proleptically and analeptically determined as the story's center, James deploys his typical anti-event moves: "She *had*, with her gliding step, diminished the distance between them, and she stood nearer to him, close to him, a minute, *as if* still charged with the unspoken. Her movement *might have been* for some finer emphasis of what she was *at once hesitating and deciding* to say" (526, my emphases). Here though – as with the plot of "The Beast" as a whole – James also provides a concrete *image* of not-happening, in the eerie "minute" of May's stasis, which outlasts and frustrates Marcher's retrieval of any "movement" that "had" preceded it.

May now usurps the function of the Beast and of Jamesian narrative: "She only kept him waiting, however; that is he only waited" (ibid.). This sentence repeats in miniature the entire thrust of the story: a default of event, at first presented as the fault of the hero's virtual antagonist, is then interpretively relocated ("that is") as a fault of his own. Marcher spends most of his life under the impression that he is being "kept waiting" by another – fate, the Beast – only to revise this formulation at the end: the problem all along has been that "*he* only waited," the leap having really been his to take.[17] But in thus encapsulating the story, this self-revising sentence also helps to produce a theatrical dispersion of time: the "minute" of Marcher's waiting is rendered multiple, not only by the fact that we get two different accounts of it (one where May only keeps Marcher waiting, one where Marcher only waits) but also by the fact that this "minute" will turn out upon rereading to have contained "*all that is in*" the story. This specifically Jamesian "scenic consistency," however, is not simply a matter of moments pregnant with meaning. Rather James constructs, for the reader as for Marcher, the experience of an utter *refusal* of meaning in any dramatic sense – the scene's absolute refusal to signify within the here-and-now in which it (only barely) occurs. "[W]hat he saw in her face was the truth," we read (ibid.): but in the Jamesian *theatron*, "the truth" can be "seen" without thereby becoming accessible, without granting us anything now. Staging this refusal, James offers a breathtaking preview of Weber's "theatricality as medium": "Since no narrative sequence succeeds in framing or enclosing the places it traverses," Weber writes, "it winds up being traversed by them, being opened, every time it tries to conclude, toward other scenes, which remain inconclusive" (22). For James, too, the theatrical "distance between them" – between Marcher and May, audience and performer – turns out to be an intervening, mediating space through which seeing the truth is exactly not getting it.

The vehemence with which space intervenes, not only between characters but between reading and "getting" more generally, manifests itself here in the odd eruption of yet another typical Jamesian peculiarity: what Ezra Pound called James's "dam'd fuss about furniture" ("Henry" 308).[18] There is no end of moments, throughout James's work, when the material trappings of a room rise to such prominence in narrative consciousness that they seem to menace the story's continuity. One of the most startling occurs in the middle of the passage we've been discussing:

> Her movement might have been for some finer emphasis of what she was at once hesitating and deciding to say. He had been standing by the chimneypiece, fireless and sparely adorned, *a small, perfect old French clock and two morsels of rosy Dresden constituting all its furniture;* and her hand grasped the shelf while she kept him waiting, grasped it a little as for support and encouragement. She only kept him waiting, however; that is he only waited. (526, my emphasis)

By the standards of dramatic storytelling, the excursus on tchotchkes is simply bizarre. It is only James's brazen commitment to another theatricality that lets "*all that is in* the hour" rise up at this moment; that lets the multiplicity of space assert itself, in a veritable aggression of *mise-en-scène*, as a violent distraction from the drama of May's love and John's greed. The clock, with its outrageously nested adjectives, seems to flaunt an ability to suspend the present occurrence, stopping the narrative in its tracks and insisting that *something else* must be acknowledged. James's passage illustrates this theatrical capacity of objects: they assert themselves at the most outrageous possible moment, in blithe defiance of our desire to follow the plot. They are like the dark doubles of the Chekhovian rifle, with its promise of dramatic significance. Unlike that emphatically meaningful weapon, Jamesian things mark a theatrical excess of differential space, the irruptive disabling of synthesizing comprehension.

"something ... had been wanted in the picture": Disrupted Image in The Ambassadors

When things also go awry for Lewis Lambert Strether in Book XI of *The Ambassadors*, the explicit theatricality of this incident brings us to a different, but related, mode of Jamesian theater. In "The Beast in the Jungle," theater operates as a mode that pulls apart its own present. Simulating the multiplicity of theater space, James's narrative undermines the "now" of reading – and the fluid progression that drama tries its best to impose. In the scene I want to look at next, however, the "stream" of temporal flow is not the target but the agent of theatrical disruption. In what we might call the *disrupted image*, a differential element of motion comes to disturb an essentially static "picture," mobilizing the difference of change over time against the relative stability of a pictorial surface. In either mode, theater emerges as the disruptive opening of an additional dimension; we might say that while devices like prolepsis and hypothesis let James theatricalize narrative *time*, the disrupted image lets him theatricalize presentational *space*. Moreover, the fact that the former mode always remains in play means that "action" in the latter still fails to centralize, or focus, the scene. Instead, space and time rend dramatic unity along both axes.

In the scene at hand, Strether has embarked on a day in the countryside, in search of "that French ruralism, with its cool special green, into which he had hitherto looked only through the little oblong window of the picture-frame" (452). The "picture" seems at first to be a metaphor for Strether's naïve romanticization of the land, but James soon grounds it in a surprising (one might even feel, excessive) literality: Strether's desire for this landscape turns out to be bound up with his onetime desire for an actual picture. "[H]e could thrill a little at the chance of seeing something somewhere that would remind him of a certain small Lambinet that had charmed him, long years before, at a Boston dealer's and that he had quite absurdly never forgotten ... The little Lambinet abode with him as the picture he *would* have bought" (ibid.). The identification of the painting as "the picture he *would* have bought" already invests it with a kind of multiplicity, splitting it between the actual nonevent (of purchase) and the hypothetical act. At the same time, though, the apparently perfect coincidence of the countryside with Strether's desire suggests – in a Jamesian context – that the picture may be a repressively limiting conceit. "The oblong gilt frame disposed its enclosing lines; the poplars, and willows, the reeds and river ... fell into a composition, full of felicity, within them": the landscape becomes the picture only as the effect of the "enclosing" frame, whose odd grammatical position as the subject of the first clause underscores the sense of this synthesis as forced. We are also invited to notice that the pictorial metaphor itself depends on the additional dimension the metaphor promises to exclude. Thus Strether can find himself "freely walking about" in the painting only insofar as the painting is *more than* its pictorial surface: by "boring so deep into his impression and his idleness that he might fairly have got through them again and reached the maroon-coloured wall" (ibid.).[19] This playful suggestion contains the serious reminder that the picture can be violated, precisely because it has – as no ideal plane does – an *other side*. Only apparently manifest as surface, the image holds its own alterity in reserve. In quartering Strether for the day, the French countryside hints at its own hindquarters – its "other parts."

We might think, here, of John Marcher's final posture in "The Beast in the Jungle": "he flung himself, on his face, on the tomb" (541).[20] In this position, he at once exposes himself to the Beast he hallucinates and, by refusing to "meet" his fate, extends the tale's postdramatic refusal of immediacy to its very last sentence. This theatrical obtrusion of "other parts," in both passages, might further remind us of Antonin Artaud's desire to activate theater space "*in its undersides (dans ses dessous)*" (*Theater* 124): to seize it in its dimensional difference, which traditional theater represses for the sake of "a culture without shadows" (12). And indeed, in Strether's idyll, the jocular prospect of "boring" too deep heralds his eventual realization that the picture has not offered a sufficient analogy for his day after all: "this had been all day *at bottom* the spell of the picture – that it was essentially more than anything else *a scene and a stage*, that the very air of the play was in the rustle of the willows and the tone of the sky" (458, my emphases).

What prompts this medial transformation is Strether's dawning awareness that "though he had been alone all day, he had never yet so struck himself as engaged with others and in midstream of his drama" (457–458). That "drama" is young Chad Newsome's affair with the married Madame de Vionnet, and the question of how this drama is, and isn't, "his" (Strether's) is the novel's central problematic. But in the imaginative context of a static picture, the "drama," and specifically the "stream" of its temporality, provides the dimensional disruption that makes the painting erupt into theater. As Rowe observes, "visual impressions" in James are "always already involved in complex semantic, social, and historical determinations" (194); Strether's "hopes of finding nothing but surfaces" in the countryside are therefore destined to be dashed (197).[21] The "sharp fantastic crisis" (*Ambassadors* 462) that takes place when Chad and Madame de Vionnet show up, evidently in the country on an adulterous overnight trip, does not exactly destroy Strether's Lambinet; rather, their disturbing presence now seems to have been the *telos* of the entire afternoon, "as if these figures, or something like them, had been wanted in the picture, had been wanted more or less all day" (461). And the foregoing revelation, that the picture "had been all day . . . a scene and a stage" *because* it could still be traversed by the "stream" of drama, prepares us to understand the "crisis" of the episode as theatrical. Theatricality bursts forth, that is, as the manifestation of what the pictorial surface in itself lacked – and as what Strether, unbeknownst to himself, must have "wanted."[22]

This sense of picture as both in want of (lacking) and wanting (inviting) the dimensional irruption of scene and stage corresponds to standard Jamesian poetics: "The picture is to set the stage in every needful way for the action of the scene" (Wiesenfarth 34). We should, by this point, have complicated our sense of the Jamesian scene as "action"; but by literalizing the "picture" of novelistic description, the *Ambassadors* episode enacts both the tension and the cooperation between static and (spatio)temporal media, where the picture's "want" opens the space of performance, or "sets the stage" for the scene that will come to disturb its planar surface. Perhaps the clearest illustration of this dynamic appears in the role of the *river* in Strether's countryside. Explicitly bound up with the pictoriality of the landscape, the river is twice marked as a site of ignorance. At first "the poplars and willows, the reeds and river – *a river of which he didn't know, and didn't want to know, the name* – fell into a composition" (453, my emphasis): Strether's willful unknowing is set off in the discourse as if to produce the "want" it denies. Then later, shortly before his friends' appearance, Strether arrives for dinner in "a village that affected him as a thing of whiteness, blueness and crookedness, set in coppery green, and that had a river flowing *behind or before it – one couldn't say which*" (457, my emphasis). The river marks precisely the depthlessness of the pictorial impression, which denies the difference between "before" and "behind": denies the theatrical space of undersides and backsides, even as here, too, the discourse registers that denial as a lack. But this same river will emerge with a vengeance from the indifference of the pictorial: it is *by way of the river* that Chad and Madame de Vionnet invade Strether's picture, rather violently literalizing and affirming Strether's perception that he has been "in midstream of his drama" all along. The river has twice marked Strether's pictorializing repression of alterity, his refusal to acknowledge either the differentiations of history (the river's name) or the differential resources of space ("behind or before"). As if in retribution, the river now comes to disrupt all pictorial self-evidence: it becomes the conduit of movement whereby the "others" we hadn't seen turn out to make all the difference in the world. In the process, we come to understand Strether's initial exclusion of such "others" as a symptom of "want" in both senses: a lack, but also, perversely, a desire.

Just as the strategies of Jamesian syntax diffract the linear stream of narrative events into a spatializing diachrony, the Jamesian disruption of picture mobilizes that stream against the immediacy of the planar image in a "crossing of time and space" (Rowe 216). Both of these operations, I contend, respond to a theatrical desire for a heterogeneous, differential medium. And the two operations collaborate: Strether experiences the scene that has exceeded his Lambinet most significantly, and typically, in retrospect, as the "belated vision" of a subsequent vigil: "He then knew more or less how he had been affected – he but half knew at the time" (465). Alone in his rooms, Strether revisits the day's events; describing his ride back to Paris with the lovers, the discourse passes between pluperfect and narrative past, so that it becomes impossible to locate his realization firmly in either scene: "The eating and drinking, which had been a resource, had had the effect of having served its turn . . . and it was during their somewhat tedious progress to the station, . . . their silences in the dim compartment of the much-stopping train, that he prepared himself for reflexions to come" (466). Consciousness, here, is half anticipation and half retrospect; experience slides back and forth between these two moments, unable to take place in either one.

This temporal dispersion of the event of consciousness, moreover, is inseparable from *what* the consciousness is *of*: the fact that Madame de Vionnet's disposition all evening "had been a performance" (ibid.). Here as so often in James, that is, a character's behavior gets recognized *as theater*, and while this recognition seems somehow illuminating, its meaning proves resistant to any other formulation. "Performance" is by no means, for instance, just a synonym for "deception," even though the substance of Madame's performance is indeed the falsehood that she and Chad "had left Paris that morning, and with no design but of getting back within the day" (467). Strether's response to this "lie" (466) is not only moral but also keenly appreciative, a response to her virtuosity: "From the point of view of presence of mind it had been very wonderful indeed, wonderful for readiness, for beautiful assurance, for the way her decision was taken on the spot, without time to confer with Chad, without time for anything" (ibid.). "A performance" is not merely a metaphor for what Madame has done; she has literally engaged body, voice, and language in creating an aesthetic experience, as she constantly does throughout the novel (we already know that as a child she had "made a clean sweep ... of every 'part', whether memorized or improvised, in the curtained costumed school repertory" [224]). Strether becomes this particular performance's producer only in tortuous Jamesian retrospect, and he produces it as a performance of immediacy: that "*presence* of mind," that punctual temporality of acting "on the spot ... without time for anything." But by making it the imaginative product of Strether's "belated vision," James shows us how this dramatic ideal of action as self-contained, undistributed unity arises out of – and, in spite of itself, remains within – a theatrical space of diffraction. The theater where Madame de Vionnet's performance can be "seen" is precisely the differential space that arises when the moment of recognition is pulled apart, distributed between preparation (when Strether "but half knew") and recollection (when he "knew more or less").

Ultimately, too, Strether's retrospective focus shifts from the performance itself, which disturbs him with "the quantity of make-believe involved," to "the other feature of the show, the deep, deep truth of the intimacy revealed" (468). Like the "truth" John Marcher sees in May Bartram's face, this "truth" never unfurls discursively; it maintains the maddening ineffability of an object whose dimensions – "deep, deep" – resist sublimation into dramatic logic. The theatricality of the Jamesian "show" is just this kind of depth, the evasive recess whereby narrative manages to withhold what it "reveals." The afternoon-as-painting had promised total accessibility, with Strether "freely walking about in it" (453) in recuperation of the lost but, in principle, accessible Lambinet. Reconceived as theater, the same day gives out onto a depth that is irreducibly a distance, and Strether finds himself excluded from the very "show" he attends (or at which, we might say, he assists). But this distance is also the dimension of desire. The space between Strether's lonely rooms and the colorful village – and the space between both of these and those other rooms, somewhere upstream, where Chad and Madame de Vionnet must have enacted their "intimacy" – describes the stage on which Strether can finally unleash his nocturnal fantasies. These now exhibit the riotous multiplicity of the experimental stage: "He recognized at last that he had really been trying all along to suppose nothing. Verily, verily, his labour had been lost. He found himself supposing innumerable and wonderful things" (468).

For James, theater carries us away; it works on us by pulling us apart. Marcher and Strether are both subjected to this theater, and neither will succeed in "getting back, as he might put it, into his own presence" ("Beast" 536). And yet this gap determines the playing space of Jamesian erotics, where love itself is the individual's subjection to anachrony, the dispersive force of a desire that knows no present. This ceaseless undoing constantly interferes with the drama of James's writing; but it opens the page into a space of theatrical departure.

2 Gertrude Stein

Reflecting, as she so often did, on her own earlier work, Gertrude Stein observed that her sentences "had a balance which was the balance of a space completely not filled but created by something moving as moving is not as moving should be. As I said," she continued, "Henry James in his later writing had a dim feeling that this was what he knew he should do" (*Writings* 132). This chapter began by observing that Stein identified James as "her forerunner" in *The Autobiography*; here, Stein conceives herself as developing a particular Jamesian tendency. We might note, however, that this recognition itself takes place by way of a temporal gymnastics that makes James's own innovation proleptic: it's not James who influences Stein, but as it were the other way around. Beyond reversing the logic of influence, Stein's insistence that writerly space is "completely not filled" might make us think of the exactly opposite terms in which James had extolled drama: "the real [dramatist] gets down on his knees, disposes of his goods ... and at last rises in triumph, having packed his coffer in the one way that is mathematically right. It closes perfectly; between one object and another you cannot insert the point of a penknife" (qtd. in Edel 39–40). In discerning a language that opens space rather than filling or "clos[ing]" it, Stein begins to identify the theatricality by which James exceeds his own dramatic ideal of communicative compaction – the pen/knife that disruptively pushes its way into every scene. And this identification proceeds by way of a literary historicity we can now recognize as itself a piece of Jamesian theatricality: Stein constitutes the event of James's writing retroactively, as anticipation. James, in other words, becomes not a writer who was, but a writer who will have been going to be – i.e., to be Stein. "He came not to begin but to have begun," she writes of him in *Four in America* (*Writings* 291).

If Stein positions her own writing here as the culmination and even, paradoxically, the origin of James's, elsewhere she frames her work's value in terms of its kinship with the visual art of her contemporaries, specifically cubism. As we can now observe, however, Jamesian theater seems to haunt this affinity too. Stein identifies cubism's "triple foundation" as the "composition of which one corner was as important as another corner," the disappearance of "faith in what the eyes were seeing," and the pictures' new desire "to leave their frames" ("Picasso" 19); this is the same perspectival rebellion we have discovered in James's theatrics of undersides and backsides. Nevertheless, Stein would most likely want to qualify the similarity; although she acknowledges James's importance, she is always careful to distinguish his achievement from her own. James, Stein writes in *Four in America*, "is a combination of the two ways of writing" (291), which are "the way when you write what you are writing" and "the way when you write what you are going to be writing or what some other one would have written if they had been writing" (282). The latter "way" certainly does describe the strategies of Jamesian scenography as we've analyzed it; by contrast, "the way when you write what you are writing" would seem to denote the ideal of a unified, self-contained present. And indeed, Stein proclaims her dedication to the present throughout her work. In "Portraits and Repetition," for example, she criticizes "intelligent people" because "although they talk as if they knew something [they] are really confusing, because they are so to speak keeping two times going at once, the repetition time of remembering and the actual time of talking" (*Writings* 106). She describes her "portraits" as an attempt at "making what I know come out as I know it, come out not as remembering" (107), and in "Plays" she insists that "The business of Art ... is to live in the actual present, that is the complete actual present, and to completely express that complete actual present" (65).

Given this poetics of the present, it is surprising that the piece in which she formalizes her binary of "the two ways of writing" should bear the name of, and keep returning to, a figure who she insists *combines* them. This fact alone suggests that Stein's present is inherently permeable. If it can exclude the "two times at once" of "remembering," it still maintains relations with the "going to" and "would have"; these can impose themselves productively upon the present in such a way as to yield, for instance, the general who Henry James "was or was not" (283). Just as Henry James, in the ways this chapter has been tracing, explodes the dramatic integrity of the narrative present, "Henry James" seems to undermine the poetic present as a time that must be fully or "completely" its own. This composition signals to Stein's reader that her "complete actual present" is more conceptually complex than we might assume. In what follows, I'll be examining the theatrical ramifications of that complexity.

Nevertheless, Stein does continually makes it clear that in her own most important writing, she has attempted to make the present her sole temporal site.[23] She frames her ability to recognize and achieve this goal – to activate "something moving as moving is" rather than "as moving should be" – as her advance beyond James, who keeps one foot stuck in the dispersive temporality of recollection, anticipation, and hypothetical that Stein will (have been going to) transcend. Her commitment to the present makes her cast James's innovation "in his later writing" as an approach to presentness; she is no doubt responding to the outrageousness of his syntax, the incredibly elaborate and processual – because never finished – construction of sense, glaringly driven by imperatives other than communicating narrative information, or telling what happened. This is, of course, the quality that makes James's later work look modernist, or writerly: the degree to which it draws our attention to its own textual procedure, rather than its represented fiction.[24] In different ways, Charles Caramello explains, James and Stein *both* "present acute cases of the tension between referentiality and autoreferentiality that has haunted formalist aesthetics in music, painting, and literature for more than a century. They are difficult, in sum, for the same general reasons that most modernist writers are difficult" (193).

This shift of emphasis from story to discourse, or from the narrat*ed* to the narrat*ing*, easily evokes an ethos of the present moment.[25] Indeed, the very word "modernism" seems to name an ascendancy of the present moment, deriving from the Latin *modo*, or "just now" ("modern"). But while some modernisms have certainly provoked audiences through their assertion of the "now" as such, this chapter has pursued a different temporality of outrageousness in James. Far from asserting the present, James's texts operate as an explosive dispersion of the present, constantly reorienting the reader toward *other* temporal sites. In so doing, his texts simulate the spatial heterogeneity of theater; they become theatrical precisely by subverting presentness. Given this understanding, how do we make sense of Stein's concerted effort to embrace the present in her writing? Must we find her "modernism" antithetical to James's theatricality?

To arrive at this conclusion would mean shoring up a binary familiar from both literary and visual art criticism: theatricality on one side of an aesthetic divide and modernism on the other.[26] On the contrary, however, I claim that we can read key aspects of Stein's modernist innovation *as* theatrical, in a sense that directly relates to Jamesian techniques. To make this argument, I begin by reviewing the discourse on Stein's supposed antitheatricalism in light of her 1935 lecture "Plays," in which she challenges the very assumptions that make the antitheatricalist reading possible. I then turn to two of Stein's "landscape" plays: *Paisieu* (1928) and the surprising Broadway hit *Four Saints in Three Acts* (1927, produced in 1934). It is true that Stein does not subject actuality to an all-out attack, as James does. But neither does her treasured "present" correspond to the present James tries to demolish. The unifying immediacy of drama's "*so ist es*" (Brecht) could not be farther from Stein's landscape; her "present" is not a communion with what is happening here and now, but a movement that splinters the here-and-now beyond recognition. For Stein, this is the promise and pleasure of theater: a fundamentally dispersive, discontinuous field.

Beyond Antitheatricality: "Plays"

The theater of James's texts, as we have been reading them, offers an alternative ground for understanding the theater of Stein's – alternative, that is, to the fundamentally *dramatic* sense of theater that seems to have grounded the interpretation of Stein's work as antitheatrical. If we align theatricality with "unities of space, time, [and] action," then Stein's "utterly broken and fragmentary stage," in works like *Four Saints in Three Acts*, must indeed seem antitheatrical (Puchner, *Stage* 109). But by treating the dramatic and the theatrical as separate concepts, we can begin to trace Stein's construction of an iconoclastic *but still emphatically theatrical* logic. James's writing in particular helps us see how theater is itself conducive to the "broken and fragmentary." Returning once more to Samuel Weber, we might say both James and Stein anticipate his argument that theatricality is the "*separability* of place 'itself'" (294): for the earlier writers too, theater is what *undermines* any attempt at spatial, temporal, or subjective "unity." The playhouse is a riotous space; dramatic continuity can only impose itself upon this space in an act of repressive violence. If Stein's plays institute a fragmentary experience, then, this need not be understood as an attack on the theater medium itself. On the contrary, Stein activates theater's own resources *in excess of* the integrating dramatic present. We might thus switch the terms of Martin Puchner's claim that Stein devised an "antitheatrical drama" (*Stage* 105): it's precisely when we look past the rules of drama that her theatricality becomes legible.

To begin with, Stein makes it clear that she understands the province of theater as utterly distinct from the narrative ambition basic to drama: "I concluded that anything that was not a story could be a play," she writes in "Plays" (73). Indeed, the fact that this sentence occurs in a lecture devoted to "Plays" might make us miss the breadth of its scope: it articulates, not just a sense of theater, but a radical *theatricalism*, claiming not only that plays should not be stories, but that *anything* other than story can make for theater. This claim should encourage us to regard Stein's marking as "plays" some very un-play-like texts, not as an attack on theater's presumed integrity, but on the contrary as an aggressive expansion of theater into new realms. For example, the following text is from her 1928 piece *Paisieu: A Play*, which I'll discuss later in this chapter:

> **ACT ONE**
> Geronimo in season.
>
> **ACT ONE**
> Seasonable dishes.
> Scorpions and butterflies and scorpions are
>   non-existent so she could be easy.
>
> **ACT ONE**
> Its beginning is twenty twenty-two.
> Nobody counts poplars.
> Nobody counts poplars.
> Nobody.
> Counts.
> Poplars.
> Nobody counts poplars as counts counts poplars.
> Next. (155–6)

Although the piece preserves one remnant of dramatic form – the designation of "Acts" and, later, "Scenes" – it is not at all clear what exactly these terms designate. Needless to say, their repetition confounds their original function of marking progressive stages; the architecture of drama seems to have crumbled into found artifacts, to be rearranged at will. Perhaps more troubling is the fact that none of these lines are attributed to speakers, nor do they obviously describe onstage actions. Instead, they have the feel of a single, authorial discourse, not radically unlike the voice of non-"play" texts like 1914's *Tender Buttons*:

> A seal and matches and a swan and ivy and a suit. (4)
> [. . .]
>
> **COLD CLIMATE.**
> A season in yellow sold extra strings makes lying places.
>
> **MALACHITE.**
> The sudden spoon is the same in no size. The sudden spoon is
>   the wound in the decision. (12)[27]

Either of these pieces, like all Stein's work, is unsettling enough on its own. Regarded side-by-side, they bring the question of genre to a kind of crisis. "I think and always have thought that if you write a play you ought to announce that it is a play and that is what I did," she writes in "Plays," remarking as well: "I have written a great many plays and I am quite sure they are plays" (73, 69). What, she dares us to wonder, makes her so sure? By insisting that *Paisieu* is "A Play" while *Tender Buttons* is not (but presumably "could" have been[28]), Stein challenges her readers to interrogate their assumptions about theater. Her "plays" are not plays in the sense that I will take up in subsequent chapters: they do not use familiar formal conventions to evoke the conflation of script and scene, and hence we are unlikely to feel that we are "seeing" *the* play as we read. Stein withholds this experience from her reader; by marking her texts as "plays" nevertheless, she produces a dissonance that goads the reader toward a new logic of staging. She assigns us the task of discovering what might make her works appropriate to performance. We have no legitimate basis, she argues, for assuming that such works cannot suit the stage.

Critics have been oddly eager to dismiss this provocation, however, and to apply more commonsense parameters of theatricality in judging Stein's work antitheatrical. Sarah Bay-Cheng helpfully suggests another approach, by situating Stein's work within the tradition of avant-garde performance. Yet Bay-Cheng also claims that Stein's "dramatic writings before 1920 are distinctive for their antitheatricalism ... As many have argued previously, these early texts labeled 'plays' are not terribly stage-worthy (though numerous productions have been attempted)" (35).[29] I am not sure how one might distinguish an "attempted" production from, say, a fully accomplished one, although this kind of distinction consistently subtends such readings. Bay-Cheng disputes Puchner's account of Stein as a writer of closet drama, on the basis of his failure to note "the progression of Stein's drama over three decades" (48), but she approvingly quotes his statement that "[t]he transformations that were necessary for staging *Four Saints* can serve as a measure for the distance Stein's text maintains from the theater" (*Stage* III, qtd. in Bay-Cheng 54). It is not clear to me, however, that Virgil Thomson's active manipulations of Stein's text really constitute radical "transformations" of that text, nor that the particular interventions Thomson made "were necessary." Surely there are innumerable ways one could bring this play into production, which begin suggesting themselves the moment one approaches the text with that question in mind. To insist that Stein's collaborators had to *make* her script theatrical, as it were rescuing *Four Saints* from its own literariness, is to ignore another possibility: that in such texts, Stein pursues theater itself beyond dramatic limits.

Jane Palatini Bowers, in her 1991 study *They Watch Me As They Watch This*, elucidates various ways in which Stein sets text and other aspects of performance in productive opposition. *Four Saints*, for instance, "counteracts the very performance it initiates in a kind of counter-text, a written text which asserts itself at every moment of performance" (48), while 1936's *Listen to Me* is "a collision that [Stein] engineers" between "conception and its projected enactment" (91). Bowers's analysis is strongest where it presents Stein's texts as *engaging* theatrical performance in order to investigate its possibilities and impossibilities in a kind of immanent critique. The "adamantly and self-consciously 'literary'" quality of these plays (2) emerges, as Bowers shows, through their orientation toward, anticipation of, and (sometimes) realization in theater. In many places, Bowers's readings provide an inspiring precedent for my own project: in showing the ways in which these texts at once demand and resist enactment (as, for example, in her wonderful consideration of verbs in the early plays [17–19]), she is revealing what I would call their negative theatrics. In these moments, Bowers shows Stein exploiting specific formal possibilities inherent in the medium. For example: "In the theater the forward march of time is inexorable," but it is equally true that the "flow of speech and action is checked, as it were, by the way the eye perceives performance in space – instant by instant. Really then, the dynamism of performance ... is at once continuous and discontinuous" (49–50). Thus *Four Saints*, far from ignoring the "reality" of performance, simply "emphasizes the discontinuity of performance rather than its continuity" (50).[30] With this formulation, Bowers neatly preempts much of the discourse on "antitheatrical" Stein.

Ultimately, Bowers concludes that Stein's plays are "a performed poetry, at once textual and theatrical" (135). At other points in her argument, however, she seems unduly bound by dramatic norms, as when she characterizes Stein's *A Play Called Not and Now*, in which "No one acts; nothing happens; no one speaks," as accordingly "a play that cannot play in the theater" (91). Similarly, while her claim that Stein's *A List* asserts "the primacy of the written text ... over the performance text" is suggestively Adornian, it rests on the problematic argument that some of the play's clarity would be lost in performance (31–32). Bowers writes that "[o]nly the written text can set us straight" if, for instance, we hope to follow Stein's extensive play with homophones like "for" and "four" (ibid.). But as we have seen, being "set straight" is a specifically dramatic requirement. In Stein, such ambiguities are not brakes on theatrical performance, but projections of a theater where meaning is never available to a synoptic gaze, where we are always being invited to zig and zag between different possibilities. The sound that might either be "for" or "four" *is* theatrical in this sense: the word never stops referring to its own alternatives, or "other parts." If written text is ascendant here, its primacy lies not in correcting performance, but in anticipating and providing for this dynamic.

Throughout the rest of this chapter, I try to explicate the logic of Stein's fundamentally discontinuous theater. This reading should unseat the conception that her work is antagonistic toward theatrical performance. Still, the "Plays" lecture does seem to provide ample justification for the claim that Stein shows at least a "conflicted relation to the theater" (Puchner, *Stage* 102). In particular, Stein objects to the "nervousness" she associates with many of her experiences at the theater, a discomfort she ascribes to the "syncopated time" that arises between spectator and spectacle ("Plays" 58–59). As if in response to the same sense of theater we've traced in James, Stein here records an agitating discontinuity. This feeling arises for her, before the show has even begun, from the sight of the curtain: "the curtain already makes one feel that one is not going to have the same tempo as the thing that is there behind the curtain" (59). The potentially disruptive presence of other viewers compounds the effect: "the audience and the fact that they are or will be or will not be in the way when the curtain goes up that too makes for nervousness and nervousness is the certain proof that the emotion of the one seeing and the emotion of the thing seen do not progress together" (ibid.). Stein seems acutely aware of everything *but* the drama that is to be presented, beset by the space and time of theater as a matrix of disparities. This is, as I have been repeating, a specifically Jamesian experience; similarly, when Stein writes that "before it had commenced it was over" (71), she could just as well be describing the anachronic Jamesian "scene." And yet the two writers' confluence is far from complete: Stein *objects* to the theatrical discomfiture James had ultimately embraced. We might therefore wonder if Stein's "nervousness" implies a renewed dramatic impulse to centralize the stage.

It would be convenient for my argument if "Plays" told the story of Stein learning to embrace the theatrical "nervousness" she describes: the spatial discontinuity embodied by the curtain, and the temporal discontinuity of "syncopated time."[31] Instead, however, her lecture continues to treat these features as problems: "This thing, the fact *that your emotional time as an audience is not the same as the emotional time of the play* is what makes one endlessly troubled about a play," she writes, "because not only is there a thing to know as to why this is so but also there is a thing to know why perhaps it *does not need to be so*" (58, my emphases). For Stein, as for dramatic authors, the bifurcation between the audience and the play is a problem that must be creatively *overcome*. By repeatedly casting the problem in the terms that "there is a thing to know," however, she also seems to luxuriate in the critical task thus generated, suggesting a desire to dwell on the theatrical terrain where this conceptual "thing" is "there" to engage her.[32]

Puchner claims that Stein tries to solve the problem of the "two times" through "the attempt to import [the] quality of synchronized reading into the dramatic form," since "[i]t is only in private and ideal circumstances, Stein and so many modernists argue, that a perfect synchronicity between story and the affective reader can be achieved" (*Stage* 102). As we observed earlier, however, Stein by no means regards the written-and-read medium as a guarantee of "perfect synchronicity." In "Plays," she suggests that theatrical syncopation has its analog in the realm of reading: "in a book it is always a strange doubling, the familiarity between the characters in the book is a progressive familiarity and the familiarity between them and the reader is a familiarity that is a forcing process . . . It makes of course a double time [. . .]" (67). Ridding the written text of *its* "two times" is for Stein an ambition as necessary, and as new, as the corresponding project for theater. It is clear, therefore, that the solution to theatrical syncopation will not simply consist in writing plays meant to stay on the page.

And indeed, Stein goes on to describe an irreducibly *theatrical* model for this reform: the experience of going, in her youth, to see Sarah Bernhardt's company. "[I]t was all so foreign and her voice being so varied and it all being so french I could rest in it untroubled. And I did . . . It was better than the theatre because you did not have to get acquainted" (71). This theater was "better than *the* theatre" – that is, the theater as normative, and as normally available to young Gertrude. It was, therefore, barely recognizable *as* theater, much as innovative forms (as Stein herself knew) generally go unrecognized.[33] And yet it succeeded for her, as theater, precisely by being "foreign": by keeping its distance, offering an alternative to the normal sociality of "the theatre." The repeated "all" ("all so foreign . . . all being so french") emphasizes the spatially distributed copia of performance, just as the "voice being so varied" describes the temporally differential experience of Bernhardt's virtuosity. Of course the performance might, on its own terms, have been the height of drama; but it is precisely the freedom from *taking* it on its own terms – from having to get acquainted – that Stein celebrates here. Nor does this distance have anything to do with a "fourth wall"; on the contrary, Stein's pleasure ensues from her own elimination of the dramatic fiction, which opens a space for her to "rest in."

Stein thus describes a theatrical sensibility that arises first with her own *in situ* revision of other artists' work. Not only "french" or "foreign" plays are susceptible to this reshaping, moreover: the Bernhardt play "awakened in me a desire for melodrama on the stage, because there again everything happened so quietly one did not have to get acquainted and as what people felt was of no importance one did not have to realize what was said"; her favorite melodramas "made the whole stage the whole play ... silence stillness and quick movement" (72). Here again, Stein blithely dispenses with the play's own self-conception – imagine a melodrama for which "what people felt was of no importance"! Restaging these works as a kind of abstract ballet, what Stein excises is not theater as such, but the centralizing emotional coercion of *dramatic* theater. By refusing to let the melodramas engage her on the Aristotelian level of sympathetic fiction, she is able to enjoy the sensory qualities of the performance. Thus reimagined, "the whole play" is dispersed over "the whole stage." Theater is valuable as a sensory panoply ("all so foreign") that can add up to a powerful impression *without* imposing the continuities either of human interest or of discursive meaning (of "realiz[ing] what was said"). By "eliminating progression" (Davy 116), Stein's kind of theater abandons not its own theatricality but the dramatic *unification* of theater's spaces and times.

In her girlhood, Stein found her "desire" "awakened" when theater's dimensional copia could manifest itself outside narrative compulsion. The "clothes, voices, what they the actors said, how they were dressed and how that related itself to their moving around" are, for Stein, "things over which one stumbles *over which one stumbled*" ("Plays" 71, my emphasis): the shift in verb tense is decisive. Costume, sound, text, and movement remain to Stein as the heterogeneous "things" of theater, that is, but one *no longer* stumbles over them – provided one has found a way to stop the headlong vector of progressive dramatic narrative.[34]

2 Gertrude Stein

Negativity beyond Contradiction: Paisieu's *Differential Landscape*

Clearly, then, Stein does not object to theatrical multiplicity in itself. What bothers her is rather the experience of that multiplicity jarring against the expectation of continuous unity. Stein's desire to overcome the "two times" of theater is not a pseudodramatic intolerance of discontinuity or discrepancy as such. The problem of the two times is rather that they keep theater trapped in a binary struggle. The conflict between drama's demand for immediacy and theater's own dimensions of distance crowds out the differential pleasures of the *variously* discontinuous experience that results when dramatic expectations are released altogether. Accordingly, Stein's solution is perhaps less to prescribe a drama of "perfect synchronicity" (Puchner, *Stage* 102) than to remove the dramatic ideal itself. Temporal syncopation and spatial separation stop being problems once we set aside the standards from which they deviate: continuous immersion, maintained by narrative momentum, in drama's "absolute" present (Szondi), and the unbroken togetherness of a theater that demands we "get acquainted." Stein's problem is not with theater's multiplicity but, so to speak, with its *du*plicity, the way her experience of its phenomenal disposition contradicts its prevailing norms. If the viewer can come to accept theater as a panoply of differentially distributed contents – and herself as one alien among others – then a maddening bifurcation will dissolve into a texture of potentially infinite, nonexclusive variants. Stein initiates this process, in "Plays," by developing a contentedly alien persona: the young woman we see at the theater seems utterly immune to twenty-two hundred years of dramatic expectations and desires, rather as if she had just dropped in from outer space.

In thus dismissing drama altogether, Stein does indeed move away from the twoness she had noticed in "Henry James." She also announces a mode of nondramatic theatrical pleasure quite unlike the one we have traced in James's work. For him, theater emerges as a difference or "descent" from drama's centralizing ideal. In this mode of theater, drama never disappears completely; instead, it is perpetually subjected to subversion, distraction, and rupture. In fact, as we saw in the Jamesian device of the "disrupted image," the "stream" of dramatic action can itself be mobilized to produce theater as against the stasis of the pictorial. It is the violent interplay between drama and "other parts" of the playing space that produces theatrical pleasure for James. For Stein, by contrast, theater's essential operation is not the interposition of disruption and disparity *between* drama and its others but, instead, the cultivation of difference *within* an already-decentralized perceptual field. The delights of this theater are exploratory and, as it were, distributive – a rhizomatic pleasure of lateral textures, as compared to the more oedipal pleasure of chopping away at dramatic tradition's towering tree.[35] In Stein, Bonnie Marranca writes, one is "continually absorbed by the pleasure of tracing the endless diverging lines impressed upon constantly transforming surfaces, and at every turn discovering winding, wider pathways leading to ever more mysterious corridors of experience" (24). The difference that structures this theater is not fundamentally a force of opposition. Rather, to quote *Tender Buttons* again: "The difference is spreading" (3).

Jamesian theater thus ceaselessly contends with dramatic and narrative norms, while Stein's theater simply discards them. This difference typifies the authors' respective senses of their own relation to literary tradition more broadly: "James was preoccupied with his predecessors and with himself as their terminal point, Stein with herself as successor and as originator of a new lineage" (Caramello 20). But the distinction also speaks to the sharply different facts of their respective theatrical careers. If James painfully came to release his long-held dream of being a prominent playwright (Edel 55, 108, 115), Stein's biography shows something like the opposite trajectory: theatrical success at sixty, followed by twelve more years of work addressed to the stage. So the logic that led us to explore James's prose fiction as a kind of refuge for his renegade theatricality – which neither the institutional theater of his day nor his own dramatic standards could accommodate within playwriting – does not apply to Stein, who continues to insist that her pieces can actually "play." A theatrical reformer at long distance, she sought to provide for a radically new theater, one that would correspond to her singular experiences of some of the old. James, much more deeply invested than Stein in existing theater, maintains his theatricality as a negative relation to the dramatic: divergence and distraction, his various techniques of fracturing the narrative present. These techniques simulate the "stumbling" Stein sees as expendable, since her theater will simply eliminate the dramatic norm such divergence is *from*. As Ryan remarks, "Ibsen did not exist for her" (1); dramaturgically speaking, neither did Aristotle.[36]

In the empty space created by this full-scale eviction of precedent, Stein decided to construct "a play [that] was exactly like a landscape" ("Plays" 75). Stein's "landscape plays" are like nothing James would have recognized as theater – and yet they proceed from an intuition of theater as a differential space of riotous multiplicity, an intuition we can recognize as Jamesian. Included in Stein's notion of landscape is the sense that these plays will provide their own context, establish their own terrain; unlike Strether's *paysage* in *The Ambassadors*, these landscapes will not find themselves perforated by someone else's "drama." But this is because they perforate themselves: they are already structured as a network of incommensurabilities. We should not mistake Stein's espousal of "untroubled" pleasure for a dismissal of negativity altogether. Rather, her plays generate their own theatrical negativity internally, precisely because they no longer have a dramatic norm against which to react. A part of Stein's job therefore consists in *manifesting* the negative, giving it the substance of a topographical feature. This occurs quite literally in the opening lines of *Paisieu: A Play*:

> Not Paisieu a play.
> Arbuthnot or hollowed is constant eggs and grasped.
> Failure in white clouds.
> Arbuthnot
> Geronimo (155)

The first line seems flatly to deny its own premises. But this cheekiness is really a kind of showing-off: the play will be capacious enough to accommodate its own negation, which becomes a generative moment *within* it. Although the lines in *Paisieu* are not attributed to characters, I find it particularly rewarding to imagine this statement spoken by a performer, as if correcting the assumptions of an audience who, perhaps, hold programs emblazoned with the very referent being denied (and created). The question that would then arise is not just "then what is it?" but also "then where am I?", a question to which we would at once know *and* not know the answer: we are in Stein's landscape, a field that harbors incommensurable alternatives simultaneously. The second line enacts this tension through its translation of "or" into "and," as well as through the outrageous zeugma of each pair of terms, held together only at great strain: "Arbuthnot or hollowed," "constant eggs and grasped." The play thus alerts us that its challenge will be to perceive radically *different* terms *together*. As Andrzej Wirth observes, Stein enacts a "splintering [*Zersplitterung*] of language, whose fragments ('bits') let themselves align with different constellations of meaning" ("Gertrude" 67). Her procedure will be, to use Stein's own words, "a combination and not a contradiction" ("Plays" 58; cf. Schultz, "Combination") – but despite the "eggs," a combination that refuses to emulsify.

To support this radical heterogeneity, the negative emerges as a phenomenon operative within the perceptual field, rather than as its limit: the "other parts" of Jamesian theater are, for Stein, already *here*. Accordingly, the first word – "Not" – becomes "Arbuthnot," the name of a definite historical entity. John Arbuthnot was an eighteenth-century doctor and satirist, friendly with Jonathan Swift and Alexander Pope; but more important than this particular association, I think, is the sense Stein conveys of the "not" as a fundamentally mobile quantity, now negating phenomena and now filling them out. Things "are, but not": the "not" is a modification, not a cancelation, of their being.[37] "Arbuthnot" then becomes "Geronimo," the improbable surname of a family whose members will become, if not the play's characters, the subjects and objects of much of its language. Stein's negative doesn't erase the world, but populates it. We may start out with the expectation that these "nots" will yield to a "but . . .," but by withholding the negative's negative, Stein retrains us to regard the "no" as a phenomenon in its own right, equal in status with the objects it negotiates. In the same way, "Failure" is no longer an attribute *of* something ("white clouds") but manifests as an element "in" an arrangement, a compositional feature in itself. Negativity operates here not as binary opposition, nor even as dialectical negation, but as the ongoing parsing of specificities within a fundamentally accommodating field. "There is no no in no," Stein writes in her 1936 play *Listen To Me* (419); negativity doesn't cancel or transcend itself here, but – as it were – nests.

That the negative has a place *within* Stein's theatrical world returns us to the question we encountered earlier: how should we understand Stein's conviction that "The business of Art [. . .] is to live in the actual present, that is the complete actual present, and to completely express that complete actual present" ("Plays" 65)? I've been arguing for a tradition of "negative theatrics" that treats the present not as an ideal but as a problem; that operates by, in various ways, negating its own actuality. Must we place Stein entirely outside this tradition? Marranca suggests as much when she claims that Stein's "affirmation of life, untouched by modern and at times fashionable alienation, is a joyous modernism" (20). This kind of observation certainly speaks to a real affective difference between Stein and the other writers treated in this study. But as we have already begun to see, Stein's difficult work effects an "alienation" of its own; and whatever "affirmation of life" she may evoke, I think the life of her language is far too various to support any totalizing affirmation *or* negation.[38] There is thus no question of *attacking* the present, as in James. Nor is Stein's negative theatricality a *determinate negation* of the actual, as we will see in the more obviously alienated Beckett; rather, hers is a fundamentally differential, ramifying movement, within a present too complex to brook totalizing rejection.

And yet Stein's landscape, like those of James and Beckett both, unfurls at the expense of any phenomenal immediacy. In fact, even in the above sentence about "The business of Art," Stein's words multiply in a manner that undermines the "complete actual present" to which they refer. Characteristically courting redundancy at every turn, this sentence produces a discursive present which is never "complete," but submits to continual adjustment and elaboration. The nested emphases of the phrase "complete actual present," as well as its repetition, promote a heightened sensitivity to each word's distinctiveness, each time it occurs, while at the same time creating a system of echoes. This is language hard at work disabling any synthesizing moment of uptake. Its present is *not* the "complete," absolute present of drama; rather, it is divided and provisional, constantly yielding to supplementary excavations.[39]

Stein's theater operates this way too. Her landscapes preempt the dramatic "*so ist es*" by investing every word with its own vector of movement: there can be no single surface of reception, no point at which to converge. Between Scene III and Scene IV of *Paisieu*'s first act, we find:

> Scene in preciseness
> Whole button come can couple with all division in
>   antics of required lame and dew.
> Germaine and her child.
> Germaine and her child. (159)

Here again, Stein's "preciseness" consists of acknowledging the *difference made* by increments of space and time. If it is not enough to say something once, this is because the stage is continually criss-crossed by microcurrents of difference, such that no moment's content can be identical to the last. This is not, as many have claimed, a poetics of "stasis."[40] Rather, it is a theatrics for which the passage of time and the shifting disposition of space emphatically *count*. If one were to stage this passage, one might bring the lights up on a woman and a child, then dim them, then bring them up again; the audience would experience a tableau divided from itself (a "couple with all division"?). Repetition here is not an attempt to impose "synchronicity," but a display of fundamental variation: "A matter of fact is that there is a blue sky of different colors. A blue sky of different colors"

(*Paisieu* 159). Or again, on the next page: "It is the difference between very quickly and very quickly" (160).

It's tempting, once again, to regard such lines as invitations to staging: just think of all the ways performance could produce "the difference between" two iterations of the same phrase. Certainly these lines instance the *invitation to co-creation* that so many have found in Stein: "Whatever you find" in her plays "depends on your own way of looking" (Marranca 7). Far from being unstageable, that is, Stein's texts are uniquely appropriate to theater as a collaborative medium. But the theatricality of these lines goes beyond their appeal to creative collaboration. Already on the page, they exhibit and promote a sense of language as spatially and/or temporally distributed: one "very quickly" is different from the other "very quickly" because there are two of them, that is, because they occupy different places on the page simultaneously, or because they occupy two distinct moments of writing or reading. By emphatically occupying a particular position, each word exceeds the signification that makes it the same word wherever it is. Stein thus emphasizes the way words can take up space and time. "Stein treats her words as though they are material objects related to each other spatially, that is, visually on the page and sonorously in the air," Bowers writes (26). The word becomes thinglike, in the sense Stein identifies elsewhere: "a thing that seems to be exactly the same thing may seem to be a repetition but is it" (*Writings* 103). As in the Jamesian parlor, these "things" arrange themselves to the consternation of any sublimating gaze.

If Stein's theater text beckons collaborators' innovation, then, it also demonstrates writing's ability to *stage itself* – an effect that aligns it with the more formally conventional playwriting we'll encounter in subsequent chapters. In Stein, the effect of self-staging occurs through the use of repetition, but also through her work with parts of speech – in particular, her refusal to let "little" words play a merely supporting role in the construction of sense.[41] Prepositions and other inconspicuous terms swell with a newfound materiality:

> Disuse of in between. (*Paisieu* 158)
> [...]
> To be called to be. (161)
> [...]
> Thanks for it as in by kept call. (162)

"To be called to be" is, we might say, the state of such words in Stein – and the state of the playscript in general. By summoning these words to positivity, Stein's syntax simulates the theatrical vector that thrusts text into the actual. But it would be wrong to assume that the newly emphatic presence of words like "in," "to," and "by" corresponds to an ideal of absolute, immediate being – "purely present existence ... directly and immediately perceived" (Ryan 37). The positivity being foisted on these words is not something that "purely" or "directly" *happens*; instead, their new substantiality feels burdensome, like a mission the small words – or our imaginations – can't quite discharge. Numerous readings of Stein bear witness to this difficulty, which often leads critics (I don't exclude myself) to make "sense" of her works by bracketing the very words she wants us to notice. Thus, for instance, Pamela Hadas cites a passage from *Two: Gertrude Stein and Her Brother* that includes the sentence "This was the remainder of *there were having been or being* any martyr" and notes: "Leo [Stein] might easily have seen himself as a martyr" (66, my emphasis). The temptation of reference interferes with our perception of precisely those words Stein wants to make us see, words whose very impropriety should discourage us from trying to "get acquainted." These words exist *among* the others without qualifying or reducing them; they do not coalesce, via signification, into a unity. And this coexistence of terms in undecidable relation – in a relation that only yields determinate meaning at the cost of active exclusion or reduction – anticipates theater's ability to dispose things (and people) in an unresolvable sensory multiplicity.

The (Dis)continuous Present: Four Saints in Three Acts

The second subtitle of *Paisieu* is "*A Work of Pure Imagination in which No Reminiscences Intrude.*" This description, like many passages throughout Stein's writing, seems to announce an unquestioning dedication to the present; but as we have seen, Stein consistently troubles the very immediacy she announces. If "No Reminiscences Intrude" upon her theatrical landscape, this does not yield a dramatic "absolute present," with spectator and spectacle plunged into the unity of the here-and-now. Rather, the play distributes itself through a structure of relays and echoes:

> There are passes in a mountain and if a tree can be used they will put it where they are.
> Leave where they went. Leaves are where they are where they went.
> Leaves where they went. (176–177)

It is true that the utter unpredictability of this language, its freedom from narrative or discursive logics such as that of "reminiscence," compels our attention to each moment of the text anew. But we risk mischaracterizing the particular consistency of these moments if we adopt the vocabulary of the "present" too quickly. Especially treacherous is Stein's own term for her aesthetics: the famous "continuous present," which she mentions repeatedly in the lecture "Composition as Explanation" (*Writings* 21–30). With this term, as with the subtitle of *Paisieu*, Stein espouses a refusal to ground language in the authority of what has been or will be. Only a sustained attention to the present in its uniqueness, she suggests, can ward off the reifying force of convention.[42] By calling her present "continuous," Stein emphasizes the ongoing dedication and perpetually renewed effort this project demands. And yet what determines the present, for her, is precisely the perceptual *absence* of continuity. As Wirth observes, Stein's continuous present entails the "abandonment of the chronological linearity of succession and progression" ("Gertrude" 71). What is "continuous" about it is only that the singular moment *perpetually refuses* to situate itself among its precursors and successors. To experience presentness in this sense is exactly not to experience continuity.

Stein's "continuous present," in other words, is not only an experience of rupture, "a gap, where past and future . . . are momentarily unhooked" (Stewart 39). It is also a concept that redoubles this gap as the disjuncture between theory (the "continuous present" as a *term*) and creative or receptive practice (the experience to which the term refers), marking the discontinuous work off from the discourse that formalizes its procedure as "continuous." This present, in other words, not only displays but perpetuates a constitutive disparity. This explains why Stein would forego the textual conventions of drama, which use recognizable conventions to imply the structure of a performance event: for her, the promise of each writerly choice lies in the way it *doesn't* accord with a predictable structure, or extend a causal logic. The title of her 1927 play *Four Saints in Three Acts* gives a nod to dramatic convention, but it also conveys a sense of disjuncture: how will *four* saints fit into *three* acts, without something sticking out? As one scene heading puts it: "Could Four Acts be Three" (462)?

Indeed, once the play gets under way, we find Stein's eccentric arithmetic operating directly in service of a triumphant *dis*continuity. As in many of her plays, Stein employs Acts and Scenes out of sequence, conveying her commitment to a language that determines its own procedures anew at every (dis)juncture. But *Four Saints'* obsession with number goes beyond this characteristic Steinism. The phrase "How many" arises again and again, and – as has frequently been observed – seems to emerge as a question about the text's own production:

Saint Therese. How many saints are there in it.
Saint Therese. There are very many many saints in it.
Saint Therese. There are as many saints as there are in it. (*Four* 458)
[. . .]
Saint Therese. How many windows and doors and floors are there in it. (463)
[. . .]
How many saints are there in it.
How many saints are there in it.
How many acts are there in it.
[. . .]
How many Acts are there in it.
Four Acts. (478)

These questions of number emphasize multiplicity, implying that the important determinations of textual production and reception are choices among infinite alternatives, rather than between binary options – and that these choices can be made anew at each moment: "It is very necessary to have arithmetic inestimably" (479). Defiantly inestimable, Stein's numbers are *not* the signs of an inevitable succession. She treats the sequence of "natural numbers" – normally the privileged register of the *a priori* – as manipulable verbal material, their sensory qualities rising to prominence:

> One two three all out but me.
> One two three four all out but four
> One two all about but you. (ibid.)

Number is de-idealized; we are asked to imagine it as equal among the other features of a verbal landscape, rather than as an *a priori* category that would structure a work in advance. "Scene VII" is thus followed by "Scene Eight" (458–460): numbering is an act of language that must be renewed each time with a conscious, discontinuous gesture. The implication, consonant with Stein's model of radical independence from tradition (rather than perpetual rebellion against it), is that *nothing* need be taken for granted: we are free to reimagine not only the rules of grammar, but the grammar of experience itself.[43] Thus, for example, in Act I, "Scene IV" is followed by "Act Two," "Scene One," "Scene One," and "Act One" before we reach "Scene V" (453–454); in Act II "Scene V" occurs nine times in a row, each time with a different content (456–457). Act I's "Scene VIII" reads simply: "Saint Therese in time" (454). Time itself has become an empirical, malleable, topographical feature.[44] Stein refuses simply to mark time's passing; rather, she posits time – like the negative – as a member of the perceptual field, subject to (and of) unpredictable divagations and specificities.

Does this kind of usage deny the inherent temporal conditions of performance? Are these tricks that only "work" on the page? Yes, if we assume "the spatial and temporal continuity of the theater" (Puchner, *Stage* 110); but again, this is just the assumption Stein's insights consistently unsettle. As "Plays" makes clear, dramatic conventions don't always succeed in organizing our theatrical experience as a seamless passage of time. This means that, for instance, the familiar sequence of Act I, Act II, Act III may itself turn out to be "unstageable," since it implies a linear continuity that the heterogeneity of theatrical space, and our perceptual existence in *relation* to it, can always subvert. We should not, therefore, simply dismiss the possibility of staging the kind of event Stein's texts demand, or assume that such passages are being pragmatically "transformed" when we adapt them for performance. Rather, we need to take these features seriously as reminders that theatrical production *can't count on* the continuity for which dramatic structure aims. No longer assumed to be the constant vector that sublimates spatial heterogeneity into meaning, time fissures into a multiplicity of its own.

If in *The Ambassadors* Strether's countryside landscape explodes its own pictorial integrity through the movement of the "others" it has harbored, Stein's landscapes never present themselves as integral in the first place: discontinuity is the principle of their formation. "I felt that if a play was exactly like a landscape then there would be no difficulty about the emotion of the person looking on at the play being behind or ahead of the play," she writes in "Plays," "because the landscape does not have to make acquaintance. You may have to make acquaintance with it, but it does not with you, it is there" (75). Stein is not claiming that the landscape play is immediately and entirely accessible, simply "there" for us in a rapturous continuity of life and art once the interference of the fourth wall has been removed. Rather, she acknowledges in landscape an asymmetry between subject and spectacle, through the latter's carefully cultivated independence: "it" does not have to return your attentions. The following lines from *Four Saints* seem to imitate this configuration:

> A pleasure April fool's day a pleasure.
> Saint Therese seated.
> Not April fool's day a pleasure.
> Saint Therese seated.
> Not April fool's day a pleasure.
> Saint Therese seated.   (*Four* 445)

The lines about "April fool's day" pursue a train of thought with which the tableau of "Saint Therese seated," in its impassive repetition, seems utterly unconcerned. Stein thus celebrates the way a composition can abide, impervious, while the mind busies itself in rumination. "What is the difference between a picture and pictured," says the text a few pages later (452); that difference, which had caused such a disturbance in Stein's early theatergoing experience, has now become the very terrain of her theatrical landscaping. The dramatic work entices us with the promise of emotional confluence, then fails to accommodate – has no space for – our perceptual idiosyncrasy, as the curtain itself seems tacitly to admit. The landscape, however, doesn't dog us with the offer of "acquaintance," of mutual recognition, of fellow-feeling, then punish us when our singular perceptual apparatus shifts us out of line. Instead, it opens out into expanded possibilities of relation between essentially discontinuous elements – elements among which we can therefore place ourselves. "[T]he landscape not moving but being always in relation, the trees to the hills the hills to the fields the trees to each other any piece of it to any sky and then any detail to any other detail" Stein writes in "Plays" (77): the sky itself, no longer an all-encircling dome guaranteeing unity (and symbolizing the "unities"), becomes subject to differentiation as its relational possibilities multiply.[45] Similarly, Strether's heightened awareness of a shifting "engagement with others" is what makes his landscape theatrical, makes him perceive it *as* theater "at bottom." In Stein as in James, landscape becomes theater when we perceive it, not as the continuous extension of life as we (already) know it, but as a system of relations *with others*, relations built on constitutive disparities that keep space and significance open.

> Saint Therese and Saint Therese and Saint Therese.
> Many saints as seen and in between as many saints as seen.
> [...]
> Saint Therese and sound. (*Four* 448)
> [...]
> Saint Therese can know the difference between singing and women. Saint Therese can know the difference between snow and thirds. Saint Therese can know the difference between when there is a day to-day to-day. To-day. (453)

Just as Saint Therese appears multiply divided from herself, so the saints "as seen" seem to harbor a fleet of others "between" them, in a multifarious agglomeration of what we see and what we don't. "Saint Therese and sound" recommends precisely the kind of theatrical attention that will appreciate irreducibly different media (the corporeal, the aural) *without* synthesizing them: like the saint, we "can know the difference between" these features of experience by entertaining them, strangely, together. And as the end of the second passage above reminds us, "the difference between" can always insert itself where no *two things* were evident. In fact, this "difference" can wedge itself into the very consistency of the present: the fact that "there is a day to-day." Stein's usage seems to delight in the standard hyphen that keeps "to-day" in pieces.

The landscape play's perpetual inscription of discrepancies between "any detail" and "any other detail" thus extends to the theatrical present itself. This present bears no resemblance to the absolute present of drama; Stein's plays grasp and magnify the heterogeneity that dramatic narrative tries to reduce. Because these pieces look more like Stein's other experimental texts than like plays as we usually encounter them, many readers have concluded that Stein was uninterested in, or even downright hostile toward, the particularity of the theater medium. It is true that *Paisieu* is no more a drama than *Tender Buttons*; but to forsake drama is not necessarily to reject the theatrical itself. Far from eviscerating theater of its medial specificity, Stein's insistence that "anything that was not a story could be a play" demonstrates her rigorously *expansive* approach to theater. This far-flung definition indicates not a lack of interest in the properly theatrical, but a desire to destabilize that "properly" – and in particular, to leave its dramatic investments in continuity, unity, and immediacy far behind. Nor can it be maintained that Stein's work becomes "theatrical" only in hindsight: James, her avowed "forerunner," had set a precedent for her landscapes in the disruptive, dispersive spaces of his own scenic poetics.

These readings have tried to show how two modernist *writers*, whose uncompromising literariness has sometimes seemed to thrive on a rejection of the theatrical, were in fact using writing to pursue and proliferate the theater they loved – a theater whose manifold elements perpetually retreat from, and interfere with, drama's totalizing display. The shift to a theater beyond drama plays out within the formal structures of their texts. Once we recognize this dynamic, it becomes harder to maintain that theatrical experimentation must belong to the stage *as distinct from* the page. In James and Stein, writing enacts specifically theatrical evasions, subversions, and ruptures of its own. This theatrical capacity still inspires some of today's writers; and it helps solve the baffling riddle of the contemporary playwright, who perversely chooses to approach performance through the medium of text. In Part II of this book, I'll explore the work of two contemporary playwrights who, though much closer than Stein to traditional forms of playwriting, nonetheless extend her emphasis on theater as a radically differential medium. These writers pursue Stein's intuition that "there is something much more exciting than anything that happens" (*Writings* 113), an excitement whose theatrical ramifications we have also traced in James. And indeed, like James, Suzan-Lori Parks and Mac Wellman maintain pleasurably violent relations with the dramatic norm; for them, the moment when Stein's theater could imagine itself thoroughly "untroubled" by drama's ideals belongs to a different modernism.

In between Stein's landscape plays and the landscape of contemporary playwriting, however, there arises another kind of textual scene: "*A country road. A tree. / Evening.*" In Samuel Beckett's *Waiting for Godot*, the very idea of landscape will come to feel laughably insufficient to the horror at hand: "You and your landscapes! Tell me about the worms!" (207). Beckett's foreclosure of landscape corresponds to a theatrical attitude toward the present that differs, once again, from either James's or Stein's. In Beckett, the absolute present of drama reasserts itself with a vengeance; the reification of "how it is" becomes a compositional obsession. Determined to exacerbate the text's complicity with the here-and-now of performance, however, Beckett thereby inscribes a rigorously utopian movement, which transcends actuality through the very determination to manifest it. Before passing on to the theater of our era, we need to spend some time on the well-worn terrain of *Godot* and its vexing relationship to the actual. For Beckett's theater there is no longer "a blue sky of different colors" (Stein, *Paisieu* 159); there is only a sky "like any sky at this hour of the day" (Beckett, *Waiting* 121). This is a theater for which the heterogeneity of the stage no longer promises difference, or rupture. The prospect is bleak; but as we will see, in turning to meet the terrible *continuity* of "this hour," Beckett will draw theater's writing into the breathtaking stringency of a negative dialectic.

CHAPTER 3

"Gesture towards the universe"
Theater as Utopia in Waiting for Godot

> No other writing so steeps us in total aversion from whatever the present immediacy may be: absorption, possession, by a time and place cloudily remembered, elsewhere, nowhere.
> (Hugh Kenner)
>
> Life at the time was too demanding, too terrible, and I thought theatre would be a diversion.
> (Samuel Beckett)[1]

Few scholars have taken Beckett's well-known statement that his early playwriting was "a diversion" as a cue not to treat his plays seriously.[2] On the contrary, these texts have received an overwhelming amount of scholarly attention since they were first produced – to the point where any attempt to revisit them critically must be haunted by a slight sense of the gratuitous. This chapter will nevertheless focus on one of the most tirelessly worked pieces from this oeuvre: the smash-hit, era-defining *Waiting for Godot*. This is not only, I hope, evidence of my having been infected with the "gratuitousness provoking acts without use or profit" that Artaud offers as a definition of theater (*Theater* 24) – a notion by no means alien to the piece in question. I'm focusing on *Godot* because its very ubiquity has made it a text that rings in our collective theatrical ears, and in those of the artists I'll discuss in Part II of this book. Mac Wellman and Suzan-Lori Parks belong to a trajectory for which *Godot* is a decisive moment; while these writers were already at it when Beckett died in 1989, they have also been the inheritors of his early work, and I want to be able to chart that inheritance.

Waiting for Godot constitutes a crucial step in the development of what I've been calling "negative theatrics." In Chapter 1, drawing on a range of theorists, I described this as a mode for which theater's heightened implication in the actual – which drama fundamentally affirms – has become a *problem*. I also argued that this theatrical problem lends itself to textual exploration, whereby it also becomes a problem of writing. In the previous chapter, we saw two writers embark on this exploration. For both James and Stein, theater harbors the potential to diffract drama's "absolute" present (Szondi), dismantling the narrative continuity that functions as that present's delivery system. James thus devises a prose fiction that subjects "dramatic" narrative to the ongoing interference of theater's "other parts"; Stein writes plays for a theater without narrative, a theater whose present is unrecognizably dispersed into differential spatial and temporal relations. For both writers, drama's reifying affirmation of the present – in Brecht's words, drama's "*so ist es*" – is thus overcome by structures of alterity, structures they find within theater itself.

James and Stein, that is, both discern a theater where what goes on *here, now, before our eyes* is only a slender part of the entire experience. In Beckett, by contrast, that here-and-now becomes total: his theater insists that there *are* no "other parts" anywhere. We thus encounter something like the furious return of the dramatic present: an actuality that asserts itself as such more explicitly, and tyrannically, than ever before. This tendency has not passed unnoticed, and from its earliest moments, the critical discourse on Beckett's theater has invoked "presence" and "the present" as key terms. While this orientation has drawn poststructuralist critique, deconstructive insights have ultimately been absorbed into an ongoing conversation that continues to place the issue of actuality at the heart of Beckett's theater – a trajectory that (sometimes explicitly) makes Beckett scholarship look like a kind of microcosm for theater studies as a whole. Theorists such as Herbert Blau, Bert O. States, and Stanton Garner have all identified a complex dynamic of presence and absence, here and elsewhere, as central to Beckett's plays.[3] In this chapter, I propose to step back from these critics' phenomenological and poststructuralist vocabularies. Instead, I suggest that the dynamic they describe in Beckett might most usefully be understood as *utopian*, in the negative sense I briefly introduced in Chapter 1. This concept will enable us to see how Beckett's emphatic staging of the actual, while enormously different from the techniques of dispersion we observed in James and Stein, winds up exceeding its own present just as forcefully. Through utopian procedure, what looks like a return to drama's "*so ist es*" becomes, instead, a determinate negation of what is.

The word "utopian" summons a host of associations, only some of which I want to activate here. For example, in *Utopia in Performance* (2005), Jill Dolan argues compellingly that "in the theater, we can encounter our inarticulate longings toward a future that ... might still remain *mute*, but can on some deeper level be *felt*" (164). The utopia of Beckett's theater does operate in this way; but I'm not sure a sense of utopia that implies "a hopeful feeling" (Dolan 5, cf. 13) can account for Beckett's emphatically, indeed pleasurably hopeless works. Still less do I mean to invoke the kind of utopianism associated with Thomas More or Plato's *Republic*: engagement in conceiving of a perfect society. Such associations go violently against the grain of Beckett's entire sensibility, and while teasing them out of his texts might be a fascinating exercise in devil's advocacy, I will be deriving my concept of Beckett's utopianism from a theorist whose work this book has already begun to engage: Theodor Adorno.

In itself, reading Beckett through Adorno is anything but novel. For half a century, Beckett scholarship has had recourse to Adorno's 1961 essay "Trying to Understand *Endgame*," a classic account of the representational logic of Beckett's text. More broadly, readers of critical theory are well aware that Beckett is something of a golden child amidst Adorno's theorization of modernist negativity; when you find yourself athwart the dizzying dialectics of Adorno's critique, a reference to Beckett is a sure sign that something is being approved of. But it seems to me that the Beckett-Adorno-utopia nexus has never really been related back to *theater* as a medium in a sustained way; even the *Endgame* essay has not received much deep engagement from writers focusing on Beckett's specifically theatrical exploration. This is an oversight, since Adorno's aesthetic theory profoundly illuminates Beckett's theatrical sensibility, and even Beckett's turn to the theater as a medium. I propose to reframe the actuality of Beckett's theater through Adorno's concept of utopia as "the determined negation of that which merely is" (Bloch and Adorno 12); in this way we can begin to see how "the present" names, for Beckett as for the writers who follow him, not just an ontological or phenomenological category that theater puts into play, but an ethical and affective crisis that theater must face. With *Godot*, Beckett is working out negative utopianism not only *in* theater, but *as* theater.

A utopian reading of the play also brings into relief the special significance that text acquires within Beckett's theater. For James and Stein, again, theater's spatial and temporal dimensions harbor an alterity that undermines the unifying present of its "happening"; theatrical writing is language that registers and simulates this experience, whether or not it also literally provides for the stage. In Beckett, by contrast, the space and time of theater have coalesced into the unrelenting identity of a single place, a single moment. Deeply entrenched within this field, writing nevertheless becomes the custodian of negativity; theater, we might say, comes to operate as a utopia *of writing*. To trace this logic is in a certain way to take Beckett at his word about playwriting being a "diversion" – but in the literal or topographical sense. How might the writing of his theater, *in its very saturation with* what Beckett calls "Life at the time," have established a utopian path *away* from that "terrible" present?

Because utopia develops as a quite specific problematic in Adorno's work, I begin by reviewing his concept below. While my treatment is necessarily brief, I hope it will ground my continued use of the term throughout this chapter. I then launch into a discussion of moments in *Godot* that establish a utopian dialectic between the actuality of performance and the virtuality of an unstaged script, considering the play's remarkable relation to drama's "absolute" present. But *Godot* by no means rigidly opposes a subversive text to a conservative scene; accordingly, in the next section, I consider the ways in which the play explores writing as thoroughly implicated in a tyrannical present. Following this, I examine the way a utopian logic develops out of this agonized complicity, whereby theater becomes a site of *attendance* in a double sense: as in English, a site of heightened presence; but also, as in the French "*en attendant*," a site of waiting, indeed longing, for what the present fails to comprehend.

Finally, I'll consider the immediate legacy of *Godot*'s theatrical discoveries, and particularly its use of *monologue*, in Beckett's 1949 novel *The Unnamable*. This last section will act as a kind of coda to Part I, by asking one last time how problems of theatrical performance might shape a text that doesn't ask to be performed. Chapter 4 will shift the terms of this question by turning to recent theater that has centered around novels and other nonplay texts, and Chapters 5 and 6 will concentrate on plays. But I hope my brief reading of *The Unnamable* will gesture toward another landscape where the twentieth century's negative theatrics might be traced out: the terrain of experimental fiction.

Adorno's insistently negative concept of utopia adheres literally to the word's etymology: *u-topia* as no-place. He adapted this concept from Ernst Bloch, a philosopher he knew and admired; in a conversation between them in 1964, Bloch identifies the negativity of utopia as their common ground. "I believe, Teddy," he says, "that we are certainly in agreement here: that the essential function of utopia is a critique of what is present" (Bloch and Adorno 12).[4] And indeed, Adorno consistently elaborates the term "utopia" in terms of the negative relation between the concrete reality of suffering and an unnamable, unspecifiable alterity which could replace – and which we know precisely as *difference from* – the present. Utopia's "inextinguishable colour comes from non-being," he writes (*Lectures* 210); utopia develops as a longing in the face of what the real fails to be. Max Blechman observes that for Adorno, "the morally necessary negation that brings the untruth of existing totality to the light of day, that reveals the whole as *not yet* what it should be, itself implies a critical knowledge of the whole – a knowledge that rests on an inkling of the whole that is *yet to be*" (181). "Utopia," that is, while irreducibly negative, always exceeds its own negativity. Its "not this!" always articulates the possibility of a different world, although it is only the possibility, and not the different world itself, that gets articulated. In an article on the concept of utopia in Frankfurt School thought, Adriana S. Benzaquén explains:

> a future that is expected to be different (utopian, reconciled) cannot be described with categories taken from the present. No present categories would be adequate to describe the radically different future, *if it is to be radically different* ... Negative thinking criticizes the existent as that which can and should change, and in so doing it marks the space of an absence. That absence, however, is not to be filled with images or given a positive content; it is to remain *as* absence, as possibility. (150–151)

This restriction applies to critical thought, but also – as Adorno's *Aesthetic Theory* continually makes clear – to art. Adorno offers *Romeo and Juliet* as an example of how aesthetic utopia operates:

> Shakespeare was not promoting love without familial guardianship; but without the longing for a situation in which love would no longer be mutilated and condemned by patriarchal or any other powers, the presence of the two lost in one another would not have the sweetness – the wordless, imageless utopia – over which, to this day, the centuries have been powerless; the taboo that prohibits knowledge of any positive utopia also reigns over artworks. (*Aesthetic* 247)

Waiting for Godot might seem like a far cry from Shakespeare's tragedy; but for Adorno, Beckett represents with sharp legibility the modern moment of the same "taboo." Now, though, even the "sweetness" of *lost* love has become suspect: contemporary art manifests a new ferocity in its refusal to represent happiness. This ferocity comes, in part, from the modernist rejection of *any* fictive imitation, a loss of relish for "the presentation of the nonempirical as if it were empirical" (19). In a world whose reality is experienced as crushing, art no longer wants to render this kind of homage, as it were, to the real: "New art is so burdened by the weight of the empirical that its pleasure in fiction lapses" (ibid.). Moreover, the emphasis on concrete detail, on the object's quiddity, that had characterized realism would now constitute a false report, since real concreteness, the quality of particularity that escapes the dominance of a general system, has all but disappeared from the world. "The concrete serves for nothing better than that something, by being in some way distinct, can be identified, possessed, and sold," Adorno writes; "[t]he marrow of experience has been sucked out," and a work of rich fictional representation would implicitly be claiming otherwise, thus participating in the charade of "pseudoconcreteness" (31; see also "Trying" 123–129). In order to avoid this complicity, "New art is as abstract as social relations have in truth become" (*Aesthetic* 31).

This situation pulls the artwork, with increasing urgency, in two opposite directions. On the one hand, reality's bleakness demands, ever more sharply, that the work produce an alternative: "art must be and wants to be utopia, and the more utopia is blocked by the real functional order, the more this is true" (32). And yet to make a utopia, even fictively, would be to induct it into the "administered world" in which it could only operate as a ruse: thus "art may not be utopia in order not to betray it by providing semblance and consolation" (ibid.). Art therefore has to nurture utopian desire without attempting to concretize that for which it longs, warding off any such representation with new levels of vehemence. As Fredric Jameson argues, utopian writing "recovers its vocation" as "the answer to the universal ideological conviction that no alternative is possible, that there is no alternative to the system ... by forcing us to think the break itself, and not by offering a more traditional picture of what things would be like after the break" (*Archaeologies* 231–232). Or as Adorno himself writes: "Through the irreconcilable renunciation of the semblance of reconciliation, art holds fast to the promise of reconciliation in the midst of the unreconciled" (*Aesthetic* 33).

Adorno also continually emphasizes, however, that the utopia of art (or of theory) is constituted through, and intrinsically depends upon, the very reality it negates. Its negation is *determinate negation* (*bestimmte Negation*, sometimes translated as "determined negation"), a concept Adorno takes from Hegel. In *Phenomenology of Spirit*, Hegel introduces this concept during his discussion of skepticism, the moment when the mind comes to doubt its own conscious experience. This doubt, which says *no* to "phenomenal consciousness," can either be a dead end or a generative movement, depending on which kind of negation this is: abstract or determinate. The former "only ever sees pure nothingness in its result and abstracts from the fact that this nothingness is specifically the nothingness of that *from which it results*. For it is only when it is taken as the result of that from which it emerges, that it is, in fact, the true result; in that case it is itself a *determinate* nothingness, one which has a *content*" (Hegel 50–51). Abstract negation, that is, detaches itself from what it negates (here, conscious experience) and thereby becomes the stance of a generalized *no*. "But when, on the other hand, the result is conceived as it is in truth, namely, as a *determinate* negation, a new form has thereby arisen" (51): a thought that is dialectically *of* that which it negates, and from which neither the negation nor the negated can be eliminated. When Adorno says that "utopia is essentially in the determined negation, in the determined negation of that which merely is" (Bloch and Adorno 12), he thus emphasizes that utopia is never entirely detached from the present reality; on the contrary, the present reality remains utopia's "content," to use Hegel's term, alongside that reality's negation. Utopia, then, is not simply nowhere, or elsewhere; its "u-" is saturated with its actual "topos," the site that it rejects. This is true of the utopian artwork as well; ultimately, the term "realism" can be rehabilitated as denoting this dialectical relationship between the real and the work that negates it. Beckett exemplifies this modern aesthetic: his "shabby, damaged world of images," Adorno writes, "is the negative imprint of the administered world. To this extent Beckett is realistic" (*Aesthetic* 31). Beckett registers the present in recoiling from it, and this preserves the longing for something else through its very refusal to make the "something else" manifest.

To read Beckett's work as utopian, as I do here, is thus hardly a daring departure – even if the word's persistently positive undertones continue to create a certain dissonance. What will be somewhat unorthodox, however, is associating Adorno's utopia with Beckett's sense *of theater* – and through Beckett, with possibilities of the theater medium as such. As I mentioned above, while readings of Beckett within theater studies often briefly cite the *Endgame* essay, they rarely engage Adorno in depth when considering Beckett's specifically theatrical dimensions.[5] On the other hand, sustained literary-theoretical analyses of Adorno-on-Beckett that claim to address the plays' "theatrical" elements too often turn out to mean by this a set of known quantities (such as the tramps' supposed "play-acting"), rather than a dimension that Beckett is actively exploring.[6] This lack of deep engagement is hardly surprising: recent developments aside, Adorno has appeared in theater studies more often as an antagonist than as a resource. When Benjamin Bennett dismissively declares in *All Theater Is Revolutionary Theater* that "[f]or Adorno,

Beckett is mainly an excuse to make pronouncements about the postwar age," he voices an extreme version of this antagonism (235 n. 13). It is true that, amidst Adorno's abundant remarks on Beckett, there is scant evidence of any interest in seeing (or imagining) the plays performed. I believe, however, that Adorno's concept of utopia is poised to comprehend Beckett's theatrical innovation. Beckett's plays do not only exemplify the utopian nature of art; they describe it and render it legible *as a theatrical operation*. For Beckett, that is, utopia emerges when writing attends to the prospect of performance: when text conceives of itself as enacted in the real.

"What is there to recognize?": *Godot* and the Dramatic Present

At the beginning of *Waiting for Godot*, the two tramps reunited, Vladimir asks Estragon where he has spent the night:

ESTRAGON: In a ditch.
VLADIMIR: *[admiringly]* A ditch! Where?
ESTRAGON: *[without gesture]* Over there. (11)

With these lines, Beckett introduces a problematic of performance that he will continue to develop: the deeply vexed relationship between language and place. Anna McMullan has observed that Beckett's work always "foregrounds the tension between text and stage" (137); in *Godot*, the conventional fact that a play is both written and staged becomes an opportunity to test the utopian force of writing amidst a heightened actuality. The first episode of this endeavor consists in a little act of omission which elegantly throws the whole scene, for a moment, out of joint: the fact that Estragon's "Over there" is "without gesture." Deprived of a referent, the utterance fails; as if unable to find semantic nourishment in the world, Estragon's words are simply wasted. The play thus announces its power to separate the verbal from the physical, and thereby also desire from pursuit, the impulse of utterance from any space where utterance would go into effect. This moment is, of course, just one more instance of Beckett's famous aesthetic of failure.[7] But Beckett discovers here that theater can provide for that aesthetic in a very particular way: by invoking its physical reality as wrong for its words.

Commenting on this passage, Martin Puchner points out that it "introduces a rupture between words and gestures that becomes increasingly central for [Beckett's] plays" (*Stage* 159). Puchner contends that this rupture should be understood as "one of the strategies with which

Beckett attacks the integrity of the actor" (ibid.).[8] It is certainly true that Beckett's performers are made to disintegrate, and go on disintegrating throughout his oeuvre; but the particular content of the line in question suggests an operation whose scope is broader than the person of a single performer: it is not just Estragon, or the actor playing him, who is made to fail here, but the entire relation between the play's language and the concrete terrain on which it occurs. Adapting Stein's famous witticism about Oakland, we might say that there is a "there," but it isn't *there*. With this direction, Beckett seems to sabotage the staging of his language. The trajectory that should lead from script to production is anticipated, and stalled. The concatenation of body and space proves inadequate to the language that should inhabit it, so that the language seems to hover, awaiting emplacement. It's as if the realization of these words, their distribution through a field of bodies, had not quite happened yet.

Within the concrete space of performance, then, Estragon's line simulates the still-unstaged script. In this moment, the play works backwards; the words resist incorporation into the performance event, as if refusing the means of production. Puchner is right when he observes that Beckett "recreates on the stage the experience of reading a dramatic text" (*Stage* 168). And yet the *negativity* of such an experience is only possible given the prospect of performance: only in the course of a theatrical event produced live, here and now, can the play constitute "the experience of reading" as an experience of refusing the actual. Arrayed on the page, these words direct us to imagine their performance; uttered on a stage, imagined or real, they declare their independence from that scene, even or especially where this comportment means they are words wasted.

This line introduces a principle that will be crucial for the play, ultimately accounting for its most famous pairing of spoken and unspoken words: "Yes, let's go. / *They do not move*," the lines that end both acts (187, 357). Meeting with actors for the London premiere in 1955, Beckett suggested the technique of "contrapuntal immobility": the strict separation of speech from movement throughout, which the last line's devastating yoking of announced movement to actual stillness would presumably crown (McMillan and Fehsenfeld 82). The humanist content of this refrain is hard to resist; Beckett had taken the title of an earlier, unfinished play from Samuel Johnson's poem "The Vanity of Human Wishes," and it would be difficult to deny that *Godot* is equally "about" our inability to enact our own projects – to produce our own plays, as it were.[9] But if the technique of isolating speech from movement seems to find its thematic justification in a fundamental sense of impotency, this also works in the other direction: Beckett's despair here comes to see itself as a specifically theatrical possibility. Not only does theater turn out to be an appropriate medium for Beckett's exploration of failure, hypocrisy, incommensurability and so on; but the exploration itself is revealed as a problematic that belongs to theater, insofar as theater forces the issue of the relationship between writing and place.

Estragon's motionless "Over there" briefly but decisively throws the situated nature of performance into crisis. On the one hand, there is a momentary lapse of the speaker's power to claim any spatial context (of his "there" to mean anything); we seem to witness a fantasy of shedding emplacement as such along with the requirements of interpersonal communication. In this antisocial instant, breaking with the rules of good conversation, the play madly behaves as if its language could separate itself from the fact of our being here, now, together. On the other hand, however, the refusal to indicate simultaneously suggests an opposite awareness: a sense that such specification would be false, because there is no "over there," no place *else* to point to. In this sense, it is as if the shared here-and-now had monstrously swollen, occluding the possibility of any other referent: as if, as Beckett will write in *The Unnamable*, "there are not two places" (*Three* 403), so that *here* is all the *there* we get. Writing thus becomes a foil for the present and the presence of performance, but not in the sense that actuality is decisively foiled, fractured or obscured. Rather, the shared here-and-now becomes more palpable than ever in the face of a language that, as it were, dies trying to escape it. In short, this moment is *both* a flight from the present *and* an affirmation of the present's overweening power.

This complex engagement with the present has long been registered by the critical discourse on Beckett's theater. In the influential 1957 essay "Samuel Beckett, or presence on the stage," published in *For a New Novel*, Alain Robbe-Grillet describes *Godot*'s innovation as the fact that its characters' "situation is summed up in this simple observation, beyond which it does not seem possible to advance: they are *there*, they are on the stage" (115). Robbe-Grillet ends the piece, however, with a remarkable twist, declaring that absence, "the common fate of all Beckett's characters," ultimately overtakes the plays too: "The stage, privileged site of *presence*, has not resisted the contagion for long … *No one was ever there*" (125). While scholars have continued to cite this essay over decades, they have tended not to discuss the twist at the end; Robbe-Grillet thus becomes the founding figure for an ongoing discourse that has (rightly, if sometimes one-sidedly) treated Beckett's theater as emphatically present.[10]

These readings have been challenged, in the wake of deconstruction, by scholars like Steven Connor. Drawing on Derrida's critique of Artaud, Connor criticizes the "live" theater/"dead" writing binary that, he argues, underlies the claim that Beckett's stage is a "theatre of presence" (115–118). Connor argues that Beckett's own work consistently undermines this metaphysical logic; in *Krapp's Last Tape*, for example, "the theatre has been transformed from a place of being to a place of writing" (131). In turn, theater phenomenologist Stanton Garner contends that such textualist readings fail to grasp Beckett's concern with embodiment, the way he "foregrounds the corporeality of actor and character within his stage's exacting field" (28). Garner proposes to combine poststructuralist insights with phenomenological sensitivity in order to trace the way "theatrical language [is] language caught up in a play of bodiedness and disembodiedness, presence and absence, self and nonself" (124) – a "play" he sees exemplified in Beckett.

While both Connor and Garner are critical of readings that "ignore the problematic status" of presence in Beckett's work (Garner 29), neither mentions the problematic, sharply paradoxical end of Robbe-Grillet's essay. But I think Robbe-Grillet's *coup de théâtre* hints at a relationship between presence and its other which is captured neither by the deconstructive supersession Connor envisions ("from a place of being to a place of writing") nor by the phenomenology of "oscillation" or "always also" that Garner identifies (85, 39). The paradox of Robbe-Grillet's essay suggests that Beckett's theater transcends its own presentness *precisely by immersing itself* in the present; this is not oscillation, but dialectical reversal. To talk about the presence of Beckett's theater, then, is not necessarily to embrace – or to claim that Beckett embraces – presence as a positive metaphysical value. But neither is Beckett's presence simply one pole of a phenomenal experience that is "also" attuned to absence. Rather, the intensification of the present itself furnishes the content of Beckett's determinate negation. The Adornian analytic helps us see that writing might put itself *through* presentness precisely in order to generate that determinate negation, thereby producing the vector of utopian desire.

Critical work that investigates the sense of presence in Beckett's theater remains indispensable for understanding this process. Jonathan Kalb's 1989 study *Beckett in Performance* is particularly illuminating here. Beckett's theater, Kalb writes, "creates scenes whose subject matter is their duration in the present time. His dramas are not *about* experiences; *they are those experiences themselves*" (3–4).[11] In this theater, the "fiction" is *of* the performance present – there is no way to separate the story from the realm of its presentation. "Any activities separating the actors from their characters, such as asides or non-realistic physical predicaments, are part of the internal fictions and require no conscious shifts of context on the performers' parts," Kalb writes (46–47). The actors onstage cannot transcend the situation in which they are placed. Unlike James's Madame de Vionnet, or Stein's Saint Therese, they can only ever be where they are, as they are; they have no "other parts" to play.[12] In this theater of what *cannot be otherwise*, actuality consumes the possible. Beckett "uses performance circumstances to dramatize the impossibility of escaping the proscenium frame, and hence of transcending life's theatrical circumstances" (47). Beckett surpasses drama's production of theater as a transfixing image *of* life by producing theater *as* life, theater whose content is ruthlessly coextensive with the here-and-now of our watching.[13]

Kalb presents this total actuality as Beckett's break from dramatic tradition, aligning him instead with "contemporary performance art and avant-garde theater" (4) and with Artaud's Theater of Cruelty (146–148). But the immediacy Kalb describes is in fact the intensification of an entirely dramatic principle: drama's assertion of an "absolute present." We saw in Chapter 1 that although the present of drama lies behind the fourth wall of its fiction, this fictional present will ideally impose itself upon the viewer with such total effectiveness as to incorporate the actual present of the performance, obliterating any trace of difference between the two scenes: "yes, that's how it is [*so ist es*]," says the viewer complacently (Brecht 237/VII: 25). To take Brecht's and Szondi's theories seriously, I suggested, means that we cannot understand the move *beyond* drama as a shift from representation to presence, from a fictional then-and-there to a concrete theatrical here-and-now, since drama *itself* shuns any quality of then-and-thereness in favor of a rigorous concrete immediacy. In ideal drama, the fictional and the actual are not antagonists but, as it were, collaborators in the name of "how it is."

This argument bears specifically upon how we understand Beckett's relationship to the dramatic. To acknowledge that his work *submits* to the actual is to appreciate its difference from either James's concerted attack upon the actual or Stein's ongoing complication and fragmentation thereof – both of which bear some resemblance to the multiplying vectors of Brecht's own "literarization." *Waiting for Godot* confronts us, for the first time in this study, with a kind of theater that problematizes the dramatic present by immersing itself *in* that present to the point of paralysis. There is a surprising continuity here between two very different theatrical projects: Beckett picks up on the reifying "that's how it is" that Brecht ascribes to drama – and, perversely enough, runs with it. Drama's "*so ist es*" is thus carried, in Beckett, to the extreme of tautology: *this* is how it is, or more simply: this is it. If we sense this tautology at work in Estragon's gestureless "Over there," his outburst in Act Two is its most sustained articulation. Vladimir is trying to coax Estragon into admitting that they were in the same place the day before:

VLADIMIR: [. . .] Do you not recognize the place?
ESTRAGON *[suddenly furious]*: Recognize! What is there to recognize? All my lousy life I've crawled about in the mud! And you talk to me about scenery! *[Looking wildly about him.]* Look at this muckheap! I've never stirred from it!
VLADIMIR: Calm yourself, calm yourself.
ESTRAGON: You and your landscapes! Tell me about the worms! (207)

This response is funny, in spite of its bitterness, because Vladimir has hardly been talking to Estragon "about scenery." That Estragon thinks he has suggests at least two things we should notice: first, that he automatically understands the referent of Vladimir's "the place" – i.e., *this* place – as theatrical ("scenery"), leaving no room for any distinction between theater and metatheater, fictional present and performance present. "A country road" is "scenery" for the characters just as it is for us, although this fact is so obvious as not to arouse much interest; it is not, for example, an occasion of proud metatheatrical demystification. Second, Estragon seems to be imputing to Vladimir's question a more broadly cultural register, one that includes visual art ("You and your landscapes!") and perhaps even idealist philosophy ("Recognize!").[14] The implication is that these spheres of experience are no longer relevant, precisely because they imply a dimension of distance that has collapsed into the total immanence Kalb describes. Landscapes are impossible because there is no standing apart, no view to an elsewhere; recognition, the knowledge of the other as such, would also require an epistemological stance apart – the very opposite of the amphibious immersion Estragon announces. There is nothing to recognize because there is only the one thing, what we cannot *not* know, body and soul: "this muckheap."[15]

But recognition is also a specifically dramatic term, describing the climactic and decisive moment when someone learns who or what someone or something is: I am my father's murderer; you are in fact a woman; this is a house for dolls. In disavowing the possibility of such a moment,

Estragon thus severs his play from dramatic tradition – but in a very particular way. After all, the possibility of recognition has always threatened to succumb to hubris or blindness or bad odds; a theater without recognition scenes might simply be a theater pessimistic about our chances of understanding our world and each other, a nondramatic theater of lonely, entropic drift. The theater Beckett announces here is different: the drama of recognition is renounced, not because we can't seem to place one another, but because there is no longer any *question* about where anyone stands: it's us, we're all right here, and there is nowhere else to go.[16] The severance from drama is thus achieved by what amounts to a terrible intensification of its laws: the "absolute present" manifests here as a hyperbolic version of the neoclassical dramatic "unities" of time and place.[17] Estragon's outburst is precisely an *agony* of the "unity of space," and it has its temporal counterpart in an analogous outburst from Pozzo later in Act Two. Pozzo has just informed Vladimir that his slave Lucky is "dumb," Lucky having delivered a tour-de-force monologue in Act One, or what Vladimir is sure was just the day before:

VLADIMIR: Dumb! Since when?
POZZO: *[suddenly furious]* Have you not done tormenting me with your accursed time! It's abominable! When! When! One day, is that not enough for you, one day he went dumb, one day I went blind, one day we'll go deaf, one day we were born, one day we shall die, the same day, the same second, is that not enough for you? (333)

Pozzo is not merely angry because Vladimir is pressing him for unimportant details; rather, his "suddenly furious" rage rehearses Estragon's, along a different axis. Whereas Estragon cries that there is only one place in his universe, Pozzo roars that there is only "one day": the play thus trumpets its obedience to dramatic law, and in the same breath denounces the life that supports such a law, that stops brutally short at the edges of the here-and-now and leaves no other space, no other time imaginable.[18]

Hardly a clean break from dramatic tradition, Beckett's "world of the now" (Kobialka 35) is drama's absolute present, hyperbolized. Overgrown, this present cannibalizes drama's other constitutive elements: not only recognition, but the even more basic principles of change, action, and meaningful communication ("ESTRAGON: *[without gesture]* Over there"). In other words, *Godot* is not promoting the absolute present as a revolutionary theatrical program, much less a metaphysics; rather, the disappearance of other space and other time, the "impossibility of escaping" that Kalb locates in Beckett's theater work, is the experiential problem the work sets out to confront. This problem is posed by a monstrous persistence of the dramatic – or rather, by the perception that drama's absolute present is true to a certain modern experience of the world. Adorno describes this experience:

> the social apparatus has hardened itself against people and thus, whatever appears before their eyes as attainable possibility, as the evident possibility of fulfillment, presents itself to them as radically impossible ... compelling them to identify with this impossibility and make this impossibility into their own affair. In other words, to use Freud, they "identify themselves with the aggressor" and say that *this* [i.e., the possible] *should* not be ... " (Bloch and Adorno 4; cf. Adorno and Horkheimer 61)

The rage with which both Estragon and Pozzo deny the plausibility of another space or another time corresponds to the self-directed aggression Adorno describes, the ferocity with which we have learned to attack our own longing for a different world. As Stanley Cavell writes of *Endgame*'s Hamm and Clov, "the power of belief ... has become, because useless, the source of unappeasable, unbelievable pain" (*Must* 131).[19] The symptomatic response to this pain, which Adorno describes and Beckett depicts, is not to cling tighter to the utopian belief that a different life is possible, but to try to gouge out that belief like an offending eye. The play translates this violence into theatrical terms as a kind of hyperdrama: the maintenance of an absolute present, as the eradication of any avenue to other time and space. This formal situation becomes the ground of Beckett's playwriting – its premise, not its goal.

The theater medium, that is, becomes an opportunity for Beckett to struggle directly with a tyrannical actuality: to engage the present in a more or less violent battle. This is the image Bert States suggests in his 1978 essay on *Godot*. "The present (of things present) is a monster to be slain," States writes, "an encumbrance (as the body is for certain mystics), above all a medium of diversion in which *being* is centrifugally spun out into what *was* ('What exactly did we ask him for?') and what *will be* ('We'll hang ourselves tomorrow')" (*Shape* 96). The monster, however, does not surrender so readily as States's remark might suggest. The inaccessibility, to the characters, of what was, and the utter unlikelihood that anything *else* will be – both born out by the same lines States cites – testify to the present as monstrously un-slayable. If present-participle "*being* is centrifugally spun out" into past and future throughout this play, this is true not in the Jamesian sense of a present that is repeatedly banished, but in the much more desperate sense of a present state that *extends* to past and future, as it were includes them, so that there is no prospect of a different time.[20] This means that the theatrical present cannot be, as in drama *or* Brechtian epic, the moment of a radical event. Nor can the stage rigorously distinguish itself from the world beyond it, since the principle of the "beyond" is precisely what is being foreclosed. "Thus, forever shuttling between memory and expectation," States continues, "[Beckett's characters] carry to the extreme the condition in which *all normal life* is lived" (ibid., my emphasis).

This last statement is worth pausing over; it fascinatingly both registers and reenacts the play's insistence on the identity between here and everywhere else, now and all the time, and in so doing, sheds light on a major tendency of (primarily early) Beckett scholarship. I refer to the fact that States, discussing the logic of actuality *within* the play, suddenly begins making huge claims about the world outside the play: "all normal life." Now, despite the brilliance and precision of States's essay and his status as a major innovator in theater studies, I think this sentence will read to many today as an example of an early, now-outmoded mode of Beckett criticism: the humanist or existentialist approach that tended to celebrate Beckett's insight into such quantities as "mankind." Paul Sheehan nicely summarizes the divide between this work and later readership: "on one side, [there are] those critics who bestowed intellectual authority on Beckett by seeing him as an exemplar and exegete of the human condition in its starkest, most essential form; and, facing them, a later generation that sees Beckett's writings as too anomalous and refractory to sustain abstractions like 'human' and 'condition' for long, and too unsettling and polymorphous to be reducible to essences" (178).[21] And yet the context of our discussion, and States's, may help to account for the power of the universalizing impulse in reading Beckett: Beckett's work is heavy with the sense that apparently individuated experience just *is* "all normal life," the fear that there *is* such an in-different creature as "man," and that we are living that indifference. This sense belongs to the vision of present reality as systematically obstructing possibilities of spatial, temporal, or interpersonal difference: the elsewhere, the elsewhen, the alterity of another's perspective. The universalizing tendency of so much Beckett reception, then, is not merely an artifact of mid-century chauvinism; rather, such readings respond to an anxiety within the work itself, which forces the prospect of a life that could not offer any resistance to our generalizations – a life for which what happens on one stage for two hours could, horrifically enough, be valid everywhere and always.

To recognize Beckett's stage as the site of "all normal life," as States does, is therefore to see its double *critical* force. *Godot* is critical not just in the sense that what happens onstage represents, say, the futility or emptiness of "normal life" offstage (the province of satire), but in that it labors to express the experience of there being no escape from, or exception to, the normal as such – onstage or off. This experience marks Beckett's fundamental confluence with Adorno. But their confluence also extends beyond the baleful: when Adorno elaborates utopia as determinate negation, he describes how Beckett's resolute vision of uninterrupted sameness becomes, dialectically, an exception to that sameness. By manifesting uniformity as a particular experience, Beckett's work contravenes that uniformity. "The more total society becomes, the more completely it contracts to a unanimous system," Adorno writes, "and all the more do the artworks in which this experience is sedimented become the other of this society" (*Aesthetic* 31). By testifying resolutely to a present reality that seems to exclude any avenue of departure, a work can create a path of departure, constituting radical otherness negatively. This notion not only accounts for the social or political value of Beckett's work; it also describes the logic of his turn to theater.

That logic differentiates Beckett from the older writers discussed in Chapter 2. For James, desire could diffract reality into "innumerable and wonderful things" (*Ambassadors* 468); for Stein, a phenomenology of discontinuous experience could announce a "difference between very quickly and very quickly" (*Paisieu* 160). For Beckett, such subversions are no longer available; his is a world of tyrannically coherent actuality. His playwriting reflects an awareness that the only escape from the present is to register the impossibility of escape as fully as possible:

> VLADIMIR: We're surrounded! *[Estragon makes a rush towards back.]* Imbecile! There's no way out there! *[He takes Estragon by the arm and drags him towards front. Gesture towards front.]* There! Not a soul in sight! Off you go! Quick! *[He pushes towards auditorium. Estragon recoils in horror.]* You won't? *[He contemplates auditorium.]* Well I can understand that. (263)

This passage makes one of Beckett's cheaper jokes, and could easily be labeled "antitheatrical." But it functions, in fact, as Beckett's declaration that he needs the theater. First, because the fundamental situation of performance is revealed as what makes the horror of contiguity palpable: what registers the burden of existing *in a space bereft of radical difference*, a space that is here identical with the social as such. Estragon's "horror" is conventionally recognizable as stage fright, but that convention now becomes an opportunity to take fright at the very fact that we are all here, now, that we are in the same place to the point of being in each other's way. Theater's "co-presence" thus becomes the embodied experience of the contracted unanimity Adorno describes.

Second, however, theater also reveals itself in this moment as perforated by an *other medium*. There is no Brechtian rupture of character here, but there *is* a confluence with Brecht in the way the suddenly heightened coincidence of the tramps' words with our bodies makes us remember that the scene is rehearsed. These gestures, which wanly pretend to respond to our presence, were in fact planned in advance – and first of all, *scripted*.[22] Moments like these feel like tricks precisely because they run us along the seam of two different systems: the performance, in which our presence participates in the inescapability of the present, and the text, which has had to anticipate this present before it was here and which therefore refers us to a scene of virtuality. This reference suggests, however improbably, that the present could have been imagined and realized otherwise. The moment when writing openly submits to the actual is thus also, dialectically, the moment when it begins to escape the actual.[23] *Godot*'s language at once colludes in the construction of its "absolute present" and, *in the same gesture*, undermines that present's authority.

This logic is at work in the following passage from Act One, just after Estragon has dozed off and reawakened:

ESTRAGON: I dreamt that –
VLADIMIR: DON'T TELL ME!
ESTRAGON: *[gesture towards the universe]* This one is enough for you? (39)

As in the earlier line, Estragon couples a deictic phrase ("This one") with a behavior that refuses to refer. "The universe," that is, cannot properly be the object of gestural reference; it is not something we can point to, and since it is by its very concept *not* one thing among others, it cannot sensibly be the referent of Estragon's words. We may easily feel that we know what Beckett means: reality, which gives us "enough" to worry about without having to consider an extra dreamscape. But Beckett specifically chooses "universe," the term whose hyperbolic inclusiveness is calculated to arouse a delicious dissonance in the reader: we know what he means, and we can easily imagine gestures that might try to convey this meaning . . . but could they really succeed, in the absence of any immediate cue?[24]

If our earlier stage direction makes the character do too little for his words to be meaningful, this one asks him to do – to encompass – too much. The text is recalling us to the fact that it is a piece of writing; it is briefly constructing the intimacy of a closet drama (cf. Puchner, "Stage" 164).

And yet this moment can operate on a theatrical audience too: through the strangeness of a necessarily insufficient enactment, we experience a gap between what is recited ("This one") and what takes place. Borrowing Garner's description of monologue in Beckett's *Not I*, we might say that here the universe as such is being "'deactualized' in terms of the stage present and returned to the status of 'possible world'" (132). But the fact that it's literally "the universe," or drama's "this," that gets deactualized here is significant: in this moment, *Godot* displaces the actual *precisely by committing to* the actual. What thus occurs is not only an "oscillation" between presence and absence, or actuality and virtuality, as Garner's phenomenological account suggests (85). It is a rigorous negative dialectic, in which we arrive at the utopian consciousness that "this one," our shared present, *isn't* all there is, only through the gesture that tries to register that present as fully as possible. Theater thus wrests the prospect of displacement from the dramatic principle *of* placement, to articulate that which is not this, not here, not now.

Together, the line and the stage direction inscribe a dynamic whereby the most direct apprehension of the real as such – of something very much like the "bad reality" of Horkheimer and Adorno's totalizing conception (116) – itself becomes the moment of a flight from the real. By writing down "the universe" in a line that corresponds to everything *and nothing* onstage, Beckett insists upon the page as an alternative site where the traumatic experience of the totalized actual can be inscribed and, only thus, transcended. Text and scene incriminate each other as the present's means of production, and yet a mischievous discrepancy between them glimmers like a crack in a closed, black box. The crack is too narrow to see through, much less to provide escape; but it suggests another universe beyond the walls, a stage that we do not hold, that we have not reached. In Beckett's hands, Adorno's "wordless, imageless utopia" starts taking on a distinctly theatrical – if fugitive – shape.

"All the dead voices": Writing and the Real

It would thus be too simple to say that in Beckett's theater, a utopian *text* transcends the compromising actuality of *performance*. Beckett's commitment to determinate negation means that language cannot just float free of the actual; on the contrary, Beckett continually emphasizes language's complicity in maintaining the unbearable present. Indeed, critics have sometimes framed Beckett's theater as one that empowers text above all.

As we saw, Connor describes this theater as "transformed from a place of being to a place of writing" (131). W. B. Worthen argues that Beckett's work "insists on the controlling authority of the text to govern the play" (*Modern* 140), establishing "a field in which ... subjects are qualified by and painfully inspected for a 'text' that invades, objectifies, replaces, and destroys them" (142). The notion that Beckett promotes the (more or less violent) ascendancy of the written text *over* production, however, cannot account for his ongoing exploration of the ways text can fail to be anything *but* a vessel of the real.

One way Beckett explores this failure is by instituting a poetic pattern that organizes the passage of time in a particular way: a recurring A-B-C-B in which Vladimir's expressive advancements are brusquely capped by Estragon's repetitions. The pattern appears throughout the play but reaches its climax early in Act Two:

ESTRAGON: All the dead voices.
VLADIMIR: They make a noise like wings.
ESTRAGON: Like leaves.
VLADIMIR: Like sand.
ESTRAGON: Like leaves. (211–213)
[...]
VLADIMIR: Rather they whisper.
ESTRAGON: They rustle.
VLADIMIR: They murmur.
ESTRAGON: They rustle. (213)
[...]
VLADIMIR: They make a noise like feathers.
ESTRAGON: Like leaves.
VLADIMIR: Like ashes.
ESTRAGON: Like leaves. (215; cf. 63–65, 111)

The repeated thrust of this pattern is that – like the tramps themselves – verbal poeisis isn't going anywhere. Expression can only circle back to more of the same; more specifically, it *cannot progress in time*: the passage of moments will not mean the acquisition of new poetic correlatives for an experience which (as *Godot* never stops insisting) itself has nothing new to offer. These lines imply that the effort to keep saying our world cannot get us beyond the world as we've already said it. They dramatize the negative credo Beckett famously articulated in his 1949 piece "Three Dialogues with Georges Duthuit": "nothing to express, nothing with which to express, nothing from which to express, no power to express, no desire to express, together with the obligation to express" (556). This is *Godot*'s first line, "Nothing to be done," explicated as poetics.

To treat Estragon's repeated "Like leaves" only as a brake put on Vladimir's poetic efforts, however, would be to miss the phrase's own specificity: "leaves" are also the leaves of books, and the middle part of the interchange quoted above could be a thumbnail for the dialectic between page and performance: "They rustle. / They murmur. / They rustle." In Beckett's hands, this juxtaposition constitutes a cynical comment on the afterlife of text, and on Beckett's own limited ability to revive the dead voices of his predecessors; as such, it becomes a troubling touchstone for the play's ongoing allusiveness.[25] The dialogue goes on from here:

VLADIMIR: What do they say?
ESTRAGON: They talk about their lives.
VLADIMIR: To have lived is not enough for them.
ESTRAGON: They have to talk about it. (213–215)

The graveyard humor of this exchange lies in how quickly the tramps' concern jumps from *what* the "dead voices" are saying to the fact *that*, exasperatingly, they go on speaking at all. Estragon's lines guide the conversation away from the possibility of communication: that the voices "talk about their lives" either seems so trivially true as to constitute a refusal to hear them at all, or suggests a narcissistic discourse that requires no auditor. The voices, in short, are locked up from us in their papery rustle: they are very much like Derrida's "grapheme," that unit *of writing* which mocks the phonic ideal of immediate communication by flaunting the prospect of its own ghostly persistence long after there is no one to mean it and no one to whom it can mean (Derrida, "Signature" 318). Indeed, if the "ashes" are, among other things, the ashes of recently burnt books, the "leaves" that reconstitute themselves in Estragon's rejoinder suggest a literary legacy that has, as it were, outlived itself, pages still fluttering long after our ability to revive their voices is gone.[26] Literature is precisely *not* a conduit to others in other worlds; no longer a means of escape from the present, the "dead voices" have become reified as the inarticulate topography *of* the present. As such they are so painful that the tramps will do anything – even keep on doing "Nothing" – just to drown them out: "we're inexhaustible," Vladimir observes, naming what might almost be called the play's superobjective: "It's so we won't hear" (211). In having tried momentarily to revive the voices by asking what they say, Vladimir has uttered a desire which we are encouraged to understand the rest of the play as suppressing.

Vladimir's question, however, also introduces a further complexity: he is not just asking for a report of what the voices say but, more realistically, asking Estragon to help him *invent* the dead voices' words. Taken in this sense, the question is no longer unanswerable, and it yields a bifurcation in the subsequent dialogue: Estragon might be tabling the question by reporting (deciding) that the voices just "talk about their lives" *or* he might in fact be answering it by quoting the voices *exactly as he hears (reads)* them, with Vladimir continuing the recitation. The exchange would then proceed like this:

VLADIMIR: What do they say?
ESTRAGON: "They talk about their lives."
VLADIMIR: "To have lived is not enough for them."
ESTRAGON: "They have to talk about it."
VLADIMIR: "To be dead is not enough for them."
ESTRAGON: "It is not sufficient." *[Silence.]* (213–215, quotation marks added)

The possibility of *quotation*, in other words, becomes the possibility that these lines are not *about* the voices, but are attributable *to* the voices — in which case "They" would seem to refer to the tramps themselves. And indeed, these sentences might just as well apply to Didi and Gogo, also "inexhaustible" talkers for whom, as we know, neither life nor death suffices.[27] But to understand the tramps as intoning the dead voices, here, would be to observe the very mechanism that makes playwriting possible: the personation of mute, material text. I'm not suggesting that we reject the more obvious reading of these lines, namely that the living are talking about, not for, the dead. My point is that the possibility of the alternate reading constitutes a basic structure of undecidable alternation between what is *written* (dead voices, like leaves) and what is *happening* before us (the tramps saying something). Not only have we lost access to the voices of others, then, we have lost the ability to trust that such voices *are* other: we can no longer tell the difference between the voices of the present and those which could be traces of an other site.

This structure perfectly rehearses the device with which Act Two begins: Vladimir's song about the dog. "A dog came in the kitchen"; Cook killed the dog; the other dogs buried him and "wrote upon the tombstone / for the eyes of dogs to come: A dog came in the kitchen" ... thus the song begins again (193).[28] The principle of endless repetition and the sense of a murderous world are what bind the song most obviously to the rest of the play; but just as important is the way what is sung becomes indistinguishable from what is written, so that ultimately the singer cannot know whether his object is the dog or the epitaph, or whether he himself or the "dead voice" of the tombstone's text is telling the story. In the same way, it cannot be completely clear that Estragon and Vladimir are talking for themselves rather than sounding out the dead voices for the ears *and* "eyes" of us "dogs to come" – cannot, in part because the men onstage *are* sounding the dead voices of the rustling script called *Waiting for Godot*. Their words are already leaves. Correspondingly, the repetitions that dominate the play (including that of the title line) achieve something like the textual possibility of returning, rereading, going back to check before moving on: as the time of performance flaunts its inability to advance our apprehension of the world, we are thrown backward instead. Connor has linked *Godot*'s destabilization of text/performance oppositions to its "curious *déjà vu* structure" (116–120), where characters repeatedly lose track of their place in the conversation:

VLADIMIR: Damn it haven't you already told us?
POZZO: I've already told you?
ESTRAGON: He's already told us? (135)

These quandaries are like having lost one's place in a book; ultimately, perhaps the "rustle" the characters hear is the pages of their script flipping backwards and forwards in the breeze unnoticed, sabotaging any dramatic progression. Here again, we find something like a perverse relation to Brecht, as if Beckett were presenting an ominous underside to Brechtian "literarization." In *Godot*, the stage-as-book still opposes the "single track" of dramatic plot development, but it no longer solicits relaxed, analytical mastery. Instead, the script imprisons its "readers" in a baffling structure that prevents them from getting anywhere.

At the same time, critics have often pictured *Godot*'s default of progress in terms of a *missing* text: "vulnerably scriptless" (Connor 130), the tramps "do not seem to have a text prepared beforehand and scrupulously learned by heart, to support them. They must invent" (Robbe-Grillet 121).[29] Given that *Waiting for Godot* is probably the most famous script of its century, what exactly do these critics mean? We've all seen plays in which scriptlessness is an explicit conceit, in which the performance "breaks down" and the performers pretend to go off-book; this happens, in fact, in Beckett's first play, *Eleuthéria* (142). We've also seen truly improvisatory work for which not having "learned parts" is a generative constraint. No one is likely to confuse *Godot* with either kind of piece; why, then, the impulse to imagine the play as unscripted? No doubt it's mostly a way of teasing out the logic of *Godot*'s metatheatricality. But the widespread sense that the tramps "must invent" is also a response to the play's theme of specifically verbal effort: in the midst of the characters' self-conscious performance ethic, we sense that performance itself is being imagined as a kind of compensatory writing.

That a character should appear to be inventing the words she speaks is, as we know, a fundamental ideal of drama (Szondi 9). The appearance of invention in *Godot* differs from dramatic "spontaneity," however, by its emphasis on the *work* of verbal production. This emphasis is, of course, most heightened in Lucky's monologue, where the slave pours forth verbiage on the command to "Think!" (141). We encounter it also, earlier, in Pozzo's disquisition upon nightfall (by turns "*lyrical*" and "*prosaic*") and his demand for feedback afterwards:

POZZO: [...] I weakened a little towards the end, you didn't notice?
VLADIMIR: Oh perhaps just a teeny weeny little bit.
ESTRAGON: I thought it was intentional. (125)

After Pozzo and Lucky depart, Beckett introduces a running gag in which Estragon seems to be trying to reach back *behind* the dialogue, and reconstitute it retroactively as scripted, as a series of tasks that were already there to be executed. Thus when Vladimir observes that the other two men have changed, Estragon replies: "That's the idea, let's make a little conversation" (159). The motif continues:

VLADIMIR: No no, it's impossible.
ESTRAGON: That's the idea, let's contradict each other. (219)
[...]
VLADIMIR: That what?
ESTRAGON: That's the idea, let's ask each other questions. (221)
[...]
VLADIMIR: Moron!
ESTRAGON: That's the idea, let's abuse each other. (269)

Lines like these create the sense of a world whose script is missing by imagining the characters' ability to fill in for that script – here, Estragon's ability to *read back* Vladimir's words, suspend their ephemerality as performance and reproduce them as prescriptions, instructions for tasks to be performed.

These moments feel similar to moments throughout Beckett's prose works, when the discourse breaks away from the story to comment wryly upon itself: "The above passage is carefully calculated to deprave the cultivated reader" in *Murphy* (69), or in *Malone Dies*, a line break followed by the words: "What tedium" (*Three* 181). But in a novel, a sentence *about* the novel will interrupt, and thus momentarily displace, whatever fictional scene is being conveyed. In theater, by contrast, the scene can *remain present through* those moments when literary composition declares itself as such. No longer made to vanish by the consciousness of writing, the scene now encompasses that consciousness, becoming its medium. "What is there to keep me here?" Clov asks Hamm in Beckett's next play, and Hamm responds: "The dialogue" (*Endgame* 58). Verbal invention doesn't escape but *sustains* the hegemony of the present; Beckett's stage characters root themselves more firmly in the scene as they textualize it. The "four or five leaves" that appear on *Godot*'s tree at the top of Act Two (189) are like the visual proof of this proposition, as if all the exertions of the first act had precipitated themselves as a handful of pages. Those pages now flag the impervious persistence of this muckheap, which wears them like a trophy.[30]

"What have I said?" Vladimir asks himself toward the end of the play (339). That "said" is thus substituted for "done" in the conventional expression of guilt reflects, first, the "contrapuntal immobility" through which a great deal has been said and nothing done, the thorough dissociation of language from praxis: Vladimir's asking what he has *said* thus emphasizes how little he has been able, how little people are able, to *do*. But there is also a sense in which the substitution suggests the equivalency of saying and doing in this theater, at least insofar as speech in the face of an unbearable present becomes the means of production of that present, the material of its presence to us. Beckett takes playwriting as an opportunity to present reality *as* constituted in words, a vision which amounts to a condemnation of language. "To imagine a language means to imagine a form of life," wrote Ludwig Wittgenstein, in a book published the same year as *Godot*'s premiere (7).[31] For Beckett, to suffer a language is to suffer a form of life, and likewise to inflict one: *this* one. Theater offers him an opportunity to literalize this logic: not merely through the "immediacy" of performance, but through the experience of that "immediacy" as scripted, as brought into being by language, which it reciprocally sustains. When Vladimir forbids Estragon from telling his dream, Estragon's interpretation ("This one is enough for you?") carries the same principle: he imagines that describing a "universe" means having to inhabit it, a prospect to be regarded with horror.

This is also a way to understand Beckett's infamous insistence on "faithful" productions, and in particular his insistence on the sparse set – *Endgame*'s "*Bare interior*" (1) or the comparably bare exterior of *Godot*: "*A country road. A tree. / Evening*" (7). As theater scholars like to remind us, no script could ever really postulate *a* singular, "faithful" staging; I'll revisit this common sense in the next chapter. But Beckett's settings, with their minimalist precision, suggest a world whose specificity derives from language – a space which harbors no refuge from, no excess beyond what has been written. The emptiness of the stage is marked here and there by discrete and specifiable objects recalling the images in language-learning books: *a tree, a pair of boots, a carrot*. And this austerity asserts a terrible responsibility of the writer, reduplicated by the characters in their own language-work: the responsibility of having gotten us into this mess in the first place, by means of words. Beckett's scenography, that is, points an accusing finger back at Beckett himself. In *Eleuthéria* this happens explicitly:

AUDIENCE MEMBER: [...] By the way, who put together this flop? *[Program]* Beckett *[he says Béquet]*, Samuel, Béquet, Béquet, that's got to be a Jew from Greenland crossed with an Auvergnat.
GLAZIER: Don't know. Apparently he eats his soup with a fork.
AUDIENCE MEMBER: No matter. Pulp it. (148)[32]

The script is never so overt a reference as in *Godot* or *Endgame*. Instead, the precise bareness of the stage takes up the mark of this literality, the sense of a performance executed *to the letter*. In this way, writing finds itself guilty of the real.

Utopia in Attendance

Amidst this very acknowledgment, however, an opposite trajectory begins to suggest itself: a path away from the concrete world, and in particular from the actual site of the stage. This de-realizing tendency of Beckett's work has sometimes been emphasized – we might say, taken at its word – to the detriment of productive exchange between readers and theater artists. Discussing her controversial 1984 production of *Endgame* in an interview with Jonathan Kalb, JoAnne Akalaitis expresses frustration with this impasse. She rightly points out the folly of the notion that her show at A.R.T. injected too much cultural specificity onto the scene of Beckett's blank stage:

> I think it's idiotic. I mean, everything onstage is in a specific place. At least it's in the theater. At least it's in Cambridge at the American Repertory Theatre. If you have it in a black box and put a chair onstage, the audience does not walk in and say, "We are in a no-man's-land, we are

in a vague, abstract, Platonic space." I mean, that's the thing about theater; it doesn't happen in your mind, it doesn't happen on the page, it happens in a place ... It's very academic, that whole idea that directors can't be specific. Everything is specific. I mean if you put a chair onstage it is chosen by someone and it means something. (qtd. in Kalb, *Beckett* 82)

These remarks are salutary; they remind us of dimensions of theatrical experience that are all too easy to forget – especially when the discussion, like mine, is launched in front of a pile of books and a computer screen, not a stage. The "vague, abstract, Platonic space" is only a fantasy, and indeed, as Akalaitis suggests, a literary one. And yet it is, I would argue, a fantasy that a play itself can promote.[33] Throughout *Godot*, as we've seen, the play evinces an *impracticable* wish for a stage that could sustain the virtuality of the stage direction; for a performance which would not confirm the text's commensurability with the laws of the real. This wish emerges from, and in direct opposition to, the intensified sense of the real as a textual site, of the present as that which we are always writing, to our great shame. Both the wish and the sense arise from the specifically theatrical experience of *language emplaced*.

One of Beckett's stage directions literalizes this experience in a quite particular way. Vladimir has just informed Estragon that Godot is to meet them today, Saturday:

ESTRAGON: *[very insidious]* But what Saturday? And is it Saturday? Is it not rather Sunday? *[Pause.]* Or Monday? *[Pause.]* Or Friday?
VLADIMIR: *[Looking wildly about him, as though the date was inscribed in the landscape]* It's not possible! (35–37)

"As though the date was inscribed in the landscape": is this only a joke about getting your dimensions mixed? We might recall Strether's relation to landscape in *The Ambassadors*: out for a ramble in the country, he tries *not* to see historicity in this "picture" – only to be surprised by a vector of temporal progress, Chad's and Madame de Vionnet's boat trip down the river, which explodes the still image into a "drama" of adultery. Strether, like Vladimir, is forced to consider the question of passing time, since the crux of the scandal confronting him is that his friends have obviously planned an overnight stay. But Vladimir's problem, in the moment cited above, is the opposite: he looks for the trace of time in his landscape, but can't find it. In fact, as we know, Estragon will later passionately deny that their country road qualifies as a "landscape" at all, because a landscape is something you can travel toward and away from, something you can "recognize" across a distance, whereas: "Look at this muckheap! I've never stirred from it!" So we might say that what Vladimir looks for "wildly" in this moment is not just the date but the landscape itself, as the prospect of a space that one could regard *from elsewhere*.³⁴ Such a prospect would preempt Pozzo's eventual claim, anticipated here by Estragon, that there is only "one day," by making clear that that today is one day *among others* (Saturday and *not* Sunday, today and *not yet* tomorrow). And it would put this place in relation to other places, as one that could be reached from elsewhere, recognized, by us as by an other: for instance, by Godot.

The text presents this as a fantasy, a desperate mistake. But its form is significant: Beckett tells us, not just that Vladimir looks around as if he could learn the date from the landscape, but that he searches specifically "as though the date was *inscribed*" therein. Vladimir acts, that is, as if his muckheap were a surface of inscription: a canvas, or a page, which we could not only "recognize," but read. Like the gestureless "Over there" with which we began, this moment therefore suggests a shift *back* from performance to text, a leap that displaces the character from his position in a concrete actuality and toward the virtual condition of script. It is as if Vladimir were trying to see the play in the state it was in before being made real, as if this vantage could provide some kind of leverage against the present that now engulfs him. The leverage would be history, "the date" grasped as if from without. To apprehend the present this way would entail the kind of "*Überdenflußdenken*," thinking "above the flow" (or "across the flow"), that Brecht demands (72/II: 91).³⁵ Such a perspective would make revolution possible; it would make possible the advent of Godot.

It would, and for Beckett, it doesn't. Akalaitis's point could be recast as the fact that, whether Beckett realizes it or not, the date always *is* inscribed in our cultural products: no "bare interior," no "country road," no tree but records the prejudices and expectations, the means of production of its time. The historical self-awareness of her subway-tunnel *Endgame* might be read as an attempt to render Beckett's subjunctive phrase in a truer indicative mood; and Beckett's resistance, as an effort to hold on to that subjunctive as such – even if the strangely ungrammatical "as if the date *was* . . . " seems almost to shudder against this insistence. What Beckett tries to voice, against sound common sense like Akalaitis's, is the sickening feeling that we *can't* read the date after all, that dates are irrelevant because we've reached a point at which nothing can change. This is like the admission that we can't receive the "dead voices," or can't be sure whether they are different from our own: it is the feeling of being trapped in an utterly indifferent actuality, a present that admits of no difference between now and then, and hence no difference between the now and the not-yet. Beckett's theater plays its exclusion of history in order to endow its present with the greatest possible hopelessness. "Nothing happens, nobody comes, nobody goes, it's awful!" (*Waiting* 137).

And yet this awfulness is what launches the work's rigorous utopianism: its insistence that the prospect of a radically other life remain unspoken, so that it can *be* radically other:

ESTRAGON: I was dreaming I was happy.
VLADIMIR: That passed the time.
ESTRAGON: I was dreaming that –
VLADIMIR: *[Violently]* Don't tell me! *[Silence.]* (335)

What the "*violen[ce]*" of Vladimir's repeated prohibition registers is the urgency of keeping the dream out of the actual, beyond the dramatic present into which its description would introduce it. By refusing to present the dream, Vladimir/Beckett maintains it as such: the possibility of a different universe. And in the theater, as opposed to prose fiction, this means not just the difference of one universe from another – a subject contemplated at length in *Murphy* (63–66) – but, specifically, the difference between *this one* and one that is not here, not now, not this.

The "*Silence*" that follows Vladimir's prohibition doubly marks the discrepancy between reality and its utopian other. If the silence goes off as prescribed, we may experience an emptiness where the dream would be, a gap that leaves a place for the happiness it dare not present. But if patrons are sniffling and shifting, and programs rustling like leaves, then performance itself becomes the field of interference between what could be (the utopia of silence, *as written*) and what is.[36] In this sense, the direction "Silence" (as distinct from, say, "Pause") always refers to a difference between possible and actual performances, marking the gap between what happens in the auditorium and what – the script tells us – could happen. Suddenly obtrusive, our own presence now collaborates in the foreclosure of the possible world.

Is this orientation "antitheatrical," a question merely of preferring the private copy to the public show? I think not: the audience's presence is not an annoying inconvenience for this play, but the very medium through which the violence of actuality becomes palpable, *and* through which we can experience the desire for the unrealized as such. Perhaps Beckett would have liked to be able to shut us up, or shut us out, at such moments, so that silence really would take place in the theater *as prescribed*; but to plan on this would have been wishful thinking, and Beckett's sophistication leads him to include "Silence" as exactly that: a wish, an event *manqué*, no matter how assiduously the performers themselves pause in hopes of securing it. This is not a matter of disavowing the audience; on the contrary, the audience is crucial to Beckett's theatrical poetics.[37] It is only in registering the crisis of our co-presence, the consolidation of our cruelly identical present, that *Godot* hurls itself against this shared actuality, toward something we are *not* watching, somewhere we are not.

As the play's original title declares, then, Beckett's is a theater *en attendant*. Between the "waiting" of the French term and the "attendance" of its English cognate runs a seam that must have dogged the author's bilingual imagination. For this seam is also, precisely, the seam of our presence at the performance that happens here and now and – in the same breath – our anticipation of something that has not happened, something perpetually not-here, not-yet. For Beckett, theater manifests the experience of life lived as an absolute present, or *as drama*; but it exceeds drama by exposing this experience in the light of what it doesn't contain. Theater thereby becomes the place where we attend something else.

With this understanding of Beckett's early theater, we reopen the question of what he and Adorno have to say to each other. On the one hand, it's true that Adorno likes to brandish Beckett against theoretical antagonists, and often seems to treat Beckett's work as a poetically encoded treatise. Thus he writes, for example, that in *Endgame* "Being, trumpeted by existential philosophy as the meaning of being, becomes its antithesis" ("Trying" 147) – as if Beckett's play were mainly concerned to demonstrate that existentialism is wrong. Such a claim might seem like prime evidence of Adorno's using Beckett as "an excuse to make pronouncements," as Benjamin Bennett quips: Adorno seems to look at *Endgame* and see only his own theoretical commitments reflected back at him (cf. Nowak, *Elementen* 64–65). And yet I think we are now in a position to see that even this remark of Adorno's resonates with specifically theatrical – that is, formal and medial – concerns. If we are reading with an eye toward Beckett's utopian deployment of theater's actuality, then Adorno's observation that being "becomes [the] antithesis" of its own meaning in *Endgame* also indexes the very reason why Beckett turns to theater. In theater, the space and time of *what is* can engulf us so mercilessly that meaningfulness – excluded by the airless consistency of the hyperdramatic present – flees from being, and aligns itself instead with what *isn't*: the not-this and not-yet of which writing is both the foil and the promise. Adorno would not have identified theater as the privileged medium of this negation; but as we saw in the Introduction, he does identify a special problem in the way performance stays bound to its own present. As if in rejoinder, Beckett seizes on this problem and shows how, in consigning writing to the reality of performance, he can make the here-and-now of the stage into the vivid content of a determinate negation. The landscape of alterity hovers here in shadow, "inscribed" as the longing for what isn't. Adorno's aesthetics thus turn out to function as a particular *theatrical* sensibility.

In Part II, we'll see how later artists have extended and developed these utopian theatrics. Like Beckett, both Suzan-Lori Parks and Mac Wellman – and also, as I'll argue, the company Elevator Repair Service – elaborate new relations between text and stage, reimagining the seam between the two media as a site of utopian possibility. One technique that remains central to these later artists is the use of monologue – a device whose importance for Beckett we need, therefore, to consider. I want to end this chapter by speculating on the legacy of one of *Godot*'s most striking formal quirks: Lucky's long, explosive speech.

Toward a New Monologue: Beckett's "scribal act"

Beckett places Lucky's monologue at the center of his play; as we'll see in the following chapters, this decision anticipates monologue's heightened significance in more recent playwriting, where it continues to operate as a utopian device. Here, however, I want to consider the relationship between Lucky's speech and a different kind of monologue: Beckett's novel *The Unnamable*, written in 1949 directly after *Godot*. *The Unnamable* completes the series of *Three Novels* that includes *Molloy* and *Malone Dies*, but I suggest it bears distinctive traces of the theatrical "diversion" that had intervened in the trilogy's production. With *The Unnamable*, Beckett's prose begins to simulate the theatrical dialectic we have been tracing in *Godot*. I want to suggest that *The Unnamable* is driven by the utopian dynamic Beckett had been working out in writing for theater; specifically, in writing Lucky's monologue.[38] *The Unnamable* is less an interior monologue than a novelistic mimesis of *stage* monologue, an adaptation of the latter's utopian theatricality for a medium that will stay on the page. Reading the novel this way shows us how thoroughly a theatrical problem can *be* a literary problem, demanding the creation of a new form of prose. I said above that in *Godot*, Beckett pursues Adorno's negative utopianism "not only *in* theater, but *as* theater"; in

The Unnamable he carries this theatrical project further, not only in writing, but as writing.

The Unnamable tells us, fairly early in the novel, that his[39] discourse is written. In this, he resembles the narrators who precede him in the trilogy: Molloy, Moran, and especially Malone, whose discourse is full of references to the act of writing. By comparison, writing in *The Unnamable* draws much less attention to itself, and critics have described the novel's overall effect as that of an oral, not a textual, voice.[40] As Dorrit Cohn observes, the Unnamable explicitly "contradicts his scribal act," making his discourse a contender for the category of interior monologue, a mode of writing that doesn't feel like writing (176). This contradiction is present from the first time the Unnamable mentions writing: "How, in such conditions, can I write, to consider only the manual aspect of that bitter folly? I don't know. I could know. But I shall not know. Not this time. It is I who write, who cannot raise my hand from my knee" (*Three* 295). It seems clear, however, that this self-contradiction shouldn't diminish our sense of writing's importance in the novel, as if it meant that the Unnamable were somehow just *less* of a writer than his forebears. On the contrary, the contradiction that takes place in this passage has a striking compositional significance: this is the first time the novel negates its own discursive authority outright, something it will do incessantly from this point on.

The question of writing thus establishes the novel's fundamental dynamic, instituting the impossibility of truthful self-report and with it, the endless labor of the "pensum" that will come to define the Unnamable's entire predicament (304): he must try to speak of himself, and yet finds that whatever he commits to language is a lie. "I have always been sitting here, at this selfsame spot, my hands on my knees, gazing before me like a great horn-owl in an aviary," the Unnamable had announced earlier, setting the scene (287); now, shattering the image of the "great horn-owl," the assertion-and-negation of writing marks a transition from fiction to the vexed impossibility thereof. Not only does the Unnamable "contradict[t] his scribal act" the moment he avows it, but the "scribal act" is itself a motor of self-contradiction. So when writing recedes as a topic of discourse in the pages that follow, we shouldn't conclude that textuality has disappeared into the presentness of voice; rather, writing declares itself throughout the discourse as what continually renders that presentness problematic – just as it does in *Godot*.

For the Unnamable, too, language is not spontaneous expression but interminable labor. His characteristic syntax, his extended use of commas, contributes to this sense of the written as *work*: "The slopes are gentle that meet where he lies, they flatten out under him, it is not a meeting, it is not a pit, that didn't take long, soon we'll have him perched on an eminence" (*Three* 352). Used instead of periods, the commas suggest that all is provisional and there is no time to rest; used instead of dashes, they suggest inevitability rather than interruption – interruption is not called for because no utterance takes itself to be complete in the first place. This sense that the discourse has perpetually not yet said what it has to say becomes explicit with the theme of the "pensum" itself: "it's of me now I must speak" (318). At the level of syntax, however, this ongoing deferral emphasizes the written nature of the text by creating a kind of synchronic undertow: the phrases don't merely succeed one another, but rather each one signals that the next already has a place beside it. The commas turn the discourse into a *list*, an accumulation of language rather than a fluid, phonic stream.[41] The Unnamable's problem with words is not their ephemerality but, on the contrary, their tendency to stick around – much as Vladimir and Estragon are persecuted by the abiding of the "dead voices . . . like leaves," a "charnel-house" (*Waiting* 223) whose actual scene just *is* a topography of writing.

Grasping how *The Unnamable* functions *as a monologue*, then, shouldn't depend on a sense that the novel downplays its own writtenness. This text is strikingly different from Beckett's previous novels, but I don't believe its radical form can be understood as the result of a shift from "something written down" to "a voice speaking aloud" (Brater, *Drama* 8); in Chapter 6 I'll return to the parallel assumptions that often attend readings of experimental stage monologue. Here, I want to notice how thoroughly the monologue that is *The Unnamable* is shaped by – as – the theatrical plight of writing *amidst* the situation ("situation, revolting word" [303]) of embodiment in space and time. The Unnamable tirelessly attempts to constitute and place himself, beginning with the novel's inaugural question: "Where now?" (285). His discourse acts out a crushing sense of writing as positively responsible for the actual, alongside an equally daunting awareness of writing's negativity: the way writing can refuse to seize on the situation at hand and "go on," go off, elsewhere. This double movement constructs monologue as a form of utopian critique determined equally by literature and theater; later playwrights such as Parks and Wellman will return it to the stage.[42]

It would be wrong to claim that this text/scene dialectic has no precedent at all in Beckett's earlier prose fiction: consider the way the earlier works delight in abusing the conventions of direct discourse. Near the beginning of *Watt*, Arsene, the servant whom Watt is replacing, departs: "Before leaving he made the following short statement," we read (39), and a speech of some 25 pages ensues (its length becomes all the more outrageous in retrospect, when we learn that the narrator himself is only repeating what Watt has told him). The third chapter of *Mercier and Camier*, the short novel Beckett wrote after *Watt* and before the trilogy, opens with the words "I trust an only child, I was born at P" and continues for some time in this autobiographical vein, but we learn on the next page that this is not the narrator speaking, but a talkative and "hideous" old man assailing the protagonists during a train ride (27–29). Both of these passages exult in establishing an impropriety at once social and generic: the obliterating, narcissistic garrulity of these speakers in their interpersonal contexts *is also* the unwieldy grafting of an obviously literary, i.e., *written* discourse into what has been (*Watt*) or will be (*Mercier*) established as a scene of speech. The emphatic composition of such moments disrupts the convention by which the text is supposed to convey a spoken conversation; when the character's speech begins to read like a piece of writing, the textual medium through which we encounter this speech becomes perceptible as such.

These irruptions of writing into scenes of oral speech anticipate the theatrical possibility Beckett exploits in *Godot*, where – as we've seen – script dialectically establishes its own incongruity with the scene of its enactment, as if writing cannot bear to confine itself within the scenes it has created. The part of the play that these passages anticipate most directly, however, is Lucky's monologue, which turns out to be literally *too much* for the other characters to endure:

LUCKY: Given the existence as uttered forth in the public works of Puncher and Wattmann of a personal God quaquaquaqua with white beard quaquaquaqua outside time without extension who from the heights of divine apathia divine athambia divine aphasia loves us dearly with some exceptions for reasons unknown but time will tell [. . .] it is established what many deny that man in Possy of Testew and Cunard that man in Essy that man in short that man in brief in spite of the strides of alimentation and defecation wastes and pines wastes and pines and concurrently simultaneously what is more for reasons unknown in spite of the strides of physical culture the practice of sports such as tennis football running cycling swimming flying floating riding gliding conating camogie skating tennis of all kinds dying flying sports of all sorts autumn summer winter winter tennis of all kinds hockey of all sorts penicillin and succedanea in a word I resume flying gliding golf over nine and eighteen holes tennis of all sorts in a word for reasons unknown in Feckham Peckham Fulham Clapham namely concurrently simultaneously what is more for reasons unknown but time will tell fades away I resume [...] the air the earth the sea the earth abode of stones in the great deeps the great cold on sea on land and in the air I resume for reasons unknown in spite of the tennis the facts are there but time will tell I resume alas alas on on in short in fine on on abode of stones who can doubt it I resume but not so fast I resume the skull fading fading fading [...] *[All three throw themselves on LUCKY who struggles and shouts his text.]* (141–145)

As States observes, Lucky's monologue enacts the violent transcendence of its own reality, not only in that its register moves from the local ("camogie," "Feckham Peckham Fulham Clapham") to the cosmic or elemental ("the air the earth the sea the earth"), but also by way of its explosive *form* (*Shape* 40–41). The monologue burgeons beyond the verbal patterns and proportions of anything else in the play; it not only describes but *is* a cessation of life as we (as Vladimir and Estragon) know it. "In the context of *Godot*," States writes, "this pell-mell madness functions very much like amnesia in the Beckett universe: it releases the character from bondage to a sensuous and temporal world" (43–44). The monologue's theological scope does imply the possibility of such "release" with respect to thought's object: hearing it unfold, we suddenly find ourselves faced with the prospect of the eternal, and to that extent lifted out of the "sensuous and temporal." But we might also observe that Lucky's speech is *emphatically* sensuous and temporal. It is sensuous in the feel of its sudden momentum, and its insistence on how compellingly, indeed compulsively, words can *sound* after their meaning has been exhausted: "quaquaquaqua," "penicillin and succedanea," "fading fading fading"; this exaltation of sound over sense is unique in the play.

Lucky's speech is also sensuous in its emergence from the play's most battered body, and the need of its onstage auditors to respond to it, and repress it, physically ("*All three throw themselves on Lucky*"), casting the speech itself as a physical transgression. Far from making time stop, the monologue's duration and virtuosity make time extremely palpable, heightening the question – for the onstage and offstage audiences – of how long this can go on. Beckett's stipulations for the other characters' behavior during the speech occur in four distinct phases: "*Vladimir and Estragon all attention, Pozzo dejected and disgusted*"; "*Vladimir and Estragon begin to protest, Pozzo's sufferings increase*"; "*Vladimir and Estragon attentive again, Pozzo more and more agitated and groaning*"; and finally "*Vladimir and Estragon protest violently. Pozzo jumps up, pulls on the rope. General outcry. Lucky pulls on the rope, staggers, shouts his text. All three throw themselves on Lucky who struggles and shouts his text*" (141–145). These segments emphatically mark the passage of time and, more specifically, the temporal condition of theatrical reception.[43] Stage monologue thus becomes a way for language to plunge with redoubled energy into the embodied presence of performance, and to exacerbate the sense of an imprisoning present. And yet, as States suggests, the very fury with which language digs itself into the scene also accomplishes a kind of "release" from that scene, exceeding the here-and-now by being *too much* for it. Rendered in response to Pozzo's repeated directive to "Think!" (141), Lucky's monologue is a theatrical misprision of interior monologue. It profits in comedy and in poignancy from the mismatch between this language and its concrete scene, a scene which reasserts itself, with violence, to quash it.

The unruly monologues in *Watt* and *Mercier and Camier* approach this dynamic, but the inner continuity of these novels' prose form affects the kind of havoc these speeches can wreak. If the rising duration of Lucky's monologue heightens the crisis of his language with respect to its scene, the rising page count of Arsene's monologue tends rather to abate this tension by making us forget Watt's presence: the monologist merely takes over the thread of the discourse.

Malone Dies, by contrast, dwells on "the uncomfortable and difficult materiality of writing" (Connor 68); but those difficulties are still something the novel's discourse can, as it were, be counted upon to convey. *Malone* certainly emphasizes the temporality and, indeed, the labor of writing; we receive this discourse as itself a performance, and never merely as a passive vehicle or transparent medium of sense. But the novel constructs a stable fictional setting, "here, in the bed" (*Three* 177); and with his pencil, Malone provides the discourse with a stable fictional origin – there is really no question about whose words these are. At one point, in what will seem to have been a kind of feint toward *The Unnamable*, we read:

> I fear I must have fallen asleep again. In vain I grope, I cannot find my exercise-book. But I still have my pencil in my hand. I shall have to wait for day to break. God knows what I am going to do till then.
>
> I have just written, I fear I must have fallen, etc. I hope this is not too great a distortion of the truth. (202)

Beckett teases us with an uncanny sense of displacement from the page, only to reterritorialize; the relief we feel as the narrative slides back into place is just what *The Unnamable* will refuse us. I think writing *Godot*, and especially devising Lucky's monologue, whetted Beckett's appetite for a more sustained and complex mode of disjuncture: a flight of language, a virtuosic piece of writing that is emphatically of the world (embodied, temporal) and yet *finds no place* there. Returning to prose fiction, Beckett faced a challenge that recalls James's predicament: how would he transpose this (dis)placement onto prose for the page, when the page itself seems to guarantee that language, however errant, will always be in its proper place already?

James, I argued, meets this challenge by simulating theatrical discontinuity through increasingly tortuous syntax. Beckett, in turn, creates *The Unnamable*, a book that simulates theatrical monologue by changing the way written prose relates to *its* here-and-now. In the Unnamable's famous "I can't go on, I'll go on" (407), we hear a multiple echo of *Godot*. First, in that the play's characters have literally shared these words: Vladimir says "I can't go on!" at the end of his soliloquy (339), and Estragon says "I can't go on like this" twice in the second act (239, 355) (the second time, very near the end, Vladimir chillingly replies: "That's what you think" [355]). A more profound echo, however, arises from the theatrical condition that Lucky's monologue carries to the point of crisis: the fact that "going on," as talking and talking, implies going *on*, that is, going onstage, submitting extravagant language to the hostile actuality of performance. *The Unnamable* adapts this theatrical perception by embedding the hostile actuality within the principle of discourse itself, so that the page can only house its language in the same way the stage did: at grips. Writing ceaselessly constructs *and* falls foul of its present, in a dialectic modeled on a theatrical relation between text and scene.

"The fact would seem to be, if in my situation one may speak of facts, not only that I shall have to speak of things of which I cannot speak, but also, which is even more interesting, but also that I, which is if possible even more interesting, that I shall have to, I forget, no matter" (*Three* 285–286): *The Unnamable* is certainly not modernist prose at its wildest, or its most refractory. But it is prose that contrives to trip over itself, to convert the fact that there is writing "going on" from a substrate, or given, into a palpable predicament. In this passage, the words that should help me navigate "my situation" immediately *become* my situation. "The fact would seem to be ... ": the sentence starts as an attempt at orientation, even conceptual mastery. By recognizing what the fact *is*, I might get the better of mere fact, transcend it. But the word "fact" is no sooner written than it becomes one more thing to get a grip on, confronting me as the fact of the word "fact": before I can talk with it, I have to talk about it, along with all the other "things of which I cannot speak." This same trouble recurs with the word "also," then the word "I," until the accumulated verbiage overwhelms me, crowding out whatever the main thrust of the sentence was going to be. Writing thus becomes a process by which language makes itself distressingly present: makes *itself* the very scene, or "situation," that it must then try to write itself *out* of.

The exhilarating momentum that develops in later passages of the novel comes from the intensity of this struggle, as writing starts racing, breathlessly, to outdistance itself:

> The place, I'll make it all the same, I'll make it in my head, I'll draw it out of my memory, I'll gather it all about me, I'll make myself a head, I'll make myself a memory, I have only to listen, the voice will tell me everything, tell it to me again, everything I need, in dribs and drabs, breathless, it's like a confession, a last confession, you think it's finished, then it starts off again, there were so many sins, the memory is so bad, the words don't come, the words fail, the breath fails, no it's something else [. . .] (404)

Quotation does little justice to these sentences, since so much of their power comes from their length, the headlong determination with which they go on.[44] This would be phase four of Lucky's monologue, the "General outcry" amidst which "Lucky pulls on [his] rope, staggers, shouts his text" as the others "throw themselves on" him. In *The Unnamable*, discourse has learned to become its own rope, and to pull against itself, heightening its own fury. Beckett's monologue takes shape as writing's interminable attempt to get to somewhere else, precisely through the most intense possible confrontation with the "fact" of its own emergence. It is *going on* (and on) in the mode of *going off*: fleeing, raging, exploding.

"The place, I'll make it . . . ": Beckett's fiction thus appropriates theatrical monologue as the most rigorous form of desire, one that commits itself to the thought of an "elsewhere" by digging its heels into the hegemonic here-and-now. This discourse insists, in spite of everything, that there is something more than everything. Through the agony of its burgeoning, the monologue intimates what the present doesn't hold. That alterity remains necessarily unspecified, unreached; sometimes Beckett figures it as death, and sometimes as "Silence." As Vladimir observes, though, to be dead is not enough; the dream of annihilation functions, in Beckett, as the trace of a possible life so radically different from *this* that it can manifest in our imaginations only negatively, as an absolute caesura. "Only by virtue of the absolute negativity of collapse does art enunciate the unspeakable: utopia," Adorno writes (*Aesthetic* 32). Utopia has no image, but inheres in the sustained relation to the this-ness *amidst which* transcendence, like Lucky's supernova, keeps trying to occur. What Beckett discovers is that this relation is theatrical.

If monologue becomes a privileged form for utopian theatricality, this is not only because of the way its copious going-on digs into, and strains against, the present. As outrageously selfish speech, monologue also exacerbates the "co-" of theater's "co-presence": the community of characters within the scene, but also – as the savage response to Lucky's speech is meant to mark – our own presence together in the auditorium. In *The Unnamable*, monologue enacts the perpetual unmaking and remaking of successive personae; not only those of the speaker, but also those of the audience his discourse implies.

In this way, Beckett's novel fabricates the same violently negative relation to the social that stage monologue enacts in *Godot*. The last chapter of this book will take up the possibility of monologue as a form of resistant solitude which, precisely by flouting communicative aims, gives utopia a social contour. Rich in actual interpersonal proximity, the theater becomes the site of a furious loneliness, pitched toward an unrealized *other* collectivity in which we would not be the same. This is where the thought of theater leads the Unnamable, whose imaginary attendance should remind us of another Beckettian stage:

> well well, so there's an audience, it's a public show, you buy your seat and you wait [...] it's only beginning, it hasn't begun, he's only preluding, clearing his throat, alone in the dressing-room, he'll begin any moment, or it's the stage-manager [...] and the spectators, where are they, you didn't notice, in the anguish of waiting, never noticed you were waiting alone, that's the show, waiting alone, in the restless air, for it to begin, for something to begin, for there to be something else but you [...] (374–375)

"[W]hat is wants the other," Adorno writes: "the artwork is the language of this wanting" (*Aesthetic* 132). For Beckett and those who follow, theater offers a place for this wanting, this waiting. And writing whispers that we're still not there.

PART II

Beyond the Present
Playwrights at the Turn of the Millennium

Only strangeness is the antidote to alienation.

(Theodor Adorno)[1]

CHAPTER 4

Introduction
Staging Writing Today

THE HEADMISTRESS: The here and now would not be flattered to hear you talk like this.

(Mac Wellman, *Girl Gone*)[1]

Finding Texts

Part I of this book tracked the negative theatrics animating various kinds of texts: some that clearly aren't plays, and don't claim to be ("The Beast in the Jungle," *The Ambassadors, The Unnamable*); some that do claim to be plays, but in so claiming, force us to reconceive our definition of a play (*Four Saints in Three Acts, Paisieu*); and one play that is obviously a play (*Waiting for Godot*). As I explained at the outset, it's been a premise of this study that in order to understand what writing can bring to theater, we need to begin with a sense of writing's own capacity for theatrical exploration. To commit to discovering this capacity *only* in playwriting, I suggested, would be an arbitrary limitation.

In fact, a similar intuition is reflected in a wide range of contemporary experimental theater practice.[2] With what seems like increasing frequency, and across extremely diverse projects, artists have been occupying themselves in performance with writings that aren't plays. I began this book by quoting Tim Etchells of the UK company Forced Entertainment, a group perpetually investigating new possibilities for playing with text and speech. Two of their recent shows pursue this interest in very different ways: in *A Broadcast/Looping Pieces*, a solo, Etchells reads out fragments of text from fifteen years of his own notes, which are printed on cards. He improvises the selection and repetition of fragments, creating a kind of musical word-web as he shifts back and forth between cards. In *The Notebook*, two performers read text from Ágota Kristóf's 1986 novel about children in wartime, each with a copy of the titular notebook in his hands.[3]

Both pieces could exemplify a tendency Richard Schechner, writing in 2010, refers to as "text-as-text theater" (900). With this term, Schechner marks a difference from the loathéd "text theater" proper, but also slyly suggests a certain complicity. He writes:

> Rejections of literature, the text, authors, and authority were a hallmark of the historical avant-garde and even of the great burst of activity from the late 1950s through to the 1980s. Its rhetoric included burning the libraries, ransacking the museums. In theater, I was not alone in advocating rejecting the words-as-written by playwrights, starting instead with the people present in the room ... But around the turn of the century, a big change took place – text-as-text reasserted itself ... [These new performances] put the text – both as words heard and as physical object, the book – at the center of the performance. (ibid.)

Schechner's main explicit point of reference for "text-as-text theater" is the New York company Elevator Repair Service (ERS), who from 2004 through 2010 developed a trilogy of shows based on canonical American novels.[4] The first and most famous of these, *Gatz*, is a six-hour performance (plus breaks) that contains every word of F. Scott Fitzgerald's *The Great Gatsby*, most of which the actor Scott Shepherd reads aloud from a paperback.

I'll discuss *Gatz* at some length later in this chapter. But we might also apply the "text-as-text" distinction to work that foregrounds text in other ways, like Nature Theater of Oklahoma's *Life and Times*: throughout this ongoing multimedia series, the transcript of a company member telling her life story over the phone serves as a script, always verbatim. "The play does what Faulkner and Gertrude Stein did with English prose: makes us hear it in all its terrible richness and peculiarity and flatness as it struggles to express itself, or hide from its own emotional life and specious truths," wrote *The New Yorker*'s Hilton Als of Episodes 1–4 (2013). If *Life and Times* "makes us hear" the textures and adventures of language itself, Als's literary references suggest that this aural revelation occurs through an energetic avowal of writing. True, the text first came into being orally, as speech, and preserves all the tics of its orality intact (its "ahems and ahas and ehs and what-was-I-talking-about digressions," Als writes); these features could easily support a naturalizing performance, which would recapture the spontaneity of the original recording. But the company never attempts this. Instead, they find various modes of defamiliarizing delivery, such as choral singing or stylized melodrama, which keep the task of enunciation – and thus the text's status *as script* – in evidence. Nature Theater thereby inverts traditional dramatic procedure, wherein written dialogue tries to provide for its own erasure as writing by producing what can seem like spontaneous speech (Szondi 8–9). Instead, the company uses features of spoken language to highlight that language's unnatural arrest as text, in a performance which continually reminds us of this transposition.

In Chapter 5, I'll argue that Suzan-Lori Parks's plays do something similar. And yet calling *Life and Times* itself a "play," as Als does, seems at once inevitable and odd. (The project's web page says that certain episodes "work within the form of the musical/opera" and "are dealing with theater and the genre of the 'whodunit,'" but the word "play" never appears ["OK"].) It's true that the performance seems emphatically beholden to its text; the transcripts constitute the premise and through-line of the project, and the self-imposed injunction to render every syllable almost seems like a burlesque of the textual "dominance" so often associated with the theater of plays. At the same time, though, this is just as emphatically *not* the text of a playwright, an emphasis registered in Als's claim that it is "English prose" as such that "struggles to express itself" in the work. It's not that we forget that this text is (was) someone's speech; on the contrary, the transcripts offer a gratifying sense of access to the "real" woman who first uttered them, a feeling of intimacy that builds as the reality effects of her discourse accumulate. But this dynamic is maintained by the promise that no mediating *literary* consciousness has intervened in her confession, a promise each "um" and "like" seems to substantiate. And this apparent aesthetic neutrality makes the transcripts an ideal substrate for the experiments with genre and medium that shape the project's successive episodes, sustaining its artistic interest. Unquestionably, text is central to these performances; but it would feel wrong to say that they are performances *of* that text, as one can refer to performances of a play.

Meanwhile, other companies and auteurs on both sides of the Atlantic have recently been drawn to more traditionally literary texts which are also not plays: besides Elevator Repair Service's American novels trilogy and Forced Entertainment's *The Notebook*, we might think of Italian director Romeo Castellucci's *Hyperion: Letters of a Terrorist* (Berlin, 2013), in which actresses recite excerpts from Hölderlin's epistolary novel *Hyperion* amidst the director's famously anarchic sensory landscape. "I have never been interested in poetry in theatre because I have always believed it was the anti matter [sic] of the scene," Castellucci remarks in an interview. "And here I am, disarmed again by this subversive poet." Castellucci's work belongs to the longstanding tradition of *Regietheater* or "directors' theater," in which canonical plays often become the platform for directorial imagination and virtuosity. This genre is strongly associated with Germany, as in the work of Frank Castorf or Thomas Ostermeier, but has its familiar American analogs too, from the student productions many of us sat through in college ("It's *Antigone* ... but in *outer space!*") to the more compelling precedents Schechner eulogizes: "The Wooster Group in a series of well-known works from the mid-1970s through the 90s ... had its way with plays by T. S. Eliot, Thornton Wilder, Arthur Miller, Anton Chekhov, and Jean Racine," Schechner recalls, identifying these works with his own interest in "deconstructing texts; twisting them; making collages of them; and so on" (900). Schechner's virilizing language feels less disturbing once you remember that it's first of all Elizabeth LeCompte, the Wooster Group's director, who was having her "way" with Eliot et al. But regardless of who's on top, what Schechner points to here is a widely shared sense that plays force a theatrical contest: *Regietheater* versus *Texttheater*; break the play or it'll walk all over you.[5] In this context, Castellucci's remark that Hölderlin's novel has "disarmed" him is interesting: while it gestures toward a similar power struggle, it also suggests that this text somehow preempts or prevents that struggle. Does *Hyperion*'s not being a play have something to do with this disarmament?

It's not that nonplay texts always go more quietly into the mise-en-scène; clearly, many companies value the perceptual frictions such texts can introduce, and the challenges they create for performance. But whenever we hear a novel, or a notecard, or a telephone transcript in the theater – when we're made aware, as we usually are, that that's what we're hearing – we also hear, as a kind of accompanying reverb, the company's choosing of that text; the act of theatrical creativity that identified *that* text as something to bring to the stage. No matter how authoritative such a text might be when read, in the theater it will usually emit a sense of having been taken unawares, or coaxed from its orbit. In a way that might remind us of "found" objects in a gallery, its content is an inextricable combination of its own aesthetic dimensions ("text-as-text") and the fact of this audacious importation.

I would suggest that this kind of work with nonplay texts is actually the best referent for critical accounts that define theater texts as "the linguistic *material* of an autonomous stage art" (Poschmann 20, my emphasis). But are such accounts really valid for plays too? In one way, yes, of course. "Actors *use* the words on the page to produce an action, an event, to do something," W. B. Worthen remarks (*Drama* 9–10). This should be obvious to anyone who is putting on a play, which is part of Worthen's point: amidst the ongoing discursive kerfuffle of theoretical and artistic self-positioning, "'the text' functions in largely metaphorical, ideologically laden ways" that float free of what we all actually know to be true (xiii). Texts, of whatever kind, can't *make us do* anything in the rehearsal room; "while the text may seem to direct a specific act at a specific time, the recontextualization of that 'act' as performance cannot be fully specified" (ibid.). Erika Fischer-Lichte makes a similar observation in her 1985 essay "*Was ist ein 'werkgetreue' Inszenierung?*" ("What Is a 'Faithful' Production?"). Noting a "fundamental opposition" between the abstractness of verbal signs and the concreteness of theatrical ones, she explains that theatrical signs can never mean exactly the same thing as the words of a text (44–45). A production can thus only be a "transformation" of its text, and there are no objective criteria for determining whether that transformation is "adequate" to the written work (41–44). "As an instrument of criticism, the concept of faithfulness to the work thus appears to be completely unusable, if not indeed harmful," Fischer-Lichte concludes (46). Even when actors and directors think they're following or serving a text, they're actually creating something new.

Again: yes. These arguments – especially Worthen's, which engages directly with Lehmann's *Postdramatic Theater* and other recent scholarship – offer a crucial corrective to unexamined assumptions about how dramatic theater works. In their wake, claims about the erstwhile "dominance of the text" start looking not just wrong, but downright silly. And yet if we understand a written play fundamentally as a spur to independent subjective acts of theater-making (Fischer-Lichte), or as "one instrument among many that the repertoire of enactment might deploy" (Worthen, *Drama* xvii), then it does become difficult to see how plays' relationship to theater could be categorically different from that of other kinds of text.

Perhaps this isn't really a problem; after all, the assumption that there *is* such a difference is part of what get playwrights barred from the republic of really adventurous theater. If playwrights would only explain that what we're writing is just *there for performers to use*, the same way a novel or an interview is, it might get us a place at the "live art" table. Elfriede Jelinek, perhaps the most canonical living "postdramatic" writer, famously abjures control over performance. "The author does not give many stage directions, she has learned her lesson by now. Do what you like," she writes at the beginning of *Ein Sportstück* (1998); quoting this statement, Karen Jürs-Munby notes that Jelinek's texts "have given directors the freedom to ... become more like creative co-authors of the material" and that "German *Regietheater* ... has taken up the challenge of Jelinek's texts with a vengeance" ("Agon" 9).

The American playwright Charles Mee proposes an even more radical reworking in a statement on his web site:

> Please feel free to take the plays from this website and use them freely as a resource for your own work: that is to say, don't just make some cuts or rewrite a few passages or re-arrange them or put in a few texts that you like better, but pillage the plays as I have pillaged the structures and contents of the plays of Euripides and Brecht and stuff out of Soap Opera Digest and the evening news and the internet, and build your own, entirely new, piece – and then, please, put your own name to the work that results.

The earnest, pedagogical tone of Mee's exhortation contrasts with the wryness of Jelinek's seductive-ironic surrender. But they share the essential gesture, more a recognition than a bestowal of our freedom to "do what we like." Neither *creates* the possibility of treating these pieces as "a resource for your own work"; as Fischer-Lichte and Worthen remind us, that's what the texts would be anyway. The operative difference here is not between kinds of texts – say, plays or *Dramen* versus all other "theater texts" – but between authors' individual sensibilities, what they will or won't go for. Even Beckett seems to have acknowledged this after a fashion, telling Jonathan Kalb that it would be more all right for directors to flout a playwright's wishes once he's dead, "just because then you can't hurt his feelings" (qtd. in Kalb, *Beckett* 79).

Beckett's estate, however, remains notoriously tyrannical, and its intransigence may hint (however unwittingly) at another meaningful logic. The previous chapter suggested that in *Godot*, the fantasy of a production that *would* be fully determined by the text is bound up with an "intensified sense of the real as a textual site" for which the subject, as language-user, is painfully responsible. This argument implies that the claim to be dictating a whole theatrical event from the page – unreasonable as it is – is not necessarily a foible extrinsic to the work. If there are "texts in which the refusal of dominance is anchored" (Jaeger 9) there are also texts in which the refusal of that refusal plays out, thematically and formally; *Godot* is one of them.

I claim that this unreasonable resistance to *what really happens* defines a crucial current of experimental theater, enacting one of the most persuasive motivations for making theater at all. And I'd like to suggest that playwriting as such offers a privileged form for this resistance. If we return to Adorno's model of the artwork, we can reconceive the theatrical text as a monadic "force field" that asserts its "foreignness to the world" through its objectivation (*Aesthetic* 176, 183).

We can then supplement Worthen's formulation with its opposite: theatrical performance may be "a specific kind of doing that lives outside the text" (*Drama* 55), but equally, text is a specific kind of doing that *lives outside the performance*, outside the here-and-now in which performance takes place. This is true of all texts "used" in theater, but *plays* can activate this autonomy in a particular way: by acting as though writing *could* determine performance, by scripting theater as the performance *of* writing, a play can undermine performance's actuality. Beyond introducing writing's ontological alterity to the stage, a play promises – falsely but assiduously – to have disposed an entire happening to that alterity. It claims to hijack the performance here-and-now in the name of that which is neither.

This claim hovers in the words themselves: "the play" is a term whose referent is, somehow, *both* a piece of writing *and* a live, embodied event. "Did you ever see it?" "No, but I've read it": the very possibility of such commonplace exchanges proves that the word's bifurcated meaning is no mere homonymy. The play you read and the play you see are – impossibly – the same thing. By writing within the conventions that make a play recognizable as such, then, an author inscribes this conflation into her text. These conventions – dialogue attributed to characters, events (however vitiated) that could form a plot, clear distinction between the spoken and unspoken levels of text – actively promise that a performance, even *the* performance, is latent in the writing. In this sense, Beckett's insistence that his plays be performed "as written" only extends the logic of playwriting's fundamental conceit. The slippage between noun ("play*wright*") and participle ("play*writing*") redoubles this sense, as if the fundamental instrument through which a show got "wrought" were the word processor. However faintly, this language suggests an indifference to the particularities of performance and production. These terms seem to intimate that the script already constitutes the event, whose other features would thus become somehow incidental.

This effect is what makes arguments like Worthen's so necessary: plays that obey these conventions "trick" us by *not* immediately beckoning the reader's directorial intervention and invention, or appealing emphatically for coauthorship through nonverbal scenic elements, to the same degree as texts structured without these conventions. Plays lean on these conventions, that is, to perform a kind of imaginary self-staging, to make us feel as if they really do already entail a performance.[6] In fact, a "play" that demurs from these conventions might nevertheless pursue this peculiar experience by other means, thus living up to its name. We've seen this with Stein's landscape plays, in which words and phrases seem to try to arrogate the materiality of performance for the page.

Neither Stein's texts nor Beckett's nor anyone's can actually determine a theatrical event; but I want to consider the dynamic in which the *illusion* of something like this possibility becomes a powerful component in the experience of reception. Within this dynamic, a play we read on the page promises, deceptively but compellingly, that it's all ready to manifest in performance – no "transformation" necessary. And in performance, when we're aware that what we're watching is a play, we receive a corresponding promise: that a text was the origin of this performance, and that even as the performance passes by, its possibility will persist, stored up – as it were – between the pages of the script. I propose that this pair of treacherous promises distinguishes plays from other texts we see and hear in theater.

But if this illusion marks all plays, then how can it possibly take us "beyond drama," as this book's subtitle insists? If these structural conventions undergird the most normative dramaturgy, how can they be central to the rejection of that dramaturgy? Artists sometimes adopt generic conventions precisely in order to explode or deconstruct them; we've seen something similar in James's relationship to "dramatic" storytelling, another version of which will appear in Wellman's *A Murder of Crows*.[7] But unlike other elements of the dramatic norm, the "imaginary self-staging" I've been describing is not something the negative theatricalists in this study want to attack. Rather, they seize on that self-staging in order to disrupt the very ethos that sanctioned it, mobilizing it *against* the dramatic affirmation of presentness.

Here's the distinction I want to draw: while playwriting that abides by the dramatic norm will also sustain a fantasmatic equivalency of text and performance, it will do so through an ideally stable third term – the play's fiction – which should synthesize writing and performance and dissolve the medial specificity of each one. The text to which dramatic performance refers back is conceived mainly as a configuration of *story and characters*; its language serves primarily as the means of evoking these, as do the material elements of performance. Lehmann describes this process: "Fixed onto the cognitive programme 'Action/Imitation,'" he writes, "the [dramatic] gaze misses the texture of written drama as much as that which offers itself to the senses as presentational action, in order to assure itself only of the represented" (37).[8] Dramatic theater may recall us to its text, but only insofar as that text is the "home" of plot and character – Ibsen's *Hedda Gabler*, say, as the original site of Hedda and her travails, which both text and performance will do their best to *make present* for us. Here we can recall Szondi's emphasis on the absolute presence of the dramatic universe, where words are "not written" but "spoken in context" (8). Drama, on page or stage, is an experience of important things happening to people like us here and now. The fallacy that its text determines its performance "makes sense" because in performance as in text, drama strives to make events and people fully actual: im-mediate, unfettered by the particular dimensions of a specific medium.[9]

What writers like Parks and Wellman find in playwriting, by contrast, is the prospect of a theater that will ongoingly propose itself *as written*. When we watch their plays in performance, we recognize them *as* plays – a property these works borrow from drama. Remnants of plot to be enacted, characters to be embodied, and dialogue to be spoken still provide a fictional link that text and performance share, enabling us to experience the performance "of" a play. But this time, that link doesn't quite circle back to the present: through the modernist "difficulty" of their language, these plays insists on their writing *as* writing, intricate, wild, and flagrantly in excess of the demands of any present scene. In the midst of performance, instead of supporting a robustly present experience, they insistently flag the somewhere-else of a language that won't resolve itself into any concrete happening. "Anti matter" indeed: in these plays, character and plot *and* their attenuation serve to relay writing as different – as difference – from the way things happen here and now.

The following chapters will focus on this kind of playwriting in work by Parks and Wellman. First, however, I want to test out my argument about the significance, and appeal, of "imaginary self-staging" *for performance*. In order not to beg the question, I'm going to do this by considering a recent production that isn't a play: Elevator Repair Service's *Gatz*, a show that exemplifies Schechner's description of "text-as-text theater." Even more than text-forward pieces like Nature Theater's *Life and Times*, *Gatz* mirrors plays' constitutive resistance to sensible thinking: it challenges the confident critical assurance that "faithful production" is a meaningless term. In the process, it shows the fantasy that plays trade on – that a text *can* determine a performance – yielding tremendous theatrical richness. As I noted in the Preface, scholars have recently tended to validate plays as experimental theater by denying that their text commands the stage; but *Gatz* throws its theatrical energy into activating precisely that command. In so doing, it offers a logic of theatrical experiment that would be less tethered to the reasonable dictates of the real. *Gatz* thus demonstrates how the modernist negativity we traced in James, Stein, and Beckett might be reflected in a field of contemporary theatrical practice that extends beyond the staging of plays – even as it questions the teleology of that particular "beyond."

The Silly Word "Faithfulness": *Gatz*

When ERS performed *Gatz* in Zurich in 2006, a favorable review appeared in the *Tages-Anzeiger*. Its headline proclaimed "*Die Wiedergeburt der Werktreue*" – "the rebirth of textual fidelity" (Müller). In the body of the review, however, the critic Tobi Müller – who has also worked as a dramaturg at Berlin's *Volksbühne* – puts the matter differently. "The silly word *Werktreue* (it doesn't exist: every step on the stage is a step away from the text) is at once slavishly fulfilled and, again, contested" by the production, Müller writes.

That *Gatz* could move a reviewer to paradox is perhaps less remarkable than its power to summon the discredited concept of "faithfulness to the text" at all – indeed, Müller hastens to disavow this backward notion before he's even finished the sentence that both invokes and contradicts it. Could it be that his parenthetical self-interruption betrays a certain critical anxiety, which undercuts the common sense certainty its contents would convey? "Silly word! Faithfulness is just a fairytale!" proclaims the grown-up critic, a little too loudly.

As mentioned above, *Gatz* is a staging of Fitzgerald's *The Great Gatsby* – not a "stage adaptation" in the familiar sense, but a marathon performance in which we hear every word of the novel. The show is set in an anonymous office, where a man who can't get his computer to start (Scott Shepherd) discovers the novel in his Rolodex. He starts reading it out loud; eventually, all thirteen performers embody characters from the story and speak those characters' words, while Shepherd takes the part of the narrator, Nick. Unlike ERS's *The Sound and the Fury* (2008), in which a copy of Faulkner's novel circulates between performers, in *Gatz* Shepherd has the paperback through almost all of the show, while other performers speak from memory. It's a staple of downtown lore, however, that after years of touring, Shepherd "actually knows the whole book by heart" – a fact the company confirms on its web site ("Gatz").[10]

The phrase "by heart" turns out to have a particular resonance for what seems to be going on in *Gatz*: multiple reviewers have described the piece as an exercise in love. Alexandra Kedves in the *Neue Zürcher Zeitung* refers to the company's "stormy affair with the novel"; Jason Zinoman in *The New York Times* describes the show as "a rather earnest love letter to the book." This critical tendency is all the more remarkable considering that *Gatz* is hardly dominated by amorous affect. There are tender passages, but like most of ERS's work, the piece's mood is mainly playful and smart, highly energetic but wary of coercive emotion. It's as if the sheer quantity of labor, thought, and care that the company has obviously put into its work with Fitzgerald's text – and the quantity of time we see them put in nightly – demanded the excessiveness of an erotic vocabulary for its expression. Ben Brantley, in his own *New York Times* review of the long-delayed New York premiere, takes this premise furthest. "The most compelling love affair being conducted on a New York stage this season isn't between a man or a woman" he declares at the outset of his rave. " . . . It is between a man and a book." The show "chronicles one reader's gradual but unconditional seduction by a single, ravishing novel . . . Think of it as a morning-fresh variation on an ancient theatrical formula: Boy meets book. Boy *gets* book. Boy becomes lost in book."

Brantley differs from the other love-struck critics in one important respect: whereas they discern a romance in the company's real-life relationship with the novel, he insistently describes *Gatz* as a story *about* the romance of reading, with Shepherd as the "romantic lead." This interpretation gives a lot of weight to the sparse fictional frame ERS constructs around the novel: a rundown late-twentieth-century office, whose bored employees gradually take on *Gatsby*'s roles. The office "characters" have no words of their own, and their activities are at once familiar and vague, like movie or TV extras whose only job is to provide an office "feel." Certainly the piece doesn't show us much that could explain the remarkable collaborative feat of storytelling they undertake. Brantley, however, naturalizes this departure from narrative logic by claiming that the coworkers' "metamorphosis" into Fitzgerald's characters "seems to be taking place entirely in the reader's mind." This interpretation wouldn't have occurred to me, since – given my own sense of the work I'd seen from the company and its members before – I came to the show without any expectations of realist narrative coherence. In fact today, based on memory alone (I saw the piece twice, in an "underground" showing in 2005 and again in 2012), I might have said that the office setting was essentially a design concept, there to provide a specific sensory consistency and props for the company's virtuosic physical comedy. Watching *Gatz* again on video, however, I have a hard time finding anything that could invalidate Brantley's account. In other words, describing *Gatz* as a variation on a familiar kind of play – in which an unlikely hero has a whirlwind romance – may reflect a particular critical agenda, but it doesn't exactly do the piece an injustice.

Placed side by side, Müller's review and Brantley's could work as a caricature of their respective cultural universes: the European critic using *Gatz* to do some theory, the American invoking good old dramatic convention. Of course, the piece's reception overall doesn't always fall so neatly into these two camps; what I mean to bring out, here, is the way *Gatz* seems to inspire relatively extreme critical maneuvers, precisely because of its hybrid nature – as if its allegiance to one norm or another had to be established *for* it. On the one hand it's not a play, since its text is obviously written in another genre; like the other recent pieces I touched on above, *Gatz* maintains our awareness of the novel as a "found text." At least initially, we're not tempted to conflate the novel with the structure of the performance itself, the way we would with a play. Instead, as Francisco Frazão writes, we experience "a text whose use value was swerved, as it was not intended to become a piece of theatre" (142–143). For Frazão, *Gatz* functions as one more demystifying attack on the notion of faithfulness: it exemplifies the way "[p]ostdramatic theatre exposes the seamlessness between text and production for the ideological construct that it is" (151). On the other hand, several critics describe – and I would also attest to – a strong sense, by the time *Gatz* ends, that what we have experienced somehow *is* the novel, as if the theatrical apparatus had become a really incredible pair of reading glasses. "Watching 'Gatz' is a heightened version of reading the book oneself," writes Rebecca Mead in *The New Yorker*. Or as ERS director John Collins has said, "by the end, the theater has been blown away by the writing" (qtd. in O'Leary).

Is *Gatz* a staging "of" Fitzgerald's *The Great Gatsby*, or is it a devised performance that "uses" the text? Collins has objected to these categories in terms Worthen would appreciate, challenging the assumption "that you do things in [devised] work that you don't do when working on a play" (Collins, "Way" 122). *Gatz* itself, however, doesn't so much deconstruct or dissolve these categories as keep them more energetically in play, by hyperbolically extending the fantasy that produces them in the first place: the "silly" fantasy that we could ever be faithful to a text. *Gatz* proposes that even texts which deny us the conventional footholds for staging might yet demand a performance that doesn't just "use" them, but *stays true to* them – or tries to. The steps taken by such a performance would not, *pace* Müller, be "steps away from the text"; or if they were, they'd also always be circling back toward it, "borne back ceaselessly" like Gatsby toward the romance of an inaccessible past (154). "Though I listen to all the arguments which the most divergent systems employ to demystify, to limit, to erase, in short to depreciate love, I persist," writes Roland Barthes in *A Lover's Discourse*, in a section called "The Intractable" (22).

I am, obviously, suggesting that the question of theatrical ethos *Gatz* raises – does the performance "find" the text or does the text found the performance? – must be connected to the amatory theme that keeps surfacing in its reception, and that this connection occurs through the concept of *faithfulness*, which the show enlivens as a category at once artistic (*die Werktreue*) and erotic (*die Treue*).[11] *Gatz* helps us imagine textual fidelity as a desirous practice, a way of being with a text. Like a lover determined to stay true to the beloved, this theatrical project is taken up in spite of its apparent "impossibility." I realize that the *a priori* impossibility of the faithful production belongs to a different order from the supposed "impossibility" of the faithful union, which is probabilistic and rhetorical: "everybody cheats" has some force as a piece of common sense, but no one would say it's literally true, let alone conceptually necessary. I want to insist on this analogy anyway, because I think it illuminates the way *Gatz* treats its text: not as a means to an end, but as an entity with a complex and separate inner life, which the performers have nevertheless invited both to compel and to limit their own behavior.

Certainly, the piece lets us know that *it* knows that such fidelity is a fantasy. This awareness shows up most consistently in the performance of Susie Sokol, who plays the lady golfer Jordan Baker, Nick's ostensible love interest. Sokol's office persona is the only one who seems to notice, and engage with, Shepherd's act of reading; at one point, she even grabs the book and starts reading aloud herself, much to his dismay (until it turns out this passage is, anomalously, narrated by Jordan in the novel [72–75]). Throughout the show, and more markedly than other performers, Sokol frequently turns compliance with the text into a gag. Early on, for instance, while Shepherd reads about "Miss Baker who seemed to have mastered a certain hardy skepticism" (Fitzgerald 30), Sokol screws up her face and torso in an unlikely "hardy skepticism" pose; a little while later, she cartoonishly acts out a passage describing one of Gatsby's parties, embodying in rapid-fire succession the "old men," "young girls," "superior couples holding each other tortuously," "single girls dancing individualistically," a "celebrated tenor [who] had sung in Italian," and so on (52). One might say that Sokol, who appears as more of an "authority" on the text than any other performer except Shepherd, embodies a kind of text-performance reality principle: her job is to bring the dream of fidelity comically back down to earth.[12]

What happens at the climax of Sokol's party charades, though, is also revealing: the performer Jim Fletcher – whom we already suspect of being the title character – reenters the office, switching on a light; the jazz music from the party abruptly cuts out, and Sokol and Shepherd start trying to look busy. Fletcher sits down beside them and begins typing; Shepherd resumes reading, in a slightly chastened tone: "I was still with Jordan Baker. We were sitting at a table with a man of about my age" (53). The music recommences, softly, and for the first time, Fletcher speaks, assuming the lines of the unknown man; a few moments later, he reveals himself as Gatsby, taking Nick by surprise. "'What!' I exclaimed. 'Oh, I beg your pardon'" (ibid.): in reading this last line, Shepherd pauses, stares at Fletcher, and seems genuinely amazed. The moment takes on a particular weightiness, a hushed, auratic tone that lingers into the subsequent description of Gatsby's magical smile.

Fletcher, a veteran downtown performer, is a tall, solidly built man whose demeanor always conveys both gentleness and taurine strength. In *Gatz* his presence constitutes a kind of ground bass, or emotional anchor; his articulation of the text is full-throated but simple, neither emotive nor colored with irony. "I am not trying to bring out the Gatsby that I understand," he has said. "What I am doing is committing to the book" (qtd. in Mead). But it's hard not to graft Gatsby's heartbreaking devotion to Daisy onto the quiet intensity Fletcher brings to his performance, which sometimes – as in the sequence I just described – overtakes the tone of the piece as a whole. In this sequence, when Fletcher's gravity briefly supersedes Sokol's clowning, the piece seems to point up the contradictions that inhabit its own desire. As many have noted, *Gatz* decides not to turn its novel into a play: it refuses adaptation. But this is also true in the secondary sense that it refuses fully to adapt, or resign itself, to the reality principle that there's no such thing as faithfulness.

With this refusal, the piece also challenges the dominant model of contemporary experimental performance as a realm of hard-won theatrical self-sufficiency, authored only by those who are present, where "[t]he pivotal point . . . is no longer the work of art, detached from and independent of its creator and recipient," but rather "an event, set in motion and terminated by the actions of all the subjects involved" (Fischer-Lichte, *Transformative* 22). Instead, *Gatz* retains an untimely valorization of the work as what institutes "the irruption of objectivity into subjective consciousness" (Adorno, *Aesthetic* 245). It imagines what might happen if we delivered our embodied, interested, creative selves over to something that *isn't* "set in motion" by us, for us, and which disarranges our own desires with incommensurate ones.

This brings us back to Richard Schechner's observation that "text-as-text theater" like *Gatz* has abandoned the twentieth-century project of "starting ... with the people present in the room" (900). Schechner discusses various factors in the turn toward what he calls "the conservative avant-garde," including "the end to meaningful opposition to capitalism" as the century drew to a close (903) and a poststructuralist theoretical climate that has "emphasized repetition, citation, deferral of meaning, the circulation of ideas, and the impossibility of defining, no less finding, 'originals'" (905). Already in the late 1940s, however, Adorno had articulated the frustration that would make the (cryptodramatic!) ideal of originality feel increasingly suspect: an awareness that in a total exchange society, "people's last possibility of experiencing themselves has been cut off by organized culture ... and the individual is now scarcely capable of any impulse that he could not classify as an example of this or that publicly recognized constellation" (*Minima* 65–66). When you can no longer bring yourself to believe in spontaneity – in a world where "just do it" as a corporate advertising slogan will turn out to produce zero cognitive dissonance – then the criterion of being "present in the room" may not convince you of its inherent aesthetic promise. The problem is that what we will want to "set in motion" in any particular present will manifest the same values that are always being drummed into us, values that the wan specificities of any given moment and venue have little hope of unsettling.

Adorno's critique of jazz improvisation applies this awareness to the medium of music; as Gary Peters writes, "Adorno is perturbed by the deceptive disjuncture between surface malleability and structural rigidity, which creates the illusion of individual freedom where none exists" (81). Clearly the same logic would hold for improvisatory theater performance; but more importantly for our purposes, Adorno's critique might also chasten theoretical confidence in the absolute distinction between the static "work" and the dynamic, immediately cocreated "event" (Fischer-Lichte), or in the category of theater that truly originates "in the room," through spontaneous interaction in rehearsal (Schechner) – since apparently independent action will in fact reiterate the most conventional prescriptions.[13] For an Adornian mindset, what aesthetic experience offers is not the realization or expression of our putatively individual desires as these bubble forth in a given moment but, on the contrary, a chance of allowing these desires to be fundamentally disrupted by something that is foreign to them. Indeed, "allowing" may not be the best word for this process, since as

Adorno emphasizes, it demands not a relaxation but "the utmost tension" (*Aesthetic* 245).

The *discipline* Adorno thus associates with what he calls "aesthetic comportment" (ibid.) has at least a partial parallel in his discussion of love in *Minima Moralia*. Here again, it would be wrong to overstate the analogy; the aesthetic for Adorno occupies a unique position, and there is no amatory equivalent of aesthetic comportment, since private life "cannot be lived rightly" in a world of totally systematic domination (*Minima* 39). Nevertheless, the sexual ethics of *Minima Moralia* resonate strikingly with Adorno's aesthetic theory, and not least with notes he was making the same year (1946) on the performance of musical texts. As readers of the later *Aesthetic Theory* often observe, moreover, Adorno frequently describes the artwork in personifying terms. Far from being merely rhetorical, this usage points toward particular ethical and erotic elements of the aesthetic, elements we're likely to miss if we're too eager to oust "the work" from our accounts of theater. Prompted by these resonances between the aesthetic and "the intimate sphere" (*Minima* 182) in Adorno, I want to suggest that his remarkable argument for sexual faithfulness can help to articulate the logic of the "faithful production" as I've been developing it here.

Adorno begins this argument by observing that "love is supposed to be involuntary, pure immediacy of feeling" (172). This bourgeois ideal is suspect, of course, but not entirely false: it implies a truthful protest against society's absolute norm of self-preservation. But that protest is neutralized, and the radical element of love is defused, by a society that can afford to offer this modest reprieve its blessing, while also working to ensure that the supposed "immediacy" reflects "a thousand nuances sanctioned by the order to make now this, now that person seem spontaneously attractive" (ibid.). In order for love's initial involuntariness to harbor any real utopian force, it needs to be maintained actively, *against* the dictates of this calculus – which means that it can no longer afford to be involuntary. Love opposes the conformism of self-interest only "by persisting where the force of social pressure does not want it" – a force our own desires have internalized, which speaks as if it were "the voice of the heart" (ibid.). So even though sexual fidelity as a norm is deeply problematic, constituting a violent curtailment of the subject's freedom, it also becomes a conscious practice of resistance, carried out in the name of the utopian moment it has had to forsake: "only through fidelity can freedom achieve insubordination to society's command" (ibid.).[14]

To attend to the peculiar kind of freedom that *Gatz* manifests through its own "perverse, extreme fidelity" (B. Fuchs 169), we have to step away from the assurance that text in theater is only ever "used" or "found," subject to the impulses that arise anew in each successive moment of the staging process. Suspending that rhetoric doesn't mean denying what is obviously true: a text cannot determine a production, any more than a moment of erotic surrender can, by itself, secure an entire extended relationship. But it does mean being willing to entertain the possibility that a text might make a rigorous claim on performance – a demand that wouldn't dissolve either in the confident familiarity of conventional staging procedure *or* in the innovations and departures of embodied theatrical experiment, but would continue to make itself felt throughout performance, as something for performance to live up to. There is indeed something "perverse" about *Gatz*: an unwholesome eagerness to commit itself to the text, in defiance of what "everyone knows" about the limits of love and the realities of theatrical practice.

Fletcher as Gatsby embodies this commitment, and Shepherd enacts it, but the piece as a whole makes us feel it: over time, through our physical experience of the piece's duration (the "marathon") and again with each increasingly gratuitous "he said." The six-hour show is broken up by two short intermissions and a long dinner break, an arrangement that qualifies the heroism demanded of the performers and the audience, but also fosters an unusual sense that you somehow belong *to* the piece, not just *at* it – you make dinner plans with its strictures in mind; you briefly pursue your separate agenda of eating, smoking, phoning, but then you come *back* to it. There's something cozy about this procedure, which reinforces the habituating effect you feel as you settle back into the rhythms of Fitzgerald's prose; as critics are wont to point out, the show doesn't feel too long. But there are moments when the "submission to the exclusive experience of reading" (Mead) doesn't feel good either, like the scenes featuring "Meyer Wolfshiem," a character introduced as "a small, flat-nosed Jew" (69). "Every description of him includes his nose. His nose takes over his whole presence," Shepherd remarked in an interview (Collins and Shepherd).

In performance, the first Wolfshiem scene, which takes place about twenty minutes after the first intermission, is a pretty dreary affair. Shepherd has just read a piece of casually racist narration describing "three modish Negroes, two bucks and a girl," at which both he and Fletcher seemed faintly disgusted; they have been sitting together at the office table, surrounded by an otherwise dark stage, and nothing changes when the scene shifts to lunch in "a well-fanned Forty-second street cellar" (69). Shepherd dutifully reads Wolfshiem's lines in a gruff old-

New-York-Jew accent that markedly fails to draw laughter; both Fletcher and Shepherd look listless, if not depressed.[15] After a few lines, the performer Aaron Landsman enters with a bag lunch, sits down at the table facing upstage, and begins to eat with them. Landsman plays a handful of roles in *Gatz*, including George Wilson, the sad-sack car mechanic married to Tom Buchanan's mistress; at the end of the novel, Wilson shoots Gatsby and then himself, thinking wrongly that Gatsby has run over his wife. Landsman wears Wilson's garage coveralls throughout the show, one of the only costumes to depart from office plausibility. After Landsman sits down at the table, Fletcher and Shepherd both seem to expect him to take over Wolfshiem's lines, but he doesn't do so at first, instead silently eating his sandwich in the dark. Only after Fletcher-as-Gatsby departs to make a phone call does Landsman jump in, and even then, he stays facing upstage; he exits before the scene is over, leaving Shepherd to resume the Wolfshiem lines. The show thus manages to maintain the Jew as a kind of non-character: by refusing a full embodiment, it withholds support from Fitzgerald's inanely anti-Semitic characterization, while the shadow-presence of Wilson lends a profound darkness, and sadness, to the scene.

It's a deft way of handling this strain of the novel, intellectually and emotionally satisfying without being heavy-handed. But particularly at the beginning of the sequence, when one piece of predictable racism segues into another, you get the sense that the company doesn't *want* to be doing this right now. Throughout *Gatz*, the company plays with the gap between the temporalities of narrative and performance; here, that gap becomes historical – what could apparently have been amusing in Fitzgerald's day, and now really isn't – but it's also doubled by the reappearance of yet another temporal discrepancy: between the moment when ERS made its commitment to staging the whole novel (or, when we made our commitment to watching it) and the *durée* through which that commitment gets lived. As the hours pass, this same tension registers in the tone of Shepherd's voice: it's not exactly strained, or flat, but most of the time it conveys a slight sense of obligation, as if the reading is something he *has agreed* to do, rather than something he *is deciding* to do. And of course, that's the case. One function of the drab office frame is to maintain a sense of erotic agency for the reading nevertheless, by contrasting it with a kind of work that makes no claims on anyone's desire. In this contrast, reading (and performing) emerges sharply as what we *do* want to do, even though that desire can't possibly be available to experience, for Shepherd or for us, over the course of all six hours.

This is not to say that *Gatz* functions as ordeal art, although as Jonathan Kalb suggests, marathon theater may always have some kinship with "endurance performance art" *à la* Marina Abramovic (*Great* 17). Both times I saw the show I enjoyed myself a lot – and even now, squinting at the video and taking notes like a pedant, I will catch myself giggling at a gag or marveling at how dexterous the performers are, the exquisite coordination of their spacing and timing. Sara Jane Bailes incorporates discussion of the company's striking virtuosity in her account of ERS's contribution to a "poetics of failure" in contemporary experimental theater (2010). Bailes is well aware of the paradox inherent in the notion that these artists are so good at failing; nevertheless, I'd suggest that *Gatz* is actually less engaged with failure than the earlier ERS shows that her book discusses at greater length.[16] Again and again, this performance surprises us with its resourcefulness in meeting the novel's demands. For example, when Tom's lover Myrtle (Laurena Allen) asks him to buy her a dog from a man selling them outside the train station, the performer and sound designer Ben Williams gets up from the table at stage right where he's been running sound, comes over to them, and with no noticeable affect, holds up a calendar featuring large color photos of puppies. When Allan/Myrtle asks if he has "police dogs," Williams reaches into his messenger bag ("plunged in his hand and drew one up") and presents her with a floppy clown doll, which she proceeds to play and snuggle with as if it were a puppy (38). Undoubtedly, part of the humor here comes from the way the performance isn't even trying to correspond exactly to the text, a layer of comedy on the side of what I've been calling the reality principle. But this is also a joke about how malleable the materials of reality really are in the service of fantasy. The most piquant surprise isn't that what Williams pulls from his bag fails to be a puppy, thus unmasking representation as a lie. Rather, it's that a Humane Society calendar and an old toy *can* be a basket of puppies for us – and that the stage has been set for this transformation the whole time.

"There must have been moments even that afternoon when Daisy tumbled short of his dreams," muses Nick, reflecting on Gatsby and Daisy's first reunion; but ultimately, like Henry James's Strether, Nick is excluded from the truth of the lovers' intimacy: "I went out of the room and down the marble steps into the rain, leaving them there together" (89–90). Nick's confidence that Daisy's performance "must have … tumbled short" is characteristically clear-headed, but in sending him out into the rain, the novel gestures negatively toward the fulfillment its narrator deems impossible. To clock *Gatz* as one more proof that performance always tumbles short – or flies free – of its text would simply replicate Nick's repudiation, turning its back on the crazier possibility that a live art might go about submitting itself, with great energy, ingenuity, and self-awareness, to captivation in the "dream" of a past-bound medium. "'Can't repeat the past?' he cried incredulously. 'Why of course you can!'" (100): Gatsby clings to a fantasy of fidelity, and comes to grief. But is Nick's tautological cynicism really the superior gestus, for lovers or for critics?[17]

As we'll see in the next chapter, Suzan-Lori Parks would also challenge Nick's assertion that you "can't repeat the past" – indeed, her work suggests, you can't *not*. In one obvious way, though, *Gatz* resists feeling like a reiteration of the novel: as a general rule, events get enacted onstage just before the narration mentions them, rather than happening afterwards (which would be "too stupid," as Williams explained to me). Barbara Fuchs writes that this anticipation "challenges the precedence of text over action and of the narrator over the characters narrated: they are not puppets to be moved about, but instead originate the action that he describes" (173). I agree that this procedure gives the novel's other characters more autonomy relative to Nick – it creates the impression that Nick is registering the behavior he sees, rather than instituting it – and it also enforces the sense of the entire performance as a collaborative endeavor, so that Shepherd (or his office "character") seems less like a ringleader than he otherwise might. But I am not sure that the "precedence of text" itself is being challenged here. Each time we hear a line that retroactively accounts for something we've just witnessed, it brings home to us how well the performance *already* knows this novel – has known it beyond and before the present in which we're hearing it actualized as speech. What seems like anarchic spontaneity in the moment keeps *turning out to have been* a rapprochement with the text.

Similarly, about forty minutes before the end of the show, Shepherd begins flipping randomly through the pages of the book as he "reads" the account of the inquest after Gatsby's murder; then he closes the book and sets it down ("And it rested there," 141) and recites the rest of Nick's words without opening the book again. The thrill of this turn isn't just about Shepherd's breaking free of the text-as-object; after all, he's managed to do quite a lot with it in hand. More profoundly, I think, the moment packs the punch of a classic recognition scene, in a twist different from the negation we saw in *Godot*. At the end of *Gatz*, what there is to recognize is the depth of the claim the literary work, apparently something we just "found," has had on us the whole time; the fact that freedom – Shepherd's freedom, the company's freedom, the freedom of performance – might be realized as the freedom to keep faith with an entity which, though it isn't ours (it's not of our devising, so to speak) has yet reorganized the field of our desire. In this vision, the everyday logic of performance is transfigured: no longer a series of "step[s] away from the text" (Müller), liveness now means *living up to* the text.

"What is essentially mimetic awaits [*erwartet*] mimetic comportment," writes Adorno; "only those who imitate [artworks] understand them" (*Aesthetic* 125/190). Adorno makes it clear that this imitation is ideally "inward and mute," something we can do privately; it is reception he is theorizing here, not performance (125–126). Nevertheless, this strange relation to the artwork is exactly what *Gatz* does stage. To really encounter the work, Adorno suggests, is to exercise our capacity for reshaping our own conduct along the lines of something really other, learning to meet *its* demands in a reprieve from the usual need to reassert our own – a "glimpse beyond the prison that [the I] itself is" (245). *Gatz* shows how this account of reception might also describe an approach to working with text in theater.

Historically, but especially at mid-century, critics have identified a specifically American theme in Jay Gatsby's "idealism" (Beuka 34, 47–51, 76). This association takes root in the famous closing passage of the novel:

> ... gradually I became aware of the old island here that flowered once for Dutch sailors' eyes – a fresh, green breast of the new world ... for a transitory enchanted moment man must have held his breath in the presence of this continent, compelled into an aesthetic contemplation he neither understood nor desired ... And as I sat there, brooding on the old unknown world, I thought of Gatsby's wonder when he first picked out the green light at the edge of Daisy's dock. (154)

If there is a special national resonance to Gatsby's wonder, and to the struggle against disillusionment that is a current of the novel, then we might ask whether there is also something fundamentally American about the way *Gatz* lives its enchantment with its text. Is it a coincidence that a widely successful, nationally and internationally touring production that reanimates the outdated ideal of *Werktreue* would come from America? After all, the United States lacks Germany's strong tradition of "directors' theater"; common knowledge holds that our theater is dominated artistically by writers, at least in the mainstream. Not that *Gatz* comes out of this playwright-centric mainstream in any direct way; Collins was an intern with the Wooster Group, and ERS's 2013–2015 collaboration with the writer Sibyl Kempson was the first time since 1991 that the company had staged a play.[18] But *Gatz* was something of a crossover hit for ERS, appealing to wider US audiences who might not have been game for the company's earlier shows. It's certainly plausible that this boost on the home front had to do with the piece's ability to satisfy a cultural predilection for text-based work.

As we've seen, however, the contemporary critical discourse on text and faithfulness presents strong parallels on both sides of the Atlantic, aligning Worthen and Fischer-Lichte, Mee and Jelinek, Schechner and Castellucci. *Gatz* offers an unsettling rejoinder to this discourse by enacting a Gatsbyish dedication to the textual object – a doggedness which, Adorno's writings might suggest, has more to do with global capitalism than with national identity.[19] *Gatz* has spoken to audiences in eleven countries. Given the institutional structure of international festival touring, it has been able to do this in part because, for all its outrageous literariness, it can be billed as a theatrical experiment devised by an ensemble – and not a play.

But the nature of this experiment helps us toward a new understanding of what plays themselves might do, and demand. The remaining chapters of this book will pursue that understanding further, through readings of plays by Suzan-Lori Parks and Mac Wellman. I hope this discussion of *Gatz*, at the outset, has provided some illumination from the "other side" of the relations between text and performance, relations these plays will also explore. With the inroads *Gatz* has already made into international theatrical culture, might we recruit it as a kind of secret agent for these text-as-text-as-theater *writers*, whose work – particularly Wellman's – is not widely known outside the United States? Giving a screwy turn to a global conversation about what happens to text onstage, ERS's romance with the "great American novel" shows what it might mean for theatrical performance in the postdramatic era to exert itself – perversely – on behalf of writing.

CHAPTER 5

The Promise of "Playwrighting"
Suzan-Lori Parks

> if you believe that history is in the present, you can also believe that the present is in the past.
>
> (Suzan-Lori Parks)[1]

It's not news that Suzan-Lori Parks's plays have something to do with modernism. Born in Kentucky, Parks began attracting serious attention in downtown New York while still in her twenties; her play *Imperceptible Mutabilities in the Third Kingdom* won an Obie Award in 1990, and her reputation and influence have grown steadily in the decades since. Her work has proven especially fascinating to scholars, many of whom have noticed its affinity with both Beckett's and Stein's.[2] When prompted, Parks herself has agreed that the canonical modernists are an important influence: "I'm fascinated with what they are allowed to do, I guess. What Joyce was allowed to do or what Joyce allowed himself to do, what Beckett allowed himself to do, what Faulkner allowed himself to do, Woolf ... What they got away with" (Drukman 72). Parks acknowledges that aspects of her work "com[e] out of that tradition of doing whatever you want ... and saying, 'Here it is! You Mr. or Ms. Critic, you guys go away and think about it and exercise your brains and come up with something thrilling!'" (ibid.). The Critics have done their best to comply, in a wide range of scholarship that has frequently circled back to the theme of Parks's "tradition" in one way or another.

I want to propose that this continuity is most significantly grounded in the way Parks takes over and redirects the project we have traced in James, Stein, and Beckett: the theatrical imperative of undermining dramatic presence. Reading Parks in terms of this project will also put her in dialogue with Adorno, a pairing that might seem strange to some of her fans. For one thing, Adorno infamously raged against jazz, whereas Parks has frequently cited jazz as a major influence on her work and a model for her dramaturgy of "repetition and revision" ("From *Elements*" 8). It has become clear that what Adorno meant by "jazz" was a commercialized, deracinated form, bearing little resemblance to the adventurous music of Ornette Coleman and other jazz artists Parks discusses (e.g. in Jiggets 316).[3] Still, some of Adorno's fundamental aesthetic values clearly run counter to Parks's poetics as they are most often understood. For starters, critics have championed Parks as a writer uniquely attuned to embodied performance, often citing her remark that "Language is a physical act" ("From *Elements*" 11). Parks would certainly not agree with Adorno that the "ideal" of artistic experience is "inward and mute" (*Aesthetic* 126), nor that performance is "a vestige of an obsolete and usually regressive practice" (100). Indeed, the very concept of the culturally "regressive," which Adorno frequently invokes, is at odds with the creative atavism Parks espouses when she writes that her work aims to "locate the ancestral burial ground, dig for bones, find bones, hear the bones sing, write it down" ("Possession" 4). And yet the last clause of this sentence – rarely emphasized in the readings that cite it – also hints at a convergence. For Parks, as for Adorno, the fixed or objectified form of what is *written down* seems to represent the artist's ultimate achievement.

As we saw in Chapter 1, Adorno considers objectivation fundamental to the artwork's autonomy, which for him means its insistent (though always mediated) "foreignness to the world"; this foreignness, and not any manifest political content, is what gives art its essential critical leverage. In one respect, this claim resonates with most scholarship on Parks: although social concerns are clearly central to her plays, their formal complexity has discouraged most readers from scanning them for straightforward messages. So has Parks herself: "Why doesn't anyone ask me about *form*?" she demanded during a 1990 talkback at Manhattan Theater Club (qtd. in Solomon 73). But critical response to Parks's work has tended to downplay its autonomy, or foreignness, in another way: through a kind of reading we might call "cocreationist." Karen Jürs-Munby, for example, includes Parks in a very short list of English-language postdramatic authors who "require the spectators to become active co-writers of the (performance) text" and to "reflect on their own meaning-making" (Introduction 6). This kind of claim sees the work's formal intricacies as soliciting a heightened level of participation from the audience. It's a familiar way of valuing "difficulty" in theater, as in literature and other media. In this context, though, it's strikingly reminiscent of another familiar story: text relinquishing its claim to determine or "dominate" performance, and only thus becoming really experimental or postdramatic. In this particular version of the tale, the power gets redistributed among spectators, rather than among other "theatrical means beyond language" (Lehmann 55); but as usual, the text is congratulated for renouncing self-sufficiency.

As we began to see with Stein, however, the common perception of experimental texts as emphatically participatory can obscure a different, equally powerful valence of some of this work. Obscurity can constitute an invitation to our faculties, but it can also produce a sense of indifference to, even rejection of, its audience. There is a kind of defiant hermeticism in a passage like the following, from Parks's *Imperceptible Mutabilities*:

> SHARK-SEER: I dream up uh fish thats swallowin me and I dream up uh me that is then becamin that fish and uh dream of that fish becamin uh shark and I dream of that shark becamin uhshore. UUH! And on thuh shore thuh shark is given shoes. And I whuduhnt me no more and I whuduhnt no fish. My new Self was uh third Self made by thuh space in between. And my new Self wonders: Am I happy? Is my new Self happy in my new-Self shoes? (39)

Such passages may or may not leave us cruelly flummoxed, but part of their pleasure lies in a certain palpable unconcern with what we "get" or don't. In interpersonal terms, this is downright rude – as if the text were suggesting that it could manage just as well without us. This might be a delusion; after all, the work could not exist without its audience. But the work's desire to flee from that fact, its current of unsociability, creates a meaningful variant of theatrical experience which the cheering picture of collaborative reception can easily obscure.

In Parks's case the jazz metaphor, with its connotation of collaborative improvisation, may have encouraged this picture. The direct address and playful, conversational tone she uses in her critical statements – "Write with yr whole bod. / Read with yr whole bod" ("From *Elements*" 18) – have no doubt also contributed to the sense of her work as soliciting our participation. But if we frame Parks's writerly difficulty as a retreat from the audience, rather than an invitation to the audience, then we can begin to see how her compositions actively inscribe writing's critical "foreignness" within work for the stage.

"Watch Me Work": Writing as (Counter)Performance

W. B. Worthen, one of Parks's most thoughtful readers, has observed that her work "consistently locates a differential interface between writing and embodying" and "urges a rethinking of the relation between writing and performance" (*Drama* 141, 164). He notes that she "visibly brings the apparatus of writing into performance in ways that focus our attention to the duality of poetry and performance" – for example, by having characters announce their own names at the beginning of a play, thus bringing a moment that conventionally belongs to play-*reading* jarringly onstage (169–170). Arguing that Parks thus "foregrounds the involvement of writing in dramatic embodiment" (163), Worthen offers a nuanced account of the ways Parks lets text haunt the stage.

The relationship "between poetry and performance" furnishes the subtitle of Worthen's 2010 book *Drama* and the subject of his ongoing critical thought, so Parks's various ways of stressing and sometimes straining that relationship constitute an investigation congenial to his own. Unlike Parks, however, Worthen argues that written plays are "agencies," or tools, of a theatrical performance that inherently exceeds them. Where Parks's own statements of poetics suggest otherwise, Worthen proposes an adjustment: "As Parks suggests, [her use of repetition] creates 'a real challenge for the actor and director as they create a physical life appropriate to that text' ('from Elements' 9), or, *more precisely*, as they use the text to create a physical life outside it" (165, my emphasis). His readings of Parks's *Venus* (1996) and, especially, of *The America Play* (1993) present the plays as outstripping her critical statements by embracing "performance as an act of difference – from history, from writing – that creates revision, change" (176). Worthen thus offers another version of the "cocreationist" reading of Parks: her plays acknowledge and even allegorize their provisional nature as texts, awaiting and inviting theatrical collaboration as the "act of difference" that will ultimately make them meaningful.

This chapter – indeed this book – is much indebted to Worthen's valuable articulation of "the relation between writing and performance" as a central issue in Parks's plays. But I also want to lend an ear to the statements in which Parks suggests that her texts are more, or other, than "agencies" of embodied performance events. I hypothesize that Parks's vision of the actor and director who must "create a physical life appropriate to [her] text" describes a specific critical orientation that emerges in her plays as well as her poetic statements, a structure that Worthen's version of these relationships might not account for. Having watched her plays take shape in production from a young age, Parks surely knows as well as anyone that a script gets "use[d]" in creating "a physical life outside it"; and I think we should be curious about why her remarks consistently skew away from this common sense.

For example, in a 2006 interview, Kevin J. Wetmore, Jr. asks Parks: "But what is the experience for you then, when you see these things on their feet? . . . Are there moments of discovery? Does someone else take your work and show you things about it, and it's a sort of accidental genius?" Parks replies: "Moments of 'genius' are all blessings, but I wouldn't say my moments of genius are accidental ... Mostly I write something that's good, I know it ... the parts of my plays that people think are really good, I usually know beforehand. It's not a surprise" (Wetmore 130). What's fascinating about Parks's response isn't just her refusal to adopt the requisite playwright's humility, the sense of grateful wonder we expect a writer to demonstrate when her work is "brought to life" onstage. Parks seems to be unabashedly taking credit for everything that's "really good" in the productions – but in fact, she has shifted the topic of discussion from production back to text: "I write something that's good, I know it." Accordingly, we can't tell whether the "people" who like certain parts best are viewers or readers; either way, we get the sense that one *might as well be* the other.

This vision recalls the hallucination we saw *Gatz* provoking: theater starts to seem like "a heightened version of reading" (Mead). For Parks, however, this claim has different practical stakes than for the members of Elevator Repair Service. As a writer, Parks occupies a particular position within the traditional division of theatrical labor, and she is insisting on the central importance of that position. The slip whereby she shifts attention from the spectacle of production to the scene of the writing, thus interposing the writer *as* the more interesting spectacle, has since been literalized in her performance piece "Watch Me Work": on select afternoons in the fall of 2010 (and again in 2013), for 75 minutes at a time, Parks sat in the lobby of The Public Theater, typing away for all to see. Promotional material online presented the event as a fundamentally democratic experience, inviting people to work on their own projects during the piece and promising that "During the last fifteen minutes of the performance Parks will answer any questions the audience might have regarding their own work and their creative process" ("Suzan-Lori"). "Come on down and hang out with me and get some of your own work done," Parks suggested in her online statement (ibid.). And indeed, on the afternoon I attended, most people did seem to be working on projects of their own. But despite the real currency of that invitation, the title's bravado signals a different kind of project, which no amount of camaraderie could have displaced: the desire to present the scene of writing as a worthy spectacle in its own right.[4]

Occupying a liminal space and an "off" time, "Watch Me Work" supplemented the theater's onstage productions rather than supplanting them; but I would argue that Parks's emphatic presence in the lobby constituted that space as a kind of reverse-backstage, a window into the authorial "work" from which, we might even imagine, theater itself originates (at the Public, Parks has held the Ibsenesque title of "Master Writer Chair"). Powered by Parks's fame as well as her personal beauty and charisma, the performance enacted the fantasy of a writing that would not need the cooperation of other scenic elements in order to deserve our attention as theater.[5] Parks may be courting narcissism, but her act becomes an argument for the theatrical sufficiency of the writer – and, by inescapable metonymy, of writing. Her much-read essay "From *Elements of Style*" (1995), which Worthen cites in the passage quoted above, includes sections with titles like "form and content" (7), "time" (10), and "humor" (15), but ends with one called "opening night": "Don't be shy about looking gorgeous. / I suggest black" (18). Besides acting as an elegant reminder that black is beautiful, these last lines insist on the playwright's spectacular value: don't hesitate to give the show onstage some healthy competition.

Many scholars have observed that language, in Parks's plays, seems to become distinctively corporeal: her writing "has an almost overwhelming o(au)ral component to its performativity" (Dixon 52), "concretizes language" (Ben-Zvi 191–192), presents "Words ... traumatically made flesh" (Kolin, "You" 49).[6] The implication often seems to be that these qualities simply confirm Parks's particular fitness for the stage, that her writing's "performativity" makes it all the more apt for enactment.[7] Critics have rarely admitted a different possibility: that the distinctive corporeality of Parks's writing might vie with, or even preempt, that of the performance. This theatrical dynamic occurs when language "confronts the field of performance with its own competing fields of embodiment and activity" (Garner 147), operating as "a kind of alien body which is either visually or acoustically performing on the stage of language, in a confrontation rather than a collusion with the actor's embodiment on the actual stage" (Čale-Feldman 100). And indeed, Parks herself consistently provides images of a writing that commands, or demands, more than its share of attention and power within the circuit of production.

Perhaps the most outrageous of these images emerges during the Wetmore interview, when Parks is asked to comment on "the way Hollywood devalues writers." Parks agrees: "too often, there are the industry people who don't see the connection between what the writer does and the final product. Just like there are people who don't respect their parents, or don't respect the earth" (127). Although directed at cinema, the unwieldy comparison is surely meant to apply to theater too. The fantasy of the script as our parent is difficult to square with the cocreationist model of the script as our partner; and it is hard to imagine a figure more directly at odds with the assumption that performance happens "outside" text than this image of the script as "the earth."[8] What Parks envisions here, if briefly, is a writing from which performance could literally never depart, a writing that would circumscribe all the eventualities of production – a page that would already be the stage.[9] Indeed, the earlier "From *Elements*" essay contains a canny slip in this direction, one I am sure is intentional: "My interest in the history of words – where they came from, where they're going – has a direct impact on *my playwrighting* because, for me Language is a physical act" (11, my emphasis). By imagining writing as "wrighting," Parks explicitly embraces the conflation that is, as I argued in Chapter 4, built into the grammar of the "play." To write a certain kind of text, for Parks and as per the improbable logic of the terms themselves, is already to make theater.[10]

Parks's language is performative; as J. L. Austin himself realized soon after inventing that word, all language is (91–93). But in the vicinity (say, the lobby) of actual theatrical production, a text that "performs" in a specifically theatrical sense will be erecting itself as an alternative stage, thus taking a position toward theater as practiced that must be, at some level, a challenge. This need not entail procedures for sabotaging performance, or features that "work better on the page than the stage" (Muse 227). Indeed, critics have often claimed that Parks's work is at its most "difficult" in print. Shawn-Marie Garrett comments that "when reading Parks' plays, one is frequently reminded that it is much more fulfilling to see them performed," even as she acknowledges that Parks "privileges the reader" in various ways ("Figure" 15).[11] The two remarks are not contradictory: the logic of "playwrighting" privileges a reader most fundamentally by including the prospect of performance within her purview. We might even pause over the indicative mood of the "reminder" Garrett describes: the play reminds us that "it *is*," not "would be," more fulfilling to watch it in performance, as if the text could simply summon its live counterpart into our experience. Parks's plays contest production not by standing in its way but, on the contrary, by behaving as if they left little for production to do.

Like Beckett, then, Parks discovers in theater the opportunity to test out writing's place in, or purchase upon, the actual. But whereas *Waiting for Godot* exacerbates dramatic *unity* by making writing achingly complicit with the dramatic present of its performance, Parks's plays invest writing with the force of a rival performance, one that must "pull focus" from the present and presence of the stage. By appropriating the phenomenal quality of presence for the alternative site of writing, these plays forcefully inscribe a structure of alterity within the actual. The performance event is both here *and* there, so reality presents itself as inherently multiform and malleable – the opposite of Beckett's tautological "muckheap."

The rest of this chapter will trace that logic as Parks develops it in her remarkable early play *The Death of the Last Black Man in the Whole Entire World* (1990). Throughout this script, Parks's work for theatrical performance positions writing both as a medium distinct from that performance and as performance's vanishing point, its utopian *end*. After introducing the play's explicit thematic of writing, I'll examine the way Parks uses repetition and other devices to displace the audience's investment from more traditional surfaces of engagement, toward the shadowy, not-quite-present site of composition. Next, I'll focus on a figure that emerges at the end of the play – the *burning page* – and suggest that this figure emblematizes the ethical and aesthetic complexities Parks discovers in the question of writing, particularly in the play's brilliantly disturbing central monologue. Finally, this analysis will return once again to Adorno, arguing that Parks's "playwrighting" reveals surprising theatrical possibilities latent in his theory – and, like *Godot*, excavates the utopian dimensions of writing for the stage.

Writing the *Death of the Last Black Man*

Practically any of Parks's plays could serve as a point of departure for exploring her theatrical poetics of writing. Her use of footnotes in several plays – sometimes spoken aloud by performers, sometimes left on the page for the reader – has drawn much attention, as have her various adjustments to the orthographic conventions of dramatic form.[12] While her later works, such as *The Red Letter Plays* (1999–2000), *365 Days/365 Plays* (2006–2007), and *Father Comes Home From the Wars* (2014), tend not to feature the same challenging language that she develops in her early texts, they foreground writing in other ways. For example, the two *Red Letter* protagonists are, respectively, learning to write (*In the Blood*) and branded with an alphabetic wound (*Fucking A*); in *Fucking A*, several passages are spoken in a made-up foreign language, to be accompanied by "a nonaudible simultaneous English translation" (115); and the entire premise of *365 Days/365 Plays* is Parks's ambitious commitment to writing a play a day for a year, an undertaking that provides the piece's "central focus" (Muse 224). Nevertheless, of all her plays, *The Death of the Last Black Man in the Whole Entire World* (1990) works and reworks the question of writing in the most formally and ideologically complex ways, and I will focus on that piece here.[13]

The play is a series of seven scenes: an "Overture," five "Panels," and a "Final Chorus." The first, third, and fifth "Panels" present the ambiguous homecoming of a man designated "Black Man With Watermelon." Black Man has been killed in the electric chair (in Panel I) and has been hanged from a tree (in Panel III), but continues to show up in the home he shares with "Black Woman With Fried Drumstick." Before, between, and after the three domestic scenes that rehearse this story, there are choral sections in which a cast of other "figures" joins the couple in riffing poetically on themes of what we might provisionally call black experience[14] – and on the titular death itself. In the course of these passages, several refrains emerge, and one of the most striking and insistent refrains is about writing:

YES AND GREENS BLACK-EYED PEAS CORNBREAD: You should write that down and you should hide it under a rock. This is the death of the last black man in the whole entire world. (102)
[...]
Mmmm. Yes. You should write this down. You should hide this under a rock. (103)
[...]
You should write it down because if you dont write it down then they will come along and tell the future that we did not exist. You should write it down and you should hide it under a rock. You should write down the past and you should write down the present and in what in the future you should write it down. It will be of us but you should mention them from time to time so that in the future when they come along and know that they exist. You should hide it all under a rock so that in the future when they come along they will say that the rock did not exist. (104)
[...]
You will write it down because if you dont write it down then we will come along and tell the future that we did not exist. You will write it down and you will carve it out of a rock. [...] You will carve it all out of a rock so that in the future when we come along we will know that the rock does yes exist. (130–131)

These lines convey, in fairly clear fashion, the stakes of writing within the play's universe, and of Parks's ongoing "interest in the artifact" (Geis, *Suzan* 34). As Alice Rayner and Harry J. Elam argue, the play labors to present "evidence of both the reality of the African American experience and, more importantly, of its absence in written Western history ... The effect of excluding written stories in a writing culture is for that culture to be haunted by an unsymbolized loss," whereas "To place the past symbolically by telling stories, writing it down, securing it under a rock, is to end the haunting" (455–458). Yes And Greens's refrain sounds the need for a written record and legacy, a longing for what Parks calls "inclusion in the canon of history" ("Possession" 5). In the context of this piece, lack of access to writing threatens a *total* death sentence, clinching the mandate of official and unofficial white "justice" and making Black Man's death valid for all time. This is the terrifying prospect not only of existing no longer, but of never having existed at all.

Parks herself has repeatedly said that she writes against a "fabricated absence" of blacks in the dominant historical record, "the story that you're told that goes ... You weren't here and you didn't do shit!" (qtd. in Drukman 67). Critics have understandably seized upon this straightforwardly political pursuit within Parks's project, and Yes And Greens's refrain is one of its most explicit articulations within the plays.[15] But it should be clear by now that the injunction to "write it down" is not just a synecdoche for representation in general; amidst the larger project of "re-membering" occluded black histories ("Possession" 5), the desire for writing in particular emerges as a distinct formal issue apart from the overriding ethics of historical recognition. I think the resistant force of "write it down" needs to be read not only in relation to the obliterating effects of dominant historiography ("You weren't there"), but also in relation to the performance medium – the site at which, constitutively, you *are*. In the context of theatrical performance, that is, "You will write it down" is not simply a demand for manifestation, for presence where there has been absence. Rather, the refrain articulates a double demand for *remediation*: it insists on the need for a political "action of remedying or correcting something" ("remediation"), but imagines this action as a formal transposition whereby what happens in the medium of performance gets taken up into an alternate medium.[16] As the future tense of "You will" makes clear, this transcription does not take place within the thing we are watching, here and now: writing is represented as a moment yet to come.

At the same time, the temporal span of the play as a whole is structured by what we might, bending Adorno's famous "wrong life" to our own purposes, call *wrong liveness* (see *Minima* 39). Black Man outlives his own deaths through a corporeal persistence that tortures both himself and his partner. His perpetual resurrection is not a blessed immortality, but a prolonged twilight of pain and disorientation: "Couldnt find us. Think I got lost. Saw us on up uhhead but I flew over thuh yard. Couldnt stop. Think I overshot [...] Overshot. Overshot. I would like tuh move my hands" (109).[17] In the play's premiere production, Black Man's inability to stay dead became darkly comic as a torment for Black Woman, who repeatedly greeted his returns to consciousness with annoyance bordering on rage (in Panel III); her line "Dont move" (119) was delivered as an earnest plea. On the other hand, the play also suggests that Black Woman herself is complicit in keeping her man monstrously alive after his time, and revisions that took place between the play's premiere and its publication emphasize the necessity of Black Woman's gradually coming to accept his death. The other figures take part in this transformation: thus in the First Chorus, Queen-Then-Pharaoh Hatshepsut recites a litany that begins "Yesterday tuhday next summer tuhmorrow just uh moment uhgoh in 1317 diedied thuh last black man in thuh whole entire world" as Black Woman repeatedly interjects: "No"; in the Final Chorus, Black Woman herself speaks the litany, while the entire cast repeats the word "Yes" (111, 129).[18] For his part, Black Man begs to be released from his undead state. "Make me uh space 6 feet by 6 feet by 6," he implores, "[...] I would like tuh get up and go" (109). So if, as Alisa Solomon has written, "the play implies [that] the greatest death of the Black Man is his being written out of history" (80), death itself is not the unambiguous evil we might expect it to be. Rather, Parks creates a certain productive tension between the aim of *forestalling* "the death of the last black man" by inscribing black life into the record, on the one hand, and the aim of *finishing* that death, burying the dead and acknowledging his passing, on the other. The play thus articulates two very different needs at once: the need to end the denial, and deferral, of death by ratifying and thus completing it – "Yes" – *and* the almost opposite need to fend off cultural oblivion by inaugurating and maintaining a textual trace.

This double desire – to lay the Black Man to rest on the one hand, to protest his genocidal obliteration on the other – has been described as a "paradox" that animates the play (Carpio 221–222). While this is certainly a powerful tension within the work, I am less inclined to view it as a paradox strictly speaking than as the program for a particular imaginative shift. The major task the play outlines is that of converting one form of persistence into another: the fantasmatic afterlife of the *scene* into the objective endurance of the *text*. Parks positions writing at and as the end of performance – "You should write *this* down," the deictic gesture sweeping performance along into the textualizing mandate. This is not to say that Parks's logic disdains or devalues live enactment; on the contrary, the repetition and revision of Yes And Greens's words emphasize the ongoing and differential way in which the successive moments of performance generate significance. "[O]nce before you die try dancing around as you write," Parks advises in "From *Elements*" (15). Like the image of the dancing playwright, Yes And Greens's refrain advocates a writing that has moved through performance – in this play, an elaborate, collective, emphatically embodied performance of mourning. But Parks also suggests that performance *lives on borrowed time*. It arises like a "ghost" from the closure to which it will ultimately be summoned once again:

BLACK WOMAN WITH FRIED DRUMSTICK: Thuh page.
ALL: 6 BY 6 BY 6.
BLACK WOMAN WITH FRIED DRUMSTICK: Thats right. (130)

The pull of this trajectory, I think, explains the logic of a line that becomes a motif in the play's Final Chorus: "Somethins turnin. Thuh page" (128–131). The line only appears within the final scene, a choice that runs counter to the play's prevalent patterns of repetition. Positioned thus, it announces the imminent end of the play: the turning of the page, it implies, can impart finality when even "death" could not. It is because the page can be turned, the book can be shut, that the presence of performance can be captured into history. By emerging when it does, this line asks a theatrical audience to envision the script as the enclosing frame – the monumental tomb – of the live event.

It would probably be inappropriate, here, to recall the Disney device whereby we zoom out from a story's final image to see it as the last page of a hefty-looking book, "The End" scrawled beneath it. In fact, however, Parks herself will later appropriate this image for the last segment of *365 Days/365 Plays*, which reads: "Lights bump back up to white-hot. / Zoom. / Onstage, the manuscript of *365 Days/365 Plays*" (376). The ending of *The Death* anticipates this move, which asserts the completed and enduring artifact of the text – what Adorno calls its "objectivation" – as the culmination of performance. We might speculate that the Disney device, born long before the VCR, was designed to make the viewer feel that the ephemeral experience of movie-watching could nonetheless still be hers to keep, that she could slip it into her pocket or place it by her bed – and perhaps also to remind her that the experience was, after all, repeatable (for a small fee). The ending of *365* may share, to some extent, in this cozy commodification; but thingness in *The Death* is another matter. Soyica Diggs Colbert has shown this in an essay drawing on Heidegger and phenomenological "thing theory," where she argues that *The Death* constructs a logic of fundamentally dangerous, disruptive "things": "In the moment of rupture when an object becomes a thing, the thing rearranges relationality, including historical inheritances" (217). Colbert suggests that the black body itself becomes such a "thing" in *The Death*, as do material objects like Black Man's noose (212). Whereas Colbert sees this materiality as fundamentally "question[ing] the hegemony of language" (193), however, I would argue that the most crucial "thing" for this play is the play itself *as* a work of language – the work of writing that offers the prospect of a closure, if not an absolute end, to mourning.

We see this prospect in the relation between the play's opening and closing lines:

BLACK MAN WITH WATERMELON: The black man moves his hands. *(A bell sounds twice)* (101)
[...]
BLACK WOMAN WITH FRIED DRUMSTICK: Thuh black man he move. He move. He hans. *(A bell sounds once)*
ALL: Hold it. Hold it. Hold it. Hold it. Hold it. Hold it. Hold it. (131)

On the one hand, the penultimate line's doubling of the first announces the survival of repetition, the continued pertinence of an experience that has emphatically *not* been laid to rest. This could go on forever – or, in the endlessly re-citable words of Beckett's Unnamable, "I can't go on, I'll go on." Parks points up the transmissibility of language, and indeed of body language, across different bodies; buried or not, Black Man seems to possess Black Woman and to speak through her, just as – we infer – other figures must have been speaking through him. The play's very last line, though, is new, and I think we are asked to hear it as both a confirmation *and a restriction* of Black Woman's repetition. "Hold it" is a command to keep something, to maintain its existence; and as Deborah Geis writes, "'Hold it' also means an order to stop, to put an end to what they are doing; in a play that in some ways (like *Godot*) is condemned to endless repetition, there is also a request to stop destructive versions of history, to wait and think. The play itself is ultimately the final container to 'hold' the re-membering of the Black Man" (*Suzan-Lori* 73–74).[19] But Parks, in a remark Geis quotes, makes it clear that "the play itself" functions this way only as a piece of writing: Black Man's "last resting place," Parks says, "is *within the pages* of the play – *it's a grave*" (qtd. 74, my emphases). The different meanings of "Hold it" coalesce in this figure of the specifically textual tomb, which cradles, keeps, and preserves its bodies even as it fixes them in place and limits their obsessive circulation, their performance in the present. The line is seven beats long, which means that the ear adds a final, silent beat at the end to make eight: the play thus ends by silently observing its own conclusion, as if with a breath of relief at having finally passed on.

The injunction to "Hold it" participates in precisely the kind of "survival" that Rebecca Schneider (drawing on Adrienne Rich) has theorized as performance's ongoing relation to textual and corporeal remains: "a critical mode of remaining, as well as a mode of remaining critical: passing on, staying alive, in order to pass on the past *as past*, not, indeed, as (only) present" (7). For Parks, too, survival means holding "the past as past," attending to the page/grave which alone might *contain* mourning's painful presentness.

Like all the works we've read, *The Death* treats presentness as a problem; here, the problem is the unmanageable and wildly painful still-going-on of things that happened long ago. The play immerses us in the fact that slavery and lynching, for example, are *still operating right now*, whereas they exist only insufficiently in the "canon of history." The last form given to Yes And Greens's refrain begins with a threat that expresses this sense of a wrong liveness: "You will write it down because if you dont write it down then *we* will come along and tell the future that we did not exist" (130, my emphasis). Earlier it was "they" who would "tell the future that we did not exist" (104); what the play seems to discover in this shift is that, murderous as the dominant culture's historiography may be, there is also something terrifying in the prospect of letting performance have the last word. The ghost, the performer who will "come along and tell," threatens to obliterate the past and commandeer the future through her own emphatic presence – unless that presence is transfigured as writing.

"Grave departures": The Theatrics of Mourning

Throughout her work, Parks pursues a strategy she refers to in "From *Elements*" as "Rep & Rev" or "repetition and revision": "a concept integral to the Jazz esthetic in which the composer or performer will write or play a musical phrase once and again and again; etc. – with each revisit the phrase is slightly revised" (8–9). "I'm working to create a dramatic text that departs from the traditional linear narrative style to look and sound more like a musical score," Parks explains, suggesting that "the 'climax' could be the accumulated weight of the repetition" and asking: "What does it mean for characters to say the same thing twice? 3 times? Over and over and over and o-vah [...] How does this Rep & Rev – a literal incorporation of the past – impact on the creation of a theatrical experience?" (9–10) While Rep

& Rev appears, to different degrees, in all of Parks's plays, *The Death* is her fullest exploration of its compositional and affective resources. Not only the choral sections but the three scenes featuring Black Man and Black Woman cycle through repeated phrases and actions. As Parks's exposition of Rep & Rev suggests, this layering not only produces a musical consistency but also conveys a psychological content – mourning tinged with obsession:

BLACK WOMAN WITH FRIED DRUMSTICK: You comed back.
BLACK MAN WITH WATERMELON: – Not exactly.
BLACK WOMAN WITH FRIED DRUMSTICK: They comed for you tuh take you. Tooked you away: that they done did. You got uhway. Thuh lights dimmed. Had us a brownout. You got past that. You comed back.
BLACK MAN WITH WATERMELON: Turned on thuh juice on me in me in I started runnin. First just runnin then runnin towards home. Couldnt find us. Think I got lost. Saw us on up uhhead but I flew over thuh yard. Couldnt stop. Think I overshot.
[...]
BLACK WOMAN WITH FRIED DRUMSTICK: You comed back.
BLACK MAN WITH WATERMELON: Overshot. Overshot. I would like tuh move my hands. (108–109)

While Parks's use of repetition does break with the dramatic economy of progressive action, this repetition does not – as it can, for instance, in Stein – work to disable empathetic identification. On the contrary, passages like these provide a kind of affective grounding for other, more free-floating and formalistic moments of repetition, drawing them into the orbit of heartbreak: the formal refusal of dramatic progression becomes identified with the emotional state of not being able to "get past" what has happened, and the danger of not getting through it. When, near the end of the play, Black Woman finally seems to accept the reality of her Man's death, the intensity of the moment certainly brings "the accumulated weight of the repetition" to bear, creating a powerful experience of accomplished mourning. It is difficult to convey this experience by quoting an individual passage, although lines like the following suggest how forcefully repetition functions as both form and theme:

BLACK MAN WITH WATERMELON: I got uhway?
BLACK WOMAN WITH FRIED DRUMSTICK: Nope. Yep. Nope. Nope.
BLACK MAN WITH WATERMELON: Miss me.
BLACK WOMAN WITH FRIED DRUMSTICK: Miss me.
BLACK MAN WITH WATERMELON: Re-member me.

BLACK WOMAN WITH FRIED DRUMSTICK: Re-member me.
[...]
Call on me sometime. Hear? Hear?
Thuh dirt itself turns itself. So many melons. From one tuh 3 tuh many. Look at um all. Ssuh garden. Awe on that. Winter pro-cessin back tuh back with spring-time. They roll on by us that way. Uh whole line gone roun. (128)

As Rayner and Elam observe, this scene "relies on traditional sentimentality and induces radical change – the catharsis as a wife kneels at the coffin of her dead husband. Yet the coded and loaded dialogue complicates the purely visceral response of an audience, requiring not only emotional but aural and intellectual recognition" (459). The text is nothing if not complicated; I would suggest, though, that rather than undermining the scene's "visceral" force, its "aural and intellectual" reverberations themselves become viscerally charged. This interpenetration takes place by way of a particular doubleness within repetition itself, a doubleness Parks exploits with great effectiveness in this play. Repetition, that is, can operate *both* as an invitation to emotional sympathy *and* as a sign of aesthetic structure, and Parks weds these functions almost seamlessly.

To see how this works, we might start by turning very briefly to Freud's account of mourning in the essay "Mourning and Melancholia."[20] While Freud does not explicitly theorize repetition here (as he famously does in "Beyond the Pleasure Principle"), his description of mourning is suggestive for *The Death*'s resurrective repetitions:

> Reality-testing has shown that the loved object no longer exists, and it proceeds to demand that all libido shall be withdrawn from its attachments to that object. This demand arouses understandable opposition ... Normally, respect for reality gains the day. Nevertheless its orders *cannot be obeyed at once*. They are carried out bit by bit, at *great expense of time* and cathectic energy, and in the meantime *the existence of the lost object is psychically prolonged*. Each single one of the memories and expectations in which the libido is bound to the object is *brought up* [*eingestellt*] and hypercathected, and detachment of the libido is accomplished in respect of it. (243–244, my emphases)

Although Freud's "eingestellt" does not connote the raising of the dead the way the English "brought up" does, the translator's choice seems attuned to the supernatural tenor of this process of recalling, in which "the existence of the lost object is psychically prolonged." Freud's account resonates with *The Death* not only through this description of mourning as a kind of recalcitrant afterlife, which he twice calls "painful" (243), but also through his emphasis on mourning's durational character. As a task that cannot be accomplished "at once [*sofort*]" but requires "great expense of time," mourning corresponds to Parks's interest in subjecting dramatic "climax" (her quotes) to a kind of temporal distension. To return to the register of our James reading, we might say that a Rep & Rev "climax" is not, as in drama, something that *happens* "at once" but rather something that *has been happening*, much like the "accomplish[ment]" of mourning. And we might further suggest that a dramaturgy of mourning is distinctively appropriate to a play that takes persistence itself as its problem; a play that wants to deal with ongoing historical suffering not by excising a single representative moment (as in realism's loaded day-in-the-life) but by grappling directly with ongoingness as such. The durational dimension of theater thus glows, in *The Death*, with a peculiar thematic significance. The phrase "Not yet," spoken seven times throughout the play (but not in its final scene), signals this recasting of theater's constitutive "expense of time" as a mourning mode.

The expensive replaying of life as afterlife is one way, for Freud, in which repetition structures mourning; but he also draws attention to another axis of repetition in mourning, if not exactly in these terms. "It is also well worth notice," he writes, "that, although mourning involves grave departures from the normal attitude to life, it never occurs to us to regard it as a pathological condition and to refer it to medical treatment" (242–243). After further description, he adds: "It is really only because we know so well how to explain it that this attitude does not seem to us pathological" (243). Freud is, in effect, critiquing the fact that we naturalize one kind of response to loss when another, similar response (melancholia) strikes us as pathological, and as usual, he works to defamiliarize the phenomenon we "know so well." But in the process, he repeatedly points out a fundamental social fact about mourning, namely, its remarkable ("*bemerkenswert*") familiarity – the fact that we always seem to know it when we see it, that seeing it always feels like seeing it again.[21] Freud suggests that mourning is a site at which the patterning of the social fabric stretches to accommodate a maximum of difference within the pattern: mourning's resurrective repetitions are "grave departures" *and yet* they are departures we can expect to see again and again, departures everyone is supposed to make – ourselves presumably included. Mourning is repetition, that is, not only within the individual psyche of the mourner but also interpersonally, in that we recognize each mourner's extravagance as one more manifestation of a common experience.

Enacting the structure of mourning, Parks's Rep & Rev activates this empathetic circuit. At the same time, however, she also deploys repetition's deeply defamiliarizing force. Within a literary context, Steven Connor argues, "It is repetition more than any other trope which draws the attention of the reader to the medium of language. 'Natural,' non-literary language is characterized by its flowing irreversibility … It is at the moment when we recognize that a repetition has taken place that language begins to bulk in our apprehension as arbitrary, systematic, and material" (15). Repetition functions to denaturalize language, reminding us that what we are reading or hearing is something other than the spontaneous expression of someone's soul – is, in fact, an effect produced through labor in the linguistic medium. In repetitive moments, we suddenly find ourselves watching a writer – or watching writing – work. And when Parks turns the defamiliarizing technique of repetition toward the fundamentally familiar and affectively accessible phenomenon of mourning, she is not exactly reclaiming repetition for the dramatics of "natural" motivation. As Rayner and Elam's comment suggests, repetition in *The Death* always exceeds the immediacy of emotional identification that it also grounds, as in this passage from Panel III:

BLACK WOMAN WITH FRIED DRUMSTICK: Sweetheart.
BLACK MAN WITH WATERMELON: SPRING-TIME.
BLACK WOMAN WITH FRIED DRUMSTICK: Sweetheart.
BLACK MAN WITH WATERMELON: SPRING-TIME.
BLACK WOMAN WITH FRIED DRUMSTICK: This could go on forever.
BLACK MAN WITH WATERMELON: Lets. Hope. Not.
BLACK WOMAN WITH FRIED DRUMSTICK: – Sweetheart.
BLACK MAN WITH WATERMELON: SPRING-TIME.
BLACK WOMAN WITH FRIED DRUMSTICK: Sweetheart.
BLACK MAN WITH WATERMELON: SPRING-TIME.
BLACK WOMAN WITH FRIED DRUMSTICK: This could go on forever.
BLACK MAN WITH WATERMELON: Lets. Hope. Not. (127)

Like any text spoken onstage, these lines can be accounted for with actorly objectives; in the play's premiere, Black Woman's repeated "Sweetheart" became an urgent appeal. On the page, though, the passage suggests nothing so much as a musical explosion, and its assertion of form over content ultimately resists complete "domestication" even in performance. The insistent repetition of "SPRING-TIME," at a level of emphasis deliberately disproportionate to its semantic relevance, makes this feel like a scene of possession: the characters are not simply articulating what they feel, but lending their voices to the establishment of a visual, aural, and conceptual composition. If we identify emotionally with the passage's evocation of mourning, as I think we are likely to do, this happens less through our identification with the characters individually than by letting the play work on us *as* a composition, a poetic complex.

"This could go on forever": the sentence is strikingly Beckettian, recalling Vladimir's "This is becoming really insignificant" (*Waiting* 243) or Hamm's "This is deadly" (*Endgame* 28). In these moments, the character takes on a measure of autonomy from the play as such, only to cast responsibility for "This" back on the playwright. While the prospect that this could go on forever is an outright torment for Beckett's characters, there is more room for ambiguity on Parks's stage of mourning; mourning's repetitions are, after all, attempts to keep the lost one in play. But whether Black Woman's "This could go on forever" is weary or wistful (in the premiere it was both by turns), the line does seem at first to *be* hers in a way that points up the alien provenance of the "Sweetheart/SPRING-TIME" alternation – until the line, and Black Man's rejoinder, are themselves drawn into the estranging circuit of repetition.

What is remarkable about Parks's work here is not so much her departure from empathetic, character-centered identification as her determination to make such departures while retaining the mechanism of identification within an emphatically mediated structure: to make us mourn with a play, not just with the characters in it. By drawing out both the psychological familiarity *and* the defamiliarizing force of repetition, Parks keeps the dramatic circuit of identification activated but distorts this circuit, stretching it out past what we can see to include the inaccessible totality of the work itself. She appropriates the felt presence of concrete enactment on behalf of a poetic organization whose principle (and principal) is felt as elsewhere. The displacement of character in these moments is a synecdoche of the displacement that befalls the live as such, its conscription into the alternate site of composition itself: watch *me* work. Parks turns the question of *who and what* we are seeing into a process of constant relay, amidst which the performer's present body only serves as one glancing point of contact.[22]

In fact, Parks has famously established her own preference for using terms other than "characters" to refer to the people in her plays. She discusses this point in a much-cited passage of "From *Elements*," under the heading "ghost." Here is the passage in full:

> A person from, say, time immemorial, from, say, PastLand, from somewhere back there, walks into my house. She or he is always alone and will

almost always take up residence in a corner. Why they're alone I don't know. Perhaps they're coming missionary style – there are always more to follow. Why they choose a corner to stand in I don't know either – maybe because it's the intersection of 2 directions – maybe because it's safe.

They are not *characters*. To call them so could be an injustice. They are *figures, figments, ghosts, roles, lovers* maybe, *speakers* maybe, *shadows, slips, players* maybe, maybe *someone else's pulse*. (12)

This claim that her figures are "not characters" has struck many readers as an expression of Parks's departure from realist mimesis.[23] More urgent here, I think, is her insistence on the irreducibly *mysterious* nature of the entities she describes. Itself a piece of poetic dramaturgy, the passage works as a demonstration of how to enact that mystery, producing a scene that continually asserts the partial nature of its own presentation. Saidiya Hartman has argued for the high political stakes of such "opacity" in black American cultural history: "the subterranean and veiled character of the slave song must be considered in relation to the dominative imposition of transparency and the degrading hypervisibility of the enslaved, and therefore, by the same token, such concealment should be considered a form of resistance" (36).[24] In Parks, this resistance produces a distinctive, non-dramatic theatricality, which Marc Robinson captures when he characterizes her work as "a theater in perpetual retreat from visual, verbal, and physical presence, recoiling as readers and viewers reach toward it" ("Remarks").

Robinson also asserts that "writing itself slowly recoils from our attention, as [Parks's] characters burrow into private, coded modes of expression" (ibid.). I find, however, that the passage above suggests a different logic. In its first sentence, the shadowy alterity of the "ghost" becomes an opportunity for the writer to assert herself as such. She writes and rewrites the scene through salvos of language ("say, time immemorial . . . say, PastLand . . . somewhere back there") that take up the blank space of the ghost's unknown provenance. The image of the "corner" that becomes so prominent here emphasizes the geometry of this productive partial occlusion – the opposite, incidentally, of the 360-degree visibility murderously imposed upon the Venus Hottentot in *Venus*. And the rich proliferation of preferable alternatives to the term "characters" likewise asserts a kind of conspiracy between partial access and poetic possibility, both of which are contained in the unexpected (and easily elided) word "could" in Parks's "to call them characters *could* be an injustice." If figures are not characters, this distinction is meant to protect them less from the depths of psychology than from the surfaces of spectacle: Parks wants to create theatrical beings capable of withholding themselves, whose reticence becomes a chance for her own virtuosic verbal speculation.

"The Figures" listed at the beginning of *The Death of the Last Black Man in the Whole Entire World* have names that mark, more aggressively than those in any other Parks play, how writing sets up shop amidst aporias or recesses of character:

> Black Man With Watermelon
> Black Woman With Fried Drumstick
> Lots Of Grease And Lots Of Pork
> Yes And Greens Black-Eyed Peas Cornbread
> Queen-Then-Pharaoh Hatshepsut
> Before Columbus
> Old Man River Jordan
> Ham
> And Bigger And Bigger And Bigger
> Prunes And Prisms
> Voice On Thuh Tee V (100)

As several critics have observed, the stereotypes of watermelon, chicken, and grease operate as signifiers of racism here, which Parks subjects to parody.[25] But beyond lambasting that typology, Parks uses the ideological weakness of stereotypes to explode the principle of dramatic exposition itself. What she attacks is not just ham-handed stereotyping, but the basic dramatic expectation that a play will *present* the whole truth of its characters. In refusing to meet this expectation, Parks harks back to both Stein and James; her *dramatis personae* pointedly rejects the "bold strokes, black and firm" that James was faulted for withholding (Edel 212–213). As we begin reading down her list of figures, or as we hear the performers present their names in turn, we start off with a readerly confidence: "yup, stereotypes are wrong," we say, patting ourselves on the back for getting it. But the third name begins to complicate things: "Lots Of Grease And Lots Of Pork" continues the "soul food" association, but doesn't look much like the name of a person (if it were the last entry, it might seem to refer to a group or chorus). "Lots of Grease and Lots of Pork" can, however, still function at least grammatically as a subject; it is also a rhythmically simple phrase, easy on the inner (or outer) ear. The next entry, "Yes And Greens Black-Eyed Peas Cornbread" tumbles from even this degree of clarity into a Stein-type syntax, and the tongue trips over its challenging scansion.

By this point, we've become aware that there is something *other* than straightforward political parody going on, and something other than the presentation of character. And this something other – which clouds both surfaces of presentation, the characterological and the political – is an irruption of writing. Language begins to make a spectacle of itself precisely where the presentation of character becomes narratively and ideologically murky. It is no accident that the figure with the weirdest name becomes the mouthpiece for textual longing, as we saw above; Yes And Greens Black-Eyed Peas Cornbread marks a writerly spot at which the pleasure of verbal elaboration outweighs the exigency of dramatic manifestation, a place where the question of *who is here now* (on the page, on the stage) yields to a trace of the poet.

The Burnin Page

Despite these assertions of textuality, some readers have found *The Death* profoundly critical of writing as such. Malkin argues that the play "posits and develops two sets of images: images of orality, loose, unstructured, flowing, with its closeness to memory; and images of textuality, recorded, annotated, grammatically correct, with its affinity to history" (166). After quoting a passage from the play, Malkin remarks:

> Note the difficulty in reading this transcription of a form of black language. It comes alive, however, and becomes transparent when read aloud, when performed as an oral text. The obscure written form attests to a conscious rejection of standardized scripture as itself a form of control. The reader's difficulty in scanning Parks's texts is increased by her transcription of . . . the visceral soundings of her figures. Nonsemiotic noises are often written onto her page as musical moans that evoke an uninscribed – perhaps uninscribable – preliterate world. (159)

As we'll see in the final section of this chapter, Malkin is right to identify a longing for a "preliterate world" in this play.[26] But readings that emphasize the "oral" orientation of Parks's texts risk obscuring the ways in which Parks actively appropriates orality *for writing*. Far from asserting the realm of the "uninscribed – perhaps uninscribable," tran*script*ions like "thup," "uuh!" and "gaw" claim the visceral *as* inscribable, writing the body into the scansion of the textual line.

And while Parks certainly wields her right to depart from the grammar and "standardized scripture" of a dominant "standard" English, her ongoing practice has demonstrated that she is quite interested in developing a standardized grammar of her own. In naming her poetic statement "From *Elements of Style*" after Strunk and White's manual, she playfully cops to this ambition; and she has included excerpts of "From *Elements*" in the front matter of all her subsequent plays, where it functions precisely as a guarantee of consistent, if deviant, grammaticality in her writing. Her poetics are less about "(Un)Grammar" (Malkin 166) than about defamiliarizing and hence emphasizing – and enjoying – the operations of grammar itself.

Nevertheless, it would be wrong to claim that *The Death* straightforwardly or univocally validates writing. Writing in itself is not the solution to the problems the play explores; rather, it is the field where that solution might be discovered. To that end, Parks's figures are continually testing out different conceptions and strategies of writing – and in particular, different modes of relation between writing and the problematic present of performance. The question of what writing is for, or how it should function, arises strikingly in a passage in the Overture:

QUEEN-THEN-PHARAOH HATSHEPSUT: I saw Columbus comin./I saw
 Columbus comin goin over tuh visit you. [. . .] I ain't seen you since.
LOTS OF GREASE AND LOTS OF PORK: In the future when they came along I
 meeting them. On thuh coast. Uh! Thuh Coast! I – was – so – polite. But in
 thuh dirt I wrote: "Ha. Ha. Ha."
ALL: Ha. Ha. Ha. Ha. Ha. Ha. Ha. Ha. Ha. Ha. Ha. Ha. Ha. Ha. Ha. Ha.
 HHHHHHHHHHHHHHHH. (104)

The passage is so unsettling because it tells a story whose import is at once tremendously urgent and violently uncertain. On the one hand, it describes one of those "acts of defiance conducted under the cover of . . . seeming acquiescence" that we have learned to look for in the aesthetic traditions of the oppressed (Hartman 8). The sly writing "in thuh dirt" certainly invokes such traditions, suggesting an imaginative victory over the enslavers. And yet there is also something horribly insufficient about this gesture in the face of atrocity, a sense that the joke wasn't really on "them" at all.[27] Neatly marked off in punctuation, the scribal " 'Ha. Ha. Ha.' " wears the face of an enigmatic artifact, an address to some future reader who might recognize its import. But the collective performance it authorizes feels like a burden, not a liberation: a numbingly complete set of sixteen uniform beats, fading into a sigh. At the very end of the play, this passage recurs in revised form:

HAM: In thuh future when they came along I meeting them. On thuh coast.
 Uuuuhh! My coast! I – was – so – po-lite! But. In thuh rock. I wrote:
 ha ha ha.
ALL: Ha. Ha. Ha. Ha. Ha. Ha. Ha. Ha. Ha. Ha. Ha. Ha. Ha.
 HHHHHHHHHHHHH. HA! (131)

This time a more idiosyncratic fourteen beats of "Ha" fall short of the rote sixteen, as if the collective desire to sigh can now interrupt the ritual rule. The sigh is shorter than before, though, and followed by the new, ferociously powerful "HA!"[28] In its last moments, the play seems to have found a writing that can meet the urgency of the present – and thus empower mourning to conclude. This is the text not just written in the dirt but "carve[d] out of a rock," just as Yes And Greens also demands in her final refrain.

Such a text would be distinguished by its endurance, of course – it is written in stone, there for the ages, part of the "canon of history" – but also by the work required for its production, effort we can literally hear in the heaving caesurae of Ham's "But. In thuh rock. I wrote." The now-unpunctuated and unquoted "ha ha ha" becomes part of the rhythm of his lithographic labor, a text that bears the action of its emergence as it completes that action. The increased pain of "Uuuuhh! My coast!" (compared to "Uh! Thuh coast!" in the earlier passage), the extra strain of being "po-lite" (not just "polite"), seem to fuel the hard work of carving. The play suggests, here, that the only writing worth doing – the only writing that will "Hold" a people's suffering – is one that makes us Watch It Work. If this work is the working-through of mourning, it is also the enactment of writing *as* theatrical performance, at once emphatically corporeal and inherently reiterative, addressed to an audience of viewers, but issuing from the unrecuperable site of the present's prehistory. Imagining "thuh rock" as the medium of such performance, Parks offers the ultimate artifactuality as the acme of lived process, the deadest letter as the repository of the most live art.

At the same time, given that the rock gets carved precisely on the eve of transatlantic slavery, we might suspect that the work ethic involved is more complex than this reading suggests. Behind the labor of writing so keenly evoked lies the specter of forced labor, and capitalism's reduction of human value to labor's quantifiable "performance." Might not writing – and particularly writing so strongly imaged as work – be just another kind of participation in that economy? This question could return us to Parks's invocation of stereotypes, discussed above; in this connection, the discourse of stereotype in *The Death* signals not only the violence of prior representations but the underlying fact that writing, indeed any representational practice, can easily "work" in the service of domination. As Worthen rightly observes, writing appears here as "both an antidote to historical erasure and the compromised instrument of historical oppression" ("Citing" 8). Despite the play's historiographical imperative,

Worthen remarks, "Writing it down is ... problem as well as solution in *The Death of the Last Black Man*, for writing ... has also framed African American identity in history, as (for example) the stereotypes registered by the names of the characters themselves. Writing cannot undo the repetitive structure of history in Parks's plays" (ibid.). We have discussed how Parks's use of repetition invokes both its defamiliarizing literary force and its affective intensity as mourning; but Worthen here alludes to a third face of repetition that the play presents. Repetition is also, for Parks, the violent pedagogical device whereby an official discourse is gradually inscribed, through forced reiteration, into the pupil's "word hoard" (Parks, *Death* 121).

The figure named Prunes And Prisms is the most explicit embodiment of this mode of repetition: "Say 'prunes and prisms' 40 times each day and youll cure your big lips. Prunes and prisms prunes and prisms prunes and prisms: 19" (113; cf. 111, 116, 128). While this figuration of a deforming pedagogical repetition is emphatically oral, the phrase is taken from a passage in Joyce's *Ulysses* (Geis, *Suzan* 70–71) which itself cites a prominent motif in Charles Dickens's *Little Dorrit*, and thus attests to the textual transmission of such reformatory echoes.[29] The figure And Bigger And Bigger And Bigger, meanwhile, articulates a more obviously literary version of this recursive incorporation: derived from Bigger Thomas, a character in Richard Wright's *Native Son*, he "represents literary history's portrayal of the black man as both murderer and martyr" (ibid. 69–70; cf. Rayner and Elam 453). This figure's very name enacts the shaping force of a text that returns obsessively, as he himself suggests: "Rise up out of uh made-up story in grown Bigger and Bigger. Too big for my own name" (115). Like Prunes And Prisms, he bears racist discourse on his body: "Nostrils: flarin. Width: thickly. Breath: fire-laden and smellin badly" (ibid.).

While Parks's citation of Wright is not squarely a critique, it seems fair to say that Bigger Thomas haunts the play as a particularly painful representation of blackness – more seriously disturbing than the watermelon-and-chicken cartoons.[30] And Bigger And Bigger And Bigger's name enacts the basic principle of Parks's composition whereby repetition achieves "accumulated weight," since a word like "bigger" grows each time it repeats – perhaps not unlike the slur it rhymes with.[31] He thus stands doubly for a violence incipient in writing: in Wright's (and in "the canon" as such), but also in Parks's own. The fact that And Bigger's lines repeatedly double those of Black Man With Watermelon suggests a parallel between supernatural and textual bedevilment, a lingering doubt about whether the page really *does* lay to rest. It also intimates the prospect that the playwright herself could be creating a literary monster. Indeed, And Bigger And Bigger And Bigger seems to articulate a specifically theatrical danger of writing when he says "I am grown too big for thuh word thats me" (116). To author a figure, this suggests, is to authorize its corporeal burgeoning beyond the page; but this burgeoning – an analog, perhaps, for performance – is imagined as a kind of torture, since the strictures of the script remain: "WILL SOMEBODY TAKE THESE STRAPS OFF UH ME PLEASE?" (110, 111).

In such moments, Parks does seem to envision writing as "scor[ing] its performers" (Worthen, *Drama* 165), in the most painful possible sense. Repetition, here, is not separable from the kind of discipline that enforces the official (broken) record. By embracing repetition as a formal principle, Parks acknowledges the danger that the writer – and particularly the playwright – might be complicit in such regimes. One source of the play's powerful complexity is the way its refrains incorporate dominant narratives. For instance:

BEFORE COLUMBUS: The popular thinking of the day back in them days was that the world was flat. They thought the world was flat. Back then when they thought the world was flat they were afeared and stayed home. They wanted to go out back then when they thought the world was flat but the water had in it dragons of which meaning these dragons they were afeared back then when they thought the world was flat. They stayed at home. Them thinking the world was flat kept it roun. Them thinking the sun revolved around the earth kept them satellite-like. They figured out the truth and scurried out. Figuring out the truth put them in their place and they scurried out to put us in ours. (103, cf. 115)

The story about people "thinking the world was flat" before Columbus is less a piece of history than a signifier of "history" – a pop-cultural cliché that evokes the elementary school classroom. The illogical interpolation of dragons (why would the world being round make them any less frightening?) suggests a kind of compression, a compulsion to force the facts into a repeatable narrative whether or not the story makes sense. That repeatable narrative is the old one heroizing Europe's global depredation as a matter of having "figured out the truth." The speech itself undermines this spurious narrative, particularly in the sentences "Them thinking the world was flat kept it roun" and "Them thinking the sun revolved around the earth kept them satellite-like," which leaps into a poetic register with its quasineologism. The disdain implicit in the word "scurried" also suggests a revisionist impulse. But the last sentence reasserts fundamental categories of the old story, even if it also questions them: "their place" and "ours." Parks thus subjects her figures – and performers, and audience – to a painful process of reinscription, painful precisely because the vital poetic work of revision is bound up with the belaboring of tyrannical old scripts.³²

When, near the play's end, "Somethins turnin. Thuh page" morphs temporarily into "Somethins burnin. Thuh page" (130), there is thus a double urgency to this second phrase. On the one hand, the burning of the page is something that must be stopped, or repaired, insofar as it represents the extermination of the black record – an ultimate lynching. In this sense, the phrase sounds a note of peril, which motivates Yes And Greens's last lines about "writ[ing] it down." On the other hand, though, "Thuh page" also names a technology of oppression that needs to burn, and the refrain can also be hopeful, triumphant. But both of these readings are to some extent subsumed in a third, which I want to advance here. I think we need to take "burnin" as, so to speak, strongly intransitive: the page is not *being* burnt (à la *Hedda Gabler*) but burning like a torch, or like the bush through which God spoke to Moses. This association is hardly a stretch, given the impending Mosaic image "you will carve it out of a rock" (131) as well as the ongoing question of whether Black Man can find "words for partin" the river across which he might escape (129, cf. 112–113, 116). If "thuh page" is burning in this sense, then we are being asked to consider the page as a site of both violence and victory, an ongoing and inexhaustible spectacle in itself.

If I am right, then the burning page is a key figure for Parks's theatrical poetics. To see more concretely what this means, we can turn to the play's most sustained exploration of what a burning page might look like in performance: Ham's monologue in the Second Chorus (121–124). Ham's name may echo *Endgame*, but his speech – a "showstopper" (Geis, *Suzan* 64) – might well remind us of Lucky's tirade in *Godot*, with its central placement and disruptive copia. Itself a mock genealogy announced as "Ham's Begotten Tree" (121), the speech also makes explicit the troubling genealogical ties between explosive monologue, as a staple of experimental playwriting, and the American minstrel tradition – in particular the "stump speech" of minstrelsy upon which Ham's speech is modeled.³³ "Wassername she finally gave intuh It and tugether they broughted forth uh wildish one called simply Yo. Yo gone be wentin much too long without hisself uh comb in from thuh frizzly that resulted comed one called You (polite form). You (polite) birthed herself Mister, Miss, Maam and Sir who in his later years with That brought forth Yuh Fathuh [...]" (121). The "shame" echoed by the other figures after the first half of this monologue invokes the racial shaming inherent in minstrelsy, linking this to the shame imputed to Black people as the descendants of the biblical Ham:

HAM: [...] Yo in Yes Missy begottin ThissunRightHere, Us, ThatOne, She (thuh 3rd) and one called Uncle (who from birth was gifted with great singin and dancin capabilities which helped him make his way in life but tended tuh bring shame on his family)
BEFORE COLUMBUS/BLACK MAN WITH WATERMELON: Shame on his family.
LOTS OF GREASE AND LOTS OF PORK/BLACK MAN WITH WATERMELON: Shame on his family.
AND BIGGER AND BIGGER AND BIGGER/BLACK MAN WITH WATERMELON: Shame on his family gaw.
YES AND GREENS BLACK EYED PEAS CORNBREAD: Write *that* down.
OLD MAN RIVER JORDAN: (Ham seed his daddy Noah neckked. From that seed, comed Allyall.) (122)

In the context of this play's emergence, this "shame" of family ties might also infect the downtown New York theater audience, who would need to recognize their own susceptibility to the pleasures of a minstrel form, as well as experimental theater's ongoing indebtedness to that form, from *Godot* onward.[34] Parks will explore the theatricalization of blackness in *Venus*; Ham's monologue anticipates the later play's simultaneous offer and critique of such spectacular enjoyments. When the Second Chorus ends with Lots of own Grease repeating the play's signature line – "This is the death of the last black man in the whole entire world" (124) – "This" seems to refer to Ham's speech itself, as if to position death by minstrelsy alongside electrocution and hanging. And indeed, the "burnin" that would round out the play's collection of deaths takes place nowhere if not here, in the burn of shame – which, like the play's other murders, is centered on Black Man – and, at the same time, the hot spectacle of Ham's energy and virtuosity.

If Beckett's Lucky begins his tirade by describing those "plunged in fire whose fire flames if that continues and who can doubt it will fire the firmament that is to say blast heaven to hell" (*Waiting* 141), Parks too unleashes the fiery force of monologue, feeding the flames with a mixture of political and libidinal kindling. But whereas Lucky's speech is framed as a horrifying interruption, Ham's seems more like par for the course: "Thuh list goes on in on," other figures respond (122, cf. 124).[35] Ham's performance, more than Lucky's, is woven into the social fabric of its world; it already has a place, just as its content both describes and reinscribes the logic meant to "put us in ours." Although the speech does not repeat in the play, it partakes of the pedagogical mode of repetition, a narrative that "scores" as it excoriates. Just as the play as a whole contemplates the uncanny inclusion of atrocity within the cycles of the everyday ("This could go on forever"), Ham's monologue combines a maximum of dissonance with an obvious and ironic sustainability. It can thus figure the *economy* of American slavery, which becomes the explicit subject of its second half (the superscript numbers are presumably meant to be spoken aloud):

> HAM: SOLD! allyall^9 not tuh be confused w/allus^{12} joined w/allthem^3 in from that union comed forth wasshisname^{21} SOLD wassername^{19} still by thuh reputation uh thistree one uh thuh 2 twins loses her sight through fiddlin n falls w/ ugly old yuhfathuh^4 given she^8 SOLD [...] let us not forgetyessuhmassuhsuh^{38} w/thou^8 who gived up memines$^{3-0}$ SOLD we are now rollin through thuh long division [...] (124)

On one level, this turn literalizes the notion that minstrelsy perpetuates slavery's objectification, and the threat that black artists might extend this legacy by selling out (the "great singin and dancin capabilities which helped him make his way in life but tended tuh bring shame on his family"). As Ham becomes an auctioneer, his discourse shifts from recording to enacting "thuh long division" which is not only slavery's systematic breaking-up of families, but also the world-rending violence of the Middle Passage itself. By weaving this catastrophic division into the overt theatricality of the stump speech, a form of *repertory* entertainment and a virtuosic feat of *memorization*, Parks creates an analog for the Mosaic fire that burns furiously without actually consuming its medium – this time as a disaster that could "go on forever," blaze anew every evening, plus matinees. Lucky has lost his powers of speech in the second act of *Godot*; Ham, however, never gives us cause to doubt that he can go on reciting his litany nightly. In other words, Ham's speech lets Parks emphasize the theatrical structure of historical suffering: maximally live, but given to prescription, repetition, and institution. As always, it is the "showstopper" that best serves the mandate that the show must go on.

Locating the play's negotiations of minstrelsy within a tradition of late-twentieth-century black writers, Glenda Carpio points out that Parks's evocations of the minstrel show "underscore the ways that the very medium in which she works has been complicit in making black suffering into spectacle" (206). Not only theater, but the writing that scripts this debacle is thereby implicated in the perpetual motion machine of suffering. Yet Carpio argues that Parks, even while invoking minstrelsy, "makes those minstrel features abstract and unfamiliar and turns them into vehicles for remembering and honoring the dead"; Ham's speech "so expertly signifies on the language of the minstrel stage that it turns that language inside out ... [and] creates a laughter that mocks the laughter of minstrelsy" (206, 211). I agree, and I would add that Parks's outdoing of minstrelsy in this speech occurs as an emphatically *textual* intervention. Writing is more than just the score for, or prehistory of, Ham's painfully live performance; rather, his speech becomes an opportunity for Parks to explore the theatrical and political force of writing at grips with scenic enactment.

Thus, for example, the exponents that appear in the last part of Ham's speech play with and on writing as "scientific notation," suggesting that there is no purely quantitative transcription (cf. Malkin 172): this is a thesis about writing, whether we see the text or hear it. If "allyall^9" is easily naturalized in performance as "allyall the ninth," the same doesn't apply to "memines$^{3-0}$," forcing the issue of notation onto the stage (in the premiere, figures like "3–0" got pronounced "to the three-oh," revising our understanding of the earlier ordinals). Similarly, parentheticals like "You (polite)" invoke the orthographic experience of the phrasebook; carrying them off means keeping this specifically textual rhythm alive in performance.

More fundamentally throughout the speech, the comic use of pronouns and interjections as names – a device which should remind us of Stein – teases out the consistency of print. By turning "She," "That," and "Themuhns" into names (121–122), Parks transposes the reification that freezes an act of speech into a piece of text, and parodies the standardizing force of Record. But it seems no less significant that these names lose their capital letters in the slave auction: orthography may be reifying, but as such it implies the legitimate desire to claim a permanent place, to "carve it out of a rock." As long as the makeshift names *are names* they can appropriate a history; losing their capitals in the "long division" of slavery, they get swept away in the indifference of capitalist exchange. As Carpio observes, the pronouns ultimately "emphasize rather than fill the gaps of history" (212); between the heroic genealogical effort of "She (thuh 3rd)" and the bitter statistic of "she^8 SOLD" there is a difference of writing, a trajectory that cannot be drawn without reference to the page.[36] Parks signifies on writing, that is, precisely by flipping its position from the means ("agency") of performance to something performance means – from the signifier to the (still signifying) signified.

The sense that Ham's speech is centrally concerned with writing is voiced by Rayner and Elam, who remark that in Ham's monologue "Parks is signifyin(g) on the construct of writing" (459). The authors are referring to Parks's statement that as a writer she is trying to represent "the patterns of a people whose language use . . . not only Signifies on the non-vernacular language forms, but on the construct of writing as well. If language is a construct and writing is a construct and Signifyin(g) on the double construct is the daily use, then I have chosen to Signify on the Signifyin(g)" (qtd. in Solomon 75–76). Parks, in turn, is referring to the concept of "signifyin(g)" as theorized by Henry Louis Gates: "the Signifying Monkey . . . is our trope for repetition and revision, indeed our trope of chiasmus itself, repeating and reversing simultaneously as he does in one deft discursive act" (Gates 236).[37] To signify on "the construct of writing," then, would be to assert or present writing in a way that changes what writing is, what "writing" means. For Rayner and Elam, this subversion plays out in the way Ham's monologue resists being read on the page: "It is meant for an audience to hear and for an actor to perform" (459). But this intention inheres in even the most traditional playwriting, and I don't believe Parks's major thrust in Ham's speech is to undermine the textual. On the contrary, Parks's "signifying on writing" means – true to Gates's theory – *playing with* writing, or *keeping it in play*.

What this practice does undermine is dramatic convention, since as we saw in Chapter 1, drama has traditionally entailed the disavowal of pre-existing text. Parks reverses this orientation by placing writing center stage. The wounds of slavery, she suggests, demand a reckoning not only in writing but as writing; text will have to be more than a means of memory or representation in this reckoning, where its consistency as text is somehow crucial to any working-through that can occur. And in fact, besides riffing on the minstrel show, Ham's monologue also echoes a decidedly literary source: "The Bear," a story by one of Parks's favorite modernists. In "The Bear," William Faulkner's protagonist Isaac McCaslin is haunted by the ledgers that document his family's antebellum slaveholding, including – between the lines – the rape and incest corollary to such possession. As in Ham's speech, a stilted and improbable humor woven into the initial entries gives way to a sense of horror; Isaac's (and the reader's) ethical awakening is a matter of learning to *read* the ledger, just as his coming-of-age as a hunter entails learning "to distinguish the [titular bear's] crooked print" (186).[38]

Parks's own genealogy transposes this literary wrangle to the minstrel stage. At the same time, she reappropriates minstrelsy's "theft" of blackness (Lott), critiquing a seminal form of American theater. The metatheatricality of this move – wherein a piece of theater identifies theater's own complicity with oppressive structures – will receive its fullest development in *Venus*. Already in Ham's speech, however, Parks asks us to consider her metatheater as, specifically, a *remediation*[39]: inscribing the minstrel show into her own play, she also re-presents it as emphatically textual. This is not just theater that critiques the theatrics of racism, but theater that does so *as writing*. It would, again, be a gross misrepresentation of Parks's aesthetic to read the remark about "great singin and dancin capabilities" that "tended tuh bring shame on his family" as a slight against music and movement, both of which inform her work tremendously. But it seems clear that what prevents this scene from *being* minstrelsy, from collapsing into complicity with the complicity it shows, is its irreducible textual dimension – the script as that which cannot resolve into the performance's song and dance. "Shame on his family gaw. / Write *that* down": writing offers the transcendence, or remedial leap, that gets us to the "meta" in the first place; writing the shame down means no longer being consumed by it, even as it rages. Even if, as we've seen, writing has its own propensities for violence, Parks shows that the capture of embodied experience *into* text is crucial for emancipation.[40]

This need for textual capture is why, in the next scene, Black Man With Watermelon launches into a kind of Cartesian meditation: "We sittin on this porch right now aint we. Uh huhn. Aaah. Yes. Sittin right here right now on it in it ainthuh first time either iduhnt it. Yep. Nope. Once we was here once wuhduhnt we. Yep. Yep. Once we being here. Uh huhn. Huh" (126). Passages like these exhibit a tendency to drift away from the situation at hand and into theoretical speculation, which we will see again in Mac Wellman's work. More specifically here, though, Parks seems to literalize and almost parody her own rule against using stage directions: "The action goes in the line of dialogue instead of always in a pissy set of parentheses" ("From *Elements*" 15). From a playwriting point of view, the advantage of stage directions is that they can reduce the need for exposition within the line, allowing for more "natural" speech – so that, for example, characters can be made to refer to elements of their environment without having to name them. We've already seen the critical use Beckett makes of this convention; in foreswearing it altogether, Parks challenges herself to incorporate the sphere of performance within her figures' speech.

We might assume that stage directions are "pissy" because they're presumptuous authorial power grabs; Edward Gordon Craig thought so, roaring in 1905 that they were "an offence to the men of the theatre" (150). But in fact, stage directions mark the site at which the text can occlude itself as such, a moment when language trains its own replacement, so to speak. In quite a literal sense, stage directions authorize the substitution of their own verbiage by nonverbal means.[41] But by insisting that the necessary information – indeed "the action" itself – should fit within the spoken text, Parks preempts this moment. Instead of giving way to a corporeal reality, language sticks around to *double* the physical. In this passage, Black Man enacts precisely this superfluity by saying how things are: "We sittin on this porch right now aint we." This is just the kind of redundancy that "good" playwriting seeks to avoid, and yet Parks here positions it as an attempt to arrest the dizzying cycles of murder and domesticity that constitute Black Man's life onstage: he tries, in this passage, to put his present *into words* in order to transcend it. What his speech represents is thus not only the scene it describes, but the poetics that govern the play as a whole: a desire to contest the tyranny of the (still) here and (always) now by re-posing that present as writing.

"Land:/HO!": Textual Performance and Theatrical Utopia

Parks's burning page, then, would be a piece of text that leaps up in a life of its own, but also a text that burns with the live suffering it captures – and exceeds. By incorporating performance, such a text both perpetually explodes and perpetually reasserts its own fixed form, in Adorno's terms its "objectivation." This ethos of playwri(gh)ting takes seriously the fundamental, unreasonable logic of "the play," and brings that logic to bear on concrete poetic choices. Like Elevator Repair Service's *Gatz*, Parks's play offers a model for rethinking the "primacy of the text" (Adorno, *Aesthetic* 100) as a *theatrical* construction, rather than a musty myth of literary academia. Returning to Adorno in light of Parks's work, we can begin to see how a writing that emphatically embraces embodied performance – a writing that is exuberantly theatrical – can still seek the resistant, critical "foreignness" of text as a form apart. As in Beckett, Parks's complex interworkings of text and scene will turn out to make theater a utopian site. But Beckett converges with Adorno historically and affectively, and Adorno's intense identification with Beckett's work is well known; Parks belongs to a later moment and, it should be clear, manifests a sharply different sensibility. That her work nevertheless resonates powerfully with Adorno's theory shows how his poetics can extend into realms – and theaters – where Adorno himself could not have set foot.

As we saw, Adorno locates a problem with live performance in the way performance remains emphatically enmeshed in the real: only through its fixation as a textual object does a work of art "become autonomous from its genesis" (*Aesthetic* 100), asserting the "foreignness to the world" that is fundamental to the aesthetic (183). In readings of James, Stein, and Beckett, I tried to show how these writers create theaters that undermine the present, conceived as the violently unifying field of "the world" in Adorno's sense – the world into which, as he suggests, performance is perpetually being born. If Parks aims to appropriate performance's embodied reality for writing itself, this too describes an antidramatic orientation: a conviction that there is something insufficient, even monstrous, about the life that happens here and now, and a corresponding desire to refer us beyond the present by means of a text that engulfs and exceeds it.

In fact, the very ethos that might seem to separate Parks most sharply from Adorno – her insistence that "Language is a physical act" ("From *Elements*" 11), her enthusiasm for text *as* performance – actually represents a profound convergence. As we saw, Adorno's aesthetics also continually emphasize that an artwork must be understood as a dynamic process. "Artworks have the immanent character of being an act, even if they are carved in stone, and this endows them with the quality of being something momentary and sudden ... Under patient contemplation, artworks begin to move" (*Aesthetic* 79).[42] Or again: "Whatever in the artifact may be called the unity of its meaning is not static but processual, the enactment of antagonisms that each work necessarily has in itself" (176). This notion of a work "carved in stone" that nonetheless harbors enactment, movement, and struggle not only in its past history but in its very form is just the intuition Parks explores, and it resonates with the thematics of writing we have been tracing through *The Death*.

One might object, however, that Adorno's understanding of *all* artworks as action and motion is precisely what allows him to claim the phenomenal values of live performance for art in general while dismissing actual performance as "usually regressive" (*Aesthetic* 100). Indeed, when he discusses plays, Adorno insists that their inherent reference to actual performance must not be given too much attention – an argument that, as he is well aware, assimilates plays to nontheater texts. He writes: "each artwork is the recapitulation [*Wiederholung*] of itself ... Dramatic or musical texts should be regarded exclusively in this fashion and not as the quintessence of instructions for the performers ... Whether or not they are performed is for them a matter of indifference" (125–126/190). Such a statement would seem to be glaringly at variance with any truly theatrical project – although it is worth noticing the "for them" that distinguishes the texts' own "indifference" from, say, our own. More specifically, Adorno's claim would seem to negate the playwriting gospel that Parks articulates with characteristic verve in "From *Elements of Style*": "Jesus. Right from the jump, ask yourself: '*Why* does this thing I'm writing *have* to be a *play*?'" (7).

We might at first think that Parks wants us to consider how a text can be a good instrument for "use" in an embodied onstage performance; and certainly, Adorno's remark deprioritizes any such question. But is this, in fact, what Parks is asking? I think we are now in a position to understand Parks's question more aptly as: What about this text makes it a play – a piece of theater – *as I write it*? How does this text *hold* my experience of being a body among bodies in a catastrophic present – or, for that matter, my experience of "the marvel of live bodies onstage" (ibid. 6)? This does not mean that actual performance is "a matter of indifference" to the writer; on the contrary, Parks is demanding that *playwrights* write this way, that this kind of writing be applied to texts for theatrical production: "The last thing American theatre needs is another lame play" (7). Parks is encouraging writers to confront the theater with an *other* theater, the theater of the page. The playwright thus divides the space and time of performance from itself, activating the profound theatrical heterogeneity we discussed in Chapter 2, and giving the lie to any unifying dramatic present. It is through self-sufficiency, not instrumentality, that the text can revolutionize the stage. In order to do so, the play must rehearse – *wiederholen*, "recapitulate" or repeat – *itself*, trace and retrace the contours of the textual entombment that keeps it differently (a-)live.

Parks's poetics thus reveal a theatrical possibility latent in Adorno's discussion of performance. The reference to performance enables Adorno to *distinguish* the mode of reenactment proper to the textual object, theorizing this process in part through its *difference* from performance's concrete replayings. The prospect of actual, embodied enactment, that is, offers to define the space of the text as *elsewhere* than the world where performance happens. As Adorno relies on the conceptual efficacy of this opposition, Parks activates its theatrical force. In *The Death*, she elaborates with great affective intensity the need to transmute a tormenting liveness into an objectivated form which will preserve but transcend that liveness. Whereas Adorno invokes the figure of performance in order to bracket its literal occurrence, Parks's playwriting moves the text's *Wiederholung* beyond a merely conceptual dependence on the figure of the stage and into an ongoing, dialectical relation with the actuality of performance. In other words, Parks shows how the intuition that written text already has "the character of being an act" can motivate work for theater: the prospect of theatrical production offers to shape the playwright's achievement, both negatively – the text will emerge as that which exceeds and differs from the live event – and positively, the text deriving its own performance from the stage it strangely doubles. The question "*Why* does this thing I'm writing *have* to be a *play*?" both insists on the specificity of the theater medium and insists that this specificity can be mounted within the textual moment, that the urgency of the theatrical event must be cultivated on a stage internal to "this thing I'm writing." The page becomes, emphatically, the site of a rehearsal.

As we've seen, Parks's work is remarkable in its commitment to exploring the rehearsal or "recapitulation" that for Adorno is fundamental to the artwork. The power of *The Death* lies in its vivid manifestation of the recursiveness that makes all aesthetic experience a replaying. The topos of *discovery* – as in, Columbus discovered America – is a major site at which Parks works this out, suggesting that a poetics of *re*covery might have distinctly political stakes. What if, instead of setting out to claim new territory, we determined to (re)cover the same ground again (and again)?

BEFORE COLUMBUS: Land:
AND BIGGER AND BIGGER AND BIGGER: HO!
QUEEN-THEN-PHARAOH HATSHEPSUT: I saw Columbus comin Before
    Columbus coming/goin over tuh meet you –
BEFORE COLUMBUS: Thuh first time I saw it. It was huge. Thuh green sea
    becomes uh hillside. Uh hillside populated with some peoples I will name.
    Thuh first time I saw it it was uh was-huge once one. Huh. It has been gettin
    smaller ever since.
QUEEN-THEN-PHARAOH HATSHEPSUT: Land:
BLACK MAN WITH WATERMELON: HO! (116–117)

Here as elsewhere, the play thematizes the disastrous consequences of European "exploration." The cry "Land: HO!" ends the First Chorus and reappears in the Final Chorus (130); it marks a radical event, the discovery of the New World, and hence emblematizes a dramatic trajectory, pushing forward into the unknown and thus reducing the unknown's scope: "It has been gettin smaller ever since." By turning the dramatic hinge "Land: HO!" into a refrain, however, Parks rewrites colonization as repetition. This means several things: first, the thesis that African expeditions had already traveled to America long before Europeans, as Before Columbus's name records (Geis, *Suzan* 66–68), so that the revisionist-historiographical imperative is precisely to re-view a putative "first sight" as a citation. Second, the repetition of the phrase "Land: HO!" and its circulation between figures suggests the psychologically and socially traumatic quality of this history, as a wound that must be constituted *as* memory (see Malkin 163–164). Third, however, the almost unbearable poignancy of these lines comes from the irresistible upsweep of glimpsing a new world, a desire the play cannot cite without evoking. The discovery that has happened again and again still compels us to pursue it, drawn into the mimesis of history's text. "It has been gettin smaller ever since" registers both the experience of passing through this history and the sense of still having yet to do so: the Land has been getting smaller as I've been imprisoned here, growing more and more claustrophobic ("when he walks his thoughts dont got room" [102, 111, 129]) – *and* it has been getting smaller as its promise has receded, as if I hadn't yet landed on its shore at all. In returning repeatedly to the cusp, or horizon, of discovery, Parks marks and remarks not only the loss of a native land, but the unfulfilled project of utopia. Paradoxically, she locates hope within the moment already traversed, already betrayed.

This is, of course, a theatrical structure familiar to us from any replaying; as Schneider succinctly puts it, "attending the theatre at all is engaging in a repetitive event" (113). And yet the power of drama, Szondi tells us, depends on its ability to suspend that familiarity – suspend, that is, both our familiarity with the institutional reality of theater as rehearsed and repeated, and the familiarity of the play itself as a story we already know. In the absolute present of dramatic performance, there should be no past, hence no citation, no repetition, *no text*. Brecht saw this condition as infantilizing, and his "literarized" theater is one that refuses to disavow its own repetitive structure (71, 187). But where Brecht's explicit repetitions were famously designed to free the spectator from empathetic identification, Parks – as we've seen – adopts a poetics of mourning to make her audience *feel* the repetitive structure itself. By dissociating affective investment from the pretense of the "first time," Parks makes an argument for theater's value as lying in something it shares with reading (if not with reading as Brecht tends to imagine it): the possibility of *urgently* tracing and retracing a fixed form, an already-was. As in Adorno, the "act" in Parks is a moment when what has been settled suddenly flares up anew or "begins to move," not because performance has steered it to new shores, but because the text of the past – the page/grave – harbors that movement in itself.

The vision that thus emerges is, in a sense, less optimistic than the one Worthen ascribes to Parks in *The America Play*: "performance as an act of difference – from history, from writing – that creates revision, change" (*Drama* 176). The fraught "recapitulation" that Parks and Adorno both describe may well be an "act of difference," in a sense that remains to be specified here, but that difference is not exactly "change." On the contrary, a great deal of its force derives from the pathos of change unrealized: "I got uhway? / Nope. Yep. Nope. Nope" (Parks, *Death* 128). But Worthen is right to emphasize *revision*, the crucial partner to repetition in Parks's system of "Rep & Rev," and a term which my analysis has up to now largely ignored. Parks's poetics of repetition avow theater's perpetual indebtedness to and entanglement with a past; her revisions, it seems to me, do not so much outstrip that past as demonstrate the past's paradoxical liveliness, its currency *as* artifact, or text. The repeated cry "Land: HO!" expresses the reification, as cliché, of a moment of radical possibility, and as such expresses the betrayal of that possibility. But the same repetition also conveys a compulsive desire that the reification *preserves*, an uncertainty that draws us back to the horizon again and again, with re-visionary longing.

Plainly, Parks's work challenges any clean binary opposition between the dead letter and the living stage. But neither are these categories entirely disabled: it is *as* a repository of the dead, as the form of a pastness, that the "6 by 6 by 6" of the page burns on, searing us with a different kind of presence. In fact, the distinctiveness of the past as such, and the written text as the site of access *to* that past *from* a seriously fucked-up present,[43] becomes explicit in *The Death*'s First Chorus:

VOICE ON THUH TEE V: Good evening. Broad Caster. Headlinin tonight: thuh news.
OLD MAN RIVER JORDAN: Tell you of uh news. Last news. Last news of thuh last man [...] Last news leads tuh thuh first news. He is dead he crosses thuh river.
[...]
YES AND GREENS BLACK-EYED PEAS CORNBREAD: Did you write it down? On uh little slip uh paper stick thuh slip in thuh river afore you slip in that way you keep your clothes dry, man.
[...]
BLACK MAN WITH WATERMELON: I jumped in thuh water without uh word. I jumped in thuh water without uh smell. I am in thuh river and in my skin is soppin wet. I would like tuh stay afloat now. I would like tuh move my hands.
[...]
YES AND GREENS BLACK-EYED PEAS CORNBREAD: Back tuh when thuh worl usta be roun.
OLD MAN RIVER JORDAN: Uhcross thuh river in back tuh that. Yes. (112–114)

The device of the "news" broadcast which repeatedly, throughout the play, announces the Death of the Last Black Man emphasizes the presentness of the play's action, the live present in which the Death is both announced and kept painfully incomplete. The time of death is reported as "Yesterday today next summer tomorrow just uh moment uhgoh in 1317" (102, 129, cf. 111), and yet the repeated reminder that "This is the news" (123) suggests a condition in which the past and future have become subsumed within a catastrophic experience of the now, have lost their *difference* from that "now" within a structure "forcing the pasts [and futures!] to reappear as *presented* in the present" (Malkin 169).

As Rayner and Elam note (451), the temporality announced here recalls Pozzo's declaration that there has only ever been "one day ... the same day, the same second" (Beckett, *Waiting* 333). Indeed, Parks's stipulation of "The Present" as the setting of her play should at this point seem deeply Beckettian. For Parks's figures, however, the monstrous present does not extend quite so far back as it does for Pozzo and his audience. Rather, there is now a prospect of crossing over to a radically different moment, "when thuh worl usta be roun," before European predation. To rest in peace, to cross the river, would be to escape the impacted and overdetermined present by moving "back" to that time – and significantly, Parks imagines the vessel of this crossing as a piece of written text. What keeps Black Man sopping "in thuh river" – keeps him, much more horribly than James's Lewis Lambert Strether, "in midstream of his drama" (*Ambassadors* 458) – is a lack of access to the page, conceived as a lack of access to the space of what was. And accordingly, the Final Chorus envisions his escape into burial as an achievement of text: "He jumps in thuh river. These words for partin. / And you will write them down" (129). As the future tense of this last phrase suggests, writing's constitution of a radically distinct past is also its *promise*, that is, its gesture toward a *future* beyond the indifferent "today next summer tuhmorrow" in which the Last Black Man goes on dying.

We have already come across the play's concern for literary posterity in Yes And Greens's insistent "write it down" refrain; what we haven't yet discussed is the unexpected turn with which her last iteration concludes: "You will carve it out of a rock so that in the future when we come along we will know that *the rock does yes exist*" (131, my emphasis). Since "the rock" names the medium of this final writing, we can read these last words as an assertion of black literary tradition. But there is also a certain willful lack of reference at play, a refusal inherent in the turn to tautology: there's a rock, so there's a rock.[44] Declining to bait "the future" with a legible message, this refusal imagines a future so radically other that between then and now there would be nothing to communicate.

In either direction, then – backwards or forwards in time – writing navigates a radical break. A medium of crucial preservation, it nonetheless propels itself forward and back into its own disintegration, as the figures' ecstatic vision shows:

OLD MAN RIVER JORDAN: [...] Skirtin back tuh that. Come up back flip take uhway like thuh waves do. Far uhway. Uhway tuh where they don't speak thuh language and where they dont want tuh. Huh. Go on back tuh that.
YES AND GREENS BLACK-EYED PEAS CORNBREAD: Awe on uh interior before uh demarcation made it mapped. Awe on uh interior with out uh road-word called macadam. Awe onin uh interior that was uh whole was once. (114)

This vision recalls, quite strikingly, Derrida's account of the metaphysical vision wherein an inherently *whole* native landscape is imagined as being riven by the introduction of writing: "writing as the possibility of the road and of difference ... the path that is broken, beaten ... the violent spacing of nature" (*Grammatology* 107–108). Parks may not be as confident as Derrida that the unbroken "interior" is a conceptual trap in need of deconstruction, but neither does the play as a whole exactly *assert* the Edenic vision of the motherland described here. The lines that repeatedly image lost wholeness inscribe a disturbing *Nachträglichkeit* at the heart of the fantasy: "Before Columbus thuh worl usta be *roun* they put uh /d/ on thuh end of roun makin roun*d*. Thusly they set in motion thuh end. Without that /d/ we coulda gone on spinnin forever. Thuh /d/ thing ended things ended" (102; cf. 115). These lines emphasize the paradox inherent in trying to work back *through writing* to a moment before writing: before experience was "mapped" into standardization. By casting "roun" as the original version of "round," Parks is mounting a serious challenge to the commonsense assumption that the language of conquest belongs to the colonist. Here again, though, we also need to recognize not only the discernible sense of the lines, but also their active resistance to sense-making, a resistance that spikes in the parodic rationality of "Thusly." The wholeness of the pre-Columbian "worl" is figured as a construction of post-Columbian language, rendering the referent essentially elusive. Significantly, we approach this referent only through a kind of orthographicization of speech: the re*lettering* of an oral unit.[45] By insisting that "roun" is rigorously distinct from "round," sonically and semantically, Parks reorganizes an aural continuum into a scriptive determinacy. She thus suggests that writing, marked through its incursions into phonic performance, is the medium that best preserves the utopian prospect of its own disappearance: a worl(d) with no need for inscription. True to the theatrics of utopia, Parks intimates this vision only by withholding it from view.

To the repeated question "Where he gonna go now that he done dieded?" (102, 111, cf. 129), the play answers: the grave, the page. If there is a triumph at the end, it is the play's own discovery of itself as this shelter, its realization as a structure that can "Hold it." Although Parks has said that she considers *Venus* her "black belt in playwriting" (Wetmore 133), it is tempting to imagine the twenty-seven-year-old author of *The Death* reveling in a newfound sense of wri(ght)terly capacity. And yet, as I hope my reading has registered, the Death of the Last Black Man is hardly an open-and-shut case. The text's ability to "Hold" the life-after-life of its performance is also, after all, a mechanism in suspense: freeze, hold that pose, hold it right there. The strain of this effort betrays the knowledge of theater that readers have rightly brought to bear on Parks: the certainty that performance will disrupt the longed-for closure, raise the dead again and anew. When Parks seizes on the mad logic of the play as a form and imagines that writing can hold performance, what she imagines is finally an impossible writing, a text whose rightful scene is neither page nor stage. This writing would take place neither as scoring scar nor as instrumental grist for "thuh news" of the day, but as the *passage* to a realm where "nothin is familiar" (*Death* 107) – which also means, if we remember Freud, to a world without mourning. The performance "of" this utopian writing does not lie up ahead of it, in its enactment, but in the unmapped pre- or posthistory toward which it offers, outrageously, to conduct us: "back tuh that." For all the emphatic presence of Parks's text, her most powerful "re-membering" is not an act of realization here and now, but a technique of *remembrance* in Adorno's sense: "the not-yet-existing has been dreamed of in remembrance [*Eingedenken*]," he writes, "which alone concretizes utopia without betraying it into existence" (*Aesthetic* 132/200). Such remembrance is not realistic; by the same token, the future anterior implied by the play as a form, its promise that a text will *turn out to have been* the live event already, is a promise always broken. The prospect that we glimpse amidst the vault-work of Parks's playwrighting, though – haunting the corners – is exactly that of a life written into being, a life other than this one. It is the theatrical life of promise itself.

CHAPTER 6

"Small, fierce creatures"
Mac Wellman's Auratic Theater

SUSANNAH: [...] I am not among my kind, and do not even know what my kind are.

(Mac Wellman, *A Murder of Crows*)

only what does not fit into this world is true.

(Theodor Adorno)[1]

Over the past three decades, Mac Wellman's name has become shorthand for a growing subculture of intense verbal experimentation in American theater.[2] Parks, whose early plays are clearly in conversation with that scene, has since largely transitioned out of it, winning wider audiences for powerful, straightforward dramas like the Pulitzer-winning Broadway hit *Topdog/Underdog* (2001) and the more recent *Father Comes Home From the Wars (Parts 1, 2 & 3)* (2014). Wellman's work has never gained the same level of mainstream appeal, nor has it provoked anything like the reams of critical response that make up Parks's daunting academic paper trail. But he has built a reputation as "the cynosure in a heaven full of experimental playwrights" (H. Shaw vii); and his playwriting program at Brooklyn College continues to act as a centripetal focus for New York's avant-garde theater scene, boasting such graduates as Young Jean Lee, Thomas Bradshaw, Sibyl Kempson, Tina Satter (Half Straddle), and Kelly Copper (Nature Theater of Oklahoma). These artists are not all known primarily as playwrights; their theater work is widely diverse, and yet, as the artist and scholar (and co-alumna) Karinne Keithley Syers observes, Wellman's influence is clear: "not as a 'school of Mac Wellman,' but as a broadly cast license to think of plays in terms of language, and to value wrongness, ceremony, and a bit of demonism in the theatrical project."[3]

I won't try to trace out the far-flung contemporary manifestations of that "license" here; this chapter will confine itself to Wellman's own work, rather than tracking his influence on others. But his well-attested position at the heart of formally adventurous American theater today should lend the readings that follow a particular point: namely, that no account of that theater can reasonably define it in terms of a supposed distance from the literary – or from playwriting. By the same token, in placing Wellman's work within the lineage of theatrical negativity that includes James, Stein, and Beckett as well as Parks, I mean to suggest that tradition's continued relevance to a broader field of contemporary theatrical endeavor, which extends beyond the category of plays as such.

One of the hallmarks of Wellman-influenced theater is its extended use of monologue – a form whose significance in Beckett and Parks we have already considered. In this chapter, I'll argue that Wellman's monologues are part of his broader interest in turning theater's "co-presence" against itself. Somewhat ironically, since he has been a powerful force of community for downtown artists, his work relentlessly destabilizes community in the moment of reception. In the face of the present-tense assembly that helps constitute the theatrical, his plays insist that our present ways of coming together are inadequate. The words of this chapter's first epigraph, spoken by the young heroine of Wellman's 1992 play *A Murder of Crows*, capture the tenor of what we might call Wellman's own characteristic alienation effect: a negative sense of "among"-ness that arises with particular power in the theatrical situation, and puts our own belonging into question. In this way, Wellman explores theater as a medium especially suited for the cultivation of what, in Adorno's words, "does not fit into this world." Perhaps more profoundly than any other artist examined here, he pursues Adorno's insight that in a society where every relationship is compromised, "Only strangeness [*Fremdheit*] is the antidote to alienation [*Entfremdung*]" (*Minima* 94/105).[4]

Negating the actual community in the theater, Wellman's work partakes of the utopian project we traced in *Waiting for Godot*. For Wellman, as for Beckett, writing is the privileged vehicle of theater's utopian logic. But whereas Beckett writes an absolute present into his text, exacerbating language's "presence on the stage" (Robbe-Grillet) to the point of a dialectical reversal, Wellman elaborates moments of resistance to the present that, for him, inhere in the space and time of theater. The sense of imprisonment in the present that anchors Beckett's stage recedes, for Wellman, in favor of a model of theater more akin to that of James and Stein: a dispersed, differential, deeply distracting space. The urgency of negation remains, however; for Wellman, it is incited by the social mechanics that theater's audience both instantiates and figures. More specifically, Wellman takes theater's assembled community as an opportunity to break the discursive rules of that community: to make the theater operate against functional communication.[5]

To claim that Wellman's plays actively interfere with communication is not to claim that they have nothing to say to us; the readings that follow would obviously contradict this claim. While his language is sometimes intensely cryptic, and always luxuriously playful, it can also be quite straightforward, like Susannah's line in the epigraph above. Nevertheless, the overall effect of his compositions is to undermine communication *as an ideal of language*, as a standard that determines speech's right to exist. This ideal promotes what Adorno calls a "mendacious positivity of meaning" ("Commitment" 91) or "the universal law of clichés" ("Trying" 139). As a "law," communication demands the maximally efficient delivery of information from sender to receiver, with minimal ambiguity or waste. That is, it's a law of economy: "communication [*Kommunikation*] is the adaptation of spirit to utility, with the result that spirit is made one commodity among the rest" (*Aesthetic* 74/115). Its model could be the advertisement, which needs to maximize the uptake of unambiguous content per unit of time or space purchased. Fundamentally, it offers information with which we already know what to do: it serves practical imperatives that preexist it.

Wellman's best-known critical piece, a 1984 essay called "The Theatre of Good Intentions," argues that something very much like Adorno's "adaptation of spirit to utility" is an institutionally enforced expectation in American theater. As the title suggests, Wellman's essay is largely a critique of the dominance of "intention" in American plays.[6] He attacks the norm that places character motivation at the center of representational practice: "Why is it so inconceivable to our dramatists that some people do not know, or care, how they feel all the time? That some people act without a detachable motive, or from a myriad of contradictory ones?" (63). The repression of this possibility results in what he calls the "Euclidean character" (62), a stage figure whose every word is rigorously compatible with her psychological profile, itself reducible to a set of evident causes and aims. Such a character's speech is doubly shaped by the norm of communication: between characters, where it is always meant to strive toward recognizable goals ("motivation"), and also in relation to the audience, who can confidently redeem each phrase for the psychological access it grants. An intolerance of mystery or irreducible complexity means that every event onstage must be exhaustively accounted for, every action referring to intentions the spectator can immediately identify, and identify *with*: Adorno's "positivity of meaning." Well in line with this Frankfurt School resonance, Wellman links the orthodoxy of transparency to the wider cultural context of a society "obsessed with *images* of well-being" (61), a nation of "professional children" presided over by Reagan, the "Great Communicator" (69).

In his rejection of the communicative ideal, Wellman would seem to place himself at odds with Hans-Thies Lehmann's account of the postdramatic; for Lehmann, postdramatic theater highlights the communicative nature of theatrical exchange more than ever (136–137). Lehmann makes this claim by distinguishing between two "axes" of communication:

> It is possible to differentiate in theatre an intra-scenic axis of communication [*Kommunikation*] from an orthogonal axis of communication between the stage and the (really or structurally) distinct place of the spectators. Mindful of the fact that the Greek word 'theatron' originally designated the space of the spectators, not the whole theatre, we call the latter axis the 'theatron axis' ... [T]heatrical discourse has always been doubly addressed: it is at the same time directed *intra-scenically* (i.e. at the interlocutors in the play) and *extra-scenically* at the theatron. Proceeding from this well-known duality of *all* theatre, postdramatic theatre has drawn the conclusion that it has to be possible in principle to make the first dimension almost disappear in order to reinforce the second dimension and to raise it to a new quality of theatre. (127/230)

In its attempt to "reinforce" the *theatron* dimension, postdramatic theater still winds up aiming primarily for "communicative success"; Lehmann acknowledges that "an unavoidable proximity to the *criteria of mass communication*" is the "downside" of this emphasis (136–137). But Lehmann's account seems to me to elide the very possibility that Wellman's essay energetically, if negatively, implies: the possibility of a theater that would transcend drama not by changing the direction of its communication, but by rejecting the communicative norm altogether.[7] Adapting Lehmann's geometric vocabulary, we might say that if his version of the postdramatic has rotated theater's primary focus by ninety degrees, from the intra-scenic relationship out onto the "orthogonal" toward the audience, Wellman's theater would rotate in another direction: not out toward us, but somehow *off*, away. To truly exceed a "theater of good intentions," that is, we would have to shake off not only the requirement of characters who pursue intelligible aims amongst each other, but also, more radically, the requirement that performance present itself as a gesture *meant for us*.

In this chapter, I explore the way Wellman's work revokes the communicative imperative, developing the theatrics of a resistantly foreign language. Marjorie Perloff, one of Wellman's most loyal and insightful readers, has written that Wellman "is our latter-day Brecht, providing the *Verfremdung*, the 'making strange' that makes us see what has been before us all along" ("Foreword" xvii). Wellman's dogged wordplay, and his anarchic and often agrammatical juxtapositions of wildly different language registers, achieve this defamiliarization poetically.[8] But as Perloff's reference to Brecht suggests, Wellman puts a specifically theatrical twist on the famous aesthetic goal of "making strange." Syers adds that "it is not the strange surface of the ordinary that Wellman would have us encounter in his theater, but rather something more dimensionally strange – where things are strange because *we* have become strangers." As she emphasizes, Wellman's writing seizes on theater as a spatiotemporal and interpersonal event, and interferes with its functioning at precisely this level. Part of what thereby becomes strange is the "*we*" itself: our being here together. These plays engage our gathered presence negatively, by flouting the discursive procedures that allow for communicative consensus. Below, I explore the ways in which Wellman's work refuses to let "us" be, suggesting paradoxically that "we" are not its audience.

It is perhaps not surprising that monologue – a mode of speech defined by solitude – should be a privileged form for this project. And yet the critical discourse on contemporary stage monologue tends overwhelmingly to emphasize its interpersonally bonding, communicative power. These accounts often assume that a connection with the audience – a heavily trafficked *theatron* axis, as it were – defines monologue's theatrical potential, or distinguishes stage monologue from other kinds. Accounts like this comprehend the theatrical force of stage monologue by redescribing it as a fundamentally presentational, communicative or "dialogical" mode. In the following section, I discuss this critical tendency, including Lehmann's own account of postdramatic "monology," and offer my own account of how monologue works in Wellman's *A Murder of Crows*. Here I argue that monologue, as a profoundly unsociable form, takes part in Wellman's larger project of negating the community present in the theater and demanding a utopian alternative. The next, more explicitly theoretical section argues that this mode of theatre can usefully be understood via the Frankfurt School concept of *aura*, which sets a phenomenological emphasis on presence in dialectical tension with a critical allegiance to distance and alterity. Reading Wellman's sprawling essay-manifesto *Speculations*, I suggest that he reimagines aura as something that fights back, quite viciously, against the violating intimacies of the communicative norm. The chapter ends by briefly considering Wellman's 1998 play *Girl Gone*, a piece committed to imagining theater as the site of disobedient departures from the present – departures both *within* and *from* the "directly connected world" (254) where performance takes place.

Mouthing Off: *A Murder of Crows*

Roughly speaking, *A Murder of Crows* tells the story of an American family. That story might be summarized as follows: young Susannah, her war-vet brother Andy, and their mother Nella have lost Raymond, the children's father, in a fatal "avalanche by the . . . / grease pit" (14). They have therefore moved in with Nella's bigoted and materialistic brother and sister-in-law, Howard and Georgia. Resentful of this situation and especially of her aunt's meanness, Susannah obsessively watches the sky, convinced that an apocalyptic weather change is on the horizon. Eventually, Raymond shows up, disguised as "the weatherman" (28), and explains to Susannah that he faked his death and has been living "among the crows" – a refuge he's now had to give up due to a feather allergy (40–41). Raymond presses Susannah for her predictions about the weather, but she decides to give crow life a try herself, and in the last scene we see her among the crows, "trying to pass" for one of them (56).

The play is one of Wellman's most traditional, recognizably "dramatic" pieces. It constructs a plot, if an offbeat one; it offers pro- and antagonists, conflict and (provisional) resolution, and even a classic recognition scene: "Dad, it's you" (30). It would be false to deny that some of the play's power lies in the story it constructs; as we saw, this is also true of Parks's *The Death*, in which the story of a woman's mourning imbues poetic structure with great affective force. *A Murder of Crows* hews even closer to dramatic conventions; but it does so mainly in order to disturb those conventions again and again. Focusing on this text rather than on one of Wellman's more obviously "postdramatic" works – such as *Cellophane* (1988), *Terminal Hip* (1989), or *Antigone* (2001)[9] – offers the chance to analyze his closest critical engagement with dramatic values. The point is not just to show that Wellman's writing breaks the rules of conventional dramaturgy; I want to consider how his "intra-scenic" ruptures trouble the *theatron* relation as well.

Monologues are the primary vehicle of this disturbance in *A Murder of Crows*. These long speeches occur throughout the play, and yet they retain a sense of uneasy verbal excess. The play's opening tableau anticipates their outbreak:

> **SCENE ONE**
> A front porch of an American-type house. Only: no house. A woman, NELLA, stands on the porch looking out. Her daughter, SUSANNAH, stands a few yards down stage with an enraptured look on her face, also looking out. (Wellman, *Murder* 9)

Both of the characters we meet at the start of the play are "looking out"; that is, they are looking toward the audience, and not at each other. Their placement seems to correspond perfectly to Lehmann's postdramatic geometry: the women's gazes highlight the *theatron* axis, while the stipulation that Susannah stands "a few yards down" from her mother fractures the intra-scenic line. That the characters are introduced separately, one "looking out" and the other "also looking out," creates a sense of presentationally directed composition, a parallel that does not derive from any inner experience the characters share. In this context, the "enraptured look" on Susannah's face suggests the kind of revelation we tend to associate with soliloquy – "the verbalization of the speaker's interior feelings or thoughts" (Geis, *Postmodern* 9). We seem to be set up for a theatrical communication that will proceed directly from actor to audience, eschewing the mediation of dramatic dialogue. This is precisely what several accounts of contemporary stage monologue would lead us to expect; and yet, as I will suggest, the negative force of Wellman's monologues operates quite differently.

Monologue has often stood in tension with conventional dramatic requirements. As Ruby Cohn notes drily, "The respectable middle-class protagonist does not stand alone in the middle of his carpeted living room to ponder aloud on his problems or to debate with himself" ("Outward" 17). It would be a mistake, however, to conclude that the prominence of monologue always signals a commitment to experimental form. "To a striking and perhaps unprecedented degree," observes Deborah Geis in her 1993 book on monologue, "contemporary American playwrights have been inclined to draw upon the myriad dramatic and narrative opportunities to be found in monologic language. Virtually all of the established and emerging voices of the current American theater, from Arthur Miller to Spalding Gray, employ monologues as a fundamental component of their dramatic creations" (*Postmodern* 2). Although Geis does go on to make a strong argument for monologue's efficacy in engaging "the complicated fragmentation and continual reformation of subjectivity suggested by a postmodern world" (151; see also 29–44), the remarkable ubiquity she describes should discourage any blanket identification of monologue as inherently subversive or difficult, modernist or postmodern.

Similarly, in an article published the same year (and partially incorporated into his influential *New Playwriting Strategies* textbook, 2001 and 2012), Paul Castagno notes that "most writers of contemporary realistic drama utilize the monologue to service the requirements of both actors and audience towards explication and clarification of subtext" and "to clarify inner objectives" ("Varieties" 135; cf. *New* 199–200). He delineates three main functions of monologue within this framework: "exposition or anecdotal diversion in the early scenes, metaphoric or thematic analogy to emphasize or clarify points of conflict in the rising action, [and] character discovery, epiphany, or reversals located near the major crisis of the play" ("Varieties" 135; cf. *New* 200). As this vocabulary suggests, such uses of monologue fall squarely in line with traditional dramatic aims and organization.

Castagno describes this tendency, however, in order to show how two playwrights, Wellman and Len Jenkin, depart from it. Adapting terminology developed by Mikhail Bakhtin, Castagno argues that Wellman's and Jenkin's uses of monologue break not only from dramatic use but from the "authoritative gleam" of *mono*-logic language as such ("Varieties" 134). In a development that would parallel the innovation Bakhtin famously ascribed to the novel, Castagno sees these playwrights as "dialogizing" monologue, effectively undermining the univocal sovereignty of the speaking One. Castagno traces multiple "dialogic" currents in Wellman's monologues, including the internal "polyvocality" or plurality of languages that becomes a hallmark of contemporary theater in Castagno's later *New Playwriting Strategies* (51–72). In the article, however, his reading of Wellman emphasizes the "new kind of dialogism" present in the cognitive back-and-forth these speeches establish with their audience ("Varieties" 145). "[R]ather than denying the existence of the 'other' or pretending to be the 'final word', as was traditionally the case [in monologic speech]," he writes, "it is now the 'other' who becomes the site for the production of the 'final word'" ("Varieties" 143, *New* 230). The "other" in Castagno's reading is the spectator: the "barrage" of Wellman's verbiage "focuses the observer on the immediacy of the language," and she is thereby "invited into the creative process . . . to dialogize in the middle of [Wellman's] monologic 'playing field'" ("Varieties" 144).

Basic etymology would encourage us to understand monologue as fundamentally the discourse of a single speaker, and thus very likely as a discourse of solitude. For Castagno, however, monologue appears as a privileged form of collaboration. We might wonder: if dialogic interrelation really determines these playwrights' poetic ideal, why approach it through solo speech in the first place? The explanation that suggests itself is that monologue is language for which no response is already given. In other words, perhaps monologue reaches out through the very absence of onstage rejoinder – if another character isn't taking up the speech, then that becomes my job. It thus becomes easy to imagine that monologue, as speech liberated from conversation between characters, functions as a kind of "dialogue" *with the audience*, especially when the language being spoken is as provocative as Wellman's often is. And it seems instinctively obvious that this kind of interaction would be more profoundly or truly or *really* dialogical than the back-and-forth between characters – a dialogue which is, after all, only staged.

This conceptual turn, whereby monologue turns out to be a privileged form not of solitude, but instead of heightened theatrical sociability, appears in several critical accounts. Perloff writes that *Terminal Hip* and *Cellophane* "are not, in fact, lyric but insistently dramatic and curiously theatrical in their address to the audience . . . consistently posit[ing] one or more interlocutors to be questioned, bullied, or cajoled" ("Foreword" xvi). She thus implies that monologue becomes theatrical by engaging with an audience; if it did not do so, it would belong more to the realm of poetry than to theater. This understanding is by no means unique to readings of Wellman; Geis offers a similar logic, writing that although monologue can be defined as

> a speech for one or a dialogue with oneself . . . this sense of monologue is complicated by the presence, in the theater, of the audience. Since the status of a play presupposes that even a speech performed in the imagined solitude of a character will always include the audience as acknowledged or implicit witness, the inevitable status of the spectators as recipients foregrounds the "telling," or "narrating," function of the monologue. (*Postmodern* 7)

Similarly, Lehmann argues that monologue can only be considered a "disruption of communication" as long as we regard it outside the theatrical context (128–129). The idea of monologue as non-communication, he suggests, depends upon a narrowly dramatic framework: "only in the system of dialogue does the failure of speaking as communication between people [i.e. characters] become visible, while a monologue as a speech that has the audience as its addressee intensifies communication – namely the communication taking place in the here and now of theatre" (128). Lehmann acknowledges that postdramatic monologues can still sometimes "represent the absence of communication" (129), but his emphasis falls on the communicative *success* that tends to occur between the performer and her audience. Along the *theatron* axis, monologue becomes an emphatic experience of the shared "here and now." "[T]he monologue of figures on stage reinforces the certainty of our perception of the dramatic events as a *reality* in the now, authenticated through the implication of the audience," Lehmann writes, claiming that monologue's "*transgression of the border of the imaginary dramatic universe to the real theatrical situation*" accounts for its appeal to postdramatic artists (127).[10]

Lehmann coins a new word, "monology," in order to emphasize the importance of the *theatron* relationship: theatrical monologue, and especially its postdramatic adaptation, is not "simply a matter of a continuation of the monologue as a textual form" (128). As Geis suggests, however, even a written play is defined as such by its orientation toward the posited "presence" of an audience, implying that a *theatron* axis can structure the "textual form" more profoundly than Lehmann's neologism seems to acknowledge. I argued in Chapter 3 that *Waiting for Godot*, and Lucky's monologue in particular, structures itself through a rigorously determinate but negative relation to what Lehmann calls theater's "reality in the now" – and that *The Unnamable* creates an entirely textual simulation of the theatrical "monology" Lehmann would like to distinguish from text. In Chapter 5, we saw that Parks's *The Death of the Last Black Man in the Whole Entire World* uses monologue to elaborate a poetics of the "burning page" in which writing both provides for the theatrical present and promises itself as a spectacular alternative to that present. These works trouble any neat distinction between "monologue as a textual form" and "monology" as a feature of "the real theatrical situation."

At the same time, they also display an interest in monologue that deviates from monologue's supposed tendency to heighten "communication taking place in the here and now." Sara Jane Bailes has observed that contemporary experimental theater often valorizes *dis*engagement "between spectator and performance/performer," pursuing "a kind of subliminal or subterranean mode of working, resistant to the demands of an economy of exchange" (23–24). In Beckett and Parks, this resistance operates through monologues that bring the relationship between text and scene into crisis, and help establish the need for an alternative to present reality – an alternative of which writing itself becomes the sign. As much as they rupture the intra-scenic consistency of their (already fairly attenuated) fictions, that is, these monologues also declaim the insufficiency of the *theatron* transaction. They proceed neither by appeal nor by confrontation, but by withdrawal, marking the "here and now" as unworthy by refusing to deliver themselves fully to our present perception.

To characterize Wellman's monologues this way too is to question whether the audience really "becomes the site for the production of the 'final word'" in his work (Castagno, "Varieties" 143). There is no denying that Wellman's work is cognitively challenging; seeing or reading his plays can feel like an aerobic activity, and it is a short step from there to the heightened sense of participation that seems to ground such accounts. But it is at least as essential to these speeches that they *elude* our attempts to make meaning. In so doing, they hold open the dimension of a content ungrasped and unrealized, a referent that refuses to materialize here and now, for us.[11]

Coming back to the beginning of *A Murder of Crows*, we might notice that its opening monologue subtly undermines the presentational expectation set up by the performers' frontality: the first speech comes from the upstage Nella, *not* the "down stage" Susannah, a fact which gently troubles the association of monologue with communicative proximity. For a reader, moreover, the women's posture of "looking out" retroactively loses some of its determinacy two pages later, when Wellman begins using the word "out" as a synonym for "off," to denote an exit: "*They go up the porch steps, and out,*" "*She goes out,*" etc. (11, 14, 18, 25). This usage is so consistent that we might well wonder where exactly Nella and Susannah are looking, and who they're talking to, when the play begins. Is their "looking out" really a looking – and speaking – *off*? Is the auditorium just a distraction from their true discursive destination?

Of course, dramatic soliloquy often takes advantage of the dreamily raised eyeline, looking off into space rather than honing in on the audience. To some degree, Wellman's soliloquys derive from this tradition, which seeks to reconcile the frontality of long speeches with the ostensibly enclosed world of a dramatic fiction. But the attempt to naturalize long, solitary speeches by giving them the facial cast of thought is fundamentally an attempt to ameliorate the tension they produce within a realistic frame – and here Wellman's aesthetic makes a solid departure. If Wellman's characters avoid eye contact with us, this is precisely not in order to help them fit into the naturalistic scene. "Living room! A place I / loathe and look down upon," Susannah declares (23).[12]

The play's first words set us up for this turn: "My husband was of ordinary size and / so was the house," Nella declares (9). The statement refers, in stark past tense, to a particular poetics – specifically, Aristotle's famous requirement that the plot of a drama maintain "a definite size," neither too big nor too small. A "very tiny creature" cannot be beautiful, Aristotle writes:

> nor an excessively huge one (for then it cannot all be perceived at once and so its unity and wholeness are lost), if for example there were a creature

a thousand miles long – so, just as in the case of living creatures they must have some size, but one that can be taken in in a single view, so with plots: they should have length, but such that they are easy to remember. (30–31; 51a1)

The missing "husband . . . of ordinary size" would be precisely this beautiful Aristotelian animal, and the absent house is the structure that would accommodate him – and us. (Nella later imagines that in heaven, "None of the houses / are unusual houses, with respect to / size and shape" [48]). Tersely invoking the ideal of perfect calibration to the capacity of the present audience, Nella's words also satirize the assumption of a common frame of reference through their tenuous appeal to normativity: what *is* "ordinary size"? The remark at once exposes and undermines the assumption of a shared communicative context, suggesting the spuriousness of the supposedly ordinary or normal. This is quickly born out as the speech continues:

> This part of the
> country presents a problem. It don't
> fit on the map right. That's because
> we're downwind of the big reactor.
> Not to mention the county dump, where
> that hellacious grease pit is. (9)

With these words, the "ordinary" is relegated to a mythical past; and what *seems* ordinary ("the county dump") turns out to be shot through with sublime horror (the "hellacious grease pit").

But the obtrusion of un-surveyable, un-mappable magnitudes is not only Nella's subject here; it also determines the form of the speech itself, as it starts to burgeon beyond solicitude for the listener. As Nella's monologue continues, her frank *exposition* repeatedly dissolves into what we might call *speculation*, drifting from an informative mode that "sets the stage" to a more theoretical tone that grasps at ideas and images for their own sake. This begins to happen in the first sentences, in the shift from narrative content (loss of the husband and the house) to enigmatic questioning (the paradoxical "problem"). Similar shifts occur throughout Nella's speech:

> When the kids were kids the sea was
> normal. Of the logic of the sea my
> younger one, Susannah, said: It's lucky
> the shallow end is near the beach. (9–10)

The first sentence here seems to function as a classical nature metaphor: things were fine once, and now they're out of whack, hence the drama that is about to unfold. But the gesture of tautology lurking in this remark ("when the kids were kids") blossoms aggressively in the next sentence – tautology, like "the shallow end is near the beach," being the form of language that most vehemently refuses to tell us anything. This occurs in a passage that flaunts its monological nature, quoting the words of the daughter who stands right there instead of talking *with* her. From the start, then, monologue's departure from the sociality – one might say, from the family ties – of dialogue becomes identified with its departure from the function of grounding the audience.

This happens in other ways too throughout the first scene. After explaining that they lost their house, Nella goes on:

> [...] So we lived in various
> places, with various relations who lived
> variously in various places. All of them
> downwind of something. It's peculiar how
> no matter where you are you're always
> downwind of something peculiar.
> *Pause.*
> Those relations were called Howard
> and Georgia [...]
> *HOWARD and GEORGIA enter with
> shopping bags full of money. They go up the
> porch steps, and out, happy.* (11)

The first sentence, with its comical repetitions of "various," suggests a push to sum up, to be done with explaining, even at the cost of sense; abstracting vehemently, it makes a show of how much it doesn't tell. In place of this missing information, the speech wanders into speculation once again ("It's peculiar ... "). In a new twist, though, Nella then makes the baffling and hilarious claim that "Those relations," emphatically various though they were, "were called Howard / and Georgia," the names of the two very particular characters we subsequently see. The effect is to further divorce Nella's talking from the aim of grounding the action, as if the play has lost track of the "relations" between discourse and event, and also lost hold of the logic of "relation" – telling something – itself.

As these ruptured relations play out, family emerges as a shifting field of values, alternately concrete and abstract. The play presents a decidedly nebulous sense of one's responsibilities toward one's "various relations," including the cognitive *and narrative* responsibility of knowing exactly who they are (the very responsibility upon which Aristotle's favorite drama insists). We'll soon learn that Howard and Georgia are Nella's brother and sister-in-law, but her first speech waves this fact aside for the pleasure of running off its own rails. Similarly, after Susannah finally interrupts her mother, Nella introduces her as "Susie, the middle one" (12) – having previously referred to her as "my / younger one, Susannah." Family relations in themselves seem to attract a kind of interference, or static, and the dramatic imperative to tell the truth about (a) family hangs around awkwardly like an ancient curiosity – a front porch without a house to support it. Long monologues, with their many opportunities for vagary, provide a structure within which "relation" gets invoked, then gets lost.

Extravagant speech thus undermines the relations it ought to serve: we saw this conflict in *Godot*, where Lucky's monologue strains the intrascenic system to the point of physical agony. Even without a speaker who "struggles and shouts his text" amidst a hail of beatings, long speeches can build up a disturbing lack of fit with their fictional surroundings. Crucially, however, this ill-fittingness can then model the performance's relationship to *us*, implying that *we* are the locus of monologue's inappropriateness – that the characters are going on and on, not just in spite of each other's presence, but in spite of ours. This positioning of the audience emerges when Susannah interrupts Nella's opening monologue: "Mother, you're talking like a / dumb hick. Why do you do that?" (12). For better or worse, Wellman's core audience is decidedly non-hick, and Susannah's insult points this up in a heckle that puts her momentarily on "our" side. The implication is that Susannah rejects her mother's monologue, not on the terms that have been emerging within the world of the fiction, but on our terms; that we are in a position – here a social position – to miss or dismiss what we have heard.

But this alignment is not purely a function of siding with one character over another, as the end of the scene shows. When Susannah begins to talk at length, her own speech becomes even more unruly than her mother's:

SUSANNAH: No. The time is not ripe. The moment
  will come. Everything that is vertical
  will become horizontal. Seven feet, with
  unusual shoes on them, will emerge from
  seven open doors, doors previous locked
  tight shut. X will lead Y into the night,
  which will blaze up bright as day. A big
  pink passle of wind will stream out of a

>   billowy, purple cloud and ask each and
>   every one of us a thing or two he'd like
>   to know.
>   *She goes out.*
> NELLA: What in the name of Sam Hill do you do
>   with a child who talks like that? (13–14)

When Nella spoke these lines in a 2013 production at Brooklyn College, they drew the evening's first big laugh. The audience seemed to have been longing for some acknowledgement of the play's excesses of language, and the cognitive difficulties they cause. That's not to say Susannah's weirdness isn't delightful, or that the audience is barred from sympathizing with her apocalyptic hopes. But her speech exceeds what we can take in here and now, and we *don't* know what to "do / with a child who talks like that." It's as if we can't quite handle the play's wilder language, can't quite process, for instance, the assertion that "X will lead Y into the night." However much pleasure we may take in such speeches, they are still in some sense going over our heads. Their logic, their economy is not our own. The big laugh that confirms this implies that when we come together (laugh *together*, and not just in scattered chuckles), it's in order to ratify the exclusionary standards of "this part of the country." As a collective, we can't accommodate the verbal meandering of an idiosyncratic voice.

In trying to empty out theater's domestic relations, Wellman's poetics make a political retort: *A Murder of Crows* opened the same year "family values" became a rallying cry of the Republican campaign. Indeed, the play's opening description, "*A front porch of an American-type house. Only: no house*" (9), literalizes Wellman's ongoing interest in exposing the standard "American-type house" as a false front. Uncle Howard and Aunt Georgia obsessively disparage "Foreigners" (17), "Arabs" (33), and "other Asiatic filths" (38) throughout the play, their home precariously constituted through violent exclusion. The play's sense of domesticity as an ideal at once vacuous and vicious echoes a remark from Horkheimer and Adorno's "The Culture Industry": "The citizens whose lives are split between business and private life, their private life between ostentation and intimacy, their intimacy between the sullen community of marriage and the bitter solace of being entirely alone, at odds with themselves and with everyone, are virtually already Nazis" (125).[13] Wellman literalizes this notion that conventional social and familial bonds are in fact sustained by violent division. "[M]an I wish / I could've run him through a roaring buzz saw," says Howard of his brother-in-law. "[...] But don't get me wrong, I loved the guy" (36).

Monologue serves Wellman's satirical impulse, since the largesse of long speeches allows cruelty or bigotry to talk itself blue in the face. Monologue is a natural vehicle for hyperbole, and its gathering momentum can carry apparently innocuous clichés almost effortlessly to hysterical, violent conclusions – not entirely unlike the escalation Horkheimer and Adorno themselves build into the long sentence just cited. For instance, in the play's second scene, Georgia has been complaining about Howard's family, but acknowledges it would be wrong to kick them out. She goes on:

> Only Howard, I have a vision of how good
> America could be, if only it weren't for
> your family, particularly that part of it
> currently residing in our house, because
> America deserves better than this, I mean
> this overcrowded, down-in-the-dumps,
> small-time depression atmosphere, it
> just doesn't hit the nail on the head,
> it's not up to snuff, furthermore it's
> bothersome and a crying shame. And I know
> we've got to be hospitable even when we
> don't give a crap, but why oh why must they
> smell so bad, Jesus, Howard, it drives me
> crazy, the way they stink [...] Howard, could they be
> THAT INSANE that they would only pretend
> to bathe, but secretly not bathe? (19–20)

All the characters in this play go on and on, but in speeches like this – as opposed to Nella's, for example – the prattling becomes a kind of hectoring whose lengthiness ("... furthermore ...") consumes its own last shred of reliability. Yet the speech ends by swerving into a rather creative, idiosyncratic and funny fantasy. Even while it bears its speaker along toward a species of manic breakdown, this language continues producing a quotient of surprise, a pleasure never reducible to our sense of superiority over the character.

Georgia's deficient family feeling is, after all, something the play as a whole shares. In another instance of satirical monologue, Wellman makes merry with that TV hallmark, the serious, intergenerational let's-sit-down-and-talk scene. Interrupting Susannah's vigil by the porch, Uncle Howard engages her on the subject of Aunt Georgia. They agree that Georgia is "a hideous, rotten cunt," but then the conversation takes a turn for the normal: "It's / true," says Howard, "but she's got her feelings too. Life / hasn't been too easy on her" (24). If his speech stopped there, we might be at the start of a dramatically effective (and affecting) dialogue, a turning point in the characters' relations; responding to signals that have become second nature, we might find our own attitudes toward these people starting to soften. But instead Howard *keeps talking*, and as he talks, his speech conveys him irresistibly beyond the bounds of our empathy. "We old folks / don't have enough to do," he continues,

> most of the people
> we hate are dead [...] and since all we believe
> in is murder and hatred and envy of anyone
> who has more fun than we do, it's rough.
> You're lucky you can still get excited by
> the idea of causing someone pain, particularly
> if they're colored, or an Arab, or look funny.
> I know it's hard for you to imagine, but
> Georgia was beautiful once, god, when she
> put on her robes, at the big Klonvocations,
> she was beautiful, and her bigotry was beautiful
> too. Breathtaking bigotry.   (24)

Besides disabling any identification with the character, two aspects are salient in Howard's speech: first, the way this leap into the despicable works specifically *against* the generic expectation the scene begins by evoking (the meaningful heart-to-heart), and second, the way a related dissonance arises from the swerve into another linguistic register, particularly with the word "bigotry" and its alliterations. Meandering into a weirdly objective excursus on the speaker's own run-of-the-mill depravity, the speech utterly fails as a pitch for sympathy; but somehow, outrage seems equally beside the point. Together with its wildly incriminating content, the speech's comically detached tone – for instance, packing "murder and hatred and envy" into a subordinate clause – gives the impression that the character himself doesn't know what he's saying. Or perhaps more accurately: the impression that no *character* is saying this at all. Instead, alliteration and abstraction ("her bigotry was beautiful ... Breathtaking bigotry") recall us to the fact that this is a piece of writing – that someone who isn't here right now has been having fun with these words.

Approaching this moment purely as political satire, one might well feel that Wellman is setting up a "straw-man argument" (as Jon Erickson has claimed about Wellman's 1990 play *Sincerity Forever* ["Mise" 365]). Isn't a character who frankly enjoys "causing someone pain, particularly / if they're colored, or an Arab" just a modern-day, moustache-twirling Simon

Legree? Isn't this the kind of clubby, lazy liberalism that gives its audience the satisfaction of denouncing cartoon racism without engaging its real complexities? There is undoubtedly a measure of self-congratulation to be had here, as there is in recognizing and denouncing the stereotypes that give Parks's characters their names in *The Death*. But as I suggested in the previous chapter, such devices can also work to undermine the moral clarity they seem at first to promote. In Howard's speech, and in other monologues throughout the play, Wellman goes too far precisely in order to begin eviscerating our confidence in the play's political clarity. Once we have recognized Howard and Georgia as bigots, their rhapsodizing no longer heightens our sense of moral meaning. It would be truer to say that these speeches *indulge* in ethical and political detritus which they refuse to redeem as valuable information.[14] The excessiveness of this discourse tends to swamp our grasp of any message being conveyed.

How does this extravagance bear on existing critical discussions of monologue? It would be a grave misrepresentation of the theorists I've cited to claim that they imagine *theatron* communication on the model of a straightforward "message," political or otherwise. (Lehmann in fact explicitly contests this understanding; see *Postdramatic* 31–32 and "Decade" 35.) But when a play teases us with the prospect of celebrating our community values together (xenophobia *is* bad!) and then folds in on itself, curling up with an inane alliteration, the expectation aroused and then unmet produces a twinge of abandonment. In these moments, it feels as if the play has been guided by aims other than our reception. This implication comes to a head in a device Wellman uses frequently in his monologues: overlapping speech. In the flashback to Raymond's funeral, Nella, Howard, and Georgia stand around the coffin, "*quarreling, all at the top of their voices*" (33). They all speak at length so that, for example, the following three chunks are roughly simultaneous:

GEORGIA: [...] Absurd. He looked like a god damned foreigner in them shoes. What kind of standard-average person would go and put on shoes like that, and him being an American! and go and pretend he was like one of us, decent and normal? (33)
HOWARD: [...] like Raymond here, a total fizzle, a colossal existential dud, a complete and laughable failure at all he ever attempted in all his clownish, dipshit, clutzy life [...] (35)
NELLA: [...] I know, please forgive me for being such a fool; I know I've

> been a total fool with my life, all of it,
> including getting poor and homeless after
> his death and having to impose like this [. . .] (37)

As the speeches get more and more extreme, Georgia's paranoia, Howard's sadism, and Nella's self-loathing meld into a cacophony; no audience member will be able to take it all in.

Monologue's unsociability is thus brought to a climax. This is language that doesn't care who receives it; it is, we might say, the bald renunciation of dialogue, not only on the part of the characters but, more profoundly, on the part of the play itself with respect to its audience. There is great pleasure to be had in the exuberant sonic chaos that results. But much of that pleasure comes from a sense of how outrageously the play is outstripping us. The shared present of performance becomes a medium of insufficiency; our simultaneous attendance as an audience begins to feel like an *obstacle* to reception, since we know we could only access all this text by reading it. But of course, reading this scene comes with its own sense of insufficiency, since there we know we are not "hearing" the lines simultaneously in our mind's ear as we would in performance. This is writing that demands enactment, not in order to validate a shared here-and-now but in order to exploit and expose the present as a site of dissonance and interference. We are far from the "theatre of the speech-act" whose spectators "experience a deep 'relation' with the actor/performer" in a moment of "intimate confrontation" (Lehmann, "Decade" 40). Invaded by these monologues, theater's live happening is vital – but as, precisely, the medium in which communicative relations can most powerfully *fail* to occur.

The three overlapping speeches are similar in both content and structure to the characters' other monologues throughout the play. Their long-winded spiraling into hyperbole, renunciation of communicative efficiency, and indulgence in extravagant turns of phrase – together with their hilariously flagrant inappropriateness in the context of the funeral – make them seem like perfect candidates for mutual cancelation, implying that the same could be true of the play's other monologues, which also have these features. That is, this scene offers something like a theory of monologue, suggesting that its shameless proliferations are fundamentally extraneous, its words out of place to the point that, as far as anyone else is concerned, they may as well be wasted. The characters are not speaking to each other or to us; they are mouthing *off*, their language oriented by some polestar that neither "intra-scenic" nor "*theatron*" parameters can comprehend.

The resulting chaos is very funny, but it has a serious side too. A few minutes later, as Susannah and the resurrected Raymond regard the frozen flashback, Raymond's monologue brings the scene to a close with only a few words from Susannah (the asterisk indicates where their lines overlap):

RAYMOND: [...] But, hell, that's all history, and I'm like
          you. I get this kink in my side that tells
          me the weather's changing, and that makes
          an optimist of me. Even if I am homeless,
          and have lived with crows and the common people
          think I died buried in chicken shit right up
          to the butt end of my boot.
SUSANNAH: Dad,* I love you.
RAYMOND: Hell yes, I'd still be living with crows
          if I weren't allergic to feathers. (41)

More than any other speech in the play, Susannah's words here go straight for the gut, hailing us into an empathetic identification. And yet the pathos of Susannah's line comes not only from what it says, but more profoundly from the fact that what it says cannot be fully heard within the structure of the play. Wellman uses Raymond's monologue, his talking-too-much, to muddy the waters of emotional transmission and interfere with the response we feel ourselves wanting to have. This is a gesture that raises the prospect of a fulfilling and straightforward communication along both axes – and, at the same time, withholds it. Once again, the overlap circulates between performance and text: in print, the asterisk simulates the interference of simultaneous performance. In fact, by adopting asterisks for this purpose instead of the slashes other writers use, Wellman heightens the sense of his presentation as incomplete. Following an asterisk like a footnote, Susannah's "I love you" is "subtext" in a specifically Wellmanian sense, discourse that is not fully *here* for our consumption.[15]

There is something cruel about this moment, in which monologue shows its claws: not merely a variation on dialogical intercourse, Raymond's monologue becomes a discourse of utter selfishness in order to renounce the possibility of *communicating* love. "In our time only bad artists name what they cherish," Wellman writes in "The Theatre of Good Intentions," "because what is cherished, or revered, or loved, will immediately be used as a tool by the powers that be" (66). Resisting what Adorno calls the "mendacious positivity of meaning," Wellman makes theater a space where such transactions are held at bay. Such theater, we might say, recuperates the value of loneliness.

As we saw above, critics have often claimed that the solitary quality of literary monologue vanishes in work for the stage. Wellman's speeches should make us ask if "the inevitable status of the spectators as recipients" (Geis 7) is really so inevitable. Instead he seems to maintain the "deviant" nature of literary monologue, theorized by Ken Frieden as a discourse of "counternormative swerves" (190):

> deviation from convention always threatens meaning, for how can an individual invent new forms and still be understood? By asserting an individual style or a deviant form of expression, monologue borders on meaninglessness. Literary monologues provide the basis for inquiry into semantic solitude, associated with idiolects that strive to preserve their autonomy while reaching for an elusive otherness. (194)

Wellman puts this deviance to work in the theater. If we recall Parks's depiction of the ghostly figure who "will almost always take up residence in a corner" ("From *Elements*" 12), we can see that these writers share a desire for theater that does something other than present itself to us – a desire we can also trace back to James and Stein. In *A Murder of Crows*, Wellman's use of monologue works in tandem with his cheerful thematization of the dysfunctional family and the literally broken home to emphasize the (anti)social dimension of this project. Withholding, exceeding, or blocking the communicative speech that would unite us in confidently sympathetic understanding, the play enacts an energetic denial of our togetherness in the theater.

This impulse bespeaks a utopian conviction that the longing for a *radically different* community needs to be cultivated *as* longing, not bought off with the unifying affirmation of a dramatic "*so ist es.*" Theater can neither constitute nor present such a community "in our time" without assimilating it to the structures of the present world. To that end, as we saw earlier, theater has to avoid the kind of presentation that would *accomplish* a collectivity within the terms of the present – an "adaptation of spirit to utility" (Adorno) that would channel our discontent into the satisfying payoff of a lesson learned, a "good intention" well met. Unless theater finds a way to defer communication, it will end up as one more variant of the same old murderous meet-and-greet, sold out, as Wellman puts it, to "the powers that be."

Wellman allegorizes this concern through the eponymous crows of his play. The crows appear at the beginning of the fourth scene: "*Three big, evil-looking* CROWS *on a tree-limb in the distance*" (26). They are deliciously ominous, a muted visual correlative to Susannah's visions of global destruction; they appear in a moment when Susannah is alone, as if they can only be summoned by solitude. And they are marked as an alternate form of life by their position "in the distance" (in a production photograph of the premiere at Primary Stages, taken by Marvin Einhorn, they occupy a catwalk). Recalling Beckett again, we might say that such a figure is precisely what *Godot* resolutely refuses: the crows embody the prospect of being somewhere else, an outside perspective from which "this muckheap" could become one landscape among others. The crows' alternative perspective effects a Brechtian "literarization" in the sense we have been tracing: their positioning creates an internal distance that breaks up the stage. Indeed, Wellman's crows might be described as specifically textual figures.[16] The color of ink, they embody the play's title, which announces more than anything a peculiarity of language: the improbable and oddly exciting term "murder of crows." As any vocab geek knows, "murder" is the standard collective noun for these birds, like a "pride of lions" or a "quarrel of gnats." The play's crows are thus a figure of speech first of all. This figural, textual quality compounds a sense that the crows are *not quite here*. Before Susannah has even noticed them, they seem to promise the possibility of an escape from the "bubble of / sham, pure sham" (13) in which she feels trapped:

> I'm tired of this boring weather, I want
> some other, more interesting weather than
> this [...] when we emerge from the other
> end we may not even be "people" any more, we'll
> be something else, something finer, harder,
> cleaner, more murderous but much more spiritual. (27–28)

Through the mischievous polyvalence of language, the exciting prospect of becoming "something ... more murderous" than human crystallizes into the possibility of joining the murder of crows.

When Susannah does join them, however, this vision undergoes a rather sad banalization. Swapping murder as ecstatic vision for "murder" as social structure, Susannah ends up in a family distressingly like the one she has fled. The crows turn out to have their own repressive ideology: "The basic order of things has long been established," Crow 3 rebukes Crow 2. "[...] Face it: anything else smacks of heresy" (58). Susannah is mute now, "trying to pass for a crow by imitating Crow 1" (56). As a positivity, as an *achieved* community and no longer a shadowy prospect, the crows cannot sustain the thrilling alterity they previously figured. To actually join the crows, the play suggests, is to rob them of the "distance" that was their promise, reducing them to a kind of taxidermy – that is, murdering them. When the crows begin to speak at the end, with Susannah among them, the stage directions reveal for the first time that "they look more like mynas or parrots than real crows: i.e., they're *fake* crows" (56). And the *"Crow's Song"* they sing pointedly contrasts with the breathtaking virtuosity of Susannah's earlier speeches:

> Boom-boom, boom-boom, boom-boom,
> boom-boom, boom-boom, boom-boom,
> boom-boom [...]
> One potato, two potato, three potato, four potato, five potato, six potato, seven potato, eight!
> *And repeat, etc.* (56–57)

In this way, the play suggests that the community we can "have" here and now is not worth having. The crows' pedestrian song trumpets the play's refusal to offer us a theatrical model of triumphant community. Frustrating any desires for an image of crow utopia, Wellman constructs theater as the perpetual displacement, not the enactment, of a fulfilling togetherness.

Nevertheless, the last scene does bring its own zany satisfactions. In a startling and funny genre shift, Crows 2 and 3 begin engaging in something like a miniature conversation play:

> CROW 2: Did it ever occur to you that we
> don't have to talk about things
> the way we do? [...] I mean "caw caw" does not
> shed much light on the basic
> issues of Being, nor of where
> we come from, nor of whither
> we are headed. Not to mention
> the problem of who we are ...
> CROW 3: I don't know what you're
> talking about. Everyone
> knows god created our people
> out of marsh gas [...]
> CROW 2: What about the problem of other minds?
> CROW 3: Heresy. Errant heresy. (57–59)

This conversation seems to distill, or formalize, the play's ongoing conflict between the forces of normality and a defiant strangeness that manifests as wild speech. Crow 2's insistence that we "don't have to talk about things / the way we do" could be a central statement of Wellman's poetics.

Crow 2 thus becomes a final avatar for the monologic voice of the play; but that voice has changed significantly from previous scenes. Susannah's lyrical wildness, Nella's meandering curiosity, and Howard and Georgia's vicious hyperbole all seem to have been sublimated into a mélange of philosophical jargon: "Being," "the problem of other minds," and later, "Type A entities," "infinite regress" (60). On one level, of course, this is just another of Wellman's characteristic "swerves," a change of register that combats dramatic closure and keeps us on our toes. But in its sustained reference (however garbled) to an existing discursive practice – that is, to philosophy as a field of intellectual endeavor – I think Crow 2's speech articulates a desire on the part of the play to join *some* conversation, some community, whose locus is decidedly somewhere else. Throughout Wellman's work, theoretical reference functions as a check on dramatic "immediacy"; here, the hilarious inappropriateness of Crow 2's scholastic efforts seems to me to suggest a voice aimed over the head of anyone who can hear it, reaching for a linguistic relationship at long distance.

As the scene draws to a close, this desire becomes increasingly urgent. "Think / about it! That's all I'm asking," Crow 2 begs; "I mean, really fellas [...] REALLY. / I mean you gotta think about these things [...]" (59–60). The emphatically addressed quality of this last monologue, in the face of Crow 3's continued rejection, leaves us with a sense that all the play's crazy talk is striving for the contact it can't find. "*CROW 1, 3, and 4 start up the song as CROW 2 rambles on during a slow blackout,*" we read (60). Monologue "rambles on" extravagantly, uselessly. Its irrelevance isn't limited to the fictional scene, within which the other characters elaborately ignore it, but extends to the theater itself: the very building demonstrates its indifference by fading to black, as if the rambling were literally putting us all to sleep. And yet this last speech implies that there has always been a "really fellas!" concealed in the deviant voice of monologue – an appeal to fellowship that no given community, including the theatrical one, can satisfy.

Combining the discourse of the university seminar with those of the street corner and the pop song in its manic invitation, this speech in fact performs its own vision of fellowship: a vision not based in the co-presence of bodies in a theatrical here-and-now – crows on a branch – but in the constellation *of languages* referring to multiple, incommensurable sites. Applying Bakhtin, Castagno perceptively describes this multiplicity in Wellman as "an internal dialogism among various language systems" ("Varieties" 137). But it is also important that here, the "internal dialogism" of Bakhtin's *literary* models occurs within a speech *theatrically* marked as a mode of solitude, a discourse positioned as failing to reach anybody, which in this sense remains outrageously "mono-". That is: the meeting of voices within Wellman's monologue is offset by its defiant unsociability in the scene of performance. As the play is realized, brought forward into our world as someone's pointless act of speech, dialogism lingers as the trace of poetic composition. Which means that one of the theatrical functions of Wellman's monologue is to make us sense a dialogue that *isn't* happening here and now: a coming-together that does not *happen* at all, but haunts the intercourse of "our time" the way the shadow of a rapturous violence haunts the pedestrian "murder of crows" – or the way a script haunts a stage.[17] By squandering theater's power to communicate, these speeches speculate on a form of togetherness yet unheard-of, a communion still radically strange.

If "the truly political dimension of theatre has its place ... in the situation, the relation, the social moment which theatre as such is able to constitute" (Lehmann, "Decade" 35), then Wellman stakes his politics on the social moment theater *can't* constitute here and now. His monologues put in a pitch for Herbert Blau's claim that "the enduring gravity of theater is not collective but solitary" (*Audience* 90). As anyone who has felt miserably alone in an audience can attest, theater often brings us together to keep us apart – to show us how little we share. For Brecht, this possibility is crucial to theater's revolutionary potential, a potential traditional theater has suppressed. "It is a common truism ... that the audience, once it is in the theatre, is not a number of individuals but a collective individual, a mob," he writes (122). Brecht acknowledges that in dramatic theater, "a collective is created in the auditorium *for the duration of the entertainment*, on the basis of the 'common humanity' shared by all the listeners"; but his own theater "is not interested in creating such a collective. It divides its audience" (92). Brecht values theater as a site where seamless collectivity can spectacularly fail to happen. Lehmann himself suggests that postdramatic theater has continued to embrace this possibility:

> The "community" that arises is not one of similar people, i.e. a community of spectators who have been made similar through commonly shared motifs (the human being in general), but instead a common contact of different singularities who do not melt their respective perspectives into a whole ... Some critics may see in this only a socially dangerous or at least artistically questionable tendency towards an arbitrary and solipsistic reception, but perhaps this suspension of the laws of sense formation heralds a more liberal sphere of sharing and communicating that inherits the utopias of modernism. (83–84)

This kind of theater courts utopia by refusing its audience the immediate community produced through drama. Lehmann's description applies to a wide range of contemporary theatrical practice; but it should be remembered that Brecht conceived such division as a corollary of literarization, that is, as something produced in part by bringing *writing* forward within the theatrical scene. Wellman's monologues work this way, defying our copresence as his verbiage exceeds any communicative aim. By refusing to let the present comprehend its content, his writerly theater "heralds," as Lehmann writes, "a more liberal sphere" than the one that brings us together, under this roof, now.

The Other Axis

When Wellman writes that "in our time, only bad artists name what they cherish, because what is cherished, or revered, or loved, will immediately be used as a tool by the powers that be," he echoes Adorno's complaint that "The concrete serves for nothing better than that something, by being in some way distinct, can be identified, possessed, and sold" (*Aesthetic* 31). For Adorno, Beckett's "abstractness" exemplifies the right response to this situation, withholding the particularity that would otherwise be commodified: "In the act of omission," Adorno writes, "that which is omitted survives through its exclusion, as consonance survives in atonal harmony" ("Trying" 124–125). Although Wellman's procedures are very different from Beckett's, we have begun to see how his writing also withholds what it seeks to preserve – withholds the prospect of love, or coming-together, from the communicative economy that would "sell" us those experiences now. Reading *A Murder of Crows*, apparently one of Wellman's most conventional works, I have tried to show how its language works to defer both intrascenic and theatrical communication, launching an idiosyncratic and fundamentally extraneous discourse that is never quite "for" its audience.

According to J. M. Bernstein, the cultivation of language beyond communication is central to Adorno's theoretical project too. Like Lehmann, Bernstein adopts a terminology of "axes" to elucidate his claim. For Adorno, he writes, the "communicative axis of language" represents "the striving for transparent, intersubjective communication without loss or remainder, the complete fitting of language to the demand for intersubjective consensus" (283). This ideal represses language's other axis, its "expressive, sensible, truth-oriented relation to the world" (ibid.); this "expressive" axis is what Adorno wants to restore.[18] Now, Bernstein's reference to a "sensible ... relation to the world" might at first make us think that the "expressive axis" has its analog in Lehmann's *theatron* axis, as a link between the speaker and the actual present of her situation. On this understanding, the goal (for both Adornian dialectics and postdramatic theater) would be to shift from an act of representation to an act of presence: really being here now. But Bernstein makes it clear that expression for Adorno cannot be reduced to a moment of straightforward presentness. On the contrary, the expressive relation concerns an "excess beyond phenomenal appearing" that "relates to what has *powers* of resistance to the subject and its own ends, possesses a 'life' of its own (and thus, so to speak, turns away from the subject as its mode of appearing to the subject)" (193). In fact, Lehmann approaches a similar ideal when he describes the "coolness" of many postdramatic productions as an "attitude of deviating and turning away" (119). For a theoretical or theatrical sensibility that values this attitude, the problem with "communicative" language is not just that it abandons the concrete reality of its object, a problem we could try to solve by facing into what is "really" present. More distressingly, communication denies the object's ability to execute a turning-away of its own; in this sense, it is an *imposition* of presence. Locating everything on the same plane of commensurability, communication seeks to fill in the cracks and crevasses, closing off any hollows into which meaning might retreat.

What communication denies, then, is not presence, but distance. Asha Varadharajan observes that Adorno pursues "a philosophy whose very proximity to its object ironically confirms its distance *from* that object" (60–61). In the context of theater, we might say: the dramaturgy Wellman wants to counter is one that would reduce performance to an ideal of total givenness, presence *for us*. If we consider drama's totalizing "*so ist es*" an attempt to found just such an "intersubjective communication without loss or remainder," then we can see how theater's collective structure brings the Adornian problem of communication to a head. The model of postdramatic theater as a shift from fictional representation to immediate presentation, moreover, offers no resistance to the communicative norm. On the contrary, in identifying such theater with the "criterion of communicative success," Lehmann acknowledges this norm's affinity with the *theatron* axis. Bernstein's "expressive axis" would therefore have to be a *third* axis, one which does not describe a relation of immediate connection.

This cultivation of distance has its theatrical counterpart in the strand of experimental work that Wellman's writing exemplifies. Combining

Lehmann's and Bernstein's geometric models, then, we would get a structure like this:

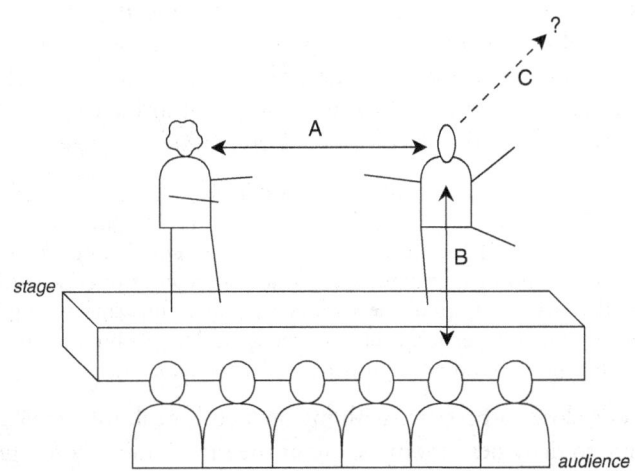

Illustration 1   A = intrascenic axis of communication (between characters)
B = *theatron* axis of communication (performer-audience)
C = noncommunicative axis: Adornian "expression" (Bernstein); negative theatrics

Displacing the intrascenic dynamics of drama's fiction (A), Lehmann's "communicative success" along the *theatron* axis (B) nevertheless still potentially seeks the "intersubjective communication without loss or remainder" that both Adorno and Wellman repudiate. Syers registers this demand for a third axis when she recommends that stagings of Wellman's work "create an environment for the play to happen that shrugs off the habit of either the model (traditional realism) or the spectacle (which traffics in the commerce of desire and pleasure between the stage and the audience)." Wellman himself lampoons such "commerce" when he characterizes the "theatre of good intentions" as a theater desperate to cut out *waste*. All the elements of its plays, he writes, are meant to be "cunningly interconnected in such a way that nothing is wasted. Waste is a great obsession of the writer of the American well-made" (64). Dramaturgically speaking, "waste" occurs when the audience does not "get" anything in particular, when – for instance – the people onstage are just talking on and on. When such extravagance occurs, we are in mode (C): an expression that cannot be subsumed in the economy of the present, but orients itself toward an eventual, utopian reception which cannot take place here and now.

By embracing this kind of excess, Wellman's theater rejects the sound economic calculus of cause and effect, communication, and uptake. It also contests the assumption that theater's social value is produced directly through its ability to bring us together in a shared experience. On the contrary, Wellman's work is characterized throughout by a prickly suspicion of closeness that recalls Adorno's critique of intimacy. The "intimate sphere" demands "critical scrutiny," Adorno argues, because

> intimacies estrange, violate the imponderably delicate aura of the other which is his condition as a subject. Only by the recognition of distance in our neighbor is strangeness alleviated: accepted into consciousness. The presumption of undiminished nearness present from the first, however, the flat denial of strangeness, does the other supreme wrong, virtually negates him as a particular human being ... "counts him in," incorporates him into the inventory of property. (*Minima* 182).

The other's close co-presence with my own corporeal, subjective existence tempts me to deny her otherness; but at the same time, my recognition of her alterity – her "imponderably delicate aura" – depends on my registering this danger *within* the situation of our being here together. For Wellman, our "nearness" in the theater can likewise activate, and sustain, a rigorous cultivation of separateness. The task of theatrical imagination is to inscribe this distance in the midst of co-presence, in order to make the recognition of aura possible.

The idea of theater as a particularly auratic medium doesn't come from Adorno, but from Walter Benjamin's canonical 1936 essay "The Work of Art in the Age of Mechanical Reproduction." Benjamin describes aura as a phenomenon of the artwork's "presence in time and space, its unique existence at the place where it happens to be": this uniqueness constitutes the work's "authenticity" and thus, ultimately, its cultic "authority," all of which are nullified by technical reproducibility (220–222). One of the paradigms of auratic art, for Benjamin, is the theatrical performer, whose compelling role (e.g. Macbeth) is further suffused with the commanding force of his own live presence (229–230). But Benjamin's conception of aura is not simply an idea of proximity, of an immediately shared space and time; on the contrary, auratic presence implies distance, a dimension within which the object is fundamentally inaccessible (222). This means that aura is not enhanced but destroyed by "the desire of contemporary masses to bring things 'closer' spatially and humanly" (223): technological reproduction disables auratic presence by making the object maximally available. Theater is auratic precisely insofar as it *limits* the "co" in co-presence; its actuality becomes the medium of something that eludes our grasp, and chastens our grasping.

Although "The Work of Art" largely associates aura with mystification and celebrates its decline, in other essays Benjamin writes more mournfully about the loss of aura.[19] When Adorno returns to the concept in his *Aesthetic Theory*, he faults the "Work of Art" essay for devaluing aura – precisely, Adorno suggests, by granting insufficient emphasis to aura's quality of distance:

> What slips through the wide mesh of this theory ... is the element opposed to cultic contexts that motivated Benjamin to introduce the concept of aura in the first place, that is, that which moves into the distance and is critical of the ideological superficies of life. The condemnation of aura easily becomes the dismissal of qualitatively modern art that distances itself from the logic of familiar things ... (*Aesthetic* 56)

Aura cannot, Adorno suggests, be written off as mystification; rather, it needs to be understood as a dimension of resistance to the existing world. Aura "is whatever goes beyond [the work's] factual givenness," he writes (*Aesthetic* 45).[20] Returning this idea to Wellman, we can see that the problem with the "theatre of good intentions" is that its presence is all "givenness": it holds nothing back, producing only what can be subsumed into "the logic of familiar things." The auratic presence that, for Wellman, constitutes the theatrical is a presence produced as distance – which is also to say, a particularity that resists being grasped or "brought closer" in the way Benjamin describes.

I think it is for the sake of that resistance that Wellman's poetic statements tend to include language of the kind this book has largely been questioning: language that values the performance here-and-now against an "elsewhere" that supposedly dominates conventional theater. In the introductory paragraph of "The Theatre of Good Intentions," for example, Wellman complains about American theater's emphasis on "content" in these terms: "What is shown annihilates the showing. The true play comes to take place somewhere else, and the physical and spiritual being of theatre vanishes in a cloud of hermeneutical epiphenomena ... This is also why American drama, for the most part, lacks theatrical presence" (59). He goes on to bemoan a "loss of theatrical presence, there-ness, or actuality" (61), complaining that characters in the "theatre of good intentions" are "merely theoretical" (62). Such statements can fit in all too well with the familiar discourse privileging emphatic actuality ("presence over representation") in theater – a discourse that, as we saw in Chapter 1, generally fails to observe its own attunement to traditional dramatic norms. But we should ask: if "there-ness, or actuality" is something Wellman wants, what does he want it for?

We have seen that Beckett strives for maximum actuality in order to suggest, dialectically, its opposite; and that Parks devises a writerly presence alternative to that of the stage. Neither of these projects is entirely foreign to Wellman. He adds to them a desire to locate and exploit the rifts *within* actuality, a conviction not only that the present is always already internally discontinuous (as in Stein), but also that the here-and-now is a precarious system harboring its own destruction:

> The whole, entire fabric
> of the heavens will burst open, like a ripe fig,
> and a whole new sky we never dreamt was there,
> will appear. Only it *has* been there all along,
> only we humans haven't been able to see it,
> on account of being chronically short-sighted. (*Murder* 32)[21]

"Theatrical presence" is valuable, for Wellman, precisely as the hidden dimension of actuality that includes ("all along") the undoing of what actually is. To the confident "*so ist es*" of drama's absolute present, Wellman opposes a present already constituted by its own imminent negation: this is how it is *but already almost not*. The "there-ness" Wellman wants theater to attain is just this precariousness. It is neither the robust embodiment of people and things in three-dimensional space, nor the pure ephemerality of performance's passing-away. Rather, it is the densely phenomenal arena within which the fault lines of the present begin to suggest themselves – "revealing," as Adorno writes in an early lecture on modernism, "the very cracks that reality would like to cover over in order to exist in safety" ("Why" 129).

"This will kill that": *Speculations*

Wellman's most sustained attempt to articulate this ideal of theater is *Speculations*, a long aphoristic essay periodically interrupted by enigmatic symbols and other forms of typographic play.[22] The piece is full of allusions to philosophy, theoretical physics, and literature, from which Wellman assembles an arsenal of terms and ideas about the nature and value of theater. These terms, including "scatter," "repression," "Hoole Space," and "Wild Time," seem to constellate rather than define an inherently elusive object. For example:

> Scatter conceals the theatrical as well; becomes a felt presence, the enabler of what is termed the "uncanny". This presence is a kind of theatrical presence in the absence of what is not . . .
>
> Scatter shows us only the outlines, as a kind of event, but also as a species of presence. But as we do not know what it is, we do not know what to do about the matter.
>
> This not knowing about the matter is intrinsic and inescapable. (10)

Wellman's notion of theatrical presence as "presence in the absence of what is not" recalls the utopian negation we saw in *Godot*, while his description of theater as a *showing* that provides for neither recognition nor action might well remind us of May Bartram's performance in "The Beast in the Jungle." Wellman suggests that theater is worth caring about exactly insofar as it "turns away from the subject as its mode of appearing to the subject" (Bernstein). This should be a radically unsettling experience, in which we are forced to acknowledge a reality not fully available to us.

"Because the hidden parts of the sleeping cat are hidden," Wellman writes, "does not mean that the hidden parts are not there" (16). This theater, like those we have encountered in previous chapters, is a theater of "other parts" (Bersani). But Wellman gives theatrical alterity a new, menacing twist: as any mouse knows, the most salient "hidden parts" of a "sleeping cat" are the sharp ones. In "turn[ing] away" from its beholders, this theater also threatens to turn *against* us; it is "alive with surprises, as the GOOSE discovered when she fell down the wrong hole . . . and was devoured by small, fierce creatures with wicked claws" (20). *Speculations* is populated throughout by these "small, fierce creatures." Beyond defying the midsize respectability of the beautiful Aristotelian animal, these imps – at once unknowable and destructive – embody the negativity at the heart of Wellman's conception of theater. In his hands, auratic "turning away" becomes a mode of malevolent threat: "the What You Will of theater will always go another way; go another way, as though she were a small, dangerous creature, chittering and snarling. perhaps venomous" (11). These descriptions, like the apocalyptic fantasy that takes wing in *A Murder of Crows*, attest to a condition in which aura can only keep itself alive through an imaginary violence. It's as if theater had to cover its retreat from communication with tooth and nail – as if only "snarling" and "venom" could protect it from dissolving into fungibility.[23]

For James, as we saw, theater emerges as both the spatializing distraction of temporal stream and the temporalizing disruption of pictorial space. In *Speculations*, Wellman returns explicitly to that dynamic, both literalizing and enlivening the violence it implies:

> This is how theater works. Time and space move
>   slowly and silently but the animosity between
>   is of an unimaginable intensity.
> Profusion devours one; then the other.
> . . .
> Space thinks, Something something something.
> Time thinks, This will kill that. (23–24)

The special value of the theater medium depends on the potential antagonism between its spatial and temporal dimensions, the way temporal movement in space or spatial persistence in time can boil up into a campaign of each *against* the other. In the midst of this unthinkable contest, something else arises – a "Profusion" that might make us think equally of James's "innumerable and wonderful things" (*Ambassadors* 468) and of Stein's "blue sky of different colors" (*Paisieu* 159). More explicitly than either of these writers, however, Wellman imagines theatrical Profusion as a kind of pandemonium. Theater's "scattering" of time and space in his vision not only diffracts both dimensions, but alienates them from each other, as if the consistency of time and space in everyday life were merely the result of a tenuous interdimensional accord that could be broken at any moment. For Wellman, theater takes up residence within the present *as* the present's liability to tear itself apart.

More specifically, this simmering antagonism defines the importance of *writing* in Wellman's theatrical universe. *Speculations* as a whole – with its dizzying array of allusions, its startling and delectable imagery, its over-the-top declarative pomp – is a shameless display of writerly virtuosity, an invitation to the theatrical pleasures of the text. Those pleasures are prickly, a flash of tooth and claw as the object ducks out of view:

> accordingly, the other (Force ∏∏) is called *Pleasure*; pleasure, the
>   rubicund and starling-eyed Ramificator. . . .
> (Here the manuscript breaks off apparently torn with great violence.
> The remaining pages, crumpled and wadded, were discovered in the
>   nest of certain, evilish Emerald-hued *Macaws*, deep within the
>   central regions of impenetrable, forest wilderness at Brooklyn
>   College.) (70–71)

Withdrawing abruptly from its own presentation, the text suggests that the only kind of story worth showing is the story of a violent disruption *of* showing. At the same moment when Wellman insists on the materiality of the page ("crumpled and wadded"), he frames that page as the medium of an auratic turning away, a flight into "impenetrable" realms. We might recall here the "little slip uh paper" Parks imagines as the vessel of escape into utopian freedom (*Death* 112). Where Parks paradoxically and poignantly conceives writing as the medium of transit to a world *without* writing, however, Wellman can't resist stamping his utopia with literacy: "Brooklyn College," whose "forest wilderness" probably houses the English Department's playwriting program.

These collegiate Macaws should remind us of Crow 2, the similarly "evil-looking" avian academic. Indeed, we might speculate that they are the very same "mynas or parrots" who have appeared in *A Murder of Crows* as "*fake* crows," now glimpsed in their (un)natural habitat. I remarked earlier that the crows are "textual figures"; the macaws seem to literalize this association by appearing as both the guardians of text (demonic, wingéd librarians?) and the agents of a violent ambush wrought directly via text's artifactual form. Here again, the work's aura is simultaneously its retreat and its threat. The wilderness/College into which the text withdraws is a refuge from "the Already known" (*Speculations* 4ff). Superimposing this wilderness onto Brooklyn College is more than a moment of whimsical autobiography on Wellman's part; harking back to Crow 2, it also invokes the possibility of a radically refigured community – a Murder, let's say – of readers and writers.

Speculations thus suggests that for Wellman, the "literarization of theater" means the cultivation of a theatrical "axis" that extends neither between characters nor between the stage and the present audience; instead, it could be described as a dangerous line of flight, "opening paths into strange spaces" (Syers). The phrase "This will kill that" comes from Book Five of Victor Hugo's *Notre Dame of Paris*:

> The archdeacon contemplated the gigantic cathedral for a time in silence, then he sighed and stretched out his right hand towards the printed book lying open on his table and his left hand towards Notre-Dame, and looked sadly from the book to the church:
>
> "Alas," he said, "this will kill that." [...] Then he added these mysterious words: "Alas and alack, small things overcome great ones! A tooth triumphs over a body. The Nile rat kills the crocodile, the swordfish kills the whale, the book will kill the building!" (187–188)

The archdeacon means, the narrator subsequently tells us, both that "The press will kill the church" and that "Printing will kill architecture" (189). If Hugo goes on to expound upon the world-historical significance of these revolutions, Wellman stays fixed on the "small things" with which the archdeacon identifies them: that "Nile rat" could be the first of Wellman's "small, fierce creatures with wicked claws." For Wellman as for Dom Claude, these creatures embody text's almost occult capacity to fissure institutional reality: the "church" of theatrical and social convention, the edifice of a communicative norm grounded in an economy of totalized exchange.

Of course, in appropriating the archdeacon's famous phrase for a late-capitalist moment, Wellman also partly inverts its logic. Hugo's murderous "this" is a vanguard of capitalism and secularization; it is not writing *per se* but the printing press, a "particularly important ... case" of the mechanical reproduction Benjamin would credit with the destruction of aura ("Work" 219). In Wellman's theater, the subversive power of text – whether printed or spoken or "torn with great violence" – lies in its potential *restitution* of aura. This writing resists appropriation, even – especially – amidst the nearness of performance. Instead of "lying open on the table," it wriggles away.

Coda: *Girl Gone*

To end this chapter, and the book, I'd like to turn to a production that has haunted me since I saw it as a teenager. Wellman wrote *Girl Gone* for the New York company Big Dance Theater, who premiered the piece in 1998.[24] What stayed with me wasn't the story – later I would dimly recall a garden party, witchcraft, spontaneous combustion – but an overwhelming sense of crystalline precision. An absolutely specific choreography seemed to move in a *pas de deux* with Wellman's words; the words themselves were peals of playful and mysterious philosophy, spoken with bell-like clarity by the company's lithe performers. My own plays don't tend to involve much physical movement, and people who have seen them might be surprised to hear me name an elaborate choreographic piece as a major influence. But *Girl Gone* helped give me a new sense of the way language can exist in theater space. Not just as people telling each other things (character to character, performer to audience), and not just as one sensory "material" among others: in that production, language glistened as something strange and precious, something my understanding could glimpse, but not exhaust. For all its musical aurality, this speech *felt*, to me, *like writing*: a thing-like enigma whose verbal density wouldn't dissolve into the immediacy of the performance, because its logic was somewhere else, somewhere beyond us.

A decade later, when I began studying theories of theater in grad school, I was excited to find so many accounts that resonated with the experimental work I loved, from Brecht's call for "true attentiveness" (28) to Stein's insistence that "anything that was not a story could be a play"

("Plays" 73) to Lehmann's description of "*events, exceptions,* and moments of *deviation*" on the postdramatic stage (105). But I also found myself frustrated by a recurring theoretical gesture that consigned writing to the prehistory of performance, as if writing were something you had to get over in order to grasp "theater itself." Big Dance's production of *Girl Gone* was at the back of my mind when I began devising this book's argument about the theatrical force of writing. When I finally read the script, I realized it had also been also a source of my desire to locate a value in theater *other* than, indeed opposed to, presentness. The title alone should be a tip-off: perhaps more explicitly than any of Wellman's other plays, *Girl Gone* explores and theatricalizes the prospect of escaping toward an elsewhere – or, in the play's shorthand, "Going Away." "To go away is to experience, or cause to suffer, / a break in the continuum," one character explains (257).

The play follows a group of girls at Saint Lulu's prep school, including the sinister trio Lissa, Lisa, and Elyssa; the eager and ingenuous Buggins; and the "sweet, buttery smooth" Hope (248). The "evil sisters" – who, we learn within the play's first two lines, are "not related" (245) – seem to have invented an alternative world called "Vadoo (or Vadu)" (244) and a system of dark practices, including the dematerialization of lovely Hope, a "darling" who "doesn't complain about violin lessons, / and can do cube roots in her head" (248). After Hope's disappearance, the girls' teacher Madame Tomba and the frightening Headmistress confront the three sisters, who defeat them both; then Lissa and Lisa disappear themselves. During a sleepover at the remaining sister Elyssa's house, Buggins receives a visitation from a strange man who calls himself "The Black Tulip" and claims to be "the Vademecum of Vadu [...] the Vademecum / of Vadoo" (275). He convinces the hesitant Buggins to cross over to that world with him, mostly by appealing to her jealousy:

THE VADEMECUM OF VADU: Your wicked nemesis, Hope Fleming, who you
    thought
   had been destroyed; yes, Hope, Hope has been
   reborn in Vadoo; bright, beaming, wide-eyed Hope,
   with all her solar radiance and golden beneficence.
   [...]
   You must help us destroy her.
BUGGINS: Okay. I'm going. (276)

At the end of the piece, the vanished sisters return and lead the rest of the characters in the play's final song:

ALL: All this could happen,
    only in Vadoo,
    only in Vadu.
    [Softly, as lights dim,]
    All this could happen;
    all this could happen;
    all this could happen.
    [Blackout.] (282)

This synopsis should already suggest how strongly this play resonates with the questions we have been pursuing throughout this chapter and the book as a whole. To begin with, the play is oriented around – but doesn't stage – the elsewhere of Vadu/oo. It might be a stretch to see the famously ambiguous "u-" of utopia in this shifting syllable.[25] But whether or not we make this connection, Wellman's Vadu/oo is a place whose salient detail is its awayness; it is a literal vanishing point, and beyond its status as a receptacle of those who have gone away, all the Vademecum can tell Buggins about it is that "In / Vadu we have a very fine time [. . .] a fine old time indeed. Not like here" (275–276). The shifting spelling not only emphasizes the shifting, ungraspable quality of the referent; it also grounds this elusiveness in Vadu/oo's status as something written, a specifically literary creation. Once again, a textual element offers to harbor the "break in the continuum" of what is "here."

The weird sisters Lissa, Lisa, and Elyssa also activate literary echoes: most obviously *Macbeth*, but also Chekhov's three, who are likewise obsessed with an imaginary elsewhere. The girls' nearly homophonous names suggest a form of community based, queerly, in words:

FORREST: Look at them. The evil sisters.
DINAH: But they're not related, Forrest.
FORREST: Evil is a bond stronger than flesh.
DINAH: Nothing is stronger than flesh.
FORREST: Oh yes there is. Oh yes there is, Dinah. Sibilance constitutes a kind of
    sibness. (245)

This "sibilance" refers at once to the esses in the girls' names and to the serpentine quality of their "evil." Forrest is hardly a mouthpiece for the play's value system, and yet his almost unwitting wordplay demolishes his wife's cliché ("Nothing is stronger than flesh") on the strength of the words themselves, reiterating the content of his claim at the level of form. We might say that the idea tested out in these lines is the hypothesis of all Wellman's theater: that the social ties of flesh-and-blood immediacy can be outfoxed by stranger connections, deviant verbal bonds.

Such connections would transcend spatial and temporal contiguity. They would thus also remain sites of *dis*connection, rather as Stein's "continuous present" turned out to name a radical discontinuity. This emerges in the scene where Madame Tomba tries to catechize the girls on the subject of Going Away – a subject upon which the three sisters, at least, have their teacher outmastered. When Tomba quizzes the students on Hypatia of Alexandria and other "women who have [. . .] Gone away, and in so going, gone / astray," Elyssa replies:

> [. . .] it is possible to live in a period
> without being of it [. . .]
> For instance, to how many of us are the
> conceptions on which the life of our time
> is based – evidence, sequence, causality –
> strange and unintelligible. These
> people, those who have gone away, without
> actually leaving, live fragmentary and,
> as it were, piecemeal existences, in a
> directly connected world. A world of cause
> and connection.   (253–254)

Where the teacher frames "going away" as a narrative of "brave, but / foolish" deviation from a presumably stable present experience (253), Elyssa argues for a patently nonnarrative concept of perpetual and self-perpetuating disconnection, in which an inherent and internal discontinuity *within* consciousness is redoubled as the discontinuity *between* consciousness itself and the "directly connected world" from which the discontinuous subject is necessarily alien.

But the "fragmentary," disconnected lives Elyssa describes are also subject to a certain mode of connection, one that reaches past the present and into other times: "The medieval mind / survives among men and women of today" (ibid.). In the play, the space for expounding on this possibility arises because Elyssa subversively appropriates the day's "lesson" (252): from the Latin, *legĕre*, to read ("lesson"). Hypatia of Alexandria, a fifth-century philosopher and mathematician, is also the subject of Wellman's text *Hypatia* (written in the same year as *Girl Gone*). She figures a scholarly lineage of anomalous reader/writers; a precarious fellowship that emerges in a dialectic of connection and disconnection.[26] Elyssa continues:

> In her time, Hypatia proved the riddle
> of living connectedly in an unconnected,
> and therefore fragmentary world.   (254)

The "piecemeal" outsider of modernity's "directly connected world" is mirrored in the medieval genius who could "liv[e] connectedly" in a world of disconnection: "living connectedly" is thus itself a feat of rupture and discontinuity, specifically in relation to one's present. Hypatia's fate dramatizes this ideal: "The mob [...] cut away her flesh with oyster shells. / She was torn limb from limb" (257). Hypatia is a figure for "living connectedly" in, and as, a state of maximal fragmentation. Elyssa's oddly anachronistic phrase "proved the riddle" emphasizes the unfixed, riddled quality of such connectedness: the riddle is never solved, but proved – proved to *be* a riddle.

Here Wellman anticipates Jacques Rancière's characterization of the "aesthetic community" as "a dissensual community ... structured by disconnection" (59), and the work of art as "the very tension between the apart and the together" (78; see 51–82). In turn, Rancière's account suggests that in *Girl Gone*, the girls' labor to create/discover Vadoo is really the project of producing aesthetic experience itself, making the play itself a kind of a Portrait of the Artist as a Bunch of Young Witches. Their weird collectivity also resonates with Nicholas Ridout's suggestion that a special "communist potential" might inhere in

> a theatre in which there is always some kind of distance; in which participants are always separated from one another rather than merged with one another in an achieved community of the event ... it may also be a theatre in which this distance is not just a spatial separation in the present, but also a temporal articulation, in which the apparent presentness of the present is complicated by the appearance within it of people, things, and feelings from other times. (*Passionate* 11)

The mode of radical community that Hypatia (dis)embodies in *Girl Gone* is likewise not one that can simply be mapped onto the assembly present in the theater. If our co-presence is present anywhere in the Hypatian model for theater, it's in the image of the viciously intolerant "mob." For Wellman, as for Beckett, the co-present audience personifies the present itself:

THE HEADMISTRESS: And where do you imagine going away from?
ELYSSA: From the here and now.
[...]
THE HEADMISTRESS: The here and now would not be flattered to hear you talk like this. (269)

The textual lesson of Hypatia and her "sisters" harbors the possibility of outpacing the wholesomely embodied "here and now." In fact, by implying that "the here and now" *can't hear* Elyssa's words, the Headmistress suggests that this entire conversation has somehow already been secreted away from our present.

But it's the play's continued *engagement* with the "here and now" that gives point, and content, to the fantasy of "going away." Instead of picturing the vaporous Vadoo and thus transporting us there, it sets about imagining a "here and now" whose very materiality shelters secret trails of departure:

> [*Only now do we see, along with CHAZ, that HOPE has spontaneously combusted. All that remains of her is a small pile of char, and her smoking shoes.*]
> [CHAZ:] ... where did they all go? Where did they go? Where? (250)

The "small pile of char" is the sign of a departure, an absence, an escape. But it is also an eruption of materiality, emphasizing the present body's resources of retreat: its capacity for phase change, here mapped on to the real feat (and feet) of the performer's actual vanishing act. Staging this moment in the 1998 production, choreographer Annie-B Parson and director Paul Lazar made Hope's disappearance happen just as magically as Wellman's direction implies, using deft maneuvers with a long cape to hide the performer's withdrawal. The punch line is that theater's physical reality is *trickier* than we might have thought. Presence is theatrical when it can reverse into awayness; this devious instability is what defines the stage as an auratic site.

Hope's smoking shoes might recall us to another tricky piece of theatrical footwear: the boots Estragon wrestles with in *Waiting for Godot*. Estragon's emblematic opening line, "Nothing to be done," refers to his inability to get them off his feet (9). Wellman's empty shoes seem to offer a cheeky rejoinder to this predicament, as if to suggest that Estragon only had to take *himself* off, and leave the shoes behind, to find relief. But of course something like this (minus the relief) happens in *Godot* too: at the end of Act One, Estragon leaves his boots "*at the edge of the stage*" (179), and at the top of Act Two they are still there, "*front center, heels together, toes splayed*" (189). The "trick" is only that when Estragon returns, he doesn't recognize them:

> [*Estragon goes towards the boots, inspects them closely.*]
> ESTRAGON: They're not mine.
> VLADIMIR: *[stupefied]* Not yours!
> ESTRAGON: Mine were black. These are brown. (237)

Eventually Estragon puts them back on and acknowledges that they fit (245); by the end of the play, he has taken them off and placed them at the edge of the stage again. Mute witnesses to the play's final acknowledgment of immobility ("Yes, let's go. / *They do not move*," 357), the boots stand for the impossibility of making a difference, or real departure. Their material abiding becomes the sardonic proof that alterity can only be a desperate illusion: *of course* they're the same, they've been here in the room with us the whole time; this fact defines the rigor of theater. To Beckett, Hope's smoking shoes (or, say, the smoking shoes of hope) would probably feel like a cute evasion, a disavowal of the terrible sense in which we *can't* get away from our present. But to Wellman, Estragon's doggedly constant boots would feel like a premature surrender to the laws of common sense. The laws of Wellman's theatrical present, by contrast, really are made to be broken.

Wellman has accordingly sought out theatrical partners who share his faith in theater's ability to attack its own givenness. In a review of another Wellman/Big Dance Theater collaboration, Una Chaudhuri observes that "Like Wellman, Lazar and Parson relish searching for the secret affinities among things, and they trust in theater's power to contain the multiplicities from which connections might be made" ("Mac"). That trust is what distinguishes Wellman from Beckett, and what links him most closely to James and Stein. Wellman's theatrical aim is to "prove the riddle" like Hypatia: to let a network of irreducible alterity gleam out through the presence of the "here and now." If this is a theater of "secret affinities" it is also, just as profoundly, a theater of incongruities: "an unconnected ... world." Its self-displacing bodies warn us not to count on their availability. Instead, like James's Madame de Vionnet or Stein's Saint Therese, its figures cultivate a propensity to recede, to divide. Refusing the intimacy of co-presence, they rebuff our attempts, as Stein puts it, to "make acquaintance." And in so doing, they reach out – like Hypatia and her evil sisters – toward a different kind of fellowship, a pact of deviation that spans temporal and geographical gaps without closing them. Committed to fracturing the cohesion of any present, these plays make us attend to something *else*, something we can't quite grasp in the here and the now of our presence together.

This auratic distance has its counterpart in the nature of Wellman's collaboration with Big Dance. "I had never written for a dance-theater company before," Wellman writes in his prefatory note to *Girl Gone*, "and asked Annie-B for some suggestions. Write a lot of stage directions, she said. The imaginary dances of *Girl Gone* were the result" (243–244). One might suppose, on reading this account, that Wellman provided instructions which Parson and Lazar executed. In fact, their staging lets the script's dances remain "imaginary": while these directions make for terrific reading – "*All do a strange thing with only / fingers and toes; nobody knows / what it is*" (260) – they are rarely recognizable in the actual choreography. Smoking shoes aside, most of Parson and Lazar's staging departs from Wellman's notes altogether. It's as if, in asking for "a lot of stage directions," Parson was requesting concrete points in the text from which to diverge – which Wellman was happy to provide. Such moments install an Adornian "recognition of distance" within the logic of the piece, keeping text and performance *apart* in the midst of their collaboration.[27]

One sequence in particular stands out, for me, as an emblem of the negative theatrics this book has been following. It takes place early in the play, after Hope has vanished but before any mention of Vadoo. At the end of recess, the three sisters are smoking, holding their schoolbooks; Buggins sneaks a puff, then sets up the tiny portable writing desk she carries with her. Lissa, lying on a nearby bench, muses:

LISSA: When I go away, I shall go terribly
    terribly far away. So far I shall
    leave no trace. So far ... no trace at all.
BUGGINS: No one goes that far. That far
    is beyond heaven and ... and ...
LISSA: The Bad Place? Ha.
BUGGINS: No. A place beyond that. (252)[28]

After this exchange, Wellman's directions read simply:

[All become solemn and thoughtful.
Pause.
It becomes completely still for a time.] (ibid.)

At this point in the production, however, something else is happening, which the text doesn't specify. A simple, eerie tune has begun to play, and the lights are fading to black. Buggins, kneeling in front of her little escritoire, slowly raises its hinged lid. The desk's opening faces upstage, and we see that a bright, white light is spilling out of it, illuminating the performer's torso and, eventually, her face. The three sisters gather around in the dark, and they all peer intently at whatever it is that's inside the desk. As in the script, the teacher's voice booms out: "You have one minute, girls" (ibid.). The four girls lean in even closer; then, as the teacher begins counting down from sixty, Lisa, Lissa, and Elyssa stand up and slowly file away. Buggins, however, remains kneeling at the desk a while longer, staring into its depths. Finally, about halfway through the minute, she slowly closes the desk, picks it up, and carries it back to the "classroom."

In performance, then, it is the writing desk that opens the prospect of the "place beyond" – opens it, that is, to the four girls, not to us. In the performer's illuminated form we see only the reflection of something that is otherwise inaccessible. Unlike the stage lights that would deliver her to us more fully, the light inside the desk divides her from us, claiming her for a site where we cannot be. The desk becomes a metonym for writing as it functions in Wellman's theatrical imagination, and – in different ways – in James, Stein, Beckett, and Parks: a fissure in the present, an axis reaching out to some place where we're not. It gleams with the artwork's Adornian "foreignness to the world."

And yet the occasion for this dislocation *is* the world: this one. As the evil sisters cluster in the dark, they body forth the darkness in which *we* cluster, staring, like them. In this conspiratorial tableau there is a kind of threat-promise, a tenuous foreshadowing of the weird collective we could be.

Then the countdown begins, the stage lights brighten; we shift in our seats and come back to the present.

Notes

Preface

1. More recently, in a lecture written by Etchells and read by the actress Kate Valk at the 2013 Crossing the Line festival in New York City, Etchells discussed his ongoing fascination with the process of putting text onstage. "What is it that makes a text present?" he asked; what lets language "take or make a place in space and time?" The fact that Etchells has worked so deeply and fruitfully with such questions throughout his career makes the earlier jab at playwrights all the more striking.
2. As Martin Puchner has observed, "the familiar story of the emancipation of theatrical performance from the dramatic text" animates "a century-long polemic ... launched by actors, directors, and theater visionaries" ("Drama" 292–293).
3. For an intellectual history of the disciplinary distinctions between literature, theater, and performance, see Shannon Jackson's *Professing Performance* (2004).
4. Parenthetical citations of "Lehmann" refer to the English edition of *Postdramatic Theatre* (2006). Where it has seemed useful to include Lehmann's original German words in brackets, the page number of the English translation is given followed by the corresponding page number in the original, e.g. "(37/54)." The same applies to quotations from Bertolt Brecht and Theodor Adorno.
5. Already in *Postdramatic Theatre* Lehmann announces that "in the course of this study the often dismissively used term 'text theatre' will turn out to mean a genuine and authentic variant of postdramatic theatre, rather than referring to something that has supposedly been overcome" (17). For more on this question, see Jürs-Munby, "The vexed question of the text in Postdramatic Theatre in a cross-cultural perspective" (2011); see also Tomlin (58).
6. All quotations taken directly from texts in German are my own translations.
7. Foreman, who has described his avant-garde staging as "finding ways to make the writing inhabit a constructed environment" and as "a CONTINUATION of my writing process" (6, 13), is an avid reader of Stein ("his artistic mother," as

Marc Robinson observes [*Other* 159]); he also directed the 1996 premiere of Parks's *Venus*.

Part I Modernism's Negative Theatrics

1. Adorno, *Aesthetic Theory* (132).

1 Introduction: Negative Theatrics

1. Beckett, *Waiting* (39).
2. Similarly, Małgorzata Sugiera writes that in postdramatic work, "the theatrical 'here and now' no longer keeps up the pretence of creating an illusory 'there and then' . . . presentation (understood as presence) ousts traditional representation, turning into an interactive act of creation" (25). See also Lehmann 85 and 95.
3. Recently, scholars like Stephen Bottoms and Theron Schmidt have challenged such accounts of the postdramatic; as Bottoms points out, the "logic of representation is not something whose 'governance' we can arbitrarily suspend" (74; cf. Schmidt 189–190). Bottoms sees Lehmann's conception of the postdramatic as fundamentally continuous with a Greenbergian art-historical modernism, a "notion of artworks as autonomous and self-present" (69); for Bottoms, the disavowal of representation thus goes hand-in-hand with a theoretical exclusion of the viewer (68). It seems to me, however, that the claim to have moved "beyond" representation is often associated with a *heightened* creative role for the audience (see Chapter 6, this volume); Erika Fischer-Lichte's account of performance as an "event" rather than a "work" throughout *The Transformative Power of Performance* (2004) exemplifies this tendency.
4. See Phelan, *Unmarked* (1993). Throughout *Performing Remains* (2011), Rebecca Schneider discusses and challenges the critical tendency to understand performance in terms of ephemerality; see especially 87–110.
5. Other artists Fuchs discusses in the essay include Len Jenkin, Adrienne Kennedy, Daryl Chin, Richard Foreman, and the Wooster Group.
6. In *The Domain-Matrix* (1996), Sue-Ellen Case makes a parallel critique of the discourse on "queer performativity" as exemplified by the work of Judith Butler and Eve Kosofsky Sedgwick. Case writes: "It is confounding to observe how a lesbian/gay movement about sexual, bodily practices and the lethal effects of a virus, which has issued an agitprop activist tradition from its loins, as well as a Pulitzer Prize-winning Broadway play (*Angels in America*), would have as its critical operation a notion of performativity that circles back to

written texts, abandoning historical traditions of performance for the print modes of literary and philosophical scrutiny" (17).
7. For example: "When a cast-iron pot is 'played' by a cast-iron pot, imported from actual use, *the transparency of fictional semiosis is pressured by a material opacity*, and the stage announces itself as a territory of surfaces, dense, particularized, sensory, radically actual" (Garner 92, my emphasis).
8. In *Liveness*, Philip Auslander argues that "relationship between the live and the mediatized is volatile and subject to significant change over time, as is the definition of liveness itself" (187). His contention that we may not value live performance as much as we think we do, and will likely come to value it less and less, suggests that we may be approaching a post-metaphysical relationship to performance.
9. Power suggests a different reorientation of the presence debate. "It is not so much a question of affirming or rejecting presence," he writes; "theatre, I will argue, has the potential to interrogate our experience of the present ... play[ing] out the possibilities and problematics of presence (*Presence* 7, 12). I take (and appreciate) Power's point that theater can do more with presence than just affirm it or reject it, but I remain interested in gestures of rejection – particularly when these gestures are less about debunking metaphysics, and more about refusing the existing world.
10. Stanley Cavell pursues the question of reality in (and on) film throughout his 1971 book *The World Viewed*.
11. Lehmann glosses Giorgio Barberio Corsetti's argument that "the theatre needs the *text as a foreign body*, as a 'world outside the stage'" (146). This notion of the text's fundamental foreignness echoes Adorno's aesthetic theory, as I discuss below.
12. All citations of Brecht in English refer to the 2015 edition of *Brecht on Theatre*. Where an original German phrase is also given, the volume and page numbers after the slash refer to the Suhrkamp edition of *Schriften zum Theater*.
13. Invoking the early twentieth-century performance theorist Max Herrman, Erika Fischer-Lichte writes: "The bodily co-presence of actors and spectators enables and constitutes performance. For a performance to occur, actors and spectators must assemble to interact in a specific place for a certain period of time" (*Transformative* 32). This co-presence is "the specific mediality of performance" (38); Fischer-Lichte makes it a crucial criterion of the distinction between "works" and "events" that underlies her demand for an aesthetics specific to performance (see Chapter 4, this volume).
14. Brecht derives this concept of drama in part from Goethe and Schiller, who try out various formulations for the epic/dramatic distinction in their correspondence at the end of the eighteenth century; see especially Schiller's letter of December 26, 1797 (Goethe and Schiller 248–249).

15. As Will Daddario observes, however, "The dialectical movement never ceases in [Adorno's] critiques of Brecht ... Adorno never sides with or against Brecht" (129; cf. Nowak, *Elemente* 18). Daddario even argues that Adorno's treatment of Brecht should itself be understood as "dramaturgical" because it attends to the way Brecht's plays "live in the world as politically charged objects" (129).
16. Thus, understandably, the essays in the strong recent collection *Adorno and Performance* (ed. Daddario and Karoline Gritzner, 2014) tend to handle Adorno's subordination of performance to text either by drawing on other moments in his work that qualify this claim, or by thinking about ways in which Adorno sees textual practice itself as a kind of performance. In itself, Adorno's text-centered conception of theater still registers as essentially lamentable (and old-fashioned); Anja Nowak, for example, writes that "[t]he blind spots of a theory that does not really treat theatre as an autonomous art form clearly limit the possible insights that can be gained on behalf of its contemporary practices," although performance remains conceptually important for Adorno's aesthetics ("Theatricality" 143). Nowak's *Elemente einer Ästhetik des Theatralen in Adornos Ästhetischer Theorie* (2012), to my knowledge the only book-length study of Adorno and theater, frequently reasserts this limitation, though Nowak also thoughtfully draws out ways in which Adorno's theory resonates with theater studies today. Sara Jane Bailes approaches an Adornian framework when she draws on Ernst Bloch's utopian theory for *Performance Theater and the Poetics of Failure* (2011), and she briefly discusses Adorno in her chapter on Elevator Repair Service, to which I'll refer in Chapter 4 below. Other studies that have drawn on Adorno to think about theater aesthetics include Geoffrey Baker's 2003 "Nietzsche, Artaud, and Tragic Politics," and essays by Brandon Woolf and David Barnett in *Postdramatic Theatre and the Political* (2013, ed. Jürs-Munby, Carroll, and Giles).
17. In *Stage Fright: Modernism, Anti-Theatricality, and Drama* (2002), Martin Puchner incorporates Adorno into his argument that "a suspicion of the theater plays a constitutive role in the period of modernism, especially in modernist theater and drama" (1). For Puchner, Adorno's criticism of Wagner and Stravinsky extends Nietzsche's fundamentally "anti-theatricalist" critique of mimetic gesture (35–40); as Puchner rightly points out, Adorno tends to identify performance as a "regressive" aesthetic practice (e.g. *Aesthetic* 100). My own argument in this book is obviously indebted to Puchner's; nevertheless, I will want to question his concept of antitheatricality in Chapter 2.
18. Muñoz's work on utopia, which draws extensively on the writings of Adorno's friend Ernst Bloch, has encouraged a swell of interest in this term during

recent years, particularly in queer theory and performance theory, as has Jill Dolan's *Utopia in Performance* (2005). I hope my book will resonate with their beautiful readings of utopian queer texts and performances, although I suspect my own readings sometimes indulge in the "romance of singularity and negativity" to which Muñoz objects (10–14).

19. Adorno also makes this argument in his essay "Commitment," where he writes that "it is now timely to speak in favor of autonomous rather than committed works in Germany" (92). Again, the work's utopianism, its rejection of empirical reality, *is* its engagement: "As pure artifacts, products, works of art . . . are instructions for the praxis they refrain from: the production of life lived as it ought to be" (93). Nevertheless the work has "no content, no formal category . . . that does not, however transformed and however unawarely, derive from the empirical reality from which it has escaped" (89).

20. Puchner writes: "Both the friends and the detractors of the theater have always suspected that along with its collaborative production and collective reception came a more direct relation to the social and the public spheres" (*Stage* 10); he suggests that theater can "be considered the art form that is most directly tied to social normativity" (17). Similarly, Shannon Jackson characterizes theater as a "highly fettered space" and observes: "For those of us identified with performance, the language of autonomy is a conflicted one, as the art form's interdependence with ensembles, technologies, and audiences has always been hard to disavow" (*Social* 162, 15). Jackson proposes that, rather than "bemoan" this heteronomy, we might see it as performance's challenge to the very notion of autonomy: "What if performance challenges strict divisions about where the art ends and the rest of the world begins?" (15). For works in the tradition I am trying to elucidate, however, that challenge is what spurs a redoubled negativity: this theater's consciousness of its own inextricability from "the rest of the world," or actuality, becomes painful enough to drive an impossible utopianism.

21. States, whom Garner interpretively glosses here, describes "points at which the floor cracks open and we are startled, however pleasantly, by the upsurge of the real into the magic circle where the conventions of theatricality have assured us that the real has been subdued and transcended" (States, *Great* 34). For States such moments, which let us "see the familiar in the defamiliarization" (ibid.), are fundamental to theatrical experience.

22. A poststructuralist framework that follows Roland Barthes in positioning "the work" as the locus of "filiation," "conformity," and epistemological stability ("From Work") will not share Adorno's sense that performance risks conformity in *failing* to be a work; see e.g. Weber (43, 259) and Worthen, "Disciplines." I am suggesting that there are dispositions for which

performance's nonobjectivation, rather than automatically constituting subversive "play," can begin to feel more like a risk of playing along – and I am asking what kind of theater such a disposition might produce. For alternative accounts of Adorno's critique of performance that center on his concepts of semblance and mimesis, see Sarkoparnig (62–66) and Quent (137–138). See also Rei Terada's account (and compelling critique) of Adorno's insistence on the "facticity" or nonephemerality of the artwork (173–190).

23. In an argument itself informed by Frankfurt School theory, Judith Rodenbeck contends that the happening should "be understood in its critically *negative* relation – that is, its dialectical relation – to theatrical and performance practices" (56). Far from a naïve affirmation of everyday experience, the "fundamentally mediated, split, antiempathic, and inaccessible subjectivity that produced, and was produced in, the happenings was utterly counter to the 'authenticity' of both charismatic acting and unmediated experience" (69). Rodenbeck also, however, describes happenings in terms that would seem to support Adorno's criticism of them as an anti-aesthetic "continuation of purposeful rationality" (*Aesthetic* 103; see below): "these works figured participants – *and* attention *and* senses – as objects, collage elements, exchangeable tokens" (Rodenbeck 58). In this sense, at least, the happening openly colludes with capitalism's totalization of exchange value, if it also exposes that totalization. For several artists' accounts of these works and their intentions, see Kostelanetz (1968) and Lebel et al. (1967).

24. For an alternate (Habermasian) approach to the political value of theater in particular, see Jon Erickson's "Defining political performance with Foucault and Habermas: strategic and communicative action."

25. See Chapter 5.

26. Jane Palatini Bowers does, nonetheless, argue powerfully for the latter reading of Stein; I discuss Bowers in Chapter 2.

27. See Lehmann's discussion of Stein's writing as a precursor to postdramatic theater (49–50).

2 "Something stranger yet"

1. James, *William Wetmore Story and His Friends* (259); Stein, "Plays" (70); Toklas, *What Is Remembered* (115).

2. The two authors' conceptions of literature as "portrait" is a principle theme of Charles Caramello's *Henry James, Gertrude Stein, and the Biographical Act* (1996). For briefer considerations of their work's relationship, see articles by Eric Haralson (2004), Ira Nadel (1988), and Sharon Shaw (1974).

3. On Stein's theatrical influence see also Davy, Marranca (18–23), Wirth's "Gertrude Stein und ihre Kritik der dramatischen Vernunft," Elinor Fuchs's *The Death of Character* (92–107), and Ryan (137–156). Lehmann observes that "[f]or postdramatic theatre Stein's aesthetics is of great importance, although more subconsciously so outside America" (63), and points out that her plays are "unplayable" only when "measured by the expectations of dramatic theatre" (49), an insight I hope to develop here.
4. David Kurnick usefully summarizes a substantial tradition of James scholarship that sees his late fiction as a victorious effort to make the novel "displace and replace the drama as an embodied social event" (*Empty* 1, cf. 110, 229 n.11; "Horrible" 109–110). To my mind, the most insightful exploration of James's antitheatricalism is Joseph Litvak's reading of *The Tragic Muse* (*Caught* 235–270). The reading of Stein as antitheatrical is most clearly elaborated in the fourth chapter of Martin Puchner's *Stage Fright* (101–116), which I discuss below.
5. The notion of a theatrically productive antitheatricalism also appears in Stanley Cavell's reading of *King Lear*, "The Avoidance of Love" (*Must* 267–356), and more faintly in Michael Fried's famous 1967 essay "Art and Objecthood" (139–140); see also Barish (450).
6. As Nicholas Ridout has argued, modern discomfort in the theater is inextricable from the pleasures theater offers, as well as from its critical potential; see *Stage Fright, Animals, and Other Theatrical Problems* (2006).
7. Jane Palatini Bowers also criticizes Ryan's interpretation: "This idea that Stein's plays are pure theater, in harmony with the physicality and immediacy of performance, is a common misperception about these texts, but in fact "Stein's plays oppose the physicality of performance" (2). While I agree with Bowers that "immediacy" is a mischaracterization of Stein's plays, Bowers here shares Ryan's assumption about the "immediacy *of performance*" – an assumption Stein's work itself questions (as Bowers notes elsewhere; see below).
8. See, respectively, Edel (115); Seltzer (296); Rivkin (168); A. Frank (77–95); and Litvak (198) and Sedgwick (*Touching* 39).
9. This "Rowean" element of my reading in fact represents a departure from Kurnick's argument, since for Kurnick, theater is summoned as "the present tense . . . of actual spectatorship," itself "a collective present" ("Horrible" 125). I will be investigating the ways in which both James and Stein complicate the notion of "actual spectatorship." Still, Kurnick's project is highly resonant with mine, especially where he reads *The Awkward Age* as "creating an 'event' whose very failure to take place made it a rich site for imagining relational possibilities beyond the constraints of the given" (111, cf. *Empty* 129–130) – although Kurnick suggests that this "failure to take place" is the result of

dramatic and social convention and of novelistic form, rather than (as I argue throughout this book) an experiential possibility formed within the theater medium itself.

10. Readers of Ohi's brilliant *Henry James and the Queerness of Style* (2011) will find echoes of his analysis throughout this chapter. I hope it's clear that by aligning what Ohi calls "the (perpetually retrospective) discovery of discontinuity" in James (39) with his relationship to theater, I don't take myself to be proposing an *alternative* to the category of queerness; rather, I'm pursuing the ways in which theater is a structuring element of the late texts' queer desire.

11. One beginners' playwriting textbook informs us that "Compelling plays" have an "essential simplicity and clarity at the core," and that "Writing plays is about picking the crucial moments of your story and putting only those on stage" (Parra 12, 14). Marc Robinson observes that critics of contemporary American experimental playwrights (including Suzan-Lori Parks and Mac Wellman) often suggest that a writer "clarif[y] her vision" (Robert Brustein, qtd. in Robinson, *Other* 195). I discuss the resistance to communicative efficiency in Chapter 6.

12. Likewise, James's early protest against theater whose "whole is a pictorial whole, not a dramatic one" (*Scenic* 231) might now be read as protesting, from beyond the grave, against experimental "landscape theater" in the tradition of Gertrude Stein and Robert Wilson. Elinor Fuchs theorizes this tradition in her essay "Another Version of Pastoral" (*Death* 92–107).

13. To sustain the "expert" gaze of a reader, Brecht implies, theater would have to be *better* than ever because it would, so to speak, have no place to hide: "Actors would never dare serve up to these experts the few sorry scraps of mimicry they currently cook up 'somehow or other' in the course of a few rehearsals, putting no thought into them whatsoever. Nobody would accept the material in so raw and unfinished a state" (72).

14. As this convergence of Brecht's "literarization" with another writer's "theatricalization" suggests, Brecht's "literarization" names a particular *mode of theatricality*, and shouldn't be confused with an attempt to strip theater of supposedly fundamental properties.

15. As Michael Moon points out, the "anachronism and atopism" of James's writing are consistent with his inheritance of an earlier queer tradition in aesthetic discourse: "from the late-eighteenth to the mid-nineteenth century the amateur of art or lover of beauty was perforce a lover of male beauty – but ostensibly the male beauty of other times and places" (31).

16. Cf. Bersani's observation about the preponderance of the hypothetical in James's prose, whereby "what presumably takes place in Jamesian fiction is reduced to mere hypotheses about it" (Bersani and Phillips 20).

17. I don't mean to imply that the "leap" that has been Marcher's to take is necessarily *toward* May, although this is what he comes to believe at the end; see Eve Kosofsky Sedgwick's classic queer reading of the story (*Epistemology* 200–212).
18. This obsession plays out during the "dramatic years" as well; not surprisingly, Margolis notes that in rehearsals for James's stage adaptation of *The American*, the author "supervised the building of new scenery (the furniture was imported from Paris) and the careful selection of new costumes" (80).
19. James here strikingly anticipates Una Chaudhuri's account of the shift from landscape *painting* to the twentieth-century phenomenon she and Elinor Fuchs call "landscape theater" (after Stein): when it enters the realm of theater, the meaning of "landscape" shifts "from a tract of land capable of being seen at a glance to an environment one can explore and inhabit" ("Land/Scape/Theory" 21; see 19–21). See also Chapter 3, n. 34 below.
20. Sedgwick's reading of "The Beast in the Jungle" ends by emphasizing the suggestiveness of this posture (*Epistemology* 212); my own emphasis on the theatricality of the Jamesian underside is indebted to her readings here and in *Touching Feeling* (35–65), as well as to Joseph Litvak's readings of James in *Caught in the Act*.
21. Rowe claims that "the uncanny coincidence of Chad and Madame de Vionnet's appearance in this apparently random scene is already governed by the secret textuality of Strether's bid for impressionistic freshness and spontaneity," a textuality figured by the book Strether carries "in his pocket" (198). Since I find it difficult to regard the textuality of the episode as "secret" even from Strether, whom I do not see as "struggl[ing] for some preartistic recognition" (197), I propose that the episode's real "secret" is not its textuality or its "formalism" (199) but rather the theatrical depths that turn out to subtend those qualities. Ohi's reading of this passage from *The Ambassadors* is especially helpful here (158–163).
22. On the insufficiency of "picture" in James's later work, see Margolis (172–173) and Caserio.
23. Allegra Stewart's *Gertrude Stein and the Present* is a book-length elucidation of this project.
24. See Kurnick for a reading of a passage from James's *The Awkward Age* that brings out this quality in the speech of its characters (*Empty* 134–135).
25. In Chapter 1, we saw a parallel assumption being made in theater studies: the idea that postdramatic theater, because it no longer focuses on conveying a fictional story, entails a shift from representation *to presence*.
26. Fried's "Art and Objecthood" has been the most influential articulation of this binary; Fried identifies "the imperative that modernist painting . . . *defeat*

or suspend theatre" as crucial to its project (135), and argues that "theatre is now the negation of art" (125). Puchner attributes a parallel vision to Stein: "What Fried and Stein share in particular is an aversion to distracting audiences as well as to human actors on the stage" (*Stage* 104). Of course, in imputing antitheatricalism to so many of modernism's most canonical writers and playwrights (Mallarmé, Joyce, Stein, Yeats, Brecht, and Beckett), Puchner effectively reanimates Fried's binary opposition: modernism is again fundamentally "a form of resistance" (Puchner, *Stage* 2) to theatricality, even if, as Puchner shows, this resistance is also productive for theater itself.

In another literary-critical example of the binary, Fredric Jameson contrasts the "theatrical" perspective of the nineteenth-century novel with Joseph Conrad's truly modernist method of sensory fragmentation, which Jameson identifies with film (*Political* 231–232).

27. In a 1982 article on Stein's "critique of dramatic reason," Andrzej Wirth observes that in Stein's plays "dialogue is dissolved into discourse; characters are only discernible as voices of the discourse . . . the basic model of her pieces [is] more like a lyric poem than a conventional drama" ("Gertrude" 64–65, cf. 68). Wirth lucidly argues that "from today's perspective, Stein's most difficult texts have gained much significance as an aesthetic program *and* a theatrical project" (64). He seems to me to impute to Stein a more profound (critical) *engagement* with dramatic convention than the plays in fact maintain, but he very helpfully elucidates several features of her *departure* from drama. For more on the contemporary significance of the shift "from dialogue to discourse," see also Wirth's 1980 essay by that title.

28. In "Poetry and Grammar," a lecture in which Stein ponders the difference between prose and poetry, she makes it clear that *Tender Buttons* is "very good poetry" rather than prose (*Writings* 138). Earlier in the essay, she notes that "words in plays written in poetry are more lively than the same words written by the same poet in other kinds of poetry," adding: "It undoubtedly was true of Shakespeare, is it inevitably true of everybody" (123). She never answers this question, but the thought suggests at once a continuity between plays and nonplay texts and a real, if elusive, experiential distinction.

29. Nick Salvato takes issue with Bay-Cheng's and Puchner's "antitheatrical" readings of Stein, and the "traditional notions of theatricality" such readings imply; he too, however, refers to Stein's "at-times complete abandonment of theatrical method and principle," which I would question (102–104). See also Fawcett's critique of antitheatrical readings of Stein (139–140).

30. Bowers characterizes theater's discontinuity as that of "a succession of present instants" (50). As I have suggested in my reading of James, I would be wary of assuming that the formation of "present instants" is the only way theater

opposes linear flow, since it seems to me that such a flow can easily be *made up of* present instants – that this is in fact exactly what drama tries to achieve. The "continuous present" in Stein's sense, however, actively resists incorporation in a linear stream, as I discuss below.

31. Laura Luise Schultz, in her study of Stein as a postdramatic writer, does claim that in this lecture Stein "decides to understand the conflicting notions of time in the theatre not as a contradiction but a combination," thus ultimately embracing discontinuity rather than rejecting it (255).
32. Thanks to C. D. Blanton for pointing this out.
33. See Stein's "Composition as Explanation" (*Writings* 21–30).
34. As Bowers writes: "The movement of language in the conventional Western play can best be represented by an unbroken, unidirectional arc. According to Stein, if the spectator tries to follow the arc, he will be distracted by the broken line of visual perception" (76). Rebecca Schneider finds a particular emphasis latent in Stein's remark that temporal syncopation "makes *one* endlessly troubled" (94, Schneider's emphasis). I would suggest that this "one" corresponds to the unifying effort of drama.
35. See Gilles Deleuze and Félix Guattari, "Introduction: Rhizome," in *A Thousand Plateaus: Capitalism and Schizophrenia* (3–25).
36. At least until Stein took to well-made melodrama with *Yes Is for a Very Young Man* near the end of her life; see Bay-Cheng (93–108) and Ryan (55–66). The fact that Stein's late plays begin to approach dramatic norms does not, I think, invalidate the notion that Stein took up playwriting in a spirit of radical independence from those norms, which remained entirely *optional* for her in a way they never were for James. Bay-Cheng's argument that Stein needs to be situated amongst the theatrical and cinematic avant-garde of her day offers a historical context for Stein's permission to abandon those norms.
37. Julia Fawcett makes a similar point in her reading of Stein's 1936 *A Play Called Not and Now*; Fawcett stresses the "and" of the title, and argues against the antitheatrical reading of Stein by suggesting that Stein values "the not-ness of performance" (153). For Fawcett, following Peggy Phelan, this means the way performance's ephemerality resists reified identity.
38. Salvato's reading of Stein's playwriting as sadomasochistic makes a refreshing intervention into the often rather warm-and-fuzzy tone of the critical discourse on her work. Salvato claims that "there is a particularly sexual charge to Stein's relentless writing, that owes largely (though not exclusively) to her relentless – and notorious – repetitions" (101). I find this argument compelling, although in my own experience, reading or watching Stein's plays tends to activate a cognitive state in which the sense of the rules she is breaking fades away: after a few minutes, her writerly antics – unlike James's

sentences – stop feeling like "a violent attack on our sensibilities and expectations" (108) because those expectations simply slip away. Then again, the same could be said about some sadomasochistic experiences.

39. Cf. Power's discussion, in relation to both Derrida and Buddhism, of an approach to theater wherein "the contemplation of presence is itself the unraveling of presence" (*Presence* 195–197).
40. For example, see Bowers (e.g. 26 and 62), Wirth ("Gertrude" 71), Puchner (*Stage* 108), and Bay-Cheng (55).
41. Ryan points out the influence of William James on Stein's practice of "treating transitives as substantive parts of the sentence" (19). William James had written: "We ought to say a feeling of *and*, a feeling of *if*, a feeling of *but*, and a feeling of *by*, quite as readily as we say a feeling of *blue* or a feeling of *cold*" (qtd. in Ryan 19).
42. See Kate Davy's thoughtful examination of Stein's "continuous present" in relation to the theater of Richard Foreman, which she presents as an extension of the landscape play.
43. Stewart suggests throughout *Gertrude Stein and the Present* that Stein's poetics imply the possibility of experiencing rare states of being. "The root experience which produced her most curiously vital and yet often unintelligible writing," she proposes, "was a serious practice of meditation – and not merely meditation but, at times, genuine *recollection*" (53). For Stein, "meditation is more than reflection: it is an act of presence – an act of communion with the ongoing reality around her" (194). The relevant implication here is that Stein's texts ask us not to assume that space and time must always work the same way – even, or perhaps especially, in the theater.
44. Bay-Cheng points out that in performance, the multiple Scene Vs could take place simultaneously (59). This would be an example of the ways Stein's abandonment of linear time makes room, so to speak, for the spatial intervention of the stage.
45. Citing this passage, Elinor Fuchs writes that in the Steinian tradition of landscape theater, "structures are arranged not on lines of conflict and resolution but on multivalent spatial relationships" (*Death* 106–107).

3 "Gesture towards the universe"

1. Kenner, *Samuel Beckett: A Critical Study* (21); Beckett quoted in Deirdre Bair, *Samuel Beckett: A Biography* (361).
2. Beckett gives a similar account in an interview with Colin Duckworth (Duckworth 17).
3. See Blau's *Sails of the Herring Fleet*, especially 115–116; I discuss States and Garner below.

4. Max Blechman, who argues that the idea of utopia is fundamental to Adorno's negative dialectics, also argues for the crucial influence of Bloch's thought here: "Adorno's 'utopian particular' is none other than Bloch's 'deepest utopian part of the consciousness' – in every instance, the consciousness that the purported identity of the universal is 'perpetuating nonidentity in suppressed and damaged form'" (189). For Adorno's own powerful account of Bloch's importance, see "The Handle, the Pot, and Early Experience," where Adorno writes: "Bloch teaches persistence in the face of what is unfamiliar and unknown, yet known ... This secret would be the opposite of something that has always been and will always be, the opposite of invariance: something that would finally be different" (219).
5. Jonathan Kalb remains an exception; his argument against historically specific stagings of Beckett's plays (particularly JoAnne Akalaitis's famous 1984 production at A.R.T.) builds on Adorno's remarks about "the horror of historical anonymity" in *Endgame* (Kalb, *Beckett* 80–82, 91–93). This argument is part of Kalb's larger argument that Beckett's playwriting already includes, and therefore to some degree preempts, the traditional domain of the director – a position that, like his engagement of Adorno, reads as rather anomalous within the context of theater studies today.
6. For example, Chris Conti's 2004 discussion of Adorno on Beckett seems to understand "theatricality" in Beckett as "word-play and rituals," empty "entertainment," "diversions," "a sense of being rehearsed to kill the time" (284–287). While I certainly agree that Beckett is attracted to these aspects of theater, the equation of theatricality with hollow entertainment seems to me to be a familiar assumption that Beckett's work itself moves beyond.
By contrast, Nowak's reading of the *Endgame* essay emphasizes ways in which it (partially) anticipates postdramatic theater discourse; see *Elementen* 66–72.
7. "[T]o be an artist is to fail, as no other dare fail," Beckett writes famously in his "Three Dialogues with Georges Duthuit" (1949); " ... failure is his world and the shrink from it desertion" (126). Also frequently cited is his comparison of himself to James Joyce in a 1956 interview: "The more Joyce knew the more he could. He's tending toward omniscience and omnipotence as an artist. I'm working with impotence, ignorance ... I think anyone nowadays who pays the slightest attention to his own experience finds it the experience of a non-knower, a non-can-er. The other type of artist – the Apollonian – is absolutely foreign to me" (qtd. in Kalb, *Beckett* 99). Practically all substantive Beckett criticism considers his espousal of failure; one of the most sustained and thoughtful engagements is found in *Arts of Impoverishment* by Leo Bersani and Ulysse Dutoit, in which the authors argue that most prior readings consider Beckett's representation *of* failure rather than his project of failing to represent, or express, at all (12–14). See also Bailes

(25–30); Bersani's essay "Beckett and the End of Literature"; Wolfgang Iser's "The Art of Failure: The Stifled Laugh in Beckett's Theater"; Peggy Phelan's "Samuel Beckett: Lessons in Blindness"; and Daniel Albright's *Beckett and Aesthetics*.

8. Puchner interprets Beckett's "attack" on the actor's integrity as an attack on theater itself (*Stage* 159–172). This argument seems to me to assume that theatricality depends, at some baseline level, on an experience of the actor's wholeness or complete mimetic efficacy – an assumption I would want to question.
9. The unfinished play, which was about Dr. Johnson's last years and his love for his younger friend Mrs. Thrale, would have been entitled simply *Human Wishes*. For discussions of this early project in relation to Beckett's completed plays, see McMillan and Fehsenfeld 25–29, and Ruby Cohn, *Just Play* 143–162.
10. Critics who cite Robbe-Grillet approvingly in this "presence" vein include Duckworth (46–47), Ruby Cohn (*Back* 138), and Kalb (*Beckett* 47). For a summary of the "theatre of presence" tradition of Beckett reception, see Connor (115–118).
11. Here Kalb is adapting Beckett's own remark in "Dante ... Bruno. Vico.. Joyce" that Joyce's "writing is not *about* something; *it is that something itself*" (503).
12. Stanley Cavell makes a similar observation about Beckett's difference from Brecht: "in Beckett there *is* no role towards which the actor can maintain intelligence, and he has nothing more to *tell* his audience than his character's words convey" (*Must* 160).
13. Especially in this respect, Beckett's theatrical utopianism differs sharply from the kind Jill Dolan theorizes; for Dolan, "performance ... rests lightly in its own moment, referring to all of time in the images of its spectacle, in the projection of its presence, in its gesture of hope toward the wishes, predictions, and resolutions of its future" (14). While we might well say that *Godot* is "referring to all of time ... in the projection of its presence," this is so in the horrifying sense that the presence of the present engulfs the past and future and neutralizes their alterity.
14. Beckett's English version departs from his French quite considerably here: "And you talk to me about scenery!" renders "*Et tu veux que j'y voie des nuances!*" (literally "And you want me to see nuances!") The French does not provoke the same dissonance as the English, nor does it harbor any particular theatrical reference. On the other hand, the cultural reference of "You and your landscapes!" is already active in "*tes paysages*" (206).
15. In taking Estragon's outburst here seriously, I don't mean to discount what Enoch Brater has called the "various textures" of *Godot*'s setting (*Ten* 37). The play doesn't, of course, provide an utterly undifferentiated experience;

Notes to pages 81–83 229

but it does ask us to imagine an undifferentiated world as the ground on which its variations play out – I don't think we can account for its pathos if we deny this. So I can't completely concur with Brater's claim that "[t]o the question, who or what is Godot, we might very well want to add this: just *where* is *his* offstage drama taking place?" (38). That is, we might very well want to, but as Estragon's fury suggests, a particular kind of frustration attends this desire.

16. I am stealing this line from Cavell, who articulates this sense of entrapment in Beckett while describing what he calls the "hidden literality" of language in *Endgame*: "The logician's wish to translate out those messy, non-formal features of ordinary language is fully granted by Beckett, not by supposing that there is a way out of our language, but by fully accepting the fact that there is nowhere else to go" (*Must* 126).

17. Adorno writes of *Endgame*: "The three Aristotelian unities are retained, but the drama itself perishes" ("Trying" 136; cf. Halpern 234–235). Richard Halpern observes that Beckett takes the unities "more seriously than perhaps any other modern playwright" (253). There may also be a pun lurking in the play's title, as Ruby Cohn points out that "French concern with the unity of time begins with Chapelain's 'Lettre *á Godeau* sur la règle des vingt-quatre heurs'" (*Just Play* 36, Cohn's italics). In 1931, while teaching at Trinity College Dublin, Beckett apparently had some fun with the unities in a parodic student burlesque called *Le Kid* (which he may or may not have written); see McMillan and Fehsenfeld 19–20.

18. There is also a kind of pun that implicates narrative itself in this relentless universality: "One day" is first of all the announcement of storytelling, of a fiction not liable to historical specificity: One day a rich man started off for the fair with his slave, in order to sell him . . . So Pozzo's "One day, is that not *enough* for you" may suggest that – contrary to what we might have believed – our habit of telling ourselves stories is bound up with, and binds us up in, the maintenance of a tyrannical present.

19. Or, as Cavell writes later in the same essay, *Endgame*'s characters perceive that "[o]nly a life without hope, meaning, justification, waiting, solution – as we have been shaped for these things – is free from the curse of God" (*Must* 149). We might say that what Adorno's concept of utopia rejects is precisely a utopia "we have been shaped for."

20. Cf. Robbe-Grillet's comment: "In this universe where time does not pass, the words *before* and *after* have no meaning; only the present situation counts" (119); also Ruby Cohn's remark that in *Godot* "The present is thick *and ubiquitous*" (*Just Play* 42, my emphasis). Here I disagree with Connor, who sees *Godot* as emphasizing "the paradox of all time; that is, that the only tense we feel has real verifiable existence, the present, the here-and-now, is in fact

never here-and-now ... Vladimir and Estragon ... can never *be* fully in their present either" (120). No doubt *Godot*'s present lacks metaphysical integrity – as States's account of it "spin[ning] out" in fact also suggests. I am arguing, however, that an experience of the present is crucial to the play's sensibility, and central to its hyperbolic appropriation of drama. The particular pathos of *Godot* is not that we lack access to the "here-and-now," but that we seem to lack egress from it.

21. In fact, Adorno anticipates the development Sheehan describes; in the *Endgame* essay he writes of "Humankind, whose general species-name fits badly into Beckett's linguistic landscape" ("Trying" 126).

22. McMullan writes of this moment: "While the audience's actual position in the auditorium is alluded to, they are simultaneously displaced by their textual reflection: 'not a soul in sight'" (141). While I agree that Beckett touches on a potential for displacement here, I would suggest that this particular displacement is not quite carried off: "not a soul in sight" functions more as an insult to us (asserting that the audience is soulless), or an insult to Estragon (telling him an obviously transparent lie), than as a real displacement. The line is about the performer seeing us, not about his failing to see us; the ruse doesn't work.

23. An anecdote from *Godot*'s production history is telling here: in 1956, when the American director Alan Schneider suggested that *Godot* be staged in the round, Beckett objected, opining that the play "needs a very closed box" (McMillan and Fehsenfeld 80). According to historians, Beckett "preferred a proscenium production because it retained the formal confrontation with the audience, allowed for clearly defined entrances and exits, and heightened the sense that the characters are 'all trapped'" (ibid.). The logic of this list is suggestively odd: if the aim is to trap the characters, why would "clearly defined entrances and exits" be desirable? Beckett's theatrical mind seems to imagine the form of the most rigorous enclosure as the form that best allows for egress: here we have a picture that could almost illustrate the dialectics of utopia.

24. The French is slightly more determinate, since Vladimir's shout is "*NE LE RACONTE PAS!*" (38): don't tell *it*, i.e., the dream. Estragon's "*Celui-ci te suffit?*" thus more clearly means: this *dream*, the one we can't wake up from, is enough for you? With this sense established, the French audience is less likely to search for a referent for "*celui-ci*"; but the question then arises why Beckett needs to stipulate the gesture ("*geste vers l'univers*") at all.

25. One particular book Beckett recalls here is Dante's *Divine Comedy*; he combines the *Purgatory*'s exhortation to let "dead poetry ris[e] again" (199; canto 1, line 7) with the *Paradise*'s more sobering comment that "mortal usage" – mortal language – "is like a leaf on a bough" (467; canto 26, line 137).

Discussing Beckett's reference to the passage in the *Purgatorio*, Michael Worton writes that "the leaves here and the tree throughout the play . . . must be perceived less as objects with an allegorical meaning than as signifiers in a complex web of intertextuality" (78). My thanks to C. D. Blanton for pointing out the pertinence of the Dante reference.

26. Bersani and Dutoit beautifully articulate this dead materiality of cultural tradition in Beckett, although they do not link it explicitly to writing: "There is no agonized reevaluation of tradition; rather, much like the derelicts of his fiction, he evokes art and philosophy of the past as if he were rummaging through a junkyard, giving an amused kick now and then at some useless and irrelevant relic of a dead imagination" (19). To say that the voices of the past cannot undergo "agonized reevaluation" is another way of saying that we can no longer converse with them.
27. "Do you remember the day I threw myself into the Rhône? [. . .] You fished me out" (*Waiting* 183).
28. According to Martin Esslin, this is an "old German student song" (76).
29. Cf. Kenner (135) and Fletcher and Spurling (42).
30. This sense of being imprisoned in the present *by* writing was apparently seized upon in George Tabori's 1984 production at the Münchner Kammerspiele. As described by Kalb, the production began by simulating an early rehearsal, with texts in hand: "At first, the points when they drop their scripts seem like sections that the actors happen to have memorized, allowing them to experiment with movement, as often occurs at early rehearsals of a play. Later those sections seem like improvisations, the actors attempting to depart from the text, or at least to lose themselves sufficiently in the action that they may call it 'theirs.' But each time the familiar exchange arises, ending with, 'Wir warten auf Godot,' [Thomas] Holtzmann [the actor playing Vladimir] holds up his crumpled paperback as if to say that they cannot leave because of the play, *Waiting for Godot*, and not because of any fictional character named Godot." (*Beckett* 92)
Kalb observes: "this is the only altered setting I know of that Beckett tolerated" (91).
31. Richard Begam points this out in his essay on *Godot* and performativity (140); for more on Beckett and Wittgenstein, see Perloff (*Wittgenstein* 115–144) and Furlani.
32. A note in the 1995 Foxrock edition of *Eleuthéria* points out that a "*béquet*" is "a small part of a scene that an author either adds or alters during rehearsals" (195). Beckett's very name, then, comes to signify an obtrusion of the writer at the site of performance.
33. Kalb, who interviews Akalaitis, seems to me to dismiss her point somewhat unfairly (*Beckett* 82); but it is true that his own larger argument itself develops

out of a sustained engagement with concrete theatrical productions – and his whole book could be described as an attempt to show how Beckett productions can achieve the kind of effect Akalaitis suggests is impossible.

34. On landscape as a form predicated on distance and removal, see Chaudhuri, who writes: "The founding paradox of perspective as employed in landscape painting is that it appears to 'give' us the world . . . just at the very moment that it removes it from us – or rather, us from it – most decisively" ("Land" 19). In Chaudhuri's analysis, the "alienation" thus established is anything but empowering: the spectator is "[u]nable to enter or alter the space of the world she or he is gazing upon" (20). But she explains that landscape *theater* – a term derived from Stein – concerns itself with immersion rather than alienation, shifting landscape "from a tract of land capable of being seen at a glance to an environment one can explore and inhabit" (21). I'd suggest that the "landscape" that is conspicuously lacking in *Godot* cuts across this distinction: the possibility of change is eliminated along with the perspective of distance; we "inhabit" the space so completely that there is nothing to "explore."

35. The translators of the recent edition of *Brecht on Theatre* have chosen "across" instead of "above" to translate the preposition "*über*," but I take it that both meanings remain active.

36. As Garner observes, silence "is always rendered virtual by the inescapable sounds of a peopled auditorium" (40).

37. Herbert Blau writes: "A subterranean drama, appearing to care for nothing but its interior life, [*Godot*] searches the audience like a Geiger counter. No modern drama is more sensitively aware of the presence of an audience, or its absence" (*Sails* 33). These last three words reflect Blau's own ongoing preoccupation with the audience as a site of lack (see *The Audience*), but they also suggest the specifically utopian dynamic we have been tracing.

38. For an account of *Godot*'s importance for *the Unnamable* that grounds this relationship in dialogue rather than monologue, but is still highly resonant with a utopian approach, see Abbott. Ruby Cohn argues for the central importance of soliloquy throughout Beckett's plays ("Outward"); Cohn defines this as speech "for oneself" rather than for an audience (23), so she doesn't discuss Lucky's command performance.

39. Some critics refer to the voice of *The Unnamable* only as "it," since that voice's radical ontological instability would seem to preclude any stable gender. It seems to me, however, that the specific references to sex and gender throughout the novel foster the sense of a male voice.
The narrator twice mentions having a penis (321, 326), and at one point wonders "what can be worse than this, a woman's voice perhaps" (357). Accordingly, since it helps with clarity, I use masculine pronouns in what follows.

40. See R. Cohn (*Back* 118), D. Cohn (177), and Brater (*Drama* 8).
41. Halpern considers this syntax in relation to the paradoxes of Eubuledes and Zeno invoked in *Endgame*, suggesting: "We might even think of the comma as a diacritical 'grain' or minim which cannot, through addition, make up the heap" (300n39).
42. To claim that *The Unnamable* manifests a kind of intermedial hybridity may be to contravene the critical commonplace that Beckett was rigorously dedicated to the purity of each medium in which he worked. Martin Harries has summarized this consensus and taken issue with it, arguing that "Beckett's awareness of and involvement with forms of media" including film, radio, and television "altered his work for the stage" (12). My argument for theater's "diversion" of the prose might be seen as parallel to Harries's claim about the effect of mass media on Beckett's theater.
43. Especially in this respect, Lucky's monologue seems to have recalled Beckett to a theatrical possibility he had explored as a performer many years before. Bair writes that in the 1931 Trinity skit *Le Kid*,

> Beckett, as Le Kid's father, Don Diegue, portrayed a very old man with a long white beard holding a small alarm clock in his hands. Don Diegue had a long soliloquy and Beckett wrote it to be the funniest scene in the parody. As Beckett talked, Pelorson, at the rear of the stage, began to move the hands on the clock, slowly at first, then faster and faster ... Suddenly the alarm clock in [Beckett's] hands began to ring ... By this time, Beckett was shouting at full speed and his speech had degenerated into a series of nonsense phrases and syllables, wilder and wilder, with less and less coherence, until after a time it didn't matter what he said because the audience was roaring with laughter ... years later members of *Le Kid*'s audience remember the uncanny feeling they had when they first saw *Waiting for Godot* and heard Lucky's speech. (127–128)

44. Jane R. Goodall has written that Lucky's monologue is "the most visibly energetic and climactic episode in all of Beckett's dramatic works" (188); I think the last sentence of *The Unnamable* can give it a run for its money.

Part II Beyond the Present

1. Adorno, *Minima Moralia* (94/105; translation modified; see Chapter 6 n. 4 below).

4 Introduction: Staging Writing Today

1. Wellman, *Girl Gone* (269).

2. For a particularly rich portfolio of the ways in which a range of contemporary theater and dance artists, centered in downtown New York, relate to text in their practices, see the statements collected in "Writing & Performance," a special section of *PAJ* 100 (2012).
3. Information about these pieces is available on Forced Entertainment's web site.
4. The company also did some early work on the first of these pieces, *Gatz*, in the summer of 1999 and in September 2003.
5. Peter Boenisch has recently criticized theater discourse that "positions the director of 'directors' theatre' *opposite* and in opposition to the text, suggesting an insurmountable antagonistic tension between director and playwright," such that "[o]ne of the positions must always appear as 'underprivileged,' in need of ... advocacy, engagement, and liberation" (7).
6. Stanton Garner writes that a play contains "a field of perceptual and corporeal activity that exists as a latency within the text ... phenomenological reading seeks to reembody, materialize the text, draw out this latency – not simply as a teleological point of realization beyond the playscript, but as an intrinsic component of dramatic textuality itself" (7). This sense that performance exists "within," and not just "beyond," the play's text is what I want to seize on here.
7. Thus Liz Tomlin argues that Martin Crimp's play *The City* "maintains the markers of the dramatic text, precisely in order to destabilize the coherence and completeness of the 'world' as understood through the lens of a logocentric dramatic realism" (62); for such works, Gerda Poschmann offers the category of "critical use of dramatic form," a subset of the "no-longer-dramatic theater text" (95).
8. Jürs-Munby extends this observation, writing that the text in postdramatic theater "precisely does *not* disappear as in conventional productions, but makes its reappearance as a resistant object" ("Vexed" 91); postdrama is thus uniquely capable of "honouring the written text in its very own materiality and dynamic" (92). Sara Jane Bailes makes a similar point, noting that in what she calls "performance theatre," "language is liberated from its singular function as narrative driver" (19).
9. See, for example, Pierre Corneille's famous 1660 essay on the three unities, which recommends the unity of time for its ability to dissolve the difference between the medium of representation and what it represents:

> The dramatic poem is an imitation, or rather a portrait, of human actions, and it is beyond doubt that portraits gain in excellence in proportion as they resemble the original more closely. A performance lasts two hours and would resemble reality perfectly if the action it presented required no more for its actual occurrence. Let us then ... compress the action of the poem

into the shortest possible period, so that the performance may more closely resemble reality and thus be more nearly perfect (125–126).

10. For a particularly rich description of what happens in *Gatz*, see Jonathan Kalb's 2013 article "Marathon Theater as Anti-Monument: The Curious Case of *Gatz*." Sara Jane Bailes is the leading scholar of Elevator Repair Service's work, and articulates the company's aesthetic with great precision in her 2010 *Performance Theater and the Poetics of Failure* (148–198). Kalb also provides a brief history of, and rationale for, marathon theater in the first chapter of *Great Lengths: Seven Works of Marathon Theater* (2011). I'm grateful to ERS for letting me access *Gatz* on video, and to John Collins and Ben Williams for answering my questions about the piece.
11. Marcus Quent makes a similar observation in relation to Adorno's concept of interpretation as itself a "faithful performance": Quent suggests that this idea implies "an erotic practice of interpretation; interpretation understood as a *moved* movement of analysis" (134). I am likewise suggesting that *Gatz* explores the way performance can be "moved" by text. See also Gustavus Stadler's "'My Wife': The Tape Recorder and Warhol's Queer Ways of Listening" (2014), which considers marital sexual fidelity and "high fidelity" music recording as related "forms of normativizing privacy" (427). Since "fidelity to the text" in theater aims to convert the object of a potentially private experience (reading) into a necessarily public one (performance), it complicates the association of fidelity and privacy in ways that might be related to the alternative, queer mode of "fidelity" Stadler discovers in Andy Warhol's practices of tape recording (449, cf. 439) and transcription (442).
12. Ironically, though, this performance is itself "faithful" to the novel's presentation of Jordan, "who, unlike Daisy, was too wise to carry well-forgotten dreams from age to age" (120): Jordan also functions as a kind of deflationary device amidst the story's romance.
13. Schechner acknowledges that his own theory of performance as "twice-behaved behavior" may have helped to undermine the mid-century ethos that pitted spontaneous live creation against text (906–907).
14. Adorno's notes on music from 1946 contain a strikingly similar thought, but this time on textual fidelity and the historical rise of musical scores. Adorno writes: "Autonomy and fetishism are two sides of the *same* truth . . . It is only the social obedience of that fidelity that enabled music to oppose the existing society" (*Towards* 53).
15. Collins told me that he doesn't recall the audience ever laughing at Shepherd's "Wolfshiem" voice – which is striking, giving how many times and places the show was performed.
16. Of the three shows in ERS's American literature trilogy, I'd suggest that the notion of a "poetics of failure" has most purchase on *The Sound and the Fury*

(which stages the first chapter of Faulkner's novel), and least on *The Select* (2010), an amazingly entertaining but fairly straightforward adaptation of Hemingway's *The Sun Also Rises*.

17. Robert Beuka observes that questions about whether Nick can serve as a reliable moral center for the novel "do not go away; they have kept critics and teachers busy since this debate first surfaced in the 1950s" (47).

18. Collins has said that seeing the Wooster Group made him "realiz[e] you didn't have to build a work for theater directly from a play script" (qtd. in O'Leary). More recently, however, he has questioned the division between "devised" and text-based work that theater discourse tends to take for granted (see Collins, "Way"). The Wooster Group's well-known work with exact reenactment of film (and filmed theater) would provide a different entry point for this discussion of "fidelity"; anticipating Müller's review of *Gatz*, Schneider writes of the Wooster Group: "it is the force of [the actors'] literal precision itself that both upholds the entire enterprise of fidelity to event and, at the same time, challenges that enterprise" (112; see 111–128). I'm suggesting that *Gatz* manages *not* to let the "challenge" to fidelity have the last word, an achievement that draws on the different kinds of mimesis, and literality, that a text (as opposed to a performance on film) makes possible.

19. Kalb discusses the way *Gatz* "sensitively taps" the frustrations of workers "in the information age" ("Marathon" 242).

5 The Promise of "Playwrighting"

1. Parks quoted in Jiggets, "Interview with Suzan-Lori Parks" (317).
2. Stein's *The Making of Americans* furnishes the epigraph for Parks's early short play *Betting on the Dust Commander*; on Parks's relationship to Stein and Beckett, see Geis (*Suzan*, esp. 6–7, 23–37). E. Fuchs (*Death* 103–105), Drukman (57–58, 70–72), Wood (who also discusses Brecht) (34), and Colbert (192). Scholars have also placed Parks in a modernist lineage by including readings of her work in such books as *The Other American Drama* (Marc Robinson, 1997) and *The Theatrical Gamut: Notes for a Post-Beckettian Stage* (ed. Enoch Brater, 1995). Parks's modernism even became the target of a rotten tomato when John Simon of *New York Magazine* called *The America Play* "a farrago of undigested Beckett and distantly ogled Joyce" (qtd. in Backalenick 27); Robert Brustein (rather disturbingly) described Parks's *Topdog/Underdog* as "the homeboy equivalent of *Waiting for Godot*" ["Homeboy"]) in his 2002 review. Parks herself has identified Faulkner and Woolf as her most decisive modernist influences; see Drukman (72) and Jiggets (310).

3. For an analysis and contextualization of Adorno on jazz which, to my mind, dispel the pertinence of his "jazz essays" for a discussion of Parks, see J. Bradford Robinson's 1994 study "The Jazz Essays of Theodor Adorno: Some Thoughts on Jazz Reception in Weimar Germany." See also Peters (75–89).
4. I don't mean to suggest that the project's participatory rhetoric was just a front for showing off. When I attended "Watch Me Work" on an afternoon in March 2013, I seemed to be the only one watching Parks the whole time, though the woman sitting next to me did snap a picture of the playwright. It even seemed possible that some of the people there didn't realize there was a performance going on – although the sound of Parks's typewriter dominated the otherwise quiet space. During the question-and-answer period that ended the performance, Parks referred to the event as a "free writing class," and when I asked if I could ask her a question about the performance (rather than about my own writing), she insisted: "It's not about me." Whether or not one buys that response wholeheartedly, it does bespeak the way Parks's own performance as a writer can come to figure, metonymically, a more general assertion of writing.
5. Similarly, Muse argues that the playwright constitutes an imposing central image within Parks's *365 Days/365 Plays* project: "Despite the festival's sincere rhetoric about democracy and leveling, the 'grassroots' festival would never have gotten off the ground without its central authorizing figure, a Pulitzer-Prize-winning celebrity powerhouse of the American theater" (224). Philip C. Kolin writes: "Suzan-Lori Parks herself has played many diverse roles, all spectacular shows, performances" ("Puck's" 8).
6. See also Bernard (694) and Louis (148).
7. For example, in Drukman's interview with Parks and her longtime director Liz Diamond, he proposes that they are "both artists dedicated to the same thing: that is, theatre texts and theatre productions that accrue meaning in the performance, that are performative in the sense that they give up some authorial hold on meaning" (58). Parks interestingly resists this idea of authorial relinquishment (59).
8. Parks does prudently adjust this analogy in the following sentence, bringing writing down to the size of "the thing we all play with" (127); but I think the initial aggrandizing impulse is significant.
9. In this sense Parks's vision recalls the poetics of *auteur* director Richard Foreman, a formidable presence in the downtown New York scene where Parks found a home in the late 1980s and 1990s. Foreman conceives of staging as "a series of problem solving tasks which 're-concretizes' the text. It's a matter of finding equivalencies for the densities and special 'auras' established by the graphics – typological as well as drawn – of the original manuscript" (Foreman 13; qtd. in Davy 120). Foreman directed the premiere

production of Parks's *Venus* at Yale Rep; for an analysis of this collaboration, see Garrett, "'For the Love of the Venus.'"
10. Harry J. Elam, Jr. activates the same conflation, in coining the term "(w)righting history" to analyze the plays of August Wilson (xvi), as does Jon D. Rossini in his study of Latina/o theater (25).
11. See also Malkin (159–172) and Dixon (49–50). For an argument that Parks's sprawling *365 Days/365 Plays* is actually a closet drama, see Muse (225–231).
12. As Young notes (29), scholars who write about Parks's work rarely fail to engage with these features, even where this is not their explicit focus. Jennifer Johung's article on Parks's "spells" and Elizabeth Dyrud Lyman's analysis of her scripts' page layouts, both of which focus on *Venus*, are particularly sustained examples of this kind of attention. On Parks's use of footnotes see Bullock (82), Dixon (62–63), Malkin (156–157), and Geis (*Suzan* 19–22). For treatments that focus on the thematization of writing as such in Parks's plays (as the current chapter does), see – in addition to Worthen's *Drama* – Johung, Malkin (155–182), Sullivan (242–267), and Dixon.
13. All references to the script refer to the version published in *The America Play and Other Works* (1995). This version significantly revises an earlier script, published in *Theater* in 1990, before the play had been produced.
14. This phrase, and its variants, circulate uneasily throughout Parks criticism. Parks has said she finds it "insulting to say my plays are only about what it's about to be Black – as if that's all we think about, as if our life is about that" (qtd. in Solomon 74); this and other remarks echo the Introduction to Henry Louis Gates's *Figures in Black* (xv–xxxii), a work Parks cites elsewhere, in which "the Black Experience" appears repeatedly in scare quotes. Most critics acknowledge the danger of pigeonholing Parks (often quoting her on the subject) but proceed to read her plays in terms of something like "black experience" – rightly, I think, especially for the early plays. See e.g. Solomon; Robert Brustein's prickly review of *The Death* in *The New Republic* ("What Do Women Playwrights Want?"); Malkin (156–157); and Rayner and Elam, who write helpfully: "the play is not 'about' the 'black experience' or about 'sorrows and frustrations and angers of people who have been wronged.' Yet, it is not *not* about them either, for those sorrows, frustrations and angers of the historical memory gather in the theatrical space to demand ritual remembrance" (456).
In her article "Digging out of the pigeonhole: African-American representation in the plays of Suzan-Lori Parks," Andrea J. Goto focuses on Parks's resistance to pigeonholing. For Parks's own playful meditation on what makes "a black play," see "New Black Math."
15. See e.g. H. Frank (5), Kolin ("You" 60), and Brewer (165). Heidi J. Holder usefully points out, however, that this "corrective" function whereby black

playwrights "attempted to fill a perceived void in their history" actually belongs to an earlier dramaturgy, from which she differentiates Parks: "In the plays of Parks, in particular, this business of staring into an absence and attempting to see it clearly has involved not a simple filling of a blank spot, but an intensification of and obsession with absence" (19). Rayner and Elam argue that *The Death* "takes stories and figures that have been excluded from history, not simply for their usefulness in writing a more comprehensive truth, but to put those images together in a theatrical, performative 'body'" (456).

16. As Louise Bernard observes, Yes And Greens's refrain "speaks not only to the urgency of History and the need to reclaim experiences and traditions, but also to the complex creative process of transcribing the oral . . . into the scribal and then into the theatrical space of performance" (690). I agree, but I want to focus on the scribal as much more, for Parks and for this play, than a midpoint between the oral and the theatrical. On remediation, see n. 39 below.

17. Soyica Diggs Colbert notes: "Importantly, Black Man's return is not a sign of the black body's otherworldly resilience typified by the ability to overcome any form of violence. The play presents him as wanting nothing more than to be laid finally to rest" (214).

18. In the play's Overture, too, Black Woman with Fried Drumstick speaks these lines, anticipating the acknowledgment she will arrive at in the last scene. Parks thus bends the dramatic "character arc" into a full circle, a geometric move she discusses in "From *Elements*" (8–11). In the premiere, however (and in the version of the play published earlier in *Theater*), Black Woman spoke these lines also in the First Chorus; that is, she never didn't speak them, so the lines didn't carry this particular "arc" at all, circular or otherwise.

19. Geis quotes Marc Robinson's observation that the play's ending "capture[s] the contradiction between fixity and flux that gives the play such energy" (*Other* 189, qtd. in *Suzan-Lori* 73). Robinson continues: "Her characters always try to mark the sensations and perceptions of their lives, but know too that nothing holds for more than a moment. The play is a portrait of the ensuing desperation" (*Other* 189). Colbert reads the last line as an "implicit critique of catharsis . . . cautioning the audience against the seductive allure of resolution or even 'clarification'" (196).

20. Malkin suggests this intertext, observing: "In a metaphoric sense, *Last Black Man* is clearly a play of mourning, approximating Freud's description of actively 'working through' the trauma of loss by remembering, repeating, and 're-experiencing' that loss" (172). Glenda Carpio also argues that Parks's early plays (including *The Death*) should be understood as "staging the work of mourning," in part by creating a "metadiscourse on mourning" that refuses the sensationalism of black suffering (194–195).

21. As Peggy Phelan writes: "What psychoanalysis makes clear is that the experience of loss is one of the central repetitions of subjectivity ... perhaps the human subject is born ready to mourn" (*Mourning* 5).
22. As Jennifer Johung writes of *Venus*, "subjecthood is a figuration that is formally displaced through the imprint of [the] name on the page" (45). Dixon links the audience's heightened sense of structure to Parks's use of "audible cue[s] such as a gunshot or a ringing bell" (56), a feature that again connects Parks with Richard Foreman (see n. 9 above and Geis, *Suzan* 59).
23. See Garrett ("Figure" 8); Ben-Zvi (191); Geis (*Suzan* 18). Worthen questions this idea, noting that "Parks's roles are difficult to assimilate to Stanislavskian acting, but perhaps no more so than Sophocles' or Shakespeare's" (*Drama* 169).
24. Opacity is crucial to Adorno's philosophy as well; as Asha Varadharajan writes, his negative dialectic "is animated by the opacity of the object" (74).
25. See e.g. Ben-Zvi (200–201), Malkin (167), and Goto (114).
26. Malkin is also careful to note that the play "charts [the] intersections" between "the recorded and the experienced," rather than positioning these terms in a rigid logical binary (166). Similarly, Kimberly D. Dixon argues that Parks's plays actively explore "the tension between o(au)ral and textual performativity" (55), concluding that "Parks does not favor either o(au)ral or written textuality, but explores each side's capacity for the performative, even as she underscores their inadequacies" (62). But Dixon, like Malkin, tends to assume that orality and textuality are at odds in moments where, I would argue, Parks is in fact asking us to imagine that the oral can be textually rendered and specified to an unprecedented degree. For example, Dixon points out that Parks "uses numerals instead of the full word, even for smaller numbers, a distinction only readers will see" (63); but I think that by making a choice like that *within a play*, Parks is actually insisting that such distinctions *can* be rendered in performance – and offering the textual surface as a model of that performance.
27. Carpio interprets this passage using Beckett's darkly ironic doctrine of "the *risus purus*, the laugh laughing at the laugh, the beholding, the saluting of the highest joke, in a word the laugh that laughs – silence please – at that which is unhappy" (*Watt* 48, qtd. in Carpio 210).
28. The premiere production lacked some of this specificity, since performers broke into actual laughing both times, rather than upholding a precise number of articulated "Ha"s. As noted above (see n. 18), that version of the play did not develop the "arc" from denial to acknowledgment of death that Parks would cultivate more strongly in her subsequent work on the script, so the stronger similarity of the two "Ha ha ha" moments is not surprising. Nevertheless, in that production the first passage did end with a weary

collective sigh, while the second ended with an energetic final "HA!", as in both versions of the published play.

29. "Papa, potatoes, poultry, prunes, and prism are all very good words for the lips: especially prunes and prism," says *Little Dorrit*'s Mrs. General, introducing a phrase that continues to accumulate meaning throughout the novel (500). Although the motif isn't clearly racialized in Dickens as it is in Joyce, its agglomeration with other "food" words (potatoes, poultry) seems to echo in Parks's list-of-food character names in *The Death* (my thanks to Richard Halpern for pointing this out).

30. On the nature of Parks's citation of Wright, see Goto (113–115).

31. Of *The America Play*, whose protagonist is described as "a Digger by trade. From a family of Diggers" (160), Parks has said: "The relationship between 'digger' and 'nigger' was the whole play for me" (Ong 48).

32. The sense of writing as an instrument of violence recurs throughout Parks's work, but is most pronounced in the third section of her first full-length play, *Imperceptible Mutabilities in the Third Kingdom*. In this dreamlike scene, a dying slave is bullied, cajoled, and robbed of her teeth on the eve of Emancipation by the sinister Miss Faith, who continually refers these proceedings to "the book": "Mrs. Saxon, book says you are due for an extraction ... Find solace in the book and – bid your teeth goodbye" (44); "Think of it as getting yourself chronicled, Mrs. Saxon. You are becoming a full part of the great chronicle!" (46). Both Worthen ("Citing" 7–8) and Malkin (161–166) cite this play as evidence of Parks's suspicion of the textual; while I agree, it seems to me that in *The Death* Parks produces a more complex and ultimately celebratory account of writing, as this chapter attempts to show.

33. See Rayner and Elam (459). A hallmark segment of the minstrel show, the stump speech was a long, comically malapropist blackface monologue, "a species of inflated Barnum-speak" that, according to Eric Lott's *Love and Theft*, "appear[s] to have grown out of white observation of black churches and black street oratory" (77, 247 n. 9). When blackness "came to represent laziness and license, the determining factor in white men's dread of miscegenation," Lott writes, "these fantasies were partly represented by a vexing and unmeaning linguistic creativity, a proliferation of huge, ungainly, and onomatopoeic words that were meant to ridicule the speaker but which also called attention to the grain of voices, the wagging of tongues, the fatness of painted lips" (122; cf. Carpio 216). Lott's groundbreaking study of the erotics of minstrelsy has been important for my own reading of Ham's monologue.

34. Geoffrey Jacques argues that Lucky's monologue, the tramps' dialogue, and other features of *Godot* have antecedents in the minstrel show, claiming that

"Beckett repeatedly returned to the use of minstrel tropes in his work" (106; see 101–109). Beckett's *Stories and Texts for Nothing* contains an oddly wistful reference to minstrelsy, when the narrator imagines "great clusters of bones, dangling and knocking with a clatter of castanets, it's clean and gay like coons, I'd join them with a will if it could be here and now . . ." (102). Even if *Godot*'s obvious links to vaudeville and music hall performance offer a more immediate precedent for the play's comic pleasures than does minstrelsy, the minstrel show certainly helped audiences develop the structure of enjoyment that a speech like Lucky's, or Ham's, can still activate.

35. In the premiere, the chorus of figures actually seemed outraged at Ham's speech, a choice I find to be in tension with the script's suggestion that his performance is a familiar occasion within its world. For instance, the speech is ushered in by Old Man River Jordan's advice: "For that you must ask Ham" and immediately preceded by the sound of a bell; Ham himself begins his speech with the parenthetical phrase "(catchin up to um *in medias res* that is we takin off from where we stopped up last time)" (121). In general, director Beth Schachter seems to have approached this scene with a desire to limit its comic appeal – an understandable choice, but one that I think curbed its most disturbing ambiguities.

36. Carpio also remarks that "The fact that the numbers in superscript are apparent only typographically . . . suggests that the number of ancestors who perished can be ignored depending on the kind of representation, oral or textual, in which their fate is represented" (216).

37. Scholarly treatments of Parks frequently invoke Gates on "Signifyin(g)"; see e.g. H. Frank (especially 3–10), Bernard (693ff), Geis (*Suzan* 15–17), and Malkin (160).

38. My thanks to C. D. Blanton for suggesting this connection.

39. I am taking this term from Philip Auslander, who borrows it from Jay Bolter and Richard Grusin (*Liveness* 6). When used this way in reference to what happens in one artist's work, the term no longer names a "historical logic" as it does for Auslander; but I would suggest that Parks's appropriations of performance for writing bear some relevance to the "incursion . . . into the live event" that Auslander analyzes throughout his book (7).

40. Jacques makes a similar point in reading a description of an early twentieth-century performance by the African-American blackface minstrel Bert Williams. After making his way downstage at the top of his act, Williams would take a notebook from his pocket, look through it, and find his first song inside. Jacques writes:

> The appearance of the illiterate 'darky' who finds his verse in a notebook is precisely the sort of character that gives audiences both the comfort of the stereotype and the discomfort of the unknown. If the stereotyped blackface

clown also has access to the "talking book" (to borrow Henry Louis Gates Jr.'s phrase), then how comforting is the stereotype? In a sense, by using the gesture of the notebook, by his employment of the gesture of reading, Williams renders absurd the very stereotype he performs. (95)

Williams's disconcerting use of "literature, and the notion of the literary" (ibid.) to frame the theatricality of a minstrel performance would be a kind of precedent for Parks's project.

41. As Martin Puchner writes: "All stage directions are descriptions or prescriptions of the mimetic space on the stage, but traditionally the doubling inherent in this projection disappears because stage directions are considered dispensable technical appendixes that do not appear in the end product, the performance" (*Stage* 26).

42. For Daddario and Gritzner, this account of the artwork aligns Adorno's aesthetics with performance in general: "Performance is process and objectivation, temporal experience and material sensation" (17). As I discussed in Chapter 1, I am interested in developing the possible theatrical ramifications of Adorno's own worry that performance itself is *not* really "objectivation."

43. In Parks's performative essay "New Black Math" (2005), someone named "Black Playwright" says: "Audiences still ask, 'what do black people think about such and such?' Black people think the world is fucked. That's what black people think" (581).

44. At the same time, this line also (to my mind) recalls Viktor Shklovsky's famous statement that "art . . . exists to make one feel things, to make the stone *stony*" (16). Parks's final refusal to focus on *what* the rock says also echoes Shklovsky's provocative insistence that "the process of perception is an aesthetic end in itself and must be prolonged . . . *the object is not important*" (ibid.).

45. Elinor Fuchs refers to this line as "geo-orthography" ("Reading" 38).

6 "Small, fierce creatures"

1. Wellman, *A Murder of Crows* (23); Adorno, *Aesthetic Theory* (59).
2. Portions of this chapter first appeared as an article entitled "Mouthing Off: The Negativity of Monologue in Mac Wellman's *A Murder of Crows*," in *Modern Drama* 57.3 (Fall 2014): 293–314, doi: 10.3138/md.0668. Reprinted with permission from University of Toronto Press (www.utpjournals.com).
3. I have also been lucky enough to have Mac Wellman as a teacher and friend. For more on Wellman's importance as a mentor to young New York artists, see Soloski. On Wellman's influence, see also Paul Castagno's *New Playwriting Strategies*, 2nd ed. (3, 12). I can't quite agree with Castagno that the "orthodoxy" of conventional dramatic playwriting "has been largely

displaced" during the last decade in America (7), but I agree that there is more experimentation happening here than ever before, and that Wellman has played a major role in this increase.
4. I have modified Jephcott's translation: "Retention of strangeness is the only antidote to estrangement." The original text reads: "Nur Fremdheit ist das Gegengift gegen Entfremdung."
5. Cormac Power offers a powerful account of how a play can subvert theatrical communication in his reading of Ionesco's *The Chairs*. "Instead of asserting 'I-you-here-now,' in line with a long tradition of dramatic communication, the play seems to pose questions as to 'who-what-where' ... The play uses 'theatre', and its deictic foundation of a shared context, to question the nature and even the possibility of that context" ("Space" 73). In Power's Derridean analysis, *The Chairs* exposes a "failure principle" that *always* threatens theatrical communication (73–74, 76); for Wellman, I suggest, communication is not only a metaphysical ideal, but an all-too-real parameter of everyday experience, which theater has to find ways to attack.
6. Adjacent to the critique of communication, Wellman's attack on "intention" also recalls Adorno's insistence that an object's truth always lies outside the intention of its creators; see Buck-Morss 76–78.
7. In the Epilogue to *Postdramatic Theatre*, Lehmann differentiates between postdramatic-theatrical and "media" modes of communication, in a way that would seem to qualify his claim about "proximity to ... mass communication": the media present "communication as (an exchange of) information," an economy from which "postdramatic theatre tries to withdraw" (184). I agree, but it seems ironic that the statement Lehmann offers as an example of the kind of speech *not* available to "mass" communication – "The statement 'I love you' is not a piece of information but an act, an engagement" (ibid.) – is perhaps the culture industry's most reliable discursive staple. Those three little words will come up again in the next section of this chapter.
8. For a detailed discussion of Wellman as a "fellow traveller of the Language poets" (72) see Appler. Perloff makes this association earlier in her Foreword to *Cellophane* (xi).
9. *Antigone* is discussed at length by Syers, and by Martin Puchner in his 2011 article "Drama and Performance: Toward a Theory of Adaptation." Marc Robinson briefly discusses *A Murder of Crows* in *The Other American Drama* (192–196); see also Douglas Messerli's thoughtful blog post "A Linguistic Fantastia" (2013).
10. One way to describe this critical convergence would be to say that these theorists think about stage monologue on the model of "direct address." Interestingly, a few years ago when the readers of Kristoffer Diaz's theater blog

rallied in the defense of direct address – *New York Times* reviewer Charles Isherwood had complained that contemporary playwrights were using too much of it – they sometimes praised this device in terms resonant with the critical accounts I have been citing: "The direct connection with the audience is the most unique and interesting thing theater has going for it – we might as well use it!" (see Diaz). I think this exchange suggests the degree to which the critical consensus on monologue reflects conventional theater wisdom more broadly, and gives a sense of how radical Wellman's work continues to be.

11. In a 1963 lecture, D. W. Winnicott exhorts his fellow psychoanalysts: "We must ask ourselves, does our technique allow for the patient to communicate that he or she is not communicating?" (188). *Mutatis mutandis*, Wellman's work suggests that we need to start building this kind of receptiveness into the "technique" with which we study theater (and monologues in particular).

12. Bert States's account of the living room in realist theater offers an incomparably rich sense of what might be at stake in Susannah's (Wellman's) rejection of that space; see *Great Reckonings in Little Rooms*, 66–70. States writes that the realist set – emblematized for him by *Hedda Gabler* – embodies "a world in which one event sets up another within a tight system of time-space probabilities" and "says, in effect, 'It will all end here!'" (67, 69). This mode of *givenness* – epistemological and phenomenological – is what has overwhelmed Estragon in his "muckheap" speech; it is exactly what Wellman's theater wants to defeat.

13. Thanks to Zach Samalin for first bringing this sentence to my attention.

14. These speeches offer a verbal equivalent to the costumes stipulated in *Sincerity Forever*, whose teenage characters wear Klan outfits throughout the play without any explicit contextual justification. While this obviously "sends a message" about the play's critical program, the very persistence of the robes and hoods *beyond* the moment of their political legibility ultimately loosens our grasp on these signifiers.

15. In a 1997 interview with David Savran, Wellman says his plays "are somehow the subtext for some absent realistic play. I just dispense with writing the text altogether and write the subtext because it's more interesting" (in Savran 330). This is a characteristic Wellmanian perversion: traditionally, the subtext *of* a text – made present by a reader's or an actor's interpretation – functions to convey the text's meaning. But a subtext *without* ("instead" of) a text suggests language wasting its breath in an elaboration without a referent – without anything to deliver.

16. This is true also in the sense that they are intertextual figures. Crows are a motif throughout Wellman's work, and hence they act as a kind of signature: Green Integer has published two "Crowtets" of his plays, and the

cover photo of his first major collection, *The Bad Infinity* (1994), looks a lot like a crow's head. But crows have also haunted earlier twentieth-century theater artists. In "Van Gogh, the Man Suicided by Society" (1947), Artaud suggests that Van Gogh's painted crows have "opened the door ... to an enigmatic and sinister beyond" (489) – a description Wellman would appreciate. Crows also appear in Sam Shepard's *Cowboy Mouth* (1971) and *The Tooth of Crime* (1972); and there is also the "distant magpie" that speckles Stein's landscape in *Four Saints in Three Acts* (469; cf. "Plays" 80). My thanks to Shannon Jackson for suggesting these echoes.

17. Wellman's writing thus seizes on an aspect of theater that Rebecca Schneider describes: "the live is a troubling trace of a precedent text and so ... comes afterward, even arguably remains afterward, as a *record* of the text *set in play*" (90).

18. Bernstein derives this communication/expression binary from passages like the following in Adorno:

> The effort to purge [authentic artworks] of whatever contingent subjectivity may want to say through them involuntarily confers an ever more defined shape on their own language. In artworks the term expression refers to precisely this language. There is good reason that where this term has been technically employed longest and most emphatically, as the direct *espressivo* in musical scores, it demands nothing specifically expressed, no particular emotional content. Otherwise *espressivo* could be replaced by terms for whatever specific thing is to be expressed. (*Aesthetic* 104–105)

The sense that expression is opposed not only to the communication of a specific message, but also to a communicative ethos of availability or givenness, emerges in Adorno's remark that "Through expression art closes itself off to being-for-another, which always threatens to engulf it, and becomes eloquent in itself" (ibid. 112).

19. See for example "Little History of Photography" (1931) and "On Some Motifs in Baudelaire" (1940). Miriam Bratu Hansen traces the shifting meanings of "aura" in this philosopher's work in "Benjamin's Aura": "Anything but a clearly delimited, stable concept, aura describes a cluster of meanings and relations that appear in Benjamin's writings in various configurations and not always under its own name; it is this conceptual fluidity that allows aura to become such a productive nodal point in Benjamin's thinking" (339). Among the meanings Hansen identifies, one that would be relevant to Wellman is "the ominous aspect of aura [which] belongs to the realm of the daemonic" (342).

20. For a discussion of Adorno's concept of aura that focuses on the entailed notion of distance, see Sherratt.

21. Consciously or not, this vision echoes a remark made by Adorno in his early essay "The Natural History of the Theatre" (dated 1931–1933): "The dome has long since closed over the theatre and now reflects the sounds coming from the stage, barring a view of the sky. But those who sit nearest to it, for a small sum of money, and at the furthest remove from the stage, know that the roof is not firmly fixed above them and wait to see whether it won't burst open one day . . . " (67).
22. *Speculations* was published in Wellman's 2008 collection *The Difficulty of Crossing a Field*, but has evolved through successive drafts available on his web site; I am citing "Draft seven," dated 2013.
23. Marc Robinson notes that Wellman "writes with the conviction that plays are animate, and so the writing keeps changing voices, contexts, and rhythms as a reminder of the unpredictability of all mortal creatures" (*Other* 192).
24. My thanks to Annie-B Parson and Paul Lazar of Big Dance for making a video of this production available to me.
25. Since Thomas More, that is, the "no-place" of "u-topia" has harbored its more positive homophone, "eu-topia" or "good place," often in undecidable relation (see "eutopia").
26. Throughout the play, TV figures as a comic double, or ironic shadow, of this connected-in-disconnection literary network. For instance, the Vademecum reports to Buggins that the vanished characters

    > have been dematerialized
    > and electronically reassembled beyond the mystic
    >   borders
    > of Vadoo (276)

    – a description that sounds provocatively like televisual transport. Here again, Wellman is interested in the possibility that cultural junk might harbor transcendent possibilities, not unlike the "verbal detritus" of everyday speech (*Cellophane* 151–152) or the "county dump" in *A Murder of Crows*.
27. In a discussion of *Antigone*, Wellman's subsequent collaboration with Big Dance Theater, Puchner rightly emphasizes the "autonomy" retained separately by both the text and the production ("Drama" 296, 305).
28. In the published text, there are two more lines of dialogue here: "FAY: There is no place beyond that. / LISSA: Yes there is" (252). The production cuts these lines, a choice that lets Buggins's words ("No. A place beyond that") reverberate throughout the ensuing action. By ending the book with this passage, I mean to emphasize that the vision of playwriting as central to theater's move beyond drama doesn't depend on some inflexible model of authorship. Then again, I also hope I have shown how this directorial cut resonates with Wellman's own sensibility.

Works Cited

Abbot, H. Porter. "A Grammar for Being Elsewhere." *Journal of Modern Literature* 6.1 (February 1977): 39–46.
Adorno, Theodor W. *Aesthetic Theory*. Trans. and ed. Robert Hullot-Kentor. Minneapolis: University of Minnesota Press, 1997.
— *Ästhetische Theorie*. Ed. Gretel Adorno and Rolf Tiedemann. Frankfurt: Suhrkamp, 1973.
— "Commitment." *Notes to Literature* Vol. 2. Ed. Rolf Tiedemann. Trans. Sherry Weber Nicholsen. New York: Columbia University Press, 1992. 76–94.
— "The Handle, the Pot, and Early Experience." *Notes to Literature* Vol. 2. Ed. Rolf Tiedemann. Trans. Sherry Weber Nicholsen. New York: Columbia University Press, 1992. 211–219.
— *Lectures on Negative Dialectics*. Ed. Rolf Tiedemann. Trans. Rodney Livingstone. Malden: Polity, 2008.
— *Minima Moralia: Reflections on a Damaged Life*. Trans. E. F. N. Jephcott. London: Verso, 1974.
— *Minima Moralia: Reflexionen aus dem beschädigten Leben*. Ed. Rolf Tiedemann et al. Frankfurt: Suhrkamp, 2003.
— "The Natural History of the Theatre." *Quasi una Fantasia: Essays on Modern Music*. Trans. Rodney Livingstone. London: Verso, 1992. 65–78.
— *Towards a Theory of Musical Reproduction*. Ed. Henri Lonitz. Trans. Wieland Hoban. Cambridge: Polity, 2006.
— "Trying to Understand Endgame." Trans. Michael T. Jones. *New German Critique* 26 (Spring 1982): 119–150.
— "Why Is the New Art So Hard to Understand?" Trans. Susan Gillespie. *Essays on Music*. Ed. Richard Leppert. Berkeley: University of California Press, 2002. 127–134.
Adorno, Theodor W. and Max Horkheimer. "Towards a New Manifesto?" Trans. Rodney Livingstone. *New Left Review* 65 (2010): 32–61.
Albright, Daniel. *Beckett and Aesthetics*. Cambridge: Cambridge University Press, 2003.
Alighiere, Dante. *The Divine Comedy*. Trans. C. H. Sisson. Chicago: Regnery Gateway, 1981.
Als, Hilton. "Eight Hours of, Like, Life." Rev. of *Life and Times: Episodes 1–4*, by Nature Theater of Oklahoma. *The New Yorker* 23 Jan. 2013.

Appler, Keith. "Mac Wellman and the Language Poets: Chaos Writing and the General Economy of Language." *Journal of Dramatic Theory and Criticism* 24.2 (Spring 2010): 69–90.
Aristotle, *Poetics*. Trans. Gerald F. Else. Ann Arbor: University of Michigan Press, 1967.
Artaud, Antonin. *The Theater and Its Double*. Trans. Mary Caroline Richards. New York: Grove, 1958.
   "Van Gogh, the Man Suicided by Society." Trans. Helen Weaver. *Antonin Artaud: Selected Writings*. Ed. Susan Sontag. Berkeley: University of California Press, 1976. 483–514.
Auslander, Philip. *Liveness: Performance in a Mediatized Culture*. London: Routledge, 1999.
Austin, J. L. *How to Do Things with Words*. Ed. J. O. Urmson and Marina Sbisà. Cambridge, MA: Harvard University Press, 1962.
Backalenick, Irene. "Suzan-Lori Parks: The Joy of Playwrighting." *Theater Week* 8–14 April 1996: 27–28.
Bailes, Sara Jane. *Performance Theatre and the Poetics of Failure*. New York: Routledge, 2011.
Bair, Deirdre. *Samuel Beckett: A Biography*. 1973. New York: Touchstone, 1993.
Baker, Geoffrey. "Nietzsche, Artaud, and Tragic Politics." *Comparative Literature* 55.1 (2003): 1–23.
Barish, Jonas. *The Antitheatrical Prejudice*. Berkeley: University of California Press, 1981.
Barnett, David. "Performing Dialectics in an Age of Uncertainty, or: Why Post-Brechtian ≠ Postdramatic." *Postdramatic Theatre and the Political: International Perspectives on Contemporary Performance*. Ed. Karen Jürs-Munby, Jerome Carroll, and Steve Giles. London: Bloomsbury, 2013. 47–66.
   "When Is a Play not a Drama? Two Examples of Postdramatic Theatre Texts." *New Theatre Quarterly* 24:1 (2008): 14–23.
Barthes, Roland. "From Work to Text." *Image-Music-Text*. Trans. Stephen Heath. New York: Hill and Wang, 1977. 155–164.
   A Lover's Discourse. Trans. Richard Howard. New York: Hill and Wang, 1978.
   S/Z. Trans. Richard Miller. New York: Hill and Wang, 1974.
Bay-Cheng, Sarah. *Mama Dada: Gertrude Stein's Avant-Garde Theatre*. New York: Routledge, 2005.
Beckett, Samuel. "Dante . . . Bruno. Vico.. Joyce." 1929. *Samuel Beckett: The Grove Centenary Edition*. Ed. Paul Auster. Vol. 4. New York: Grove, 2006. 495–510.
   Eleuthéria. Trans. Michael Brodsky. Introd. S. E. Gontarski. New York: Foxrock, 1995.
   Endgame and Act Without Words. New York: Grove, 2009.
   Mercier and Camier. New York: Grove, 2011.
   Murphy. Montruil and London: Calder, 1993.
   Stories and Texts for Nothing. New York: Grove, 1967.
   "Three Dialogues with Georges Duthuit." *Samuel Beckett: The Grove Centenary Edition*. Ed. Paul Auster. Vol. 4. New York: Grove, 2006. 555–563.

Three Novels: Molloy, Malone Dies, The Unnamable. New York: Grove, 2009.
Waiting for Godot. Bilingual Edn. New York: Grove, 2010.
Watt. New York: Grove, 1953.
Begam, Richard. "How to Do Nothing with Words, or *Waiting for Godot* as Performativity." *Modern Drama* 50.2 (Summer 2007): 138–167.
Benjamin, Walter. "Little History of Photography." Trans. Edmund Jephcott and Kingsley Shorter. *Walter Benjamin: Selected Writings* Vol. 2: 1927–1934. Ed. Michael W. Jennings, Howard Eiland, and Gary Smith. 506–530.
"On Some Motifs in Baudelaire." *Illuminations*. Ed. and introd. Hannah Arendt. Trans. Harry Zohn. New York: Schocken, 1969. 155–200.
"The Work of Art in the Age of Mechanical Reproduction." *Illuminations*. Ed. and introd. Hannah Arendt. Trans. Harry Zohn. New York: Schocken, 1969. 217–252.
Bennett, Benjamin. *All Theater Is Revolutionary Theater*. New York: Cornell University Press, 2005.
Benzaquén, Adriana S. "Thought and Utopia in the Writings of Adorno, Horkheimer, and Benjamin." *Utopian Studies* 9.2 (1998): 149–161.
Ben-Zvi, Linda. "'Aroun the Worl': The Signifyin(g) Theater of Suzan-Lori Parks." *The Theatrical Gamut: Notes for a Post-Beckettian Stage*. Ed. Enoch Brater. Ann Arbor: University of Michigan Press, 1995. 189–208.
Bernard, Louise. "The Musicality of Language: Redefining History in Suzan-Lori Parks's *The Death of the Last Black Man in the Whole Entire World*." *African American Review* 31.4 (Winter 1997): 687–698.
Bernstein, J. M. *Adorno: Disenchantment and Ethics*. Cambridge: Cambridge University Press, 2001.
Bersani, Leo. "Beckett and the End of Literature." *Samuel Beckett's* Molloy, Malone Dies, The Unnamable. Ed. Harold Bloom. New York: Chelsea House, 1988. 51–70.
A Future for Astyanax. New York: Columbia University Press, 1984.
Bersani, Leo and Ulysse Dutoit. *Arts of Impoverishment: Beckett, Rothko, Resnais*. Cambridge, MA: Harvard University Press, 1993.
Bersani, Leo and Adam Phillips. *Intimacies*. Chicago: University of Chicago Press, 2008.
Beuka, Robert. *American Icon: Fitzgerald's* The Great Gatsby *in Critical and Cultural Context*. Rochester, NY: Camden House, 2011.
Blau, Herbert. *The Audience*. Baltimore: Johns Hopkins University Press, 1990.
Sails of the Herring Fleet: Essays on Beckett. Ann Arbor: University of Michigan Press, 2000.
Blechman, Max. "'Not Yet': Adorno and the Utopia of Conscience." *Cultural Critique* 70 (Fall 2008): 177–198.
Bloch, Ernst and Theodor W. Adorno. "Something's Missing: A Discussion Between Ernst Bloch and Theodor W. Adorno on the Contradictions of Utopian Longing." Moderated by Horst Krüger. *The Utopian Function of Art and Literature: Selected Essays*. By Bloch. Trans. Jack Zipes and Frank Mecklenburg. Cambridge, MA: MIT Press, 1988. 1–17.

Boenisch, Peter. *Directing Scenes and Senses: The Thinking of Regie.* Manchester: Manchester University Press, 2015.
Bottoms, Stephen. "Authorizing the Audience: The Conceptual Drama of Tim Crouch." *Performance Research* 14.1 (2009): 65–76.
Bowers, Jane Palatini. *"They Watch Me as They Watch This": Gertrude Stein's Metadrama.* Philadelphia: University of Pennsylvania Press, 1991.
Brantley, Ben. "Borne Back Ceaselessly Into the Past." Rev. of *Gatz*, by Elevator Repair Service. *The New York Times* 6 Oct. 2010.
Brater, Enoch. *The Drama in the Text: Beckett's Late Fiction.* New York: Oxford University Press, 1994.
Ten Ways of Thinking about Samuel Beckett: The Falsetto of Reason. New York: Methuen, 2011.
Brater, Enoch, ed. *The Theatrical Gamut: Notes for a Post-Beckettian Stage.* Ann Arbor: University of Michigan Press, 1995.
Brecht, Bertolt. *Brecht on Theatre.* Third ed. Ed. Marc Silberman, Steve Giles, and Tom Kuhn. Trans. Jack Davis, Romy Fursland, Giles, et al. London: Bloomsbury, 2015.
Brecht, Bertolt. *Schriften zum Theater.* Ed. Werner Hecht. 7 vols. Frankfurt am Main: Suhrkamp, 1963–1964.
Brewer, Mary F. *Staging Whiteness.* CT: Wesleyan University Press, 2005.
Brustein, Robert. "A Homeboy Godot." Rev. of *Topdog/Underdog*, by Suzan-Lori Parks, dir. George C. Wolfe. *The New Republic* 13 May 2002.
"What Do Women Playwrights Want?" *The New Republic* 13 Apr. 1992.
Buck-Morss, Susan. *The Origin of Negative Dialectics: Theodor W. Adorno, Walter Benjamin, and the Frankfurt Institute.* New York: Macmillan, 1977.
Bullock, Kurt. "Famous/Last Words: The Disruptive Rhetoric of Historico-Narrative 'Finality' in Suzan-Lori Parks' *The America Play*." *American Drama* 10.2 (June 2001): 69–87.
Čale-Feldman, Lada. "Dramatic versus Postdramatic Textuality – Paradoxes of a False Opposition?" *Dramatic and Postdramatic Theatre: Ten Years after* (Conference Proceedings, Faculty of Dramatic Arts, Belgrade University). Spec. issue of *Anthology of Essays by Faculty of Dramatic Arts* 20 (2011): 97–108.
Caramello, Charles. *Henry James, Gertrude Stein, and The Biographical Act.* Chapel Hill: University of North Carolina Press, 1996.
Carpio, Glenda. *Laughing Fit to Kill: Black Humor in the Fictions of Slavery.* New York: Oxford University Press, 2008.
Case, Sue-Ellen. *The Domain-Matrix.* Bloomington: Indiana University Press, 1996.
Caserio, Robert L. "The Story in It: *The Wings of the Dove*." *Modern Critical Views: Henry James.* Ed. Harold Bloom. New York: Chelsea House, 1987. 189–214.
Castagno, Paul C. *New Playwriting Strategies.* 2nd ed. London: Routledge, 2012.
"Varieties of Monologic Strategy: the Dramaturgy of Len Jenkin and Mac Wellman." *New Theatre Quarterly* 9.34 (May 1993): 134–146.
Castellucci, Romeo. "The Dark Prince of Experimental Theater." Interview with Summer Banks. *Exberliner*, 12 Mar. 2013.

Cavell, Stanley. *Must We Mean What We Say?* Updated ed. Cambridge: Cambridge University Press, 2002.
The World Viewed. Enlarged ed. Cambridge, MA: Harvard University Press, 1979.
Chatman, Seymour. *Story and Discourse.* New York: Cornell University Press, 1980.
Chaudhuri, Una. "Land/Scape/Theory." *Land/Scape/Theater.* Ed. Einor Fuchs and Chaudhuri. Ann Arbor: University of Michigan Press, 2002. 11–29.
"Mac Wellman's Grecian Yearn." Rev. of *Antigone*, text by Wellman, performed by Big Dance Theater, Dance Theater Workshop, New York. *The Village Voice* 10 Dec. 2002.
Cohn, Dorrit. *Transparent Minds: Narrative Modes for Presenting Consciousness in Fiction.* Princeton: Princeton University Press, 1978.
Cohn, Ruby. *Back to Beckett.* Princeton: Princeton University Press, 1973.
Just Play: Beckett's Theater. Princeton: Princeton University Press, 1980.
"Outward Bound Soliloquies." *Journal of Modern Literature* 6.1 (February 1977): 17–38.
Colbert, Soyica Diggs. "'When I Die, I Won't Stay Dead': The Future of the Human in Suzan-Lori Parks's *The Death of the Last Black Man in the Whole Entire World.*" *boundary 2* 39.3 (2012): 191–220.
Collins, John. "A Way of Listening." Interview with Ana Pais. *New Dramaturgy: International Perspectives on Theory and Practice.* Ed. Katalin Trencsényi and Bernadette Cochrane. London: Bloomsbury, 2014. 115–124.
Collins, John and Scott Shepherd. "Elevator Repair Service's GATZ." Interview with Philip Bither. *Walker Magazine.* Walker Arts Center. 8 June 2006.
Connor, Steven. *Samuel Beckett: Repetition, Theory, and Text.* Oxford: Basil Blackwell, 1988.
Conti, Chris. "Critique and Form: Adorno on *Godot* and *Engame.*" *Samuel Beckett Today/ Aujourd'hui* 14 (2004): 277–292.
Corneille, Pierre. "Of the Three Unities of Action, Time, and Place." Trans. Donald Schier. *The Continental Model: Selected French Critical Essays of the Seventeenth Century, in English Translation.* Ed. Scott Elledge and Donald Schier. Minneapolis: University of Minnesota Press, 1960. 117–131.
Craig, Edward Gordon. *On the Art of the Theatre.* London: Heinemann, 1957.
Crawley, Peter. "Introduction: No Uncertain Terms." *No More Drama.* Ed. Crawley and Willie White. Dublin: Project, 2011. 9–25.
Daddario, Will. "From Pseudo-Activity to Critique: Adorno, Philosophy, Participation." *Performance Research* 16.4 (2011): 124–135.
Daddario, Will and Karoline Gritzner, eds. *Adorno and Performance.* Ed. Daddario and Gritzner. New York: Palgrave Macmillan, 2014.
Daddario, Will and Karoline Gritzner. Introduction. *Adorno and Performance.* Ed. Daddario and Gritzner. New York: Palgrave Macmillan, 2014. 1–22.
Davy, Kate. "Richard Foreman's Ontological-Hysteric Theatre: The Influence of Gertrude Stein." *Twentieth Century Literature*, 24.1 (1978): 108–126.

The Death of the Last Black Man in the Whole Entire World. Premiere dir. Beth Schachter. BACA Downtown, New York. 4 Oct. 1990. Videotape avail. at Performance Art Library at Lincoln Center.

Deleuze, Gilles and Félix Guattari. *A Thousand Plateaus: Capitalism and Schizophrenia*. Trans. Brian Massumi. Minneapolis: University of Minnesota Press, 2007.

Derrida, Jacques. *Of Grammatology*. Trans. Gayatri Chakravorty Spivak. 1976. Baltimore: Johns Hopkins University Press, 1997.

"Signature Event Context." *Margins of Philosophy*. Trans. Alan Bass. Chicago: University of Chicago Press, 1982. 307–330.

Writing and Difference. Trans. Alan Bass. Chicago: University of Chicago Press, 1978.

Diaz, Kristoffer. "The Isherwood Talkback." *The Heavy Lifting*. Kristoffer Diaz, 22 Oct.–1 Nov., 2010.

Dickens, Charles. *Little Dorrit*. Ed. Stephen Wall and Helen Small. London: Penguin, 2003.

Dixon, Kimberly D. "'An I am Sheba me am (She be doo be wah waaah doo wah)' O(au)rality, Textuality and Performativity: African American Literature's Vernacular Theory and the Work of Suzan-Lori Parks." *Journal of American Drama and Theatre* 11 (Winter 1998): 49–66.

Dolan, Jill. *Utopia in Performance: Finding Hope at the Theater*. Ann Arbor: University of Michigan Press, 2005.

Drukman, Steven. "Suzan-Lori Parks and Liz Diamond: Doo-a-diddly-dit-dit." *TDR* 39.3 (Fall 1995): 56–75.

Duckworth, Colin. *Angels of Darkness: Dramatic Effect in Samuel Beckett with Special Reference to Eugène Ionesco*. New York: Barnes & Noble, 1972.

Edel, Leon. "Henry James: The Dramatic Years." *Henry James:* Guy Domville *with comments by Bernard Shaw, H.G. Wells and Arnold Bennet*. Ed. Leon Edel. Philadelphia: J. B. Lippincott, 1960.

Einhorn, Marvin. Production photograph from *A Murder of Crows*, dir. Jim Simpson, Primary Stages, New York, 1992. Rpt. in *The Other American Drama* by Marc Robinson. Baltimore, MD: Johns Hopkins University Press, 1994.

Elam, Harry J., Jr. *The Past as Present in the Drama of August Wilson*. Ann Arbor: University of Michigan Press, 2006.

Erickson, Jon. "Defining Political Performance with Foucault and Habermas: Strategic and Communicative Action." *Theatricality*. Eds. Tracy C. Davis and Thomas Postlewait. Cambridge: Cambridge University Press, 2003. 156–185.

"The Mise en Scène of the Non-Euclidean Character: Wellman, Jenkin and Strindberg." *Modern Drama* 41.3 (Fall 1998): 355–370.

Esslin, Martin. *The Theatre of the Absurd*. 1961. London: Penguin, 1991.

"eutopia, n." OED Online. December 2012. Oxford University Press.

Etchells, Tim. *Certain Fragments*. London: Routledge, 1999.

"Lecture." Performed by Kate Valk. Crossing the Line Festival, French Institute/Alliance Française, New York, 28 Sep. 2013.
Faulkner, William. *Go Down, Moses*. New York: Vintage, 1990.
Fawcett, Julia. "Looking for the One Who Looks Like Some One: The Unmarked Subject(s) in Gertrude Stein's *A Play Called Not and Now*." *Modern Drama* 53.2 (Summer 2010): 137–158.
Fischer-Lichte, Erika. *The Transformative Power of Performance: A New Aesthetics*. Trans. Saskya Iris Jain. London: Routledge, 2008.
"Was ist eine 'werkgetreue' Inszenierung?" *Das Drama und seine Inszenierung*. Ed. Fischer-Lichte with Christel Weiler and Klaus Schwind. Tübingen: Max Niemeyer, 1985. 37–49.
Fitzgerald, F. Scott. *The Great Gatsby*. New York: Scribner, 1996.
Fletcher, John and John Spurling. *Beckett: A Study of His Plays*. New York: Hill and Wang, 1972.
Forced Entertainment (web site). Forced Entertainment, 2015.
Foreman, Richard. "How I Write My (Self: Plays)." *The Drama Review* 21.5 (Dec. 1977): 5–24.
Frank, Adam. *Transferential Poetics, from Poe to Warhol*. New York: Fordham University Press, 2014.
Frank, Haike. "The Instability of Meaning in Suzan-Lori Parks's *The America Play*." *American Drama* 11.2 (Summer 2002): 4–20.
Frazão, Francisco. "Disjunction and Theatricality: Elevator Repair Service's *Gatz* and Nature Theater of Oklahoma's *No Dice*." *No More Drama*. Ed. Peter Crawley and Willie White. Dublin: Project, 2011. 141–159.
Freud, Sigmund. "Mourning and Melancholia." *The Standard Edition of the Complete Psychological Works of Sigmund Freud*. Trans. James Strachey. Vol. 14. London: Hogarth Press, 1957. 239–258.
"Trauer und Melancholie." *Gesammelte Werke* Vol. 10, 428–446. textlog.de: *Historische Texte und Wörterbücher*. Peter Kietzmann, n.d. N. pag.
Fried, Michael. *Absorption and Theatricality*. Berkeley: University of C Press, 1980.
"Art and Objecthood." *Minimal Art: A Critical Anthology*. Ed. Gregory Battcock. Berkeley: University of California Press, 1995. 116–147.
Frieden, Ken. *Genius and Monologue*. Ithaca, NY: Cornell University Press, 1985.
Fuchs, Barbara. "Ventriloquist Theatre and the Omniscient Narrator: *Gatz* and *El pasado es un animal grotesco*." *Modern Drama* 57.2 (2014): 165–186.
Fuchs, Elinor. *The Death of Character: Perspectives on Theater after Modernism*. Bloomington: Indiana University Press, 1996.
"Presence and the Revenge of Writing: Re-Thinking Theatre after Derrida." *Performing Arts Journal* 9.2–3 (1985): 163–173.
"Reading for Landscape: The Case of American Drama." *Land/Scape/Theater*. Ed. Fuchs and Una Chaudhuri. Ann Arbor: University of Michigan Press, 2002. 30–50.
Furlani, Andre. "Beckett after Wittgenstein: The Literature of Exhausted Justification." *PMLA* 127.1 (2012): 38–57.

Garner, Stanton. *Bodied Spaces: Phenomenology and Performance in Contemporary Drama*. New York: Cornell University Press, 1994.
Garrett, Shawn-Marie. "Figure, Speech and Form in *Imperceptible Mutabilities in the Third Kingdom*." *Suzan-Lori Parks: A Casebook*. Ed. Kevin J. Wetmore, Jr. and Alycia Smith-Howard. New York: Routledge, 2009. 1–17.
——. "'For the Love of the Venus': Suzan-Lori Parks, Richard Foreman, and the Premiere of Venus." *Suzan-Lori Parks: Essays on the Plays and Other Works*. Ed. Philip C. Kolin. Jefferson: McFarland, 2010. 76–87.
Gates, Henry Louis. *Figures in Black*. New York: Oxford University Press, 1989.
Gatz. Elevator Repair Service. Dir. John Collins. The Public Theater, New York. 28 Nov. 2010. Videorecording provided by Elevator Repair Service.
"Gatz" (web site). *Elevator Repair Service*. Elevator Repair Service, 2015.
Geis, Deborah R. *Postmodern Theatric(k)s: Monologue in Contemporary American Drama*. Ann Arbor: University of Michigan Press, 1993.
——. *Suzan-Lori Parks*. Ann Arbor: University of Michigan Press, 2008.
Genette, Gérard. *Narrative Discourse*. Trans. Jane E. Lewin. New York: Cornell University Press, 1980.
Girl Gone. Production by Big Dance Theater. Dir. Paul Lazar. Choreography by Annie-B Parson. The Kitchen, New York. 1999. Videotape avail. at Performance Art Library at Lincoln Center.
Goethe, Johann Wolfgang von and Johann Christoph Friedrich Schiller. *Correspondence between Goethe and Schiller, 1794–1805*. Trans. Liselotte Dieckmann. New York: Peter Lang, 1994.
Goodall, Jane R. "Lucky's Energy." *Beckett after Beckett*. Ed. S. E. Gontarski and Anthony Uhlmann. Gainesville: University Press of Florida, 2006. 187–196.
Goto, Andrea. "Digging out of the Pigeonhole: African-American Representation in the Plays of Suzan-Lori Parks." *Suzan-Lori Parks: A Casebook*. Ed. Kevin J. Wetmore, Jr. and Alycia Smith-Howard. New York: Routledge, 2009. 106–123.
Hadas, Pamela. "Spreading the Difference: One Way to Read Gertrude Stein's Tender Buttons." *Twentieth Century Literature* 24.1 (1978): 57–75.
Halpern, Richard. *Eclipse of Action: Tragedy and Political Economy*. Chicago: University of Chicago Press, 2017.
Handke, Peter. *Offending the Audience*. *Kaspar and Other Plays*. Trans. Michael Roloff. New York: Farrar, 1969. 1–32.
Hansen, Miriam Bratu. "Benjamin's Aura." *Critical Inquiry* 34 (Winter 2008): 336–375.
Haralson, Eric L. "Rereading Gertrude Stein Rereading Henry James (After a Fashion)." *The Henry James Review* 25.3 (2004): 239–245.
Harries, Martin. "Theater and Media Before 'New' Media: Beckett's *Film* and *Play*." *Theater* 42.2 (2012): 6–25.
Hartman, Saidiya V. *Scenes of Subjection: Terror, Slavery, and Self-Making in Nineteenth-Century America*. Oxford: Oxford University Press, 1997.
Hegel, Georg Wilhelm Friedrich. *Phenomenology of Spirit*. Trans. A. V. Miller. Oxford: Oxford University Press, 1977.

Holder, Heidi J. "Strange Legacy: The History Plays of Suzan-Lori Parks." *Suzan-Lori Parks: A Casebook*. Ed. Kevin J. Wetmore, Jr. and Alycia Smith-Howard. New York: Routledge, 2009. 18–28.
Horkheimer, Max and Theodor W. Adorno. *Dialectic of Enlightenment: Philosophical Fragments*. Trans. Edmund Jephcott. Palo Alto: Stanford University Press, 2002.
Hugo, Victor. *Notre-Dame of Paris*. Trans. John Sturrock. London: Penguin, 1978.
Iser, Wolfgang. "The Art of Failure: The Stifled Laugh in Beckett's Theater." *Samuel Beckett*. Ed. Jennifer Birkett and Kate Ince. London: Longman, 2000. 201–230.
Jackson, Shannon. *Professing Performance*. Cambridge: Cambridge University Press, 2004.
Social Works: Performing Art, Supporting Publics. London: Routledge, 2011.
Jacques, Geoffrey. *A Change in the Weather: Modernist Imagination, African American Imaginary*. Amherst: University of Massachusetts Press, 2009.
Jaeger, Dagmar. *Theater im Medienzeitalter: Das postdramatische Theater von Elfriede Jelinek und Heiner Müller*. Bielefeld: Aisthesis, 2007.
James, Henry. *The Ambassadors*. New York: Penguin Classics, 1986.
"The Beast in the Jungle." *Henry James: Complete Stories 1898–1910*. New York: Library of America, 1996. 496–541.
"Nona Vincent." *Henry James: Complete Stories 1892–1898*. New York: Library of America, 1996. 1–31.
The Scenic Art. Ed. Allan Wade. New Brunswick: Rutgers University Press, 1948.
William Wetmore Story and His Friends Vol. 1. Boston: Houghton Mifflin, 1903.
Jameson, Fredric. *Archaeologies of the Future: The Desire Called Utopia and Other Science Fictions*. London: Verso, 2005.
The Political Unconscious. New York: Cornell University Press, 1981.
Jiggets, Shelby. "Interview with Suzan-Lori Parks." *Callaloo* 19.2 (Spring 1996): 309–317.
Johung, Jennifer. "Figuring the 'Spells'/Spelling the Figures: Suzan-Lori Parks's 'Scene of Love (?).'" *Theatre Journal* 58.1 (Ma. 2006): 39–52.
Jürs-Munby, Karen. "Agon, Conflict and Dissent: Elfriede Jelinek's *Ein Sportstück* and its Stagings by Einar Schleef and Just a Must Theatre." *Austrian Studies* 22 (2014): 9–25.
Introduction. *Postdramatic Theatre*. By Hans-Thies Lehmann. Trans. Jürs-Munby. New York: Routledge, 2006. 1–15.
"The vexed question of the text in Postdramatic Theatre in a cross-cultural perspective." *Dramatic and Postdramatic Theatre: Ten Years after* (Conference Proceedings, Faculty of Dramatic Arts, Belgrade University). Spec. issue of *Anthology of Essays by Faculty of Dramatic Arts* 20 (2011): 83–96.
Kalb, Jonathan. *Beckett in Performance*. Cambridge: Cambridge University Press, 1989.
Great Lengths: Seven Works of Marathon Theater. Ann Arbor: University of Michigan Press, 2011.

"Marathon Theater as Anti-Monument: The Curious Case of *Gatz*." *Anglia* 131.2–3 (2013): 236–247.

Kedves, Alexandra. "Ein Stück Glück in der Tristesse der Roaring Twenties." Rev. of *Gatz*, by Elevator Repair Service. *Neue Zürcher Zeitung* 28 Aug. 2006.

Kenner, Hugh. *Samuel Beckett: A Critical Study*. New York: Grove, 1961.

Kobialka, Michal. "Of Adorno's Beckett." *Adorno and Performance*. Ed. Will Daddario and Karoline Gritzner. New York: Palgrave Macmillan, 2014. 23–37.

Kolin, Philip C. "Puck's Magic Mojo: The Achievements of Suzan-Lori Parks." *Suzan-Lori Parks: Essays on the Plays and Other Works*. Ed. Kolin. Jefferson: McFarland, 2010. 7–19.

———. "'You one of uh mines?': Dis(re)membering in Suzan-Lori Parks's *Imperceptible Mutabilities in the Third Kingdom*." *Suzan-Lori Parks: Essays on the Plays and Other Works*. Ed. Kolin. Jefferson: McFarland, 2010. 45–64.

Kostelanetz, Richard. *The Theatre of Mixed Means*. New York: Dial, 1968.

Kurnick, David. *Empty Houses: Theatrical Failure and the Novel*. Princeton: Princeton University Press, 2012.

———. "Horrible Impossible: Henry James's Awkward Stage." *The Henry James Review* 26.2 (2005): 109–129.

Lebel, Jean-Jacques, et al. *New Writers IV: Plays and Happenings*. London: Calder, 1967.

Lehmann, Hans-Thies. *Postdramatic Theatre*. Trans. Karen Jürs-Munby. New York: Routledge, 2006.

———. "'Postdramatic Theatre,' a decade later." *Dramatic and Postdramatic Theatre: Ten Years After* (Conference Proceedings, Faculty of Dramatic Arts, Belgrade University). Spec. issue of *Anthology of Essays by Faculty of Dramatic Arts* 20 (2011): 31–46.

———. *Postdramatisches Theater*. Frankfurt am Main: Verlag der Autoren, 1999.

"lesson, n." OED Online. March 2013. Oxford University Press.

Life and Times: Episodes 1–4. Nature Theater of Oklahoma. The Public Theater, New York. 2 Feb. 2013. Performance.

Litvak, Joseph. *Caught in the Act: Theatricality in the Nineteenth-Century English Novel*. Berkeley: University of California Press, 1992.

Lott, Eric. *Love and Theft: Blackface Minstrelsy and the American Working Class*. New York: Oxford University Press, 1993.

Louis, Yvette. "Body Language: The Black Female Body and the Word in Suzan-Lori Parks's *The Death of the Last Black Man in the Whole Entire World*." *Recovering the Black Female Body: Self-Representations by African American Women*. Ed. Michael Bennett and Vanessa D. Dickerson. New Brunswick: Rutgers University Press, 2001. 141–164.

Lyman, Elizabeth Dyrud. "The Page Refigured: The Verbal and Visual Language of Suzan-Lori Parks's *Venus*." *Performance Research* 7:1 (2002): 90–100.

Malkin, Jeanette R. *Memory-Theater and Postmodern Drama*. Ann Arbor: University of Michigan Press, 1999.

Margolis, Anne T. *Henry James and the Problem of Audience: An International Act.* Ann Arbor: UMI Research, 1985.
Marranca, Bonnie. *Ecologies of Theatre.* Baltimore: Johns Hopkins University Press, 1996.
McMillan, Dougald and Martha Fehsenfeld. *Beckett in the Theatre.* London: John Calder, 1988.
McMullan, Anna. "Performing Vision(s): Perspectives on Spectatorship in Beckett's Theatre." *Samuel Beckett: A Casebook.* Ed. Jennifer M. Jeffers. New York: Garland, 1998.
Mead, Rebecca. "Adaptation." *The New Yorker* 27 Sept. 2010: 44–49.
Mee, Charles. "About the (re)making project" (web site). *Charles Mee: the (re)making project.* Charles Mee, n.d.
Messerli, Douglas. "A Linguistic Fantasia (On Mac Wellman's Murder of Crows)." *Ustheater, Opera, and Performance.* Ustheater, Opera, and Performance, 13 Jan. 2013.
"modern, adj. and n." OED Online. December 2011. Oxford University Press.
Moon, Michael. *A Small Boy and Others: Imitation and Initiation in American Culture from Henry James to Andy Warhol.* Durham: Duke University Press, 1998.
Müller, Tobi. "Die Wiedergeburt der Werktreue mit den Mitteln der Soap." Rev. of *Gatz*, by Elevator Repair Service. *Tages-Anzeiger* (Zurich) 26 Aug. 2006: 50.
Muñoz, José Esteban. *Cruising Utopia: The Then and There of Queer Futurity.* New York: NYU Press, 2009.
A Murder of Crows. By Mac Wellman. Dir. Meghan Finn. Brooklyn Center for the Performing Arts at Brooklyn College, New York. 29 Apr. 2013. Performance.
Muse, John. "Short Attention Span Theaters: Modernist Shorts since 1880." Diss. Yale University, 2010.
Nadel, Ira B. "Gertrude Stein and Henry James." *Gertrude Stein and the Making of Literature.* Ed. Shirley Neuman and Ira B. Nadel. Boston: Northeastern University Press, 1988.
Nowak, Anja. *Elemente einer Ästhetik des Theatralen in Adornos Ästhetischer Theorie* Würzburg: Königshausen & Neumann, 2012.
"On the Theatricality of Art." *Adorno and Performance.* Ed. Will Daddario and Karoline Gritzner. New York: Palgrave Macmillan, 2014. 143–154.
Ohi, Kevin. *Henry James and the Queerness of Style.* Minneapolis: University of Minnesota Press, 2011.
"OK Theater: *Life and Times*" (web site). *Nature Theater of Oklahoma.* Nature Theater of Oklahoma, n.d.
O'Leary, Alejandra. "*Gatsby*, Every Last Word of It, Onstage." *Yale Alumni Magazine* 69.2 (2005): n. pag.
Ong, Han. "Suzan-Lori Parks." Interview. *BOMB* 47 (Spring 1994): 46–50.
Parks, Suzan-Lori. *365 Days/365 Plays.* New York: TCG, 2006.
The America Play. The America Play and Other Works. New York: Theatre Communications Group, 1995. 157–199.

Betting on the Dust Commander. *The America Play and Other Works.* New York: Theatre Communications Group, 1995. 73–90.

The Death of the Last Black Man in the Whole Entire World. *The America Play and Other Works.* New York: Theatre Communications Group, 1995. 99–131.

The Death of the Last Black Man in the Whole Entire World. *Theater* 21.3 (Summer/Fall 1990): 81–94.

Father Comes Home from the Wars (Parts 1, 2 & 3). New York: Theatre Communications Group, 2015.

"From *Elements of Style.*" *The America Play and Other Works.* New York: Theatre Communications Group, 1995. 6–18.

Imperceptible Mutabilities in the Third Kingdom. *The America Play and Other Works.* New York: Theatre Communications Group, 1995. 23–71.

"New Black Math." *Theatre Journal* 57.4 (December 2005): 576–583.

"Possession." *The America Play and Other Works.* New York: Theatre Communications Group, 1995. 3–5.

The Red Letter Plays [*In the Blood* and *Fucking A*]. New York: Theatre Communications Group, 2001.

Topdog/Underdog. New York: Theatre Communications Group, 2002.

Venus. New York: Theatre Communications Group, 1997.

"Watch Me Work." The Public Theater. New York, NY. 14 Mar. 2013. Performance.

Parra, Angelo. *Playwriting for Dummies.* Indianapolis: Wiley, 2011.

Perloff, Marjorie. "Foreword." *Cellophane: Plays by Mac Wellman.* Baltimore: Johns Hopkins University Press, 2001. ix–xvii.

Wittgenstein's Ladder. Chicago: University of Chicago Press, 1996.

Peters, Gary. *The Philosophy of Improvisation.* Chicago: University of Chicago Press, 2009.

Phelan, Peggy. "Lessons in Blindness from Samuel Beckett." *PMLA* 119.5 (2004): 1279–1288.

Mourning Sex: Performing Public Memories. London: Routledge, 1997.

Unmarked: The Politics of Performance. New York: Routledge, 1993.

Poschmann, Gerda. *Der nicht mehr dramatische Theatertext.* Tübingen: Niemeyer, 1997.

Pound, Ezra. "Henry James." *Literary Essays of Ezra Pound.* Ed. T. S. Eliot. New York: New Directions, 1968. 295–338.

Power, Cormac. *Presence in Play: A Critique of Theories of Presence in the Theatre.* Amsterdam: Rodopi, 2008.

"The Space of Doubt: *The Chairs* and the aesthetics of failure." *Performance Research* 17.1 (2012): 68–76.

Puchner, Martin. "Drama and Performance: Toward a Theory of Adaptation." *Common Knowledge* 17.2 (2011): 292–305.

Stage Fright: Modernism, Anti-Theatricality, and Drama. Baltimore: Johns Hopkins University Press, 2002.

Quent, Marcus. "Thinking – Mimesis – Pre-Imitation: Notes on Art, Philosophy, and Theatre in Adorno's *Aesthetic Theory.*" *Adorno and Performance.* Ed.

Will Daddario and Karoline Gritzner. New York: Palgrave Macmillan, 2014. 130–142.
Rancière, Jacques. *The Emancipated Spectator*. Trans. Gregory Elliott. London: Verso, 2009.
Rayner, Alice, and Harry J. Elam, Jr. "Unfinished Business: Reconfiguring History in Suzan-Lori Parks's *The Death of the Last Black Man in the Whole Entire World*." *Theatre Journal* 46.4 (December 1994): 447–461.
"remediation, n." OED Online. Sept. 2012. Oxford University Press.
Ridout, Nicholas. *Passionate Amateurs: Theatre, Communism, and Love*. Ann Arbor: University of Michigan Press, 2013.
  Stage Fright, Animals, and Other Theatrical Problems. Cambridge: Cambridge University Press, 2006.
Rivkin, Julie. *False Positions: The Representational Logics of Henry James's Fiction*. Palo Alto: Stanford University Press, 1996.
Robbe-Grillet, Alain. *For a New Novel: Essays on Fiction*. Trans. Richard Howard. New York: Grove, 1965.
Robinson, J. Bradford. "The Jazz Essays of Theodor Adorno: Some Thoughts on Jazz Reception in Weimar Germany." *Popular Music* 13.1 (January 1994): 1–25.
Robinson, Marc. *The Other American Drama*. Baltimore: Johns Hopkins University Press, 1997.
Robinson, Marc et al. "Remarks on Parks: A Symposium on the Work of Suzan-Lori Parks: Part One: Critics and Scholars." 2004. Hotreview.org. Hunter College Department of Theater.
Rodenbeck, Judith. "Madness and Method: Before Theatricality." *Grey Room* 13 (2003): 54–79.
Rossini, Jon D. *Contemporary Latina/o Theater: Wrighting Ethnicity*. Carbondale: Southern Illinois University Press, 2008.
Rowe, John Carlos. *The Theoretical Dimensions of Henry James*. Madison: University of Wisconsin Press, 1984.
Ryan, Betsy Alayne. *Gertrude Stein's Theatre of the Absolute*. Ann Arbor: UMI Research Press, 1984.
Sarkoparnig, Andrea. "Performativization and the Rescue of Aesthetic Semblance." *Adorno and Performance*. Ed. Will Daddario and Karoline Gritzner. New York: Palgrave Macmillan, 2014. 53–66.
Salvato, Nick. *Uncloseting Drama: Modernism's Queer Theatres*. New Haven: Yale University Press, 2010.
Savran, David. "Mac Wellman." Interview. *The Playwright's Voice*. 311–338. New York: Theatre Communications Group, 1999.
Schechner, Richard. "The Conservative Avant-Garde." *New Literary History* 41.4 (2010): 895–913.
Schmidt, Theron. "Acting, Disabled: Back to Back Theatre and the Politics of Appearance." *Postdramatic Theatre and the Political: International Perspectives on Contemporary Performance*. Ed. Karen Jürs-Munby, Jerome Carroll, and Steve Giles. London: Bloomsbury, 2013. 189–208.

Schneider, Rebecca. *Performing Remains*. New York: Routledge, 2011.
Schultz, Laura Luise. "A combination and not a contradiction: Gertrude Stein's performative aesthetics." *Performative Realism: Interdisciplinary Studies in Art and Media*. Ed. Rune Gade and Anne Jerslev. Copenhagen: Museum Tusculanum, 2005.
Sedgwick, Eve Kosofsky. *Epistemology of the Closet*. 1990. Updated with a new preface. Berkeley: University of California Press, 2008.
 Touching Feeling. Durham: Duke University Press, 2003.
The Select. Elevator Repair Service. Dir. John Collins. 2010. The Public Theater, New York. September 2011. Performance.
Seltzer, Mark. "*The Princess Casamassima*: Realism and the Fantasy of Surveillance." *Modern Critical Views: Henry James*. Ed. Harold Bloom. New York: Chelsea House, 1987. 277–300.
Shaw, Helen. "Mac Wellman and Things of the Devil." *The Difficulty of Crossing a Field*. Minneapolis: University of Minnesota Press, 2008. vii–xii.
Shaw, Sharon. "Gertrude Stein and Henry James: The Difference between Accidence and Coincidence." *The Pembroke Magazine* 5 (1974): 95–101.
Sheehan, Paul. "Births for Nothing: Beckett's Ontology of Parturition." *Beckett after Beckett*. Ed. S. E. Gontarski and Anthony Uhlmann. Gainesville: University Press of Florida, 2006. 177–186.
Shepard, Sam. *The Tooth of Crime. Seven Plays*. New York: Bantam, 1981. 203–253.
Shepard, Sam and Patti Smith. *Cowboy Mouth. Fool for Love and Other Plays*. New York: Bantam, 1984. 145–165.
Sherratt, Yvonne. "Adorno's Aesthetic Concept of Aura." *Philosophy and Social Criticism* 33.2 (2007): 155–177.
Shklovsky, Viktor. "Art as Technique." *Literary Theory: An Anthology*. 2nd ed. Ed. Julia Rivkin and Michael Ryan. Malden, MA: Blackwell, 2004. 15–21.
Solomon, Alisa. "Signifying on the Signifyin': The Plays of Suzan-Lori Parks." *Theater* 21.3 (1990): 73–80.
Soloski, Alexis. "Mac Wellman, a Playwriting Mentor Whose Only Mantra Is Oddity." *The New York Times* 17 Feb. 2015.
The Sound and the Fury. Elevator Repair Service. Dir. John Collins. 2008. The Public Theater, New York. 15 May 2015. Performance.
Stadler, Gustavus. "'My Wife': The Tape Recorder and Warhol's Queer Ways of Listening." *Criticism* 56.3 (2014): 425–456.
States, Bert O. *Great Reckonings In Little Rooms*. Berkeley: University of California Press, 1985.
 The Shape of Paradox: An Essay on Waiting for Godot. Berkeley: University of California Press, 1978.
Stein, Gertrude. *The Autobiography of Alice B. Toklas*. New York: Vintage, 1990.
 Four Saints in Three Acts. Last Operas and Plays. Baltimore: Johns Hopkins University Press, 1995. 440–480.
 Last Operas and Plays. Baltimore: Johns Hopkins University Press, 1995.
 Listen to Me. Last Operas and Plays. 1949. Baltimore: Johns Hopkins University Press, 1995. 387–421.

Narration. New York: Greenwood, 1969.

Paisieu: A Play. Last Operas and Plays. 1949. Baltimore: Johns Hopkins University Press, 1995. 155–181.

"Picasso." *Gertrude Stein on Picasso.* Ed. Edward Burns. New York: Liveright, 1970. 1–76.

"Plays." *Writings and Lectures 1911–1945.* Ed. Patricia Meyerowitz. London: Peter Owen, 1967. 58–81.

Tender Buttons. Mineola: Dover, 1997.

Writings and Lectures 1911–1945. Ed. Patricia Meyerowitz. London: Peter Owen, 1967.

Stewart, Allegra. *Gertrude Stein and the Present.* Cambridge, MA: Harvard University Press, 1967.

Sugiera, Małgorzata. "Beyond Drama: Writing for Postdramatic Theatre." *Theatre Research International* 29.1 (2004): 16–28.

Sullivan, Mecca J. "Interstitial Voices: The Poetics of Difference in Afrodiasporic Women's Literature." Diss. University of Pennsylvania, 2012.

"Suzan-Lori Parks: Watch Me Work" (web site). *The Public.* The Public Theater, n.d.

Syers, Karinne Keithley. "This Theater Is a Strange Hole: Mac Wellman's Poetics of Apparence." *Postmodern Culture* 20.1 (Sept. 2009): n. pag.

Szondi, Peter. *Theory of Modern Drama.* Ed. and trans. Michael Hays. Minneapolis: University of Minnesota Press, 1987.

Terada, Rei. *Looking Away: Phenomenality and Dissatisfaction, Kant to Adorno.* Cambridge, MA: Harvard University Press, 2009.

Toklas, Alice B. *What Is Remembered.* New York: Holt, Rinehart and Winston, 1963.

Tomlin, Liz. "'And Their Stories Fell Apart Even as I Was Telling Them': Poststructuralist Performance and the No-Longer-Dramatic Text." *Performance Research* 14.1 (2009): 57–64.

Varadharajan, Asha. *Exotic Parodies: Subjectivity in Adorno, Said, and Spivak.* Minneapolis: U of Minnesota Press, 1995.

Watch Me Work. Suzan-Lori Parks. Lobby, Public Theater, New York. 2010 and 2013. Performance.

Weber, Samuel. *Theatricality As Medium.* New York: Fordham University Press, 2004.

Wellman, Mac. *The Bad Infinity: Eight Plays.* Cover photo by Carlotta M. Copron. Baltimore: Johns Hopkins University Press, 1994.

Cellophane: Plays. Baltimore: Johns Hopkins University Press, 2001.

Girl Gone. Cellophane: Plays. Baltimore: Johns Hopkins University Press, 2001. 243–282.

A Murder of Crows. Crowtet 1. Copenhagen: Green Integer, 2000.

Sincerity Forever. New York: Broadway, 2005.

Speculations: Draft Seven. 2013. *Mac Wellman: Damnable Scribbler* (web site). N. d.

"The Theatre of Good Intentions." *Performing Arts Journal* 8.3 (1984): 59–70.

Wetmore, Kevin J., Jr. "It's an Oberammergau Thing: An Interview with Suzan-Lori Parks." *Suzan-Lori Parks: A Casebook*. Ed. Wetmore and Alycia Smith-Howard. New York: Routledge, 2009. 124–140.
Wiesenfarth, Joseph. *Henry James and the Dramatic Analogy*. New York: Fordham University Press, 1963.
Wirth, Andrzej. "Gertrude Stein und ihre Kritik der dramatischen Vernunft." *LiLi: Zeitschrift für Literaturwissenschaft und Linguistik* 12:46 (1982): 64–73.
"Vom Dialog zum Diskurs: Versuch einer Synthese der nachbrechsten Theaterkonzepte." *Theater Heute* 1 (1980): 16–19.
Winnicott, D. W. "Communicating and Not Communicating." *The Maturational Processes and the Facilitating Environment: Studies in the Theory of Emotional Development*. London: Hogarth, 1965. 179–192.
Wittgenstein, Ludwig. *Philosophical Investigations: The German Text, with a Revised English Translation*. Trans. G. E. M. Anscombe. Oxford: Blackwell, 2001.
Wood, Jacqueline. "'Jazzing' Time, Love, and the Female Self in Three Early Plays by Suzan-Lori Parks." *Suzan-Lori Parks: Essays on the Plays and Other Works*. Ed. Philip C. Kolin. Jefferson: McFarland, 2010. 34–44.
Woolf, Brandon. "Towards a Paradoxically Parallaxical Postdramatic Politics?" *Postdramatic Theatre and the Political: International Perspectives on Contemporary Performance*. Ed. Karen Jürs-Munby, Jerome Carroll, and Steve Giles. London: Bloomsbury, 2013. 31–46.
Worton, Michael. "*Waiting for Godot* and *Endgame*: theatre as text." *The Cambridge Companion to Beckett*. Ed. John Pilling. Cambridge: Cambridge University Press, 1994. 67–87.
Worthen, W. B. "Citing History: Textuality and Performativity in the Plays of Suzan-Lori Parks." *Essays in Theatre/Études théâtrales* 18.1 (1999): 2–22.
"Disciplines of the Text/Sites of Performance" and Responses. *The Drama Review* 39.1 (1995): 13–44.
Drama: Between Poetry and Performance. West Sussex: Wiley-Blackwell, 2010.
Modern Drama and the Rhetoric of Theater. Berkeley: University of California Press, 1992.
"Writing & Performance." Special section. *PAJ* 100 (2012): 119–140.
Young, Harvey. "Choral Compassion: *In the Blood* and *Venus*." *Suzan-Lori Parks: A Casebook*. Ed. Kevin J. Wetmore, Jr. and Alycia Smith-Howard. New York: Routledge, 2009. 29–47.
Zinoman, Jason. "The Unadapted Theatrical Adaptation." Rev. of *Gatz*, by Elevator Repair Service. *The New York Times* 9 Dec. 2007.

Index

Abramovic, Marina, 127
Adorno, Theodor W., xv, 1, 13–19, 30, 82, 84, 86, 97, 105, 106, 114, 122, 123–124, 129, 132, 140, 142, 163–165, 172, 173, 174, 187, 191, 192, 197–198, 200
  aesthetic autonomy, 15–16, 19
  Aesthetic Theory, 13–14, 15–16, 17, 18, 19, 72, 73, 74, 84, 105, 106, 114, 122, 123–124, 129, 131–132, 163–164, 171, 174, 197, 201
  Beckett, importance of, 20, 70–75, 82, 84, 97–98
  communication in, 197–200
  The Culture Industry, 186
  on jazz, 123, 131–132, 237
  Minima Moralia, 15, 123, 124, 140, 173, 200
  on objectivation, 17, 132, 142, 163
  "primacy of the text" and, 14–20
  "Trying to Understand *Endgame*," 70, 74–75, 97–98, 229, 230
  on utopia, 13–14, 70–75, 82, 84, 86, 124, 229
Akalaitis, JoAnne, 93–94, 95
Als, Hilton, 110
antitheatricality, 19, 24–26, 31–32, 47–54, 84–85, 96–97
Arbuthnot, John, 58
Aristotle, 182–183, 184–185
Artaud, Antonin, ix, 3–5, 6, 41, 68, 79
  The Theater and its Double, 3
aura
  in Adorno, 200, 201
  in Benjamin, 200–201, 206, 246
  in Wellman, 176
Austin, J. L., 137
autonomy of art, 15–17. *See also* Adorno, Theodor W.

Bailes, Sara Jane, 127
Bakhtin, Mikhail, 195–196
Barnett, David, xii
Barthes, Roland, 29
  A Lover's Discourse, 120–121

Bay-Cheng, Sarah, 24, 50
Beckett, Samuel, 20, 158, 169. *See* Chapter 3
  Eleuthéria, 90, 93, 231
  Endgame, 70, 74, 82, 86–93, 95, 97, 227, 229, 230, 233
  importance to Adorno, 20, 70–75, 82, 84, 97–98
  Krapp's Last Tape, 78
  Malone Dies, 91, 98, 103
  Mercier and Camier, 101, 103
  Molloy, 98, 99
  monologue in, 20, 71, 81, 86, 91, 98–106
  Murphy, 91, 96
  presence in, 69, 71, 77–79, 85–86, 92, 96–97, 103, 106, 228, 232
  present in, 75–86, 91–92, 94, 95–96, 228, 229–230, 231
  silence in, 96–97, 105
  Three Novels, 98
  The Unnamable, 71, 77, 98–100, 103–106, 181, 232, 233
  Waiting for Godot, 20, 67, 68, 86–93, 109, 114, 158–159, 181, 185, 193. *See* Chapter 3
  Watt, 101, 103
Benjamin, Walter, 200–201, 206
  "The Work of Art in the Age of Mechanical Reproduction," 200
Bennett, Benjamin
  All Theater is Revolutionary Theater, xii–xiii, 74–75
Benzaquén, Adriana, 72
Bernhardt, Sarah, 53
Bernstein, J. M., 197–198
Bersani, Leo, 29–30, 35–36
  "The Jamesian Lie," 35
Big Dance Theater, 206, 212–214, 247
Blau, Herbert, 69, 196
Blechman, Max, 72
Bloch, Ernst, 82
Bowers, Jane Palatini, 51–52
  They Watch Me As They Watch This, 51

Brantley, Ben, 119–120
Brecht, Bertolt, 11–13, 34, 167, 196, 206–207
  "literarization of theater," 11–12, 33, 34, 79, 90, 167, 193, 197, 205

Cage, John, 13
Čale-Feldman, Lada, 136
Caramello, Charles, 27, 47, 56
Carpio, Glenda, 141, 159–160
Castagno, Paul, 178–179, 181, 195
  New Playwriting Strategies, 178–179
Castellucci, Romeo
  Hyperion: Letters of a Terrorist, 111
Cavell, Stanley, 82
Chatman, Seymour, 28, 33
Chaudhuri, Una, 212
Cohn, Dorrit, 99
Cohn, Ruby, 178
Colbert, Soyica Diggs, 142–143
Collins, John, 120, 129–130
communication
  in Adorno, 197–200
  axes of, 175, 191, 197
  in postdramatic theater, 175, 197–198
  in Wellman, 174–175, 180–181, 197–200, 244
Connor, Steven, 78, 90, 148
co-presence, 11, 85, 106, 173, 195, 197, 200–201, 210, 212, 217
Craig, Edward Gordon, 162

Derrida, Jacques, 3–4, 5, 6, 8, 11, 88, 170
  Writing and Difference, 3
Dickens, Charles
  Little Dorrit, 155, 241
disrupted image, 40–45
Dixon, Kimberly, 136
Dolan, Jill
  Utopia in Performance, 69–70, 218–219
drama
  dramatic unities, 48, 65, 81, 229
  movement beyond, 28
  presence and, 3–8, 10–11, 79, 116, 131
  Szondi's theory of, 8–14
  theater versus, 24
Drukman, Steven, 131, 140

Edel, Leon, 56, 151
Elam, Harry J., Jr., 146, 155, 160–161, 169
Elevator Repair Service (ERS), x, 98, 110, 117–118, 163
  Gatz, 110, 118–130, 135, 163
  The Sound and the Fury, 118, 235–236

epic, 9–10
Etchells, Tim, ix
  A Broadcast/Looping Pieces, 109
  Certain Fragments, ix

faithfulness *(Werktreue)*, 113, 118, 120–129
Faulkner, William
  "The Bear," 161
Fehsenfeld, Martha, 76
Fischer-Lichte, Erika, 122, 123
  "What Is a 'Faithful' Production?," 113
Forced Entertainment, x, 109
  The Notebook, 109, 111
Foreman, Richard, 24
Frankfurt School, 72, 176
Frazão, Francisco, 120
Freud, Sigmund
  "Mourning and Melancholia," 146–147
Frieden, Ken, 192
Fuchs, Barbara, 124
Fuchs, Elinor, 5, 8

Garner, Stanton, 5–6, 18, 69, 78, 86, 136
  Bodied Spaces, 5, 6
Garrett, Shawn-Marie, 137
Gates, Henry Louis, 161
Geis, Deborah, 139, 157, 166, 178, 180, 181, 192
Genette, Gérard, 33
Gray, Spaulding, 178

Hadas, Pamela, 61
Handke, Peter
  Offending the Audience, 11
happenings, 12–13, 18–19, 220
Hartman, Saidiya, 150
Hegel, G.W.F.
  Phenomenology of Spirit, 73–74
Horkheimer, Max, 86, 187
  The Culture Industry, 186
Hugo, Victor
  Notre Dame of Paris, 205

Ibsen, Henrik
  Hedda Gabler, 36, 116

Jaeger, Dagmar, xii
James, Henry, 20, 21, 23–24, 203. *See* Chapter 2
  The Ambassadors, 28, 31, 36, 40–45, 57, 64, 94, 109
  as antitheatrical, 31–32
  "The Beast in the Jungle," 28, 29–30, 32, 34–35, 37–38, 40–41, 109
  disrupted imagery in, 55
  Guy Domville, 24, 31, 32
  influence on Stein, 45–48

INDEX

James, Henry (cont.)
  "Nona Vincent," 32–33
  present in, 28, 29–30, 34–35
  reading *vs.* attending, 33
  relationship to theater, 28, 30–32, 34, 36–37, 43, 44–45
  scene/scenic method, 36
  time and space in, 34–35, 37, 40, 43
  The Turn of the Screw, 23
Jameson, Fredric, 73
Jelinek, Elfriede, xi
  Ein Sportstück, 113
Jenkins, Len, 179
Johnson, Samuel
  "The Vanity of Human Wishes," 76
Joyce, James
  Ulysses, 155
Jürs-Munby, Karen, xi, 132

Kalb, Jonathan, 127, 227
  Beckett in Performance, 78–79, 93–94, 114
Kedves, Alexandra, 118
Kempson, Sibyl, 129–130
Kenner, Hugh, 68
Kobialka, Michal, 81
Kolin, Philip, 136
Kurnick, David, 28, 33

LeCompte, Elizabeth, 24
Lehmann, Hans-Thies, 10, 178, 189, 190, 196
  Postdramatic Theatre, xi–xii, 4–5, 8, 10, 12–13, 113, 116, 133, 175, 178, 180–181, 197, 198–199, 207
literature and theater, x–xiv, 11–12, 13, 23–24, 27, 33–34, 50–52, 66–67, 93–94, 98–99, 100, 109–118, 128, 154–156, 163–164, 172–173, 193, 195–196, 205

Mabou Mines, 5
Malkin, Jeanette, 152–153, 160, 166
Manhattan Theater Club, 132
Margolis, Anne, 32
Marranca, Bonnie, 56, 58, 60
McMillan, Dougald, 76
McMullan, Anna, 75
Mead, Rebecca, 120, 135
Mee, Charles, 114
Miller, Arthur, 178
modernism, 14, 47–48, 58, 67, 202, 223–224
monologue, 176, 178–182, 191–192
  in Beckett, 20, 71, 81, 86, 91, 98–106
  in Parks, 157–162, 241–242
  in Wellman, 173, 176, 177–182, 184–192, 195–197, 244–245
Müller, Tobi, 118, 120

Muñoz, José Esteban
  Cruising Utopia, 15
Muse, John, 137, 138

Nature Theater of Oklahoma, x
  Life and Times, 110–111
negativity, xiii–xiv, xv, 6–8, 13–14, 15–16, 17, 19–20, 55–61, 68, 70–74, 76, 83–85, 100, 105, 106, 117–118, 172–173, 181, 191, 195, 198–199, 201–202, 203, 204–205, 220
Nowak, Anja, 97

Ohi, Kevin, 30

Parks, Suzan-Lori, 68, 98, 111, 128. *See* Chapter 5
  The America Play, 134, 167, 238, 241
  The Death of the Last Black Man in the Whole Entire World, 138–171, 177, 181, 189
  Father Comes Home From the Wars, 138, 172
  "From *Elements of Style*," 136, 137, 141–142, 144, 149–150, 152–153, 165
  Fucking A, 138
  Imperceptible Mutabilities in the Third Kingdom, 131, 133
  minstrelsy, appropriation of, 157–162, 241–243
  modernism and, 131
  monologue in, 157–162, 241–242
  mourning, theatrics of, 144–152
  present in, 137–138, 153, 154, 163, 164, 167, 168–169
  The Red Letter Plays, 138
  "Rep & Rev," 144–145, 147, 148, 168
  365 Days/365 Plays, 138, 142
  Topdog/Underdog, 172, 236
  Venus, 134, 150, 158, 161–162, 171, 237–238, 240
  "Watch Me Work," 135–136
  writing, as topic in plays of, 133–139, 152–171
Perloff, Marjorie, 175–176, 180
Peters, Gary, 123
Phelan, Peggy, 5
playwrights, ix–xv, 113–114, 134–135, 165, 172
Poschmann, Gerda, xii, 4, 112
postdramatic theater, xi, xii, xiii, xiv, 4–5, 8–11, 132–133, 175, 180–181, 196, 198
Pound, Ezra, 39
Power, Cormac, 7, 11
presence. *See also* co-presence; drama; present
  in Beckett, 69, 71, 77–79, 85–86, 92, 96–97, 103, 106, 228, 232
  drama and, 3–8, 10–11, 79, 116, 131
  theatrical, 3–8, 26, 141, 180–181, 200–203, 210
  theoretical status of, 3–6, 29, 123
present, 6–8, 10–15, 20. *See also* drama; presence
  in Beckett, 75–86, 91–92, 94, 95–96, 228, 229–230, 231

ephemerality and presentness, 4–5, 13, 17, 91, 100, 202
in James, 28, 29–30, 34–35
negative relation with. *See* negativity
in Parks, 137–138, 153, 154, 163, 164, 167, 168–169
in Stein, 46–48, 55, 58–59, 62, 66–67, 224–225, 226
Puchner, Martin, 24, 25, 48, 52, 53, 55, 64, 75–76, 85
Stage Fright, 25, 218, 221

Rancière, Jacques, 210
Rayner, Alice, 146, 155, 160–161, 169
Regietheater (director's theater), 111–112, 113
Ridout, Nicholas, 210, 221
Robbe-Grillet, Alain, 78, 90, 173
For a New Novel, 77–78
Robinson, Marc, 150
Ryan, Betsy Alayne, 26, 27, 56, 61

Sarkoparnig, Andrea, 18
Schechner, Richard, xi, 110, 112, 123
Schneider, Rebecca, 144, 167
Schultz, Laura Luise, 57
Sheehan, Paul, 83
Solomon, Alisa, 132, 161
States, Bert O., 7, 69, 102
Stein, Gertrude, 20, 206–207. *See* Chapter 2
The Autobiography of Alice B. Toklas, 23, 45
"Composition as Explanation," 62
continuous present, 26, 61–67, 209
experimental theater and, 23–24
Four in America, 45–46
Four Saints in Three Acts, 48, 50–51, 61–67, 109
James's importance to, 45–48
landscape, 47–48, 55–61, 63, 64–67, 226
A List, 51
Listen to Me, 51, 58
Paisieu: A Play, 48, 49–50, 55–61, 109
A Play Called Not and Now, 51, 225
"Plays," 46, 47, 52–53, 55, 65
poetics of entity, 26
"Portraits and Repetition," 46
present in, 46–48, 55, 58–59, 62, 66–67, 224–225, 226
Tender Buttons, 49–50, 56, 66, 224
Two: Gertrude Stein and Her Brother, 61
Stewart, Allegra, 62
Syers, Karinne Keithley, 172, 176, 199, 205
Szondi, Peter
Theory of the Modern Drama, 9–12, 30, 32, 55, 69, 79, 91, 116–117, 167

Terada, Rei, 13
Looking Away, 13
text-as-text theater, 110
Theater of Cruelty, 3, 79
theatricalization of literature, 34
theatrical presence. *See* presence
Tomlin, Liz, xii

Utopia, 69–70
Adorno's conception of, 13–14, 70–75, 82, 84, 86, 124, 229
in Beckett, 69–75, 82, 84, 85–86, 93–106, 228, 230
in Parks, 138, 144–145, 163–171
in Wellman, 173, 176, 192, 196–197, 199, 203, 204–205, 208

Varadharajan, Asha, 198

Weber, Samuel
Theatricality as Medium, 24–25, 27
Wellman, Mac, xv, 98, 109, 172–176, 179, 181–182, 186–187, 188, 197–200, 201, 202–206. *See* Chapter 6
Antigone, 177, 244, 247
aura in, 176
at Brooklyn College, 172, 204–205
Cellophane, 177, 180, 244, 247
communication in, 174–175, 180–181, 197–200, 244
Girl Gone, 176, 206–214
Hypatia, 209–212
influence of, 172–173, 243–244
monologue in, 173, 176, 177–182, 184–192, 195–197, 244–245
A Murder of Crows, 116, 172, 173, 176, 177–197, 203, 205, 244, 247
Speculations, 172–176, 202 206, 247
Terminal Hip, 177, 180
"The Theatre of Good Intentions," 174, 191, 201–202
Wells, H. G., 31
Wetmore, Kevin J., Jr., 134–135, 136
Wilson, Robert, 24, 35
Wirth, Andrzej, xi, 57, 62
The Wooster Group, x, 112, 129–130
Worthen, W. B., 87, 154–155
Drama: Between Poetry and Performance, xii, 112–113, 115, 133–134, 156
Wright, Richard, 155
Native Son, 155

Zinoman, Jason, 118